IRELAND

Hints for Using the Guide

Following the tradition established by Karl Baedeker in 1846, buildings and works of art, places of natural beauty and sights of particular interest are distinguished by one ★ or two ★★ asterisks – one for sights of particular interest, two for unique places of interest.

To make it easier to locate the various places listed in the A to Z section of the guide, their coordinates are shown in red at the head of each entry, e.g. Connemara C 1/2.

Coloured bars down the right-hand side of the page are an aid to finding the main heading in the guide: blue stands for the Introduction, red for the Sights from A to Z section, and yellow indicates Practical Information.

Only a selection of hotels and restaurants can be given; no reflection is implied therefore on establishments not included.

In a time of rapid change it is difficult to ensure that all the information given is entirely accurate and up to date, and the possibility of error can never be entirely eliminated.

Although the publishers can accept no responsibility for inaccuracies and omissions, they are constantly endeavouring to improve the quality of their guides and are therefore always grateful for criticisms, corrections and suggestions for improvement.

Preface

This guide to Ireland is one of the new generation of Baedeker guides. Illustrated throughout in colour, these guides are designed to meet the needs of the modern traveller. They are quick and easy to consult, with the principal places of interest described in alphabetical order, and practical details and useful tips shown in the margin. The information is presented in a format that is both attractive and easy to follow.

The subject of this guide is the whole of Ireland, both the Republic of Ireland and Northern Ireland which forms part of the United Kingdom.

The guide is in three parts. The first part gives a general account of the country, its topography, climate, flora and fauna, population, religion, language, society, education, economy, history, famous people as well as culture. A selection of quotations and some suggested routes lead into the second part, in which the principal places of tourist interest – towns, villages, landscapes – are described. The third part contains a variety of practical information designed to help visitors to find their way about and make the most of their stay. Both the sights and the practical information sections are listed in alphabetical order. The new Baedeker guides are noted for their concentration

The picturesque landscape of White Park Bay and the attractive little town of Kinsale reflect Ireland's charm

on essentials and their convenience of use. They contain numerous specially drawn plans and colour illustrations, and at the end of the book is a large map making it easy to locate the various places described in the Sights from A to Z section of the guide.

Contents

Baedeker Specials

The Emer

Green in all its many shades dominates this country, with meadows, fields and trees as far as the eye can see. Rambling fuchsia hedges and rhododendron bushes together with glorious parks and gardens set the tone. The main attraction for the visitor to Ireland is its natural beauty. The country is at its best in the sunshine but it would be a mistake to think it is always fine – it frequently rains. There is a saying that every day encompasses all four seasons. Following a heavy shower the sky soon clears up and the gentle Irish sun breaks through to bathe this hilly country with its many rivers in sunlight.

Apart from its countryside, Ireland's major attraction is its cultural history. The unique beauty of the strange features from Celtic prehistory is striking. High points of a journey looking at Irish art are the monastery sites and high crosses; the ruins, harmoniously embedded in the landscape, exert a powerful effect.

Holidays in Ireland can also be active. Top of the list of favourite sports is golf. The Emerald Isle has about 250 golf courses and new ones are always being created. The numerous clean rivers and lakes contain shoals of fish which make

Lough Erne
Lake district in Northern Ireland with innumerable little islands

Quin Abbey
One of Ireland's picturesque ruined abbeys

ald Isle

the island an angler's paradise. Many visitors explore the country on horseback or by bicycle. But you need to be fit – there are lots of hills to cycle up and down. Boating holidays on the River Shannon and its tributaries are popular – no licence is required to steer your own boat on Irish waters. There is no more picturesque way to see the countryside.

The Shannon–Erne Canal now connects Ireland's longest river with the beautiful Erne lake district of Northern Ireland. However, crossing the border from the Republic of Ireland to Northern Ireland is still difficult, and not just by boat. In the autumn of 1994 the bloody Troubles of Northern Ireland achieved a fragile peace and there are hopes for a more peaceful future with a normality slowly returning. Where Belfast and Londonderry used to resemble ghost towns in the evening, there is now life: in restaurants, discos, nightclubs, cinemas, the theatres and, of course, the pubs.

Indeed the best way to get to know the Irish is in a pub. Here, over a pint of Guinness, the locals tell stories, discuss life, sing songs or simply chat. Often the visitor is drawn into the conversation. The first word of Gaelic that the foreign guest learns is nearly always *fáilte* – it means welcome.

Advertisement
for the Irish national drink

Pubs
Imaginative decoration

Dublin
The Republic of Ireland's undisputed capital

Facts and Figures

The old Celtic language of Ireland is known as Irish or Gaelic. Since there are variations in the spelling of place names and personal names, in both their Irish and English versions, the forms adopted in this guide are those used in the publications of the Irish Tourist Board.

General

Ireland is politically divided into the Republic of Ireland (Eire in Irish) and Northern Ireland. Together with the main island of Great Britain and various smaller islands and groups of islands it forms part of the British Isles – a term of purely geographical significance. It is separated from Great Britain, to the east, by the North Channel, the Irish Sea – which can often be rough – and St George's Channel; the west coast is open to the Atlantic, with numerous rocky offshore islands and islets.

The total area of the island is 32,600 sq miles. From Malin Head in the north to Mizen Head in the south-west is 301 miles and the widest point from the east to the west coast is 180 miles.

Area

©Baedeker

**Republic of Ireland
Northern Ireland**

Location: from 51°30′ to 55°30′ N and 5°30′ to 10°30′ W

Area: 32,600 sq. miles/84,403 sq.km of which 5500 sq. miles/14,120 sq.km is Northern Ireland

Population: 3.5 million (Republic of Ireland) 1.6 million (Northern Ireland)

Capital of the Republic of Ireland: Dublin

◀ Cliffs of Moher on the west coast of Ireland

Topography

Interior

Only in the east, around Dublin, do the Central Lowlands reach the coast. The interior of the island is a landscape of extensive limestone plains with expanses of moorland, innumerable loughs (lakes) large and small, and here and there low ranges of hills; the Shannon system of rivers and lakes covers about a fifth of Ireland.

Mountains

Near the coast the pattern is different, with ranges of hills of some size and varying geology. The ranges in the south of Ireland are built of folded red sandstone, separated by river valleys, which are usually well wooded, and form a continuation of the mountains of Scotland and Britanny. The highest peak, at 3147 ft, is Carrantuohill (Macgillicuddy's Reeks) in the south-west of the island. In Connemara, Mayo and Donegal the predominant rock is granite, sometimes overlaid with quartzite. Characteristic of these areas are the isolated bare conical hills which rise abruptly out of the plain. A basalt plateau covers most of north-eastern Ireland. In the Wicklow Mountains granite again predominates. An area of particular interest both to geologists and to botanists is the karstic landscape of the Burren, near the west coast in Co. Clare.

Ireland went through at least two ice ages, which have left their traces in polished and striated rock surfaces and dark upland loughs, in the course of many valleys and in numerous moraines. The drumlins – elongated whale-backed mounds of boulder clay – which occur in great numbers across a wide swathe of northern Ireland, broadly between Sligo and Belfast, are deposits of this kind.

Coastline

Round Ireland's much-indented 1988-mile coastline, with its many bays and narrow inlets, will be found numbers of beautiful beaches. Some of

The coastal region around Donegal

View of the lakes at Killarney

the most impressive scenery along the coast is found in the Cliffs of Moher, Slieve League and the cliffs on Achill Island. Numerous sandy bays have extensive dunes.

In comparison with other European countries Ireland has so far had few environmental problems to contend with. That is partly because industrial growth has not advanced so much and partly because agriculture is primarily restricted to organic cattle farming. The strong south-westerly winds also limit the effects of air pollution. A relatively low level of population density is influential on the ecosystem.

Ecology

However, environmental problems are beginning to arise. The capacity of purification plants is insufficient, in many places industrial effluence and sewage from private houses flows untreated into the sea. The destruction of the bog country, the draining of some of Europe's unique moorland, has met with strong protests from environmentalists. In the cities of Dublin and Belfast pollution by heavy traffic is a problem.

Climate

Ireland lies in a region of mild south-westerly winds, subject to the influence of the warm waters brought by the Gulf Stream. Since no point on the island is more than 70 miles from the sea, the whole country has a relatively temperate climate, with mild winters and cool summers. Rain and wind are regular features of Irish weather, but long periods of rain are less common than in central Europe and the weather usually changes quickly. After a rainy day the sky will clear towards evening, with fine light effects and frequently also rainbows. Snow is rare except in the hills and never lies long.

Oceanic climate

Temperatures

Seasonal fluctuations in temperatures are small. While the temperature in the coldest months – January and February – ranges between 4°C in the north-east and 7°C in the south-west, the thermometer rises to 14–16°C in the warmest months – July and August – and very seldom exceeds 25°C. The sunniest months are usually May and June, and in general the south-east of the island gets the most sun.

Rainfall

The west of the island lies under the direct influence of Atlantic winds. The moisture-laden air masses are forced upwards by the coastal hills, and the cooling of the air at the higher levels brings down the rain in heavy downpours. Showers of this kind can frequently be seen coming, as they appear on the horizon and move past or draw rapidly closer. When a strong wind whips against the wall of rain, it is blown horizontally rather than falling from above. Average rainfall in the west of Ireland is around 305 mm on 250 days a year, while on the more sheltered east coast near Dublin it is only about 76 mm (on 190 days). The moisture content of the air is generally high, with the highest levels in the west.

Nature

Flora

Variety of species

The variety of flora throughout Ireland is unusually narrow. During the last ice age almost the whole country was covered in a layer of ice. Only a few Arctic plants were able to survive. When the ice melted Ireland was at first still connected to Great Britain and the continent by a land bridge. With the increase in sea level about 8000 years ago it became separated, but the post-glacial migration of plants was incomplete. So not even half the number of flowering species of plants which exist in Great Britain can be found in Ireland.

However, most visitors are not aware of this lack of variety. After all the island is covered in every conceivable shade of green – depending on the weather, cloud formation, amount of rainfall, wind direction and soil condition – which earns it the name of the Emerald Isle and attracts many visitors.

Forests

Of the forests which gradually covered the country after the ice age only a few remnants survive. The original tree cover consisted of oak, holly, birch, ash and hazel. Today only a small proportion of the country consists of forest and the government has made efforts to remedy this by extensive afforestation schemes. Most of the plantings have been of Sitka spruce, which has not in fact done particularly well in Ireland. Deciduous trees do flourish, however, and fine single specimens with wide-spreading, regular branches can frequently be seen.

Bogs

About 16 per cent of the land area of Ireland is covered with bog. There are different varieties of bog: highland bog (about 4 per cent), which reaches a depth of 23 ft; blanket bog (about 11 per cent, depth of 12 ft), which covers both upland and valley floor; and lowland bog. Various types of sphagnum moss flourish on all types of bog; on highland and blanket bog heather, cotton grass, ling, bell heather and bog asphodel are also found.

Subtropical Mediterranean and Arctic-alpine vegetation

Tropical and subtropical species originally planted in the parks and gardens of country houses have spread beyond these, particularly in the warm south-west where palm trees and evergreens are found.

Giant broom and rhododendron bushes together with flowering fuchsia hedges provide splashes of colour among the greenery. In the nature parks, however, these are not welcome as they choke the indigenous vegetation.

Found in Ireland: foxgloves ...   *... cotton grass ...*

... tall fuchsia hedges ...   *... and gigantic rhododendron bushes*

In the mild Irish climate many familiar flowering plants flourish luxuriantly and develop vigorous new forms, such as the foxglove and a bluebell with an unusually long stem and deep blue colour.

Surprisingly in the south-west and in the Burren, subtropical plants and Arctic-alpine plants are found side by side. Owing to the cool summers the latter were able to survive after the last ice age.

Fauna

Variety of species

As with its flora Ireland is also relatively poor in native fauna. There are only 56 mammals (89 in Great Britain), no snakes at all and the only reptile is the upland or bog lizard.

Birds

There is, however, a wide variety of birds. In addition to the 135 indigenous varieties there are about 250 species which overwinter in Ireland or rest here on their migratory flight. Hawthorn hedges provide nesting places for songbirds. In moorland areas the cry of the curlew and the snipe can be heard, and the song of the soaring lark. Oystercatchers leave their haunts on the coast and move far inland to wherever they can find sufficient water. Gulls and guillemots nest on crags off the Atlantic coast, and puffins with their brilliant beaks are occasionally seen. Cormorants patrol the coasts, and gannets, flapping their

Puffin

great wings, plunge down from a great height to seize their prey. Such seabirds as the storm petrel and fulmar are more rarely seen.

Fish, sea creatures

The water of Irish loughs (a term applied both to inland lakes and to major arms of the sea), rivers and streams is frequently brown and peaty, but it is almost always unpolluted and supports an abundant fish population. Salmon and trout are the most sought-after species; pike and rainbow trout are relatively recent introductions.

The seas around Ireland are home to 250 species of fish. Herring, sprat, cod, mackerel, plaice, haddock, sole and monkfish are of chief importance for commercial fishing. Round the coasts of Ireland various species of seal can be encountered.

Society

Population

With over 3.5 million inhabitants to an area of 27,136 sq miles Ireland is one of the most thinly populated countries in Europe. To the visitor travelling around the country this impression is reinforced by the fact that almost one in three Irish people live in the area around Dublin (population of Greater Dublin: 1.1 million). Northern Ireland has about 1.6 million inhabitants and a population density of about 187 per sq mile.

Population trends

In the first half of the 19th c. Ireland was one of the most densely populated countries in Europe. During the 18th c. a prolonged period of peace and intensive agricultural activity resulted in a sharp population increase; in the second half of the century the population was increasing by 15 per cent every 10 years. By 1821 the population numbered 6.8 million, by 1845 it had reached 8.5 million (figures relate to the whole country). The Great Famine of 1845–9, caused by successive failures of the potato harvest, halted this trend. By 1851 the population had dropped to 6.5 million. Almost 1 million people had died and another million had emigrated. Over the following decades unfavourable living conditions contributed to a decrease in population. In 1961 only 2.8 million people were living in the Republic of Ireland.

The Irish enjoy discussions and debates

At the beginning of the 1970s this trend began to change. A sharp natural growth in population and improved economic factors resulted in a population increase between 1971 and 1981 from 3 million to 3.4 million (growth of 13.3 per cent; in Northern Ireland the figures for the same period were only 1.7 per cent). Recently, however, despite a high birth rate for a European country, growth has been slow.

In the second half of the 19th c. a wave of emigration gradually began, which grew considerably in strength after the Great Famine of 1845–9. During the 19th c. about 3.5 million Irish people left their homes to try and build a new life in the United States or in Great Britain.

Emigration

Following the second world war emigration began again (between 1951 and 1961 over 40,000 emigrated annually). In the 1970s this trend reversed but the high unemployment of the 1980s led to further emigration. In the past it had been poorer farmers and unskilled labourers who left the country but in recent years the number of young educated Irish leaving has drastically risen.

The Irish who emigrated to the US settled in the large cities of the north where they soon dominated the market for unskilled labour (building sewers and railways). They grew into a political force to be taken seriously. Between 1870 and 1920, in every town in the US which had a sizeable Irish population, there was an Irish politician, often an Irish mayor and a large Irish contingent in the police and fire brigade. In spite of this considerable influence it was 1960 before an American of Irish descent, John F Kennedy (1917–63), was elected president. Kennedy, leader of the Democratic Party, was the first Catholic president.

The Irish in the US

Also of Irish descent was the American dramatist Eugene O'Neill (1888–1953); his plays have been performed since 1916 and in 1936 he received the Nobel Prize for literature.

Society

The 'travellers' or 'tinkers' (this last term is considered derogatory) are an underprivileged minority. Like the gypsies (with whom they are not related) they are persons of no fixed abode who in the past earned their living as tinkers and had a secret argot-like language. It is accepted today that the travellers did not come from elsewhere but are of Irish origin. They have long since exchanged their colourfully painted horse-drawn *vargos*, in which they used to travel the country and which today are a tourist attraction, for modern caravans.

Those families are described as Anglo-Irish whose forefathers from the mid-17th c., either as members of the lower English aristocracy or as former officers, were rewarded with expropriated Irish lands for their services. In contrast to earlier English settlers who learned to speak Gaelic and accepted the lifestyle of the local population, these new arrivals kept to themselves. They continued to speak English, kept their religion and shut themselves away behind high walls from their Catholic and Irish neighbours. In the worst cases they merely used their lands as a source of income, seldom coming to Ireland and appointing agents to collect the rent from the people living in mud huts on their property. Later the 'Anglo-Irish gentlemen' as the ruling class became upholders of cultural life. They built country houses and laid out large parks where many tropical plants flourished thanks to the mild Irish climate.

The Anglo-Irish were responsible for the spate of building activity in 18th c. Dublin which has been described as a windfall for European architecture. They built their own university, Trinity College, from which many important figures have graduated: politicians and philosophers as well as poets and writers.

In the 18th c. several cultural organisations were established by the Anglo-Irish. The Royal Irish Academy collected early manuscripts (including the famous Psalter of Columcille) and published a Gaelic

Traditional cottage

dictionary extending to several volumes. The Royal Dublin Society, known today for organising the Horse Show, was also dedicated to promoting cultural life. Its collections formed the foundations of the National Library and National Museum.

In the course of time the Anglo-Irish settled into a casual, rural lifestyle. With the larger part of the island becoming an independent state they became less influential. Some of the former estates were broken up by the Irish.

In Ireland it is customary to own your own house (no matter how modest) but in the cities more and more people rent a flat. The traditional house is the cottage with a pale straw roof, but living in one is not particularly pleasant. Usually the cottage consists of a central large room with a smaller room on each side. Families of six or more still live in an area of 654 sq ft. Not all the cottages have electricity and running water, so it is not surprising that there are few left which are inhabited except in the extreme barren regions in the west. Those who can afford it have exchanged their cottages, which tourists find so romantic, for a comfortable bungalow or simple farmhouse.

Living conditions

Religion

During the 5th c. the Celtic population of Ireland adopted the Christian faith as it was taught by St Patrick. There were no martyrs. Frequently the old Irish kinship groups went over en masse to the monastic life: the head of the clan became abbot and his family, retainers and servants followed him. Nunneries were established for the women. As a result there was a great flowering of religious houses and the number of monks grew rapidly; and just as the kinship group had previously lived in a ringfort, so they now sought safety within the enclosing walls of the monastic precinct. The penitentials and monastic rules that have come down to us bear witness to the hard conditions of life in the early monasteries. St Patrick is believed to have received part of his training on the Iles de Lérins, off the Mediterranean coast near Cannes, and it seems likely that while there he met representatives of some of the Eastern Churches. This may be how the idea of the *religio arctior*, the strictest form of ascetic life, came to Ireland, where it was enthusiastically received.

Celtic Christianity

Since the faithful were deprived of the opportunity of 'red martyrdom', at the cost of their own lives, many of them sought the 'green martyrdom' of voluntary exile to remote places. While the hermits of the Near East withdrew to the desert, their Irish counterparts retired to a solitary life on very small inaccessible islands off the Atlantic coast. A typical example of a monastic settlement of the 8th c. is provided by the tiny churches and beehive-shape stone cells on the upper terraces of the treeless islet of Skellig Michael.

Green martyrdom

In addition to a church and cells for the monks, a monastery would have a refectory and a guest house, scriptoria and craftsmen's workshops. Students from England and the Continent and men and women fleeing before the upheavals of the great migrations sought refuge in the Irish religious houses, some of which grew to become monastic cities. Latin as well as Irish was spoken in the monasteries, and not only religious works but the writings of Virgil, Cicero and Ovid were read. There are records, too, of monks who knew Greek.

Monasteries

At the same time there was a movement in the opposite direction. Side by side with the 'green martyrdom' there developed the 'white martyrdom', the *peregrinatio pro Christo* – the pilgrimage for Christ's sake. In frail boats made of animal hides on a timber framework, Irish monks

White martyrdom

ventured out into the 'pathless sea' and made their way as itinerant preachers by way of England and France to other European countries. With them they took not only their austere faith but also a humanist education, carrying in leather pouches their precious manuscripts, including copies of the scriptures which perhaps were already illuminated. Traces of their journeys and their settlements can still be found today. In regions devastated by war and the passage of armies they established new religious and cultural centres. Later, from the 9th c. onwards, when the process of conversion to Christianity was complete, Irish monks still found their way to Europe as scholars and as advisers to various European rulers. Thus Ireland was able to repay to the Continent, with interest, what it had earlier received from it.

St Patrick

Among the saints of the early Celtic Church there are some names which will constantly be encountered by visitors to Ireland. St Patrick (➤ Famous People) is the national saint of the Irish. Around his life numerous legends have grown up.

St Enda

St Enda was one of the first to withdraw, in the year 490, to a remote and solitary place in order to devote himself to a life of study and renunciation on the model of the desert hermits. Soon so many disciples followed him to his retreat on Inishmore, one of the Aran islands, that a large monastic settlement grew up, the fame of which spread to the Continent.

St Ciarán

Many of the monks who gathered round St Enda themselves founded monasteries and gained a reputation for sanctity, including St Ciarán, who in 548 established the monastic settlement of Clonmacnoise on the Shannon. The learning of the Clonmacnoise monks soon became renowned on the Continent.

St Kevin

Equal to Clonmacnoise in size and importance was Glendalough in the Wicklow Mountains, to which St Kevin, followed by numerous disciples, withdrew to lead a hermit's life.

St Brigid

The leading female saint was St Brigid, who founded a large double monastery for monks and nuns in Kildare in 490. In her 'fire house' there burned a perpetual fire – perhaps the continuation of some pre-Christian cult – which was extinguished only at the Reformation. A 'St Brigid's cross', woven of straw or reeds and regarded as a protective symbol, is still found in Irish houses, and also on cars and tractors.

St Brendan

St Brendan, who founded a monastery at Clonfert and gathered round him a host of monks, became the model for all those who left home for Christ's sake and ventured on to the open sea, sailing they knew not where (➤ Famous People).

St Columbanus the Elder

St Columba (521 or 543–97) is known in Irish as Columcille (the Dove of the Churches) and in Latin as Columbanus (the Elder, to distinguish him from the other Columbanus). Columba, who was born at Gartan and, like St Kevin, came from a royal house, went into exile to atone for his guilt. He had secretly made a copy of a psalter belonging to St Finian, who guarded his books jealously and demanded that Columba should give him the copy. When the two could not agree Finian brought the matter before the high king, who held that the copy belonged to Finian, on the grounds that a copy should go with the original book, as a calf goes with a cow. Columba and his supporters refused to accept this verdict, and thereupon fought a battle with the high king on the slopes of Benbulben, north of Sligo. Columba was victorious but left 3000 of his men dead on the field, and by way of penance left home and went into exile. In 563 he landed with 12 companions on the Scottish island of Hy (now Iona), where he founded a monastery. From there he carried on missionary work, mainly among the Picts and Angles. For all the strictness of his faith he is said to have been a kindly man and a lover of nature, particularly of animals.

St Columbanus the Younger, born in Ireland in 540, was of a less amiable temperament than Columba. About 590, when a disciple of St Comgall in the celebrated monastery of Bangor and already of advanced years, he resolved to go on pilgrimage. With 12 companions he travelled to the Continent and gained great influence at the Burgundian court, founding monasteries at Annegray and Luxeuil.

St Columbanus the Younger

He is described as powerful in the faith but uncompromising and irascible. After a dispute with the Burgundian king he and his companions made their way up the Rhine valley to Lake Constance and crossed the Alps into northern Italy. The last monastery he founded was in Bobbio in Lombardy, where he died in 615. The rules he laid down were an influential contribution to Western monasticism, and the disciples whom he gathered round him were thus given a definite pattern for the monastic life.

There were other Irish saints who propagated their faith on the Continent among whom was St Gallus, one of Columba's companions, who remained at Lake Constance and founded the Monastery of St Gall. The monastery possesses a set of illuminated manuscripts from the era when Irish manuscripts flourished.

St Gallus

St Kilian is said to have declared, 'Look how green and beautiful this country is,' when he arrived at the Main river with his companions Colonat and Totnan. The three stayed there and later were the few from the Celtic Church to have suffered martyrdom. These Irish are remembered still in the area around Würzburg, in prayers and pilgrimages, in churches and on wayside shrines.

St Kilian

St Virgil, the 'geometer', a prestigious scientist, is honoured as the patron saint of Salzburg along with St Rupert. He laid the foundation stone for the first cathedral in this city.

St Virgil

The influence of Irish-Scottish missionaries reached far into eastern Europe, as is shown by the existence of 'Scottish monasteries' at Regensburg, Vienna and Kiev. Thus the early Irish Church was able to transmit to other countries far afield the treasures of its faith and its learning, and its foundations became 'the store cupboards of the past' and 'the cradles of the future'.

Scottish monasteries

More than in any other country in Europe, the tradition of the faith has been maintained unbroken among the Roman Catholic population of Ireland, in spite of the oppression to which they were exposed in past centuries. When Catholic worship was forbidden, Mass continued to be celebrated in secret in the open air, at 'Mass rocks' in remote places. Those who wanted to become priests had to seek training and ordination abroad, mainly in France and Spain. When the building of churches was again permitted they had at first to be unobtrusively sited in side streets. The influence of the Roman Catholic Church, to which some 94 per cent of the population belongs, today makes itself felt in all areas of life in the Irish Republic. On Sundays the numerous services are attended by crowded congregations. Children are commonly baptised with the names of early Irish saints. Marriages are celebrated in church in the presence of the whole family; registry-office weddings are rare. Divorce is prohibited under Irish law. Abortions are also illegal even in cases where the mother's life is in serious danger (in a referendum in November 1992 a majority voted for freedom of information in questions of abortion and for freedom of travel for pregnant women, but voted against a change in the existing law).

The Church and the tradition of the faith

Religion

Priests

Priests are part of everyday life in the Republic. Irish priests and nuns are found in many countries, particularly in the Third World, as teachers, nurses and social workers. In the field of private charitable work within Ireland itself, the Irish put the inhabitants of wealthier countries to shame. There are, of course, more negative aspects, including the strict censorship of plays and books – a reflection of the influence exerted by the Church until quite recent times over the whole range of culture in the Republic – which led writers like James Joyce and Sean O'Casey to leave the country.

Pilgrimages

Some of the pilgrimages which are still popular among Catholics in Ireland indicate that the ascetic aspirations of the early Celtic Church have persisted to the present day. On the last Sunday in July every year tens of thousands of people climb Ireland's holy mountain, Croagh Patrick, in memory of the 40 days of penance which St Patrick imposed on himself on the summit of the hill in the year 441.

The ascent of this bare cone of quartzite with its steep slopes and sharp scree is exceedingly strenuous. The pilgrimage is not performed in a well-ordered procession: people go singly or in groups, such as school classes, sports clubs, military units; many are non-Catholics or foreigners. Some pilgrims go barefoot. Until a few years ago the hill was climbed on the night of Saturday to Sunday, but when, with increasing numbers of pilgrims, the number of mishaps also increased, the Church authorities moved the pilgrimage to the following day.

An island in Lough Derg is also associated with St Patrick. In prehistory a cave on the island was thought to be the entrance to the Underworld; and in the Middle Ages the place became famous throughout Europe as St Patrick's Purgatory, when a travelling knight claimed to have seen the fires of purgatory in the cave.

The pilgrims who make what has been called 'the hardest pilgrimage in Christendom' are now almost exclusively Irish (mid-July to mid-August). They spend three days on the island performing the numerous penances prescribed, mainly vigils and fasting, as well as attending Mass and praying. During the pilgrimage season in summer visitors are not allowed on the island and photography is forbidden.

Knock

Knock, in Co. Mayo, the scene of a 19th c. apparition of the Virgin, also attracts large numbers of pilgrims, including sick people seeking a cure. Few foreigners find their way to Knock.

Pattern day

In addition to the major pilgrimages there are many local ones on a particular saint's day ('pattern day'). Thus, for example, on Inisheer, the smallest of the Aran Islands, the Church of St Cavan, which is in danger of disappearing under drifting sand, is swept clear so that Mass can be celebrated on June 14th.

Holy wells

'Lourdes grottoes' are often set up at crossroads or in natural rock formations. Occasionally visitors will encounter a well surrounded by a wall, round which rosaries or coins or sometimes everyday objects have been deposited; and bushes or posts near the well are hung with rags of clothing. Such 'holy wells' are credited with the power of healing particular ailments.

Belief in spirits

Just as monks were the first to record the popular ancient legends and thus helped to perpetuate them, so too the Celtic Church tolerated and preserved beliefs that attributed some form of life to nature. Hence the various forms of spirit which survive in Irish tradition, such as the fairies or *sidhe* who dwell on tree-clad hills, and the 'little people' or leprechauns who live under hawthorn bushes. To destroy a hawthorn bush, it is believed in the west of Ireland, brings bad luck. There, too, lives a black beast known as the *pooka* which scares lonely travellers, and the *banshee*, whose wailing cry foretells the death of a member of one of the old-established families.

Language

All official papers are required to be presented in both Irish and English, since both languages have equal status. Members of the Irish parliament, the Dáil, generally begin their speeches with a few words in Irish. Even road signs are in the two languages. Normally communication is conducted in English, for it is only in a few restricted areas in the west and south of the country that Irish is the mother tongue of the people. These linguistic islands are collectively known as Gaeltacht; they have their own government minister and the inhabitants enjoy certain tax advantages. Whether these and other measures and the efforts of an Irish speaking elite will be sufficient to ensure the survival of the Irish language remains to be seen.

Bilingualism

The Irish or Erse language, also called by the philologically incorrect name of Gaelic, belongs to the Celtic group of languages and, within that group, to the insular Celtic languages. Gaelic in the wider sense includes Scottish as well as Irish Gaelic. Another insular Celtic language is Breton, which was taken into north-western France by immigrants from the British Isles. References to the Irish language in this guide are to be taken as meaning the Old Celtic language, not the regional variant of English spoken in Ireland.

Irish/Gaelic

Originally Celtic was spoken all over the British Isles. The Germanic peoples who began to settle in Britain in the 5th c. brought their Germanic languages with them, and the Old English and later English which developed out of those tongues displaced the old language so effectively that it survived only in remote regions without contact with

History

Gaeltacht

▨ Irish-language areas in Ireland

© Baedeker

the outside world – and Ireland in those days was such an area. In later centuries, during the period of English rule and of the United Kingdom of Great Britain and Ireland – that is, until the establishment of an independent Irish state – the speaking of the Irish language was not simply a means of communication but also a declaration of national identity. The latter part of the 18th c. saw an enthusiastic and almost romantic interest in Old Celtic, which prepared the ground for the appearance of such a celebrated literary fraud as MacPherson's *Ossian*. Like many languages, spoken by minorities, which have never attained the status of a national or even an official language (such as Breton, Provençal, Basque or Catalan), Irish enjoyed a regular renaissance in the late 19th c. – a recollection by the Irish people of their own language, culture and history which involved not only a stocktaking of their inheritance but also a purposeful concern with the old language as a living spoken tongue.

Ogham script

From the 4th to the 7th c. the language was written in the ogham script. Although based on the sounds of the Latin alphabet, ogham is quite different from the latter in origin and characteristics. The 20 letters of the ogham alphabet take the form of points or horizontal or oblique lines, in groups of from one to five, set on a long vertical line (which often runs down the edge of a stone slab). Later the Latin alphabet was adopted.

Language characteristics

Although the Irish language may seem strange and different to one accustomed to the Germanic and Romance languages of Europe – with no parallels to familiar structures, no immediately obvious relationships in the vocabulary – it nevertheless belongs to the great Indo-European family of languages which spans so much of the globe. Having developed independently of other European languages from an early stage, it has evolved grammatical patterns which have no direct equivalents in those languages. There is the additional difficulty, for those seeking to understand or learn Irish, that it has no 'received standard', merely a series of local variants which have equal validity and status.

Gaeltacht

Despite the nurturing of the Irish language over the last two centuries, the areas in which this language is spoken are steadily diminishing. Censuses from 1851 and 1961 show that in just over a century these areas have decreased by almost 80 per cent – although this reveals nothing about the number of Irish speakers. The latest estimate is that about 55,000 Irish speak the language.

Ogham script

State

Government and constitution

The Republic of Ireland (Poblacht na h'Éireann), established in 1949, succeeded the Irish Free State which came into being as an independent state in 1921. Under a constitution adopted in 1937 it is a parliamentary democracy governed by a House of Representatives (Dáil Éireann) and Senate (Seanad Éireann), with executive power in the hands of the prime minister (Taoiseach) and his ministers. The head of state is an elected president (Uachtarán na h'Éireann) whose duties are mainly of representative nature. Their term of office is seven years. Since 1997 the law professor Mary McAleese has been president.

Ireland

Republic of Ireland

Northern Ireland

National frontier ———
Provincial boundary ———
County boundary ———
(in Northern Ireland district boundary)

© Baedeker

DISTRICTS IN NORTHERN IRELAND

1 Moyle
2 Ballymoney
3 Coleraine
4 Limavady
5 Londonderry
6 Strabane
7 Omagh
8 Fermanagh
9 Dungannon

10 Cookstown
11 Magherafelt
12 Ballymena
13 Antrim
14 Lisburn
15 Craigavon
16 Armagh
17 Newry
   and Mourne

18 Banbridge
19 Down
20 North Down
21 Ards
22 Castlereagh
23 Belfast
24 Newtownabbey
25 Carrickfergus
26 Larne

Education

National flag

The flag of the Republic of Ireland is a tricolour – green, white and orange. Green is the ancient colour symbolising Ireland and stands for the Gaelic and Anglo-Norman element of the Catholic majority; orange is for the Protestants, derived from the colour of King William of Orange who routed the Catholic king James II in 1690 at the Battle of the Boyne; and white is the symbol of peace between the two groups.

National emblem

The national emblem is a golden harp on a blue background. With this Ireland remembers its great tradition of singers and bards. This is shown together with the three-leaved shamrock, a symbol recalling St Patrick and his interpretation of the Trinity.

National anthem

The national anthem is *A Soldier's Song* – written in 1907 by Peadar Kearney, with music by Patrick Heeney and Peadar Kearney – a marching song harking back to the fight for independence.

Parties

The two main parties in Ireland, Fianna Fáil (founded in 1926) and Fine Gael (founded in 1923), go back to the Irish independence movement Sinn Féin. Both parties, which have alternated in government since the state was founded, have conservative aims. They both suffered a substantial loss of votes at the last parliamentary elections.

Since the elections on June 6th 1997 there has been a minority coalition between Fianna Fáil and the Progressive Democrats.

Legal system

The law of the Republic is based broadly on the principles of British law. The old Irish Brehon Law (law of the judges), based on traditional Celtic concepts, was abolished by the British authorities in the 17th c.

Army

The army of the Republic (ca 18,000) is a volunteer force – there is no compulsory military service in Ireland – which has shown its mettle in United Nations peacekeeping forces in many parts of the world.

Administration

Ireland is divided into four historic provinces: Leinster, Munster, Ulster and Connaught. After the founding of the Free State of Ireland in 1921 the major part of Ulster acceded to Great Britain; the south and north-west belonging to the Republic of Ireland.

The provinces are subdivided into counties. Of a total of 32 counties 26 belong to the Republic of Ireland and six to Northern Ireland – these latter were replaced by 26 districts in 1973.

Education

Education

From time immemorial the Irish have held in esteem the spoken and the written word, and indeed all knowledge, and those who teach are also held in high regard. This respect was accorded even to the 'hedge-schoolmasters' who travelled the country during the period of the penal laws and taught the country children for a penny a week in the shelter of a hedge. It is said that they carried their inkwell on a chain round their necks and stuffed an edition of Virgil as well as a Gaelic reading book into their pockets. When the Irish were again allowed to have schools, education was mostly in the hands of the teaching orders and the secular clergy. The Christian Brothers played a particularly important part in educating the children of the poorer classes. Today education is compulsory from the age of six to 15.

National schools, secondary schools

There is a state system of national schools with a uniform curriculum, in which some of the staff are ecclesiastics. As a rule children go to these schools in their fourth or fifth year. Later they go on to secondary schools, which are not state run but are grant aided and inspected by the Department of Education. The Leaving Certificate at the end of the school course is issued by the department. In recent years some comprehensive schools have been established. The school day is from 9am to about 3pm. The yellow school buses which take children to school are a familiar sight in country areas.

For the further education of pupils aiming at a practical trade there are vocational schools – which also provide further education classes for adults – and a number of technical colleges.

Technical colleges

There are four universities in the Republic of Ireland – Trinity College and Dublin City University in Dublin, the University of Limerick and the National University of Ireland. Trinity College, the oldest university in Ireland, was established by Elizabeth I in 1591, exclusively for the sons of the Protestant Anglo-Irish. Irish students were admitted for the first time in 1793, but it took a further 70 years before they were able to receive grants, hold office and receive honours. Nevertheless Trinity College has played an important part in the intellectual and political life of Ireland. Among its students have been writers including Oliver Goldsmith and Jonathan Swift, later on Oscar Wilde and John Millington Synge, the philosopher and statesman Edmund Burke, and also men such as Theobald Wolfe Tone and Robert Emmet, both of whom died for the cause of Irish independence.

Universities

The National University of Ireland, which can trace its origins back to a college of which Cardinal Newman was the first rector, was established early in the 20th c. It now consists of three colleges in Dublin, Galway and Cork. Associated with it is St Patrick's College at Maynooth, a seminary for priests which also admits lay students; it has a department of Celtic studies. The National University has over 8000 matriculated students in Dublin, 4000 in Cork and 3500 in Galway.

While Trinity College (about 6000 students) is housed in fine classical buildings in the heart of Dublin, the three colleges of the National University are situated in suburban surroundings. Galway in particular has a fine campus on the banks of the Corrib, with handsome modern

Trinity College, Dublin

buildings. Originally all teaching in the Galway college, including that of science, was in Irish, but English is now also used. The college still sees itself, however, as the intellectual and cultural centre for the Irish speaking areas in the west of the country, and seeks to bring fresh impulses to this long-neglected region. The National Institutes for Higher Education in Limerick and Dublin became universities in 1989 and are now known as the University of Limerick (UL) and Dublin City University (DCU). In addition to the four universities in the Irish Republic, there are two in Northern Ireland: Queen's University in Belfast and the University of Ulster spread over four sites with its administrative centre in Coleraine.

Preserving the Irish language

Efforts are being made in the rest of the Irish Republic to rescue the old national language from extinction. Irish is a compulsory subject in all schools, and in 28 secondary schools the teaching is wholly or partly in that language. Classes of city children are taken during the summer holidays to places in the Gaeltacht, where they stay with Irish speaking families. Adults who want to improve their Irish can go to one of the Irish colleges in the Gaeltacht, and their regular courses are also attended by foreigners, usually of Irish origin.

Economy

Developments to 1945

After the establishment of the Irish Free State in 1921 most of the country's capital remained in the hands of wealthy Anglo-Irish, and the native Irish had little share in the profits. When Eamon de Valera's Fianna Fáil Party came to power in 1932, however, it followed a policy of economic self-sufficiency and fostered the growth of productive industry by protective tariffs. When the new Irish government refused to pay the 'land annuities' – the interest on capital originally advanced to enable Irish farmers to buy their land – as the 1921 treaty required, an economic war developed between Britain and the Free State. The British government imposed a 40 per cent duty on Irish goods, which led to a drastic decline in Irish exports. A compromise was reached under which the quota for the export of Irish cattle to Britain was increased on the understanding that the Free State would purchase all its requirements of coal from Britain. The economic war finally came to an end in 1938 when Britain withdrew from its naval bases in Ireland.

In the years before the second world war the Irish government promoted the country's economic development by a variety of means, including the establishment of partly state-controlled institutions such as the Agricultural Credit Corporation and the Electricity Supply Board. The Republic of Ireland's withdrawal from the Commonwealth in 1949 gave it greater economic independence.

Economic performance

In recent years the economy in Ireland has strengthened not least because of support by the EU. With low inflation a relatively high growth rate has been possible. In 1999 the inflation rate was 2.4 per cent and the gross national product increased by 7 per cent.

Yet Ireland still ranks as one of the poorest countries in the EU. Income per capita is about 70 per cent of the EU average. Contrary to the forecasts, however, Ireland has reduced its unemployment rate to 8.4 per cent; in the early 1990s it had been almost 17 per cent.

Minerals

Although Ireland is relatively poor in minerals, the working of metal ores has been increased in recent years – principally lead, zinc and silver (at Tynnagh, Co. Galway, Navan, Co. Meath, and elsewhere), but also copper, mercury and pyrites. A source of natural gas has been found at Kinsale.

Industry

Foodstuffs, drink, tobacco and textiles are traditional Irish industries, but since the late 1950s the government has promoted the development of new industries and the establishment of foreign firms in Ireland, manufacturing machinery, electrical and electronic apparatus, pharmaceuticals and chemicals as well as textiles and foodstuffs.

Attracted by tax advantages, relatively low wages (the average wage in Ireland is 40 per cent lower than in the US or Germany) and a low cost of living, about 1000 foreign companies have established subsidiaries in the Emerald Isle. A quarter of the working population have a foreign employer. From Germany 200 or so companies have dared to branch out to the edge of Europe, together with mainly British, American and Dutch firms.

Some 70 per cent of the country's total area is devoted to agriculture, the great bulk of it as pasture. In central Ireland cattle are reared for beef, while in the south dairy farming predominates. After cattle, the most important types of livestock are sheep, pigs and poultry. On good grazing land racehorses are bred for export. The predominant agricultural crop is barley, which is used in the brewing of beer as well as for fodder. The production of potatoes, sugar beet, wheat and oats is also of economic importance.

Agriculture

The fishing industry has long been neglected, the fishing fleet virtually obsolete. The particularly clean rivers, lakes and bays are one of the country's assets. In recent years fish farms have sprung up, breeding high quality fish.

A third of the Irish Republic's energy needs is met by hydroelectric and peat-fired power stations and rather more than 60 per cent by imported fuels, namely coal and oil. The largest of the hydroelectric stations on the country's numerous rivers lies on the Shannon.

Energy

Much of the Irish central plain and extensive areas on the north-west, west and south coasts consist of moorland and bog, and peat has long

Cattle on the edge of the Burren

been, and still is, the domestic fuel of Ireland. Since the beginning of industrialisation it has been increasingly worked by mechanical methods for use as industrial fuel, and in 1946 the government established Bord na Móna, an organisation concerned with all aspects of peat working, processing and use. There are now several peat-fired power stations; peat briquettes, factory made from milled peat, provide domestic and industrial fuel; and peat is increasingly used by gardeners to improve their soil. There is a peat research institute at Droichead Nua. Gradually the dangers inherent in the continued digging of peat on the moors are being realised. Every year some 14 sq miles of moorland are destroyed and it is feared that they will soon disappear altogether.

Exports

Britain is the principal customer for Irish exports, though the British share of the total has fallen from two-thirds in the 1960s to just over a half today. Over the same period exports to the other EU countries have risen to some 30 per cent of the total. The main exports are cattle, meat, machinery, textiles and chemicals. For some years the value of exports has exceeded that of imports.

Tourism

Despite the many ancient monuments, castles and stately homes, picturesque scenery and charming people, Ireland was for a long time regarded as an attractive holiday region by only a handful of tourists.

Not until 1988 were any efforts made to attract a significant number of visitors to the Irish Republic. In the 1990s there was a significant increase in tourism, especially to Dublin. However, there is no intention of giving the country the image of a destination for mass tourism, but rather to improve facilities at the quieter times of the year. It is hoped that these measures will create an additional 25,000 jobs in the service sector.

Many fishing boats are somewhat old-fashioned

Peat bogs – an increasingly rare sight

About 85 per cent of the 6 million international visitors to the Emerald Isle come from the UK, France, Germany, Italy, Holland, the US and Australia.

Tourism in Northern Ireland was badly hit by the outbreak of the Troubles at the end of the 1960s. After 25 years of decline an upturn is hoped for. At present Northern Ireland has accommodation for no more than 7,500 visitors but that could quickly change. Primarily in coastal regions owners of guest houses and small country hotels are hoping for wealthy foreign clientele.

History

Stone Age
(ca 7000–2000 BC)

Probably in about 7000 BC the first settlers reach Ireland and gradually bring the land into cultivation. They are believed to have come from Scotland, first establishing themselves in what is now Antrim, in the north-east, and moving on from there into the interior of the island. They initially live by hunting, gathering and fishing.

Ca 4000 BC

After a second wave of incomers the clearance of forest and scrub land begins, and the population turns to farming and herding. The first megalithic tombs are constructed.

Bronze Age
(ca 2000–500 BC)

Weapons begin to be made of metal – axes, daggers and swords are produced – and, towards the end of the Bronze Age, large pots, shields and horns.

Iron Age
(ca 500 BC–AD 400)

The Gaels, a Celtic people, come to Ireland and subjugate the native inhabitants, the Druid-ruled Tuatha Dé Danaan (People of the Goddess Danu). In the prevailing insecurity, with constant raids and cattle stealing, the people of the island seek safety in strong forts. Until AD 400 kings rule over the people. The new iron weapons are superior to the older bronze swords.

Gradually a division of Ireland into four provinces develops. Society is split into three classes – priests (*druí*), warriors and peasants. The king (*rí*) owes allegiance to an over-king (*ruiri*), who in turn is subject to a king of over-kings (*rí ruirech*), or high king. Below the king are the nobles of the warrior caste (*flaithi*), who are patrons of the *aes dána*, men of art and learning, including poets, doctors and jurists. The family unit is the *derbfhine*, a four-generation family which possesses land and rights of succession.

Early Christian period
(ca 400–1170)

Many of the Irish are converted to Christianity and numerous monasteries are founded. Viking raids on the island are repelled.

Ca 432

St Patrick, captured by Irish pirates and brought to Ireland as a slave, escapes but later returns to Ireland and converts its people to the Christian faith.

5th–9th c.

After Patrick's death numerous monasteries are founded, which during the 6th c. grow in size and influence. Many monks leave home and spread the Christian faith in Scotland (Columbanus the Elder, d. 597) and England and on the Continent (Columbanus the Younger, d. 615).

Ca 800

Viking raids. Vikings establish settlements on the east coast of Ireland which later develop into towns (including Dublin, Wexford and Waterford). They teach the Irish the art of shipbuilding.

Ca 1014

In the Battle of Clontarf, near Dublin, the Vikings and their allies are defeated by the Irish under their high king, Brian Boru, who is killed in the battle. This defeat puts an end to the Viking conquest of Ireland.

Norman period
(1170–1534)

The descendants of the Normans who had come to Britain with William the Conqueror in 1066 attack Ireland from bases in Wales and seize much land.

King Henry II of England (1154–89) establishes fiefs in Ireland for

Anglon Norman barons and receives the homage of the Irish clan chiefs. The Anglo-Normans, leaving the Irish only certain areas in western and northern Ireland, build mighty castles to defend their territories. They found numerous monasteries for the new monastic orders (such as the Cistercians and Dominicans), to which they appoint English abbots. Inland, towns come into being as centres of commerce and authority.

The Battle of Calann, near Kenmare, is one of the first signs of success-   1261
ful Irish resistance to the Anglo-Normans. Their power is weakened by
the Black Death which ravages the country.

Decline of Anglo-Norman rule. A new Irish national feeling emerges –   15th c.
fostered, paradoxically, by one of the great Anglo-Norman families, the
Geraldines. They and the Butlers, another Anglo-Norman family, dominate Irish political life in the second half of the century.

Ireland is still more closely bound to Britain, and the condition of the   English rule
Irish people grows steadily worse as English law and English govern-   (1534–1782)
ment are imposed on them.

Execution of Silken Thomas, a Geraldine.   1534

Henry VIII (1509–47) breaks with the Pope because of his divorce; disso-   Ca 1535
lution of the monasteries.

Henry VIII assumes the title of King of Ireland.   1541

Elizabeth I (1558–1603) continues the political and religious oppression   Late 16th c.
of the predominantly Catholic Irish.

After many years of resistance Hugh O'Neill defeats the English in the   1598
Battle of the Yellow Ford.

In the Battle of Kinsale the Irish are defeated.   1601–3

The traditional Irish system of Brehon Law is abolished by the British   1606
authorities.

'Flight of the Earls': the three leading figures in Ulster – O'Neill,   1607
O'Donnell and Maguire – flee to the Continent.

The central and western areas of Ulster, the last bastion of Irish resist-   1608
ance, are settled by Scottish and English Protestants, who are given land
confiscated from the native Irish.

Oliver Cromwell ruthlessly represses an Irish rebellion (1641 onwards)   1649
against the Protestants.
   The Roman Catholic King James II (1685–8), whose attempts to re-
establish Catholicism in Britain met with fierce resistance, seeks to
restore his position by a campaign in Ireland.

Battle of the Boyne (▶ picture, p. 32), in which James is decisively defeated   1690
by the Protestant William of Orange (king, as William III, from 1689).

There follows a time of severe political and religious repression in   18th c.
Ireland. Penal laws discriminating against Roman Catholics are introduced. Many Irish people emigrate to America. The poverty of the native
population is in stark contrast to the prosperity of the Anglo-Irish, who
possess fine houses and great estates.

After several rebellions against the repression of Catholicism, in 1782   **Relative**
Britain recognises an Irish parliament with a greater degree of indepen-   **independence**
   (1782–1800)

Battle of the Boyne (1690)

dence, in which the leading figure is Henry Grattan. The parliament does something to improve the plight of the poor. Its membership, however, is entirely Protestant.

During the 1790s the United Irishmen led by the Anglo-Irish lawyer Theobald Wolfe Tone, influenced by the French Revolution, call for the establishment of a republic in Ireland.

1798

An uprising supported by France is defeated.

1800

Influenced by the offer of financial compensation, offices and pensions from the British, the Irish parliament dissolves itself; it meets for the last time on August 2nd.

Religious freedom and Irish nationalism (1800–1922)

More than a century of efforts to secure equal rights for Catholics and national independence for Ireland end with the establishment of the Irish Free State.

1800

The Act of Union provides for the establishment of a single parliament of the United Kingdom of Great Britain and Ireland, meeting at Westminster. Ireland is represented in both the House of Commons and the House of Lords.

1801

On January 1st the Act of Union comes into force. Wealthy landowners leave Ireland, depriving the country of much of its economic strength.

1829

Daniel O'Connell, leader of the Irish Catholic middle classes (➤ Famous People), elected to Parliament in 1829, secures the admission of Catholics to Parliament and public office (Catholic Emancipation). His objective is to break up the parliamentary union of Britain and Ireland.

A devastating famine, brought about by the failure of the potato crop (the staple food of the poor in Ireland), results in the death of more than a million people (out of Ireland's 8 million) and the emigration to Britain and the United States of at least another million.   1845–9

An attempted rising by the Young Ireland Movement, consisting predominantly of Protestant middle classes seeking the establishment of an Irish state on the basis of religious tolerance, collapses because of the general lack of political interest resulting from exhaustion after the famine.   1848

In the United States Irish immigrants found the Irish Republican Brotherhood, a secret society aimed at achieving Irish independence by the use of force.   1858

The Land League is founded by Michael Davitt with the object of securing fair rents and security of tenure for Irish tenants.   1879

Charles Stuart Parnell (➤ Famous People), elected to Parliament in 1875, advocates Home Rule – independence for Ireland within the British Empire. Parnell is the recognised leader of the Irish people, but his attempt to secure the re-establishment of an independent Irish parliament is frustrated by the House of Lords after his bill had been passed by the House of Commons.   1885
  Most Protestants in the northern counties of Ireland are against Home Rule, since they believe they do better from the Union.

Foundation of the Gaelic League, with the objective of reviving the Gaelic language and Gaelic literature.   1893

Foundation of Sinn Féin (we ourselves), a group fighting for Irish political and economic independence and advocating passive resistance to British rule.   1905

With the conflict between Britain, Ulster and the nationalist part of Ireland reaching its climax in the years immediately before the first world war, the House of Commons passes a Home Rule bill, the enactment of which the House of Lords has power to delay until 1914.   1912
  In anticipation of the possibility that the bill will become law, the northern Irish opponents of Home Rule form a volunteer force to oppose its introduction by force if necessary.

In Dublin the Irish Volunteers are formed to support the demand for Home Rule.   1913

A new Home Rule bill is passed leaving it open to the northern counties of Ireland to opt for the continuance of the Union, but the outbreak of war prevents it from coming into operation.   1914

Easter Rising: while the British army is fighting in France the Irish Volunteers and an Irish citizen army, with the support of the Fenians, proclaim a republic in Dublin. It is repressed by British forces and a number of its leaders are executed.   1916

In a British general election Sinn Féin gain a majority over the Home Rule party.   1918

In Dublin the Irish members of the British Parliament establish their own Parliament, the Dáil Éireann, declare Irish independence and set up a government headed by Eamon de Valera (➤ Famous People).   1919

The British attempt to block Irish independence leads to civil war, in   1919–21 which the leading part on the Irish side is played by the Irish Republican Army (IRA).

1920 Parliament passes the Government of Ireland Act, which provides for two self-governing areas in Ireland, one in the six northern counties with their Protestant majority, the other in the rest of the country.

1921 The British government and the moderate leaders of the independence movement (Arthur Griffith, Michael Collins) sign a treaty establishing an Irish Free State (Saorstát Éireann) within the British Empire on December 6th. The six northern counties remain part of the United Kingdom.

1922 The Dáil Éireann ratifies the treaty on January 7th.

Irish Free State and Republic of Ireland

1922 Arthur Griffith becomes first prime minister of the Irish Free State in January, but dies in August. He is succeeded by William Thomas Cosgrave, who holds office until 1932.

1922–3 Armed resistance to the government by opponents of the treaty. The government wins the day, but at the cost of many lives.

1923 Supporters of the Anglo-Irish treaty form the Cumann na nGaedheal, which later unifies with a number of smaller groups to form the Fine Gael (family of the Irish) party.

1926 Opponents of the treaty, led by Eamon de Valera, form the Fianna Fáil (comrades of destiny) party.

1932 After Fianna Fáil's election victory over Fine Gael, Eamon de Valera becomes prime minister, a post which he holds until 1948 (with two later periods of office).

1937 A new constitution comes into force declaring Ireland to be 'a sovereign, independent, democratic state' under the name of Eire. The constitution provides for the election of a president.

1939–45 The independent Ireland remains neutral during the second world war.

1948 In a general election Fianna Fáil is defeated and the Fine Gael leader John Aloysius Costello heads a coalition government.

1949 Ireland becomes a republic, the Republic of Ireland (Poblacht na h'Éire-ann) and leaves the British Commonwealth.

1955 Ireland becomes a member of the United Nations.

1963 President John F Kennedy of the United States visits Ireland and is given an enthusiastic reception.

1973 On January 1st Ireland joins the European Community (then the EEC, now the EU).

1979 In Ireland, with its high rate of population, just under 10 per cent of all workers are unemployed.

1984 In June the United States president Ronald Reagan visits Ballyporeen, the parish from which his ancestors (known as O'Reagan) are said to have come.

In February the Irish Parliament decides by a small majority in favour of permitting the restricted use of contraceptives: the first time in the history of the Irish Republic that a government has successfully resisted the influence of the Roman Catholic Church.

In November the British and Irish prime ministers (Margaret Thatcher and Garret FitzGerald) sign the Hillsborough Agreement, arrived at after long secret negotiations, which provides for the establishment of a secretariat in Belfast and for regular meetings between Irish and British ministers and officials to discuss questions concerning Northern Ireland and particularly the fight against terrorism.

1985

A public referendum results in a clear 'No' to a government proposal to amend the constitution by legalising divorce.

1986

The growth in the rate of unemployment to almost 20 per cent results in the largest wave of emigration from Ireland for many years.

1987

Parliament passes the Extradition bill, a prerequisite to Ireland's membership of the European Convention in the Fight Against Terrorism.

1988

Lawyer and novelist Mary Robinson becomes the first woman president (in office until 1997).

1990

The European Community names Dublin Cultural Capital of Europe for one year.

1991

A majority of the Irish people approve in June the Maastricht Treaty for the foundation of a European Union.

In November 65.5 per cent of the Irish vote against a government proposal to permit an abortion in the case of serious risk to the life of the mother. At the same time 62.6 per cent approve unopposed travel abroad of pregnant women.

The early elections in November bring a defeat for the conservative parties. However, Fianna Fáil remains the strongest party with 68 seats.

1992

The British prime minister John Major and the Irish prime minister Albert Reynolds sign a declaration on December 15th which is intended to bring about the peace process.

1993

Following the bomb attack at Omagh in Northern Ireland on August 15th, 1998, at which there were 29 deaths, Parliament on September 3rd, together with the British House of Commons, proposes more stringent anti-terrorism legislation.

In accordance with the Northern Irish Peace Accord of April 10th, 1998, which prescribes the release of all prisoners belonging to the underground organisations by May 2000, the justice authorities begin releasing former members of the IRA on December 22nd.

1998–9

Northern Ireland

The counties of Northern Ireland (Ulster), districts since 1973, with a predominantly Protestant population, have been part of the United Kingdom of Great Britain and Northern Ireland since December 1920. Northern Ireland has its own parliament, at Stormont, and its own government.

1920–60

Tensions between the Protestant majority and the Roman Catholic minority lead to major outbreaks of violence. The mainly Catholic Irish Republican Army (IRA) becomes increasingly active, and the Protestant Ulster Defence Association (UDA) is formed.

The IRA is split into an 'Official' (socialist) wing, which calls for a

1969

The Conflict in Northern Ireland

The civil war between Catholics and Protestants in Northern Ireland, lasting until 1994 and coined the Troubles by the British government in order to play down its seriousness, began in 1969, but its roots go back to the 12th c.

In 1169 one of the five princes of Ireland, who were fighting each other for domination of the island, asked Henry II (1154–89) of England for help and – in violation of Irish law – offered him succession to his own principality. Henry travelled across to the island with his entire army, won land and granted fiefdoms to his Anglo-Norman barons. English settlers followed, colonising the Dublin area. The English secured their domination with the 1366 Statute of Kilkenny and began compelling the native Irish to accept their language and English law. Once the old Irish nobility of Ulster had flown, Ulster having previously been the core of resistance to the English presence, there arose a power vacuum in the north-east which the English crown now exploited by encouraging mass settlement by Protestants. As part of major resettlement programmes – the Plantations of 1608 – mainly Scottish Presbyterians came to this area, seizing the most fertile land and forcing the native Irish into the poorer areas or making them economically dependent. Ulster, formerly a bulwark against English domination, now formed the vanguard of English domination in Ireland. Although there were repeated uprisings by Catholic Irish they were always put down with much spilling of blood. After the Battle of the Boyne in 1690, the Protestant-English establishment continued its subjugation of the Irish population right into the 20th c. (Today's Irish Protestants still celebrate the defeat of the Catholics at the Boyne!)

Resistance to English domination in Ireland, united with Great Britain since 1801, gained strength with the nascent nationalism of the 19th c. The fight for Irish independence now began in earnest. In the wake of the bloody conflict of 1919–21 Ireland was divided: the mainly Catholic south received the status of a free state within the British Empire (later the Commonwealth) – the six counties of Ulster, or Northern Ireland, remained in a union with Great Britain. The great majority of people in Northern Ireland – Protestants form two-thirds of the population – voted to remain with Great Britain, partly because of the cultural ties to it as a neighbouring island and partly from fear of losing their privileges in the event of unification with the free state. The constitution established by the free state of Ireland (Eire) in 1937, making Irish the first official national language in preference to English, and granting the Roman Catholic church a special status, deepened the cleft between the Protestant north and the Roman Catholic south because it was designed to include Northern Ireland – Articles 2 and 3 provide for reunification with Ulster. Moreover, the Roman Catholics in Ulster were still disadvantaged by the Protestants, both politically and economically.

What finally triggered the civil war was an, at the outset, peaceful demonstration by the Catholic civil rights movement in October 1968. Units from the Royal Ulster Constabulary, consisting of Protestants, and the B-Specials, a Protestant troop with policing authorities, directly attacked the demonstrators in front of live television cameras. When – with tacit consent from the police – Protestant thugs attacked Catholic districts ever more frequently, the government in London was compelled to act and in August 1969 despatched 6,000 British soldiers to Ulster to reinstate public order. Very soon it became clear to the Catholics that the British army had not come for their protection alone. On January 30th 1972 the violence escalated – this was 'Bloody Sunday', when British paratroops shot 14 unarmed participants at a civil rights demonstration organised by Roman Catholics. Following this event, the Irish Republican Army resurfaced, having regained power after years of insignificance. The IRA, a secret terrorist organisation, had originally formed during the Anglo-Irish civil war (1919–21) when it had freed the major part of the island from centuries of British dominance. When Dublin agreed to the separation of Ulster in 1921, the IRA saw this as treason, continued its terror in the north and south and thereby instigated civil war in the free state of Ireland (1922–3). After 1936 nothing much more was heard about the IRA once Eamon de Valera, the prime minister of the Free State of Ireland, had banned the organisation. Between 1956 and 1962 the IRA came into the news once again in connection with terrorist attacks. The third wave of violence commenced in the early 1970s and continued until 1994.

The stated aims of the IRA were to protect threatened Catholics, drive out the British and bring about the unification of the Irish Republic, independent since 1949, with Ulster, then administered from the UK. The IRA's strategy was to wear down the British government and its representatives in Northern Ireland by instituting a permanent campaign of terror. It only found sympathy and support among the impoverished part of the Catholic minority in Ulster from which it recruited its members. The IRA's terrorist attacks were met by counter terror from its opponents, the paramilitary associations of Protestants such as the Ulster Volunteer Force (UVF), the Ulster Defence Association (UDA) and the Ulster Freedom Fighters (UFF), as well as the Protestant police unit of the Royal Ulster Constabulary (RUC) and units of the British army.

The armed conflict between the IRA and Protestant underground groups in which, in Northern Ireland alone, almost 3000 people were killed (about two-thirds of them from the IRA or its associated organisations), came to a provisional end in August 1994. The IRA declared a unilateral ceasefire in which the Protestant guerrilla groups concurred. Since then a fragile peace has reigned in Northern Ireland.

Wall paintings in Londonderry

Famous People

The following alphabetic list brings together people of historical importance who through birth, residence, actions or death are connected with Ireland and have attained international significance.

Samuel Beckett (1906–89)

Samuel Beckett is the leading representative of the Theatre of the Absurd. He was born in Dublin and from 1937 lived in Paris. After studying Romance languages and literature at Trinity College in Dublin (1923–7) he taught English at the École Normale Supérieure in Paris. Here he was part of the circle around James Joyce who, together with Dante, Descartes and existential philosophy, exerted a great influence upon Beckett's literary work. From 1931 to 1932 he taught French at Trinity College. Between 1933 and 1936 he lived in London. He was already writing essays, stories and poetry before the second world war. He first came to fame with his novel *Molloy* (1951). His earlier works were published in English; the later ones (including *Molloy*) were written in French and translated by himself into English. After publishing more novels he turned to the theatre and caused great interest with his first play, *Waiting for Godot* (1952). In all his works – novels, dramas, stories, radio and TV plays – he breaks with traditional form: action is reduced to a minimum. He pessimistically portrays – with a tendency towards the grotesque and burlesque – the absurdity of the human condition, the emptiness of an existence futilely waiting for death. In 1969 he received the Nobel Prize for literature.

St Brendan (ca 486–ca 578)

Who really discovered America? The Genoese sailor Christopher Columbus, commissioned by the Spanish, in 1492? The Viking Leif Erikson in the year 1000? The Phoenicians towards the end of the 7th c. BC? Or was it an Irish monk?

In the 8th c. a hagiography, 'The Sea Journey of St Brendan', was in circulation and became a sort of bestseller during the Middle Ages, translated into many west European languages. It tells how the Irish abbot Brendan discovered the 'Promised Land' on the other side of the Atlantic in the 6th c.

The Irish St Brendan founded several monasteries in Ireland, including Clonfert in Co. Galway. Driven by missionary zeal he allegedly travelled around the Scottish islands and Wales. When he heard that there was a 'Promised Land' inhabited by saints beyond the ocean he set off, according to legend, in 540 with 17 companions and a well-equipped ship and did not return until seven years later.

In order to prove that crossing the Atlantic in a leather boat, as would have been the case in Brendan's time, is not just pure fantasy the scientist Timothy Severin sailed in such a boat in 1976 from Ireland to Canada. He was excited by the similarity between descriptions of places in the book and actual geographical conditions on Labrador.

Chris de Burgh (b 1948)

In Ireland he has received the award of 'most successful songwriter of all time'. The 'troubadour of rock culture' has also enjoyed huge success abroad. Many of his singles reached the top of the record charts and received gold and platinum awards. The man in question is Christopher John Davidson, better known as Chris de Burgh. De Burgh was his mother's maiden name, one of the most common surnames in Ireland dating back to the Anglo-Norman de Burgo family which was rewarded by the English king with extensive lands in Connaught in the early 13th c. His parents are, however, not Irish but English. He was born in Argentina on 15th October 1948. Beause of his father's job as an official in the diplomatic service he spent his childhood on Malta, in Nigeria, the Belgian Congo and Rhodesia. He attended school in Wiltshire, England. In 1960 his parents bought Bargy Castle near Wexford and converted it into an hotel. In accordance with his parents' wishes he studied French, English and history at Trinity College, Dublin. After studying he devoted himself to music as a profession but there were no early successes. He received his first recording contract in 1974. His second LP *Spanish Train* (1977) was a great commercial success. On his fifth LP, *Eastern Wind* (1980), he abandoned for the first time the gentle, rather melancholic ballads which were often about knights and devils. He concentrated more on realism, with the first sounds of rock music appearing in this LP which he made with his own band. With the release *Don't Pay the Ferryman* from his 1983 album *The Getaway* he achieved the final breakthrough and it landed at number 1 in the American charts. Since then all the albums of this father of two, who never had music tuition and whose repertoire stretches from heartfelt ballads to rock songs, have been successful. The recipe for success behind his instinctive feel for music is – as he says himself – his Celtic-inspired melancholy. *The Lady in Red* was a major hit in Britain in 1986.

On August 3rd 1916, in London, a man was hanged for conspiring with the enemy – Germany – and plotting an Irish uprising. It was Sir Roger Casement who had been knighted only five years earlier.

Roger Casement (1864–1916)

At the age of 20 Dublin-born Roger Casement left Ireland and travelled around Africa. Early in the 20th c. he investigated conditions in the Belgian Congo and in Peru on behalf of the British government as rumours persisted concerning the maltreatment of the native population by whites. His discoveries, which were worse than the rumours, attracted international concern. His role as a lawyer helped him to international recognition and in 1911 to the nobility. As his health had suffered through the time he had spent in the tropics, he left the British civil service in 1913. He then dedicated his efforts to the Irish struggle for independence from the British Crown. He had a leading role in the Irish Volunteers, a resistance movement. Soon after the outbreak of the first world war he contacted the German government in Berlin. He sought official support for the Irish fight for independence and wanted Germany to supply them with weapons. At the end of 1914 the Imperial government declared its sympathy for Irish independence. At Easter 1916 the Irish rebels wanted to rise against Great Britain; Berlin confirmed its support and sent a fishing boat carrying 20,000 rifles and ammunition towards the Irish coast. However, the boat on being discovered by a British cruiser was sunk by its own captain so as not to let its dangerous cargo fall into enemy hands. Casement, attempting to reach Ireland in secret by German submarine, was arrested on April 21st 1916 by the British security forces as soon as he set foot on Irish soil.

The news of the sinking of the German ship and Casement's arrest made it clear to the instigators of the rebellion that the uprising could not succeed. But it was already too late: on Easter Monday, April 24th 1916, the uprising broke out. Four days later it was bloodily crushed by the British armed forces. Casement, held by the British government to be the chief instigator of the rebellion, was brought before the court. Charged with cooperating with the enemy and instigating an uprising against the Crown, the judge and jury sentenced him to death by hanging. Not content with his condemnation to death, attempts were made to destroy his reputation abroad as a lawyer for the native people in the colonies. His diaries were publicised in which alleged homosexual encounters were described. This led to the archbishop of Canterbury and the American president Woodrow Wilson withdrawing a plea for mercy for Casement. It has still not been confirmed whether the diaries were genuine or fake.

Famous People

James Joyce

Charles Stewart Parnell

George Bernard Shaw

On February 23rd 1965 the mortal remains of Sir Roger Casement were transferred from England to Dublin and buried in state on February 28th.

James Joyce
(1882–1941)

The writer James Joyce is remembered on 'Bloomsday', June 16th, in Dublin (➤ Baedeker Special, p. 164).

After being educated in church schools and at University College, Dublin, Joyce went to Paris to study medicine in 1902. His mother's death brought him back temporarily to Ireland before he began to live in self-imposed exile from 1904 (Trieste, Rome, Zurich, Paris, among other places). In 1914 *Dubliners* was published, a collection of 15 short stories influenced by Ibsen, in which Joyce depicts the ordinary life of Dubliners in its various phases of childhood, adolescence, maturity and public work. In the autobigraphical novel *A Portrait of the Artist as a Young Man* (1916) he employs the technique of inner monologue and portrays the tensions between the young artist and the world about him. His most well-known novel is *Ulysses,* published in 1922. In his final work, *Finnegans Wake* (1939), Joyce is trying to give expression to the unconscious. Written in a dream language, *Finnegans Wake* (on a superficial level about the dreams of an Irish innkeeper and his family on one night), like *Dubliners* and *Ulysses,* retains the atmosphere of his native Dublin. Despite the many difficulties in interpreting his works, the novels of Joyce have exerted a major influence on the 20th c. novel.

Joyce fled with his family in 1940 from Paris to Zurich where he died on January 13th 1941 after a serious illness. He is buried at the cemetery at Fluntern.

Daniel O'Connell
(1775–1847)

Daniel O'Connell is one of the best-known leaders of Irish resistance against the Bristish Crown. In the first third of the 19th c. he was hailed as 'Ireland's uncrowned king'. But then he had to give in to harsh reality.

Daniel O'Connell came from a privileged background. The son of a relatively prosperous Catholic landowner from Co. Kerry, he was able to go to Paris to study. Here he experienced the turmoil of revolution, its ideals together with its violence. Perhaps these experiences were responsible for his later politics in which he strove for peace. When he returned to Ireland the British laws toward the Irish had relaxed somewhat. Above a certain level of income the Irish were allowed to vote and schooling had improved. O'Connell settled in Dublin where he became famous throughout the country as a successful defence lawyer. He became increasingly involved in politics. For Ireland to break completely from the union with Great Britain, which had existed since 1801, did not at first seem feasible to O'Connell. His politics followed two specific goals: equal rights for Irish Catholics and protection for the small Irish tenant farmers against the unscrupulous English landowners. To this purpose he founded the Catholic Union in 1823 whose numbers soon reached over a million. As well as the middle classes and poor farmers it was made up of Catholic aristocracy, Protestant liberals, churchmen and even robbers. With the help of the Catholic Union, O'Connell was elected Member of Parliament for Co. Clare. But only after the British prime minister felt compelled to introduce a law allowing non-Anglicans access to all offices of state did O'Connell take his place at parliament in London. With the re-election of the Conservative government, O'Connell lost his political influence. He set up a second union whose aim now was Irish independence. London was becoming more irritated by O'Connell's mass rallies and his bold words of freedom for Ireland. He was spared a prison sentence when the House of Commons acted in his favour. When the Catholics tried to organise another rally before the gates of Dublin, the English governor intervened and sent in troops to prevent the rally taking place. O'Connell, still disposed towards a peaceful solution, called off the event the evening before. Most young supporters felt betrayed and turned their backs on him. In addition he was no longer in very good health. He left Ireland and went to Italy to recuperate and died in Genoa in 1847.

No other woman in the history of Ireland has won the hearts of the Irish population as much as the once feared 'pirate queen' Grace O'Malley. In the song and legend of the oppressed Irish people she is hailed as an early patriot.

Grace O'Malley
(ca 1530–1603)

Grace O'Malley was the only child and sole heiress of Owen Dubhdarra (nicknamed 'Black Oak'), head of the O'Malley clan and ruler of Clew Bay near Westport. The O'Malleys lived off the sea: from fishing as far afield as Scotland, France, Spain and Portugal, and from piracy. Grace, who had an unbridled love of the sea, soon followed in the footsteps of her father. At the age of nine she managed to extract permission from her father to learn seamanship. Her first marriage was arranged by her father to Donal, the 'battle-hardened', ruling prince of the O'Flaherty clan. At first she took on the duties and role of a wife but after the birth of three children she returned to the sea. Through her trading, fighting and piracy she contributed more to the family fortune than her husband did. The O'Flahertys soon came to regard her rather than her husband as their natural leader. Following the death of her husband she returned to her own family. In 1566 she was voted the first female head of the O'Malley clan. She decided upon her second husband herself. As the only region left that would give her control of the whole of Clew Bay was the land belonging to the Burke family with the strategically important Rockfleet Castle, she chose to marry Richard Burke. According to Celtic law the marriage was limited to one year, which meant that after one year either partner could dissolve the union. According to legend Grace made use of this law: from the battlements of his own castle she greeted Richard with the news that he must leave and the castle now belonged to her alone. With her 20 ships and 6000 men she soon ruled large areas of the west coast of Ireland and terrorised all the trading ships in the Atlantic. The following example illustrates how little mercy she showed her adversaries. When her lover was murdered she had the entire clan from which the murderer came wiped out except for one so that he could tell the rest of the world of her terrible revenge. Yet she held nothing against England which was making renewed claims towards Ireland under Elizabeth I. She obeyed superior strength, paid homage to the English queen and received her property as a fiefdom. In 1593 she travelled to London to plead personally for the freedom of her imprisoned son. This meeting was retold in legend as showing the patriotism of the 'pirate queen', of the unbroken confidence of Grace O'Malley towards the power of the English. Even though there are no deeds connected with Irish independence which can be attributed to Grace, in the minds of the Irish people this fearsome clan chief is seen, as the time since her death (1603) increases, as more of a Robin Hood figure and a freedom fighter for Ireland.

Charles Stewart
Parnell
(1846–91)

The statesman Charles Stewart Parnell, from a Protestant Anglo-Irish family, became a symbol of Irish nationalism in the second half of the 19th c. His political career began in the Home Rule League, a party founded in 1870, which, unlike the Republican Brotherhood (Fenier), created in 1858, broadly accepted a union with Great Britain, merely demanding a degree of independence for the Irish parliament and rejecting the use of violence against English rule. He soon became party leader and the most powerful man in Irish politics. By peaceful means he gained compromises from the English government. He achieved popularity in the country by calling a 'boycott', a word which first found its way into many modern languages through Parnell. The prime target of hatred for the Irish were the English landowners and the administrators of their Irish estates. Owing to the English settlement policy in Ireland in the 16th and 17th c. many British were able to take over the most fertile land. The estates were mainly managed by agents of the landowners who barely put a foot on Irish soil. These agents often took advantage of the tenant farmers. Such an agent was Captain Boycott. He displayed his power in the most brutal fashion. Parnell made the suggestion of ignoring him, of not trading with him, in short of boycotting him. The plan worked – Captain Boycott was forced to give in and left Ireland for ever.

His political efforts towards a peaceful approach to the Home Rule policy of the British prime minister, Gladstone, were not popular with everyone. As it became clear that Irish independence would not be won constitutionally, his political opponents, even among his own party, found a suitable reason to oust him – his relationship with Katherine O'Shea, who was married, yet separated from her husband, a party friend. This 'immoral behaviour' was systematically exploited: more and more supporters went over to the opposite camp, including Gladstone and the Irish bishops. His marriage with Katherine O'Shea did not prevent him from being deselected as party leader. A few months afterwards he died.

St Patrick
(ca 389–461)

It is said that Ireland was the only country to be converted to Christianity without bloodshed. This peaceful process was the work of St Patrick, the apostle and patron saint of Ireland.

Patrick was born in what is today Kilpatrick in Scotland, the son of a deacon. At the age of 16 he was taken prisoner by pirates and transported to Ireland where he was sold as a slave and kept as a shepherd. Six years later he managed to escape back home where he had a vision telling him to convert Ireland to Christianity. Until then there were only a few isolated Christians. In Gaul he trained as a priest and in 431 he returned to the island of his imprisonment as a bishop. He founded a string of schools, churches and monasteries and established the bishop's seat in Armagh. With much skill and empathy – he was familiar with the Irish mentality from his time as a captive here – he succeeded in converting the princes and kings, who still followed the Celtic religion, together with their subjects to the Christian faith. Unlike many other countries there were no Christian martyrs on Ireland. At the time of Patrick's death Ireland had been completely converted to Christianity.

Ireland's most successful missionary is surrounded by numerous legends. In the Middle Ages St Patrick's Purgatory became famous, a cave in Lough Derg (near Donegal) where Patrick is said to have seen purgatory and experienced visions of the next world. Erasmus, Rabelais, Dante and Calderón were all inspired by this. The cult of St Patrick became part of the Irish national and religious legacy. Since the 17th c., if not earlier, there has been a St Patrick's Day in Ireland. It is said that whenever at least three Irish people meet abroad they celebrate this day. In New York they celebrate St Patrick's Day with a big parade along Fifth Avenue.

Cynicism, satire and humour made George Bernard Shaw famous – not only with regard to his literary works.

George Bernard Shaw (1856–1950)

George Bernard Shaw was born in Dublin of an English father and an Irish mother. In 1876 he moved to London. At first he tried his hand at being an estate agent before beginning to write theatre, music and art criticism which was both admired and feared. In 1884 he founded with a group of like-minded people the Fabian Society: a society of intellectuals, who advocated non-Marxist, non-revolutionary progressive socialism. In 1891 he began to write plays. Using jokes, quick-wittedness, cynicism and satire he poked fun at conventions and overused clichés; he employed witty paradoxes, polished dialogues and outstanding punchlines. His most famous plays include *Pygmalion* (1912) and *St Joan* (1923). In 1925 he received the Nobel Prize for literature, but turned down a title.

In his private life as well as on stage there was no lack of intelligent humour and biting satire. On one occasion a famous society beauty remarked to him, 'Just imagine, Mr Shaw, a child with your intelligence and my looks!'. To which he rather ungallantly replied, 'And what if it had your intelligence and my looks?!'

The only one of his works which shows any feeling towards his native Ireland is *John Bull's Other Island* (1904) in which he states how Ireland, both good and evil, cannot be compared with any other region on earth; nobody can walk upon its green meadows or breathe in its air without becoming either a better or a worse person.

On hearing of *Gulliver's Travels* one cannot help being reminded of one's childhood. The first two books of this adventure story are among the most read children's books of world literature. And yet *Gulliver's Travels*, written by Jonathan Swift in 1726, is definitely not a children's book. In it Swift describes the adventures of the hero Gulliver in the kingdom of the Lilliputians, in that of the giants, in the land where immortality is possible and in the kingdom of the rational horses who have succeeded in forming an ideal society and whose servants are people also behave like animals. It is a furious satire on contemporary English society, on human stupidity, malice and wrongdoing. Ridicule, for example on the properties of the various religious denominations in *The Tale of a Tub* (1704), was the hallmark of Swift's literary works. He is regarded as the

Jonathan Swift (1667–1745)

Jonathan Swift

Eamon de Valera

Oscar Wilde

greatest English satirist, even as one of the greatest satirists ever. He was at the disposal of political groups, first for the Whigs, an English political party, which he began working for in 1689. After a few years he changed over to the opposition, to the Tories, when he felt his political and moral views to be betrayed by the Whigs. After the Tories lost power to the Whigs he returned to Dublin where he held the deanship of St Patrick's Cathedral until his death. In 1729 he received the freedom of the city of Dublin. Following the death of his closest friend, Stella, whom he never married, and possibly as a result of a pernicious illness which he had suffered from for a long time, his writings became increasingly cynical and gave his contemporaries the impression he was mentally ill. He lies buried next to Stella in St Patrick's Cathedral, Dublin.

John Millington Synge (1871–1909)

The writer John Millington Synge came from an Anglo-Irish lawyer's family and studied at Trinity College in Dublin before travelling around Germany and Italy in 1892. Between 1893 and 1898 Synge spent most of the time in Paris. There he met William B Yeats, upon whose advice he went to the Aran Islands to study the lifestyle and language of the inhabitants. At first he only stayed for six weeks on the islands but returned for several weeks at a time over the following years. He describes the land and its people in his prose work *The Aran Islands* (1907).

Synge, who in 1902 had settled in Dublin, was appointed director of the newly founded Abbey Theatre in 1904, a post he retained until his death.

Not only in the *The Aran Islands* but also in his plays he portrays the lives of Irish farmers and fishermen. One of his most important works is *Riders to the Sea*, which depicts the tragic life of fishermen on the west coast of Ireland and is based upon their actual experiences facing the inevitability of death at sea. Also particularly well known is the comedy *The Playboy of the Western World* (1907), in which the vigorous and yet at the same time delicate language of the islanders finds full expression.

Eamon de Valera (1882–1975)

Eamon de Valera is a major figure in 20th c. Irish history. For six decades (from 1913–73) he exerted a definitive influence on the politics of Ireland. He was prime minister three times (1932–48, 1951–4, 1957–9) and president once (1959–73). The creation of the Republic of Ireland is primarily his work.

De Valera was born on October 14th 1882 in New York, the son of a Spanish father and an Irish mother. Following the early death of his father he went with his uncle to Ireland where he lived with his grandmother. He studied mathematics in Dublin and entered the teaching profession. His political career began in 1913 when he became a member of the Irish Volunteers, a group founded that year to demand greater self-determination for Ireland. He was one of the leading figures in the Easter Rising in 1916 and commander of the batallion based in Boland's Bakery. After the defeat of the rebellious Irish he was thrown into prison by the British; the death sentence he had received was not carried out. Free again he stood as a candidate for the British Parliament and was elected. In May 1918 he was arrested once again by the British government and interned in England; however, he managed to escape to the US. At the end of 1920 he returned to Ireland. Meanwhile in 1918 the Sinn Féin party, standing for Ireland's independence and of which de Valera had been president one year earlier, won the majority of all Irish mandates to the House of Commons. The new MPs refused to enter the House of Commons. Instead they formed the Irish Council (Dáil Éireann) in January 1919 with de Valera being elected president of this illegal Irish parliament.

When on January 7th 1922 the Dáil Éireann ratified the Free State treaty negotiated with England, de Valera left Parliament. He was not satisfied with the status of British dominion for the new Irish Free State;

he sought the complete independence of Ireland and the unification of Ulster with the Free State. After the bitter civil war (1922–3) between the opponents and supporters of the new republic, which ended in victory for the republic, and after a year in prison (1923–4) de Valera's position towards the new state became rather more conciliatory. In May 1926, with opponents of the treaty, he founded the relatively moderate Fianna Fáil party (comrades of destiny). They won the 1932 election against the government party, Fine Gael, (family of the Irish) and de Valera became prime minister. He and the party quicky set about cutting the remaining ties with Great Britain. His government made a law abolishing the oath of allegiance of the Irish parliament to the British king. In 1937 a new constitution was introduced. Some of the paragraphs were written by de Valera himself. From now on the Irish Free State was a real republic (it officially came into existence in 1949). The government took over foreign policy and nominated its own diplomats. Great Britain vacated the naval bases on the coast of Ireland. In the second world war Ireland remained neutral. De Valera took his neutrality so far that on May 2nd 1945 he sent his condolences to the German ambassador in Dublin on the death of Hitler. In 1948 after the defeat of his party in parliamentary elections he handed over power to the opposition. Later he was to be head of the government twice more (1951–4, 1957–9). In 1959 he transferred office from prime minister to president, a position which he retained until 1973. Eamon de Valera ('Dev', as he was known to his followers) died on August 29th 1975, aged 93.

Oscar Wilde, full name Oscar Fingal O'Flahertie Wills, was first introduced to literature in his parental home in Dublin. Both his father, a doctor, and his mother were interested in literature and surrounded themselves with artists and Bohemians. During his studies in Dublin and in Oxford his interest in classical culture, art and highly cultivated lifestyles was awakened. In 1879 he moved to London and tried his hand at being a poet and art critic. His novel *The Picture of Dorian Gray* (1890) was a great success. The foreword to this novel and a collection of essays, *Intentions* (1891), vividly reflect his aesthetic viewpoint of *l'art pour l'art* (art for art's sake). In his satirical salon comedies, *Lady Windermere's Fan* (1892) and *The Importance of Being Earnest* (1895), he gently criticises the sham morals of late Victorian society. Wilde ranks as the leading representative of fin-de-siècle literature in England.

Oscar Wilde (1856–1900)

On the one hand Wilde ridiculed society in his comedies, on the other he sought recognition from high society. He tried to live his life according to his aesthetic ideals: his flat was richly decorated and he liked to dress ostentatiously. He married an attractive woman and had two children. He was at the height of his success in 1895, worshipped by society, but then he was mercilessly rejected. Since 1891 Wilde had had a passionate relationship with the young Lord Alfred Douglas. Rumours soon emerged that the two were having a homosexual relationship, which sent Lord Alfred's father, the violent and choleric Marquess of Queensberry, into a rage. After a few confrontations between Wilde and the marquess they went to court. Wilde was sentenced to two years' hard labour for 'immoral behaviour'. Public opinion turned against him, his publisher stopped the sale of his books. On the publication of the judgement, prostitutes danced in the streets because a 'troublesome competitor' had been removed. During his imprisonment he wrote the confession addressed to Lord Alfred, *De Profundis* (published in 1905). Two years of prison and the humiliation he suffered there made him into a broken man. His wife and two sons left England, he himself emigrated to France. He turned increasingly to alcohol and died in a Paris hotel on November 30th 1900.

Brother of the Nobel prizewinner for literature William Butler Yeats, Jack Butler Yeats dedicated his talent to painting not writing. Born in London, he spent his childhood in Sligo, Ireland, returning to London to study.

Jack Butler Yeats (1871–1957)

But in his paintings Yeats was captivated by the land of his fathers, taking as his subject the Irish countryside, the life of the pubs, the music halls and the race track. He favoured dark hues on which he applied bright spots of colour with a spatula. His works include *Sailing, Sailing Swiftly* (1933) and *The Careless Flower* (1947).

William Butler
Yeats
(1865–1939)

The poet William Butler Yeats was the leading light of the Celtic Renaissance, a movement to preserve and revive the Irish-Celtic tradition in art and culture and closely linked to the Irish people's desire for independence from Great Britain.

His childhood was spent in Dublin, London and Sligo. Throughout his life he was absorbed by the scenery of Ireland's west coast, with its legends and folk tales. From 1884 to 1886 he attended the School of Art in Dublin with the intention of becoming a painter. However, from 1886 he turned to literature – poetry, drama and story telling. Gradually he became involved in the Irish independence movement. Together with Lady Gregory, G Moore and E Martyn he founded the Irish National Theatre in 1899. Following the declaration of the Irish Free State, he became a senator. In this office (from 1922 to 1928) he proposed decorating Irish coins with the animals that appear in the Book Of Kells: hares and dogs, fish and birds.

The chief influence on Yeats early work was that of the Pre-Raphaelites, the influence of French symbolism and fin-de-siècle aestheticism being noticeable later, but his preoccupation with magical and occult phenomena is also apparent. In his early poems his symbolism is relatively clear whereas the later poems are mystical and obscure. A characteristic of all his poetry is the inclusion of Irish-Celtic legend, fairy tale and myth. His plays resemble dramatic poems, the action is symbolic, the characters are types. His later dramas are reminiscent of Japanese Noh plays in which he tries to combine drama, dance, masks and ritual acts. There is such deep symbolism in his final major works that they go beyond the scope of theatre. Two volumes of poetry, *The Tower* (1928) and *The Spiral Staircase* (1933), contain many of his most beautiful poems. Yeats was awarded the Nobel Prize for literature in 1923.

Culture

Ancient monuments and other features of interest scattered throughout the country are usually indicated by signposts, which in the Irish Republic are green and white. Many of these places are under state protection as National Monuments. They are usually open and unguarded, and visitors are asked to treat them with the respect they deserve.

Art and Architecture

Since the Romans never came to Ireland, the Celtic inhabitants of the island were able to develop their own distinctive culture and art without influences from outside, and as a result Ireland offers visitors the opportunity of discovering the characteristic forms and figures of early Celtic art in unique beauty and abundance. Monastic sites and high crosses, metalwork and book illumination are the most impressive manifestations of this in Irish Early Christian art; but after this heyday the late medieval period saw an artistic decline, since the country lacked a wealthy middle class with an interest in art. It was not until the 18th c. that the well-to-do Anglo-Irish ruling class began to build their country houses, usually in a neoclassical style, and the elegant Georgian houses in the towns, particularly Dublin and Limerick.

While elsewhere in Europe it is possible to date old buildings by reference to developing styles, in Ireland the style of building in earlier centuries showed little change. The country is littered with ruins from the past, fitting picturesquely into the landscape; and it has often been possible – as at Ballintubber Abbey and Bunratty Castle, for example – to bring an old building back into use by giving it a new roof and inserting new doors and windows in the gaping holes in its walls.

Stone Age

During the Stone Age (ca 7000–2000 BC) megalithic tombs, built of huge slabs of undressed stone, were constructed all over Ireland.

Dolmen

The term dolmen is generally applied to the earliest megalithic chamber tombs, the chamber being formed by a number of upright stones (orthostats) which support a capstone weighing many tons and often sloping down towards the rear of the tomb. A good example of this type is the gigantic dolmen on Browne's Hill near Carlow.

Passage grave

In the passage grave the chamber is approached by a passage formed of orthostats. The stones can be decorated with spirals, zigzags and other forms of ornament, and the whole structure was originally buried in an earth mound. In some of these tombs there are three side chambers opening off the main one, giving a cruciform plan. The passage graves in the Boyne Valley are particularly famed.

Gallery grave

In the gallery grave there is no distinction between the passage and the burial chamber. The wedge-shape gallery grave has a chamber which is broader at one end than the other, enclosed within a U-shaped formation of orthostats. This type of grave is particularly common in Ireland: there is a good example at Ballyedmonduff, near Dublin.

◀ *Ardmore: St Declan's Church and the Round Tower*

There is also the court cairn, a burial mound with a semicircular or oval forecourt serving some ritual purpose in front of the tomb chamber. A tomb of this kind can be seen at Creevykeel, north of Sligo.

Bronze Age

Characteristic monuments of the Bronze Age (ca 2000–500 BC) are the stone circles, probably used for cult ceremonies, which have left such impressive remains in Ireland. A good example is the Drombeg stone circle in Co. Cork.

To this period, too, belong the standing stones, known in Irish as *gallain*, in Breton as menhirs, which also had some ritual significance.

Evidence of Bronze Age wealth is provided by the finds (e.g. in the Wicklow Mountains) of valuable gold ornaments, including *lunulae*, crescent-shape collars of hammered gold sheet.

Iron Age

During the Iron Age and the beginning of the Christian period (ca 500 BC –AD 400) ring-forts surrounded by stone or earth ramparts, known in Irish as *raths*, were built to provide protection for kinship groups or clans from enemy attacks and plundering expeditions. There are said to be more than 30,000 ring-forts in Ireland, many of them preserved only in the form of an earthern or drystone enclosure.

There were also more strongly defended hill forts, commandingly situated on elevated sites. An imposing example of a hill fort (Irish *lis*) is Dún Aenghus on Inishmore in the Aran Islands.

The stone circle of Drombeg

Art and Architecture

Promontory forts

The term promontory fort (Irish *dún*) is applied to a ring-fort built on a promontory or projecting tongue of land; sometimes the rampart is built across the neck of the promontory. There is a fine promontory fort at Dunbeg on the Dingle Peninsula.

Another type of defensive structure was the *crannog*, an artificial island in a lough (lake) constructed with the aid of piles. Occasionally a natural islet might be used for this purpose. As places of particular security some of the crannogs remained in occupation into the late medieval period.

The Irish terms for the various types of fort feature in many place names, such as Dungannon, Lismore and Rathdrum.

Enamelwork

During the Bronze Age the Celtic population of Ireland learned the technique of enamelwork, producing beautifully ornamented everyday articles as well as jewellery. They are believed to have acquired this art from the Roman provinces.

Ogham script

Towards the end of the Iron Age the ogham script, named after Ogmios, the Celtic god of writing, came into use (➤ p. 22). Ogham inscriptions are usually found on the edges of erect slabs of stone or diagonally across the stone. They take the form of horizontal or sloping lines, used in various combinations to denote different letters, there being 20 such in all.

Most of those which have been preserved – some 250 out of a total of 300 – are in the counties of Kerry, Cork and Waterford. The inscriptions invariably take the form of standard formulae. The Alphabet Stone at Kilmalkedar on the Dingle Peninsula has Latin and ogham inscriptions side by side.

Ogham stone

Early Christian period

The Early Christian period (ca 400–1170) saw a great flowering of art in Ireland, notably in the form of richly carved crosses and illuminated manuscripts.

The many monastic sites established during this period, however, produced little architecture of any significance. It is known from the chronicles of the time that the buildings were of wattle and daub, or occasionally of timber. Where these materials were not available, as on the rocky islet of Skellig Michael in the Atlantic, use was perforce made of stone. On Skellig Michael a flight of more than 600 steps was hewn from the rock to give access to a relatively sheltered terrace on which the monks built their beehive cells and oratories and buried their dead. An upright slab of stone inscribed with a cross was the forerunner of the later elaborately decorated high crosses.

Beehive hut

The drystone beehive hut of this period (Irish *clochán*) is a small round hut with corbelled walls to form a 'false vault' and closed at the top by a flat slab of stone. This type of structure is also found in some stony and treeless Mediterranean countries, and probably originated there. On Skellig Michael the monks selected and laid their stones with such care and accuracy that the huts have remained watertight to this day.

Oratory

The early churches were tiny oratories used either for individual devotions or for celebrating Mass. The corbelled walls meet at the roof ridge, giving the building the form of an upturned boat. The interior is dark, lit only by the door or, later, by a narrow window over the altar. The Gallarus Oratory on the Dingle Peninsula is a perfectly preserved example of the type.

The gravestones on the monastic sites show a development from simple forms of ornament to small-scale works of art. In the later period all the arms of the cross that form the central feature are richly decorated. The inscriptions take the form of a standard formula ('or do ... ') asking for a prayer for the dead man. Built into a wall at Clonmacnoise is a notable collection of such gravestones and fragments of gravestones. The standing stones of the pagan period were now 'baptised' by the carving of a cross, often in very crude form. There are also early attempts at decorating such stones, as on the Reask Stone in Kerry, where the stylised cross resembles a flower.

Ireland's celebrated high crosses, standing up to 16 ft in height, are believed to have developed out of decorated standing stones of this kind. What are thought to be early forms of the high cross can be seen at Fahan and Carndonagh on the Inishowen Peninsula: stones, ascribed to the 7th c., in the form of a rough cross decorated with interlace ornament and crude figures in relief. The crosses at Ahenny in Co. Tipperary show a more developed form, with a slender shaft set on a base and a circle linking the arms with the upright. The whole surface of the cross is divided into panels, each filled with geometric designs: the Celts, it has been said, abhorred an empty surface. It is possible, though not certain, that such crosses were originally made of wood covered with sheet bronze, so that the crosses we have today may be merely stone copies of an earlier form. Raised bosses at the junction of the arms, possibly representing the nails used in the construction of the earlier wooden crosses, have been cited as evidence for this theory. On the base are figural representations, not easy to interpret, which may depict scenes of monastic life. The Ahenny crosses have been dated to the 8th c., on the basis of the striking similarity between their geometric patterns and the ornament in the Book of Kells.

Figure carving on Muireadach's Cross at Monasterboice

High crosses in Ireland
(a selection)

© Baedeker

1 Clonca	15 Durrow
2 Carndonagh	16 Kilcullen
3 Fahan	17 Glendalough
4 Arboe	18 Moone
5 Donaghmore	19 Castledermot
6 Drumcliffe	20 Kilfenora
7 Tynan	21 Dysert O'Dea/Ennis
8 Termonfeckin	22 Graiguenamanagh
9 Monasterboice	23 Kilree
10 Kells	24 Killamery
11 Duleek	25 St Mullins
12 Tuam	26 Ahenny
13 Bealin	27 Kilkieran
14 Clonmacnoise	

From about the 9th c. the ornamental patterns on the high crosses begin to give way to figural ornament. This is the great age of the Bible crosses, set up in monastic settlements as visible signs of piety and means of instruction. The finely carved relief figures, in rectangular panels, depict Old and New Testament scenes. Groups of panels are often devoted to miraculous deliveries from difficulty or danger – Daniel in the Lion's Den, the Three Young Men in the Fiery Furnace, the Sacrifice of Isaac, David and Goliath. Figures of Paul and Anthony, the desert saints, recall the Eastern prototypes of the Irish hermits, and the fabulous creatures depicted on the sides of many crosses seem to come from the East rather than from western Europe. The central feature, however, is almost always the message of salvation – on the west face Christ crucified, on the east face Christ in glory on Judgement Day. The cross is frequently topped by a small house-like structure in the form of a shrine with a shingle roof.

The type of stone used depends on local conditions, but it is usually a very fine-grained sandstone. There are quarries of this stone near Kells and Monasterboice in the east of Ireland. One of the finest of such crosses is Muireadach's Cross at Monasterboice (now dated to the first half of the 9th c.; ➤ picture on pp. 53, 261). The crosses at Clonmacnoise may have been hewn from erratic sandstone boulders. The stone used was of variable quality: the carving on some crosses is still as clear and sharp as on the day it was done, while on others it has been worn smooth and sometimes almost effaced by wind and rain. Where sandstone was not available and the harder granite had to be used, as at Columba's foundation of Moone in south-east Ireland, the carving was necessarily simplified almost to the point of abstraction. The figures on the Moone high cross have an appearance of uniformity, but the faces are not without expression.

From about the 11th c. the representation of biblical scenes, apart from the Crucifixion, was largely abandoned, and the crosses were again covered with ornamentation. Sometimes the crosses, with shorter arms and no ring, are carved with individual figures in high relief, such as the local limestone crosses of Co. Clare. The Dysert O'Dea Cross has a representation of the crucified Christ in a long draped garment and below this the dignified figure of a bishop wearing a mitre and carrying a crosier after the Roman fashion.

While there are a number of high crosses in Scotland and England, the round tower, or bell tower, found in early monastic settlements is a characteristically Irish development.

Round towers

It is a slender and elegant structure tapering to between 60 ft and 100 ft, with a conical stone roof – the central and most prominent feature of the monastic site. The building of round towers is believed to have begun after the first Viking raids: thus, in addition to serving as a bell tower, they also provided a place of safety in case of attack. The entrance was several feet above the ground, and within the tower narrow ladders gave access to the upper storeys. The various floors, of which there were usually five, were lit only by narrow windows, all facing in different directions, so that a watch could be kept for the approach of an enemy. In normal peaceful times the monks working in the open were called to services by a hand bell. A number of these angular forged metal bells have survived, and examples can be seen in the National Museum in Dublin and the British Museum in London, as well as in churches in remote Scottish glens.

Some 80 Irish round towers are still standing in whole or in part. While the earliest were constructed of undressed stone, without any form of ornament, later examples have elaborately carved stone friezes and decorated doorway arches in Romanesque style. Some round towers, including the one at Monasterboice, must still be climbed on ladders. The finest example of a round tower is the one at Ardmore in Co. Waterford (➤ p. 49).

Fine metalwork was also produced during the Early Christian period. The excellent examples of metalwork in the National Museum in Dublin show that the craftsmen of the period could practise and refine techniques inherited from the past, taking as their models articles of earlier periods in bronze, decorated with enamel or vitreous paste, or in beaten gold or silver. Among the examples of their work are such splendid ornamental brooches as the Tara Brooch and, as the monasteries became increasingly wealthy, precious vessels such as the 8th c. Ardagh Chalice. Later, richly decorated cases and containers were produced for objects of particular veneration, including manuscripts and bells,

Metalwork, crafts

bishops' crosiers and relics of the early saints. In work of this kind the artists made it a point of honour never to repeat themselves.

Irish crosiers have semicircular crooks, but with a straight end, and were kept in a similarly shaped bronze shrine, with a pattern of ornament which frequently ended in an animal's or bird's head. Bell shrines have the same shape as the bell contained within. The Shrine of St Patrick's Bell is of bronze, decorated with gold filigree, silver and precious stones.

The covers of a saint's prayer book were ornamented with cast bronze mountings. In one example depicting the Crucifixion the angels' garments and wings have spiral and interlace decoration.

The commonest items of this kind to have survived, however, are small house-shape reliquaries with steeply pitched roofs like those of the Early Irish churches. Made of wood with a bronze facing and decoration, they were designed to be carried on a strap round the neck.

Many works of this kind were carried off to Norway by Viking raiders and have come to light as grave goods recovered from tombs, particularly women's tombs. Some are in Norwegian museums; others have been brought back to Ireland.

The Cross of Cong (ca 1123), brilliantly decorated in gold and blue with animals and fabulous creatures, was the last great achievement of the Irish metalworkers.

Illuminated
manuscripts

The supreme intellectual and artistic contribution of the monks of the Celtic Church lay in the development of an Irish script and in the illumination of manuscripts. From the Latin script of the day they evolved a decorative half-uncial script which could be either strong and vigorous or, if the writer's artistic bent so dictated, lively and fanciful. The perfection of this script, written on thick parchment sheets, rivals the work of Islamic and Chinese calligraphers.

The urge to decorate the pages of a manuscript appears at an early stage. For example, in the Cathach (Helper in the Fight), St Columba's catechism (ca 600), the initials break out into a profusion of curls and spirals while other letters are outlined in dots.

Although in the Cathach only red and blackish-brown ink is used, later illuminated manuscripts glow in many colours. Among the shades used are crimson, bright red, emerald green, dark blue and yellow. The initials in the chapter headings of the Gospels are formed by a pattern of interlace ornament ending in human and animal heads, or sometimes by human figures shaped like articulated puppets to form the letters. Later the initials may take up the whole of a page. Above and below the lines appear the animals familiar to people of that period – cats, mice, cocks and hens, birds, fishes. Some of these figures are true to life, but most of them belong to a fantasy world. Words and syllables are linked by curving brackets of grotesque form in the shape of human or animal bodies which can no longer be accommodated within the line and are set above or below it.

The finest achievements of Irish book illumination are the full-page illustrations, comprising either a pattern of tapestry-like ornament or depicting scriptural scenes. The whole intricate pattern is drawn with such delicacy of line that it requires a magnifying glass to appreciate all the detail. There are evident similarities between these designs and the decorative motifs on metalwork and on high crosses.

The four Evangelists with their symbols are a favourite theme. Here again the artists have largely broken away from a realistic method of representation and are seeking to give pictorial expression to their own ideas. Thus we find figures with feet turned sideways (as in Egyptian tomb paintings), a double pair of hands, harlequin-like dress or blue hair. Numerous examples of Irish manuscript illumination can be seen in Dublin: in the Royal Irish Academy St Columba's Cathach and the Stowe Missal (early 9th c.); and in the Old Library of Trinity College the Book of Durrow (7th c.), the Book of Dimma (8th c., in a silver-plated bronze case or *cumdach*), the Book of Armagh (ca 807), which contains all four

Gospels, and the undisputed masterpiece of Irish book illumination, the Book of Kells (➤ Baedeker Special, p. 58).

Most of the holy men of the Celtic Church were active scribes and copyists. When they travelled they carried their manuscripts with them, and their foundations in Britain (e.g. on Lindisfarne) and on the Continent (e.g. at St Gall) also followed the style. In consequence a relatively large number of manuscripts have survived, most of them now in the major European libraries.

Occasionally the Irish scribes noted down personal remarks, or sometimes verses, in the margins of their manuscripts – observations of nature, pious statements and occasionally thoughts that are by no means pious. In some of these notes they give expression to their fear of the Vikings who brought this great flowering of art to an end.

Romanesque art

Romanesque art came to Ireland in the 12th c. with the adoption of the Roman form of the Christian faith. Hitherto the Irish had continued to build small churches with steeply pitched stone roofs of the traditional kind. The new style, too monumental for Irish tastes, was accepted only in part and was so considerably modified as to form a distinctive Irish Romanesque.

Ecclesiastical buildings

The first church in the new style, already a masterpiece, was Cormac's Chapel on the Rock of Cashel, which was consecrated in 1134. Builders from Regensburg in Germany are believed to have worked on this church, and the Schottenkloster (Scottish Monastery) in Regensburg is known to have had connections with Ireland – indeed in the early Middle Ages the Irish were known as Scoti or Scotti. For the first time in an Irish church the nave is barrel vaulted and the chancel has a rib vault. At the

Kilmacduagh – Romanesque and Gothic remains

57

The Book of Kells

In the Colonnades Gallery of the library of Trinity College, Dublin, can be seen the Book of Kells, one of the greatest artistic treasures in the world. Written by monks, it contains the four Gospels; one page is turned every day.

It has not yet been clearly established when and where the book was written, who commissioned it and who the artists were. The most widespread scientific theory of its origin and age is that it dates from the end of the 8th c. and came from Iona, a barren island off the west coast of Scotland. The monastery of Iona, which St Columba had founded in 563, was the place from which missionaries travelled to the mainland of Scotland, to northern England and then to the Continent. Here they influenced the founding of monasteries such as in Würzburg (Germany), Luxeuil (France), Bobbio (Italy) and St Gallen (Switzerland). In 791 the abbot Connachtach assembled in Iona the best artists and calligraphers of Europe. Further evidence that the Book of Kells must have originated on Iona can be found in the picture of the Apostle Luke on page 201. On the upper part of the apostle's hand can be seen the word 'Jonas' – another name for Iona. In 806 Vikings landed on the island and proceeded to plunder and burn it. Connachtach, the abbot, and 86 of his monks were slain. According to one theory precautions to preserve the book had been made after the Vikings had attacked Iona for the first time in 795. Shortly before their second invasion the Book of Kells, still incomplete, is said to have been taken by ship across the sea to the security of the Irish monastery of Kells (Ceananus Mor). Here it is presumed to have been completed at the beginning of the 9th c. In the 11th c. it was stolen but found again three months later, although the gilded cover had been torn off. According to another theory the entire book is said to have originated in Ireland and as far as the date of origin is concerned many scholars presume this to have been at the beginning of the 8th c. Whatever may be the true explanation, it is a fact that in the 12th c. the book was in the possession of the Monastery of Kells, for at this time the rules of this community of monks were written on the plain pages of the masterpiece. When Cromwell's marauding Protestant troops stormed over Ireland, the book was taken for security to Trinity College, Dublin.

The text of the Book of Kells is based on the Vulgate, the Latin translation of the Bible made by Hieronymus in the 4th c. but the Book of Kells does not entirely follow this version. This may be due to the fact that several sources were consulted when it was being written. Some have expressed the view that, as this work of art is larger in format than other examples of the Gospels made between the 7th and 9th c., it was orignally created to be used on the altar; this would account for the extraordinary illumination of its pages.

No costs were spared in creating the Book of Kells. The parchment for the pages was made from the hides of hundreds of calves. Pigments for the colours were obtained from all over the world: ultramarine from the Hindu Kush mountains along the route from Persia via Constantinople; carmine from southern France; and purple and gold pigment from Spain. In view of the differences in style in the artistic arrangement of the book, it is thought that several artists – probably four – were engaged on the work.

In the Book of Kells each passage of the four Gospels begins with an illuminated initial. There are 2000 of these, each different from any other. At the beginning of the account of the birth of Christ in St Matthew's Gospel, a whole page, measuring 13 by 10 inches, is devoted to the chi-rho monogram (a combination of the first two letters of 'Khristos' – 'XP' in Greek). The long diagonal arms of the 'X' lie obliquely across the page, while the 'P' can be seen in the lower part of the right side. Among the artistically decorated ornamentation well-drawn figures and animals can be seen.

These letters celebrate the incarnation of Christ and are reminiscent of the finest goldsmith's work. Anyone looking at the Book of Kells is inevitably reminded of the Orient, and yet this book is fundamentally insular – that is, Irish and northern British in character. In the combination of its ornamentation and figurative composition it constitutes the highpoint of the tradition of Irish book illumination.

Monogram of Christ

junction of nave and chancel stand two square towers. The pitched roof, however, follows earlier Irish models, and the carved fabulous beasts and human heads are typically Irish.

The Celtic head motif is also found in other Irish Romanesque churches, for example at Dysert O'Dea, where the principal doorway has animal masks between bearded human faces, or in Clonfert Cathedral, where the richly decorated west doorway is surmounted by a high gable with geometrically arranged human heads and ornament. Zigzag mouldings on the doorway and richly sculptured chancel arches are to be found on other Romanesque churches in Ireland.

After a national synod in 1110 the Irish Church was gradually assimilated with the Roman Church. Diocesan government was introduced, and the power and influence of the old monasteries declined sharply.

At the same time Bishop Malachi of Armagh introduced the Cistercians, the first of the great new religious orders to come to Ireland. Mellifont Abbey, where a Burgundian architect built the fine monastic church, was the prototype for some two dozen other foundations.

These new abbeys had a whole complex of buildings in addition to the church, including cells for the monks, a refectory, a cloister and domestic offices. The church was often called a cathedral, even though it was not one in the strict sense of a bishop's church. The monks from the older monasteries now flocked to these new foundations, bringing about the final demise of the Celtic Church.

Fortifications

When the Anglo-Normans conquered Ireland they built castles to provide security in a hostile country. An early form of castle was the motte and bailey, with a timber tower built on a circular or oval mound (the motte) and an outer court (the bailey) defended by wooden palisades.

A more substantial fortification was the stone keep, with thick walls and few windows. This might either stand by itself or be enclosed within an outer ward surrounded by curtain walls. Many ruins of these almost indestructible strongholds have survived to the present day.

In the course of time still more powerful fortresses were built, on the pattern of English castles, with corner towers and massive battlemented walls.

Gothic art

Ecclesiastical buildings

During the so-called Norman period, from the 13th c. onwards, the Gothic style came to Ireland. Buildings in this style were erected only by the Anglo-Norman incomers, with the help of native craftsmen, and by the new religious orders – first the Cistercians and Augustinians, later the Dominicans and Franciscans.

The churches and cathedrals, built in disturbed times and with limited means, were sturdy structures with little decoration and were smaller than their counterparts on the Continent. The monasteries were built in accordance with the rules and requirements of the various orders, but these, too, were on a smaller scale than elsewhere. Ruins such as those of Rosserilly, Co. Galway, with tower and cloister, refectory and reader's desk, bakery and fish tank, are like a miniature edition of a Franciscan friary.

Sculpture

Ireland's contribution to the art of this period consists of gravestones of traditional Irish type and a few works of sculpture. Most of the artists are practically unknown. One of the most gifted stonemasons of the Kilkenny area was Rory O'Tunney, whose work is to be seen in Jerpoint Abbey, in the form of figures in the cloisters and sarcophagi, in Kilcooley Abbey (near Urlingford), in the form of sarcophagi, and also in Kilkenny Cathedral. On these tombs the figure of the dead man, in full armour, lies on a stone sarcophagus under a sculptured canopy, which sometimes has late Gothic tracery, along with figures of angels, Apostles, saints and holy men around the sides; in 15th–17th c. tombs the dead man and his wife may be lying side by side. The figures are notable for

Franciscan Quin Abbey (15th c.)

the meticulous treatment of the hair and garments and for the curiously impenetrable expression on the faces.

Also typically Irish are the *sheila-na-gigs* – small carvings of obscene figures which may be fertility symbols or intended to ward off evil spirits – which can be found in unobtrusive positions in a number of churches.

Early modern period to the 20th century

At the end of the Middle Ages, given the poverty of the native population, art and architecture stagnated for several centuries.

It was not until the 18th c. that the Anglo-Irish ruling classes, having risen to prosperity and wealth, began to build country mansions and town houses appropriate to their status. Following the models provided by Palladio in Italy and Inigo Jones in England, they built mostly in the classical style. A typical example is Castletown House, near Dublin, a mansion with wings and colonnades built by Alessandro Galilei and Sir Edward Lovett Pearce in 1722–32 for William Conolly, speaker of the Irish parliament, with plasterwork by the Francini brothers.

18th c.

This flowering of architecture was followed, on a much more modest scale, by the other arts. Since the owners of the new country houses preferred an outdoor life, they were more interested in the layout of their parks and gardens than in the interior decoration of their houses. Exotic trees, immaculate lawns and terraces (as at Powerscourt in the Wicklow Mountains) meant more to them than pictures, furniture and carpets. Nevertheless there were some notable achievements in the minor arts, such as the elegant silver of the period. Some of the more eccentric wishes of the landowners were given expression in the follies they built on their estates – Greek or Egyptian temples, obelisks or artificial ruins.

Art and Architecture

Dublin

From the middle of the 17th c. a period of great building activity began in Dublin, and within barely a hundred years what had been an unimportant and not particularly salubrious little town was transformed into the second city of the British Empire. Four new bridges were built over the Liffey, its banks were lined with quays, and the old town centre was surrounded by wide modern streets and squares laid out as gardens. The Royal Hospital for old and disabled soldiers, designed by the architect Sir William Robinson on a French model, was built in 1670–87. This building activity reached its peak in the 18th c. when Dublin Castle and Trinity College were rebuilt. The short-lived Irish parliament was housed in a new building – now the Bank of Ireland – designed by Edward Lovett Pearce. As in the rest of Europe, architects of different nationalities were at work in Dublin. Richard Castle or Cassels (1690–1751), a German, built Tyrone House and Leinster House, which is now the parliament building. James Gandon (1743–1823), an Englishman of Huguenot origin, built King's Inns in northern Dublin, along with the Custom House and the Four Courts. Francis Johnston (1761–1829), who built both in the fashionable classical and neo-Gothic styles, was responsible for the Chapel in Dublin Castle and the General Post Office which featured so prominently in the fighting of 1916.

Georgian style

In addition to large public buildings this period also saw the construction of the handsome mansions of the aristocracy and the prosperous business classes, with imposing façades behind railed front gardens. This was the heyday of the 'Georgian style'. The brick fronts of these Georgian houses with their tall windows are beautifully proportioned; their only form of ornament, in endless variation, lies in the painted doors with brilliantly polished knockers, flanked by columns and surmounted by an architrave and a semicircular fanlight with a lamp or the house number. The interior of these houses is often decorated with fine plasterwork by (for example) the Francini brothers. Dublin's terraces of Georgian houses remained almost intact until well into the 20th c. Since then they have fallen victim, individually or in whole streets, to demolition to make room for new development. It is only in recent years and with great effort that it has been possible to save and to restore properly some of the city's finest streets and squares. Good examples may be seen by the visitor (on foot), particularly around St Stephen's Green, Merrion Square and Fitzwilliam Square. Similar houses and terraces can be found in other towns including Limerick and Cork.

Stained glass

During the 19th c., with Catholic Emancipation, many new churches were built, and the art of stained glass enjoyed a great flowering. The first workshops soon developed into schools of stained glass; new techniques were tried out and links were established with the Continent. Pioneers in this

Georgian doorways

development, which was considerably influenced by art nouveau, were Michael Healy, Harry Clarke, Sarah Purser and Evie Hone.

Ireland did not develop an independent style of painting. Famous during the latter half of the 18th c. were the portrait painters Robert Hunter (1748–1803) and James Barry (1741–1806), who made names for themselves with history painting, allegorical representation and etchings. Painters during the 19th c. largely concentrated on landscape, history and genre painting, among them Nathanlel Hone (1831–1917) and William Mulready (1786–1863).

With the turn of the century, naturalism and Impressionism reached Ireland. William Orpen (1878–1931) was the most popular painter of English society during that period. Jack Butler Yeats (1871–1957; ➤ Famous People), started off as an Impressionist, but gradually his works became ever more abstract. The bold colours used in the paintings of Roderic O'Conor (1860–1940) are reminiscent of the expressionists.

It is interesting to see how Irish architects and artists of the present day have taken up the forms and themes of the early period of Irish art. In church building, architects such as Liam McCormick have designed circular churches of notable quality, reflecting the plan of Ireland's prehistoric stone forts. Such new churches, and churches reconstructed on the remains of older buildings, contain tabernacles, Stations of the Cross, fonts and doors of modern design by such artists as Imogen Stuart, a native of Munich.

Among the nonecclesiastical buildings the architect Michael Scott stands out; he designed the Abbey Theatre in Dublin (1959) and the Bank of Ireland (1973). Also worthy of note is the new library of Trinity College, Dublin, by Ahrends, Burton & Koralek (1963–7).

Smaller objects in bronze, by Edward Delaney, Oisín Kelly and others, again showing the influence of the historic Celtic period, have also evolved their own characteristically Irish style. An affinity can perhaps be detected here with the brush drawings of Louis le Broquy, who illustrated Thomas Kinsella's modern version of the *Cattle Raid of Cooley*.

Literature

In the ancient Celtic period poets occupied a prominent position in Irish society. Seers as well as poets, they acquired their skills in special schools, usually under the direction of Druids, where, lying in the dark, they learned their texts and verses by heart.

During this period there came into being the great cycles of Irish-Celtic heroic sagas, which took the form of prose epics and were set against a pagan background. In the early years of the Christian period the sagas were written down by monks; but alongside this written record an oral tradition was maintained by the *shanachies*, men skilled in the art of telling tales. A number of different cycles can be distinguished.

In the tales of the mythological cycle mortals still hold intercourse with divinities, who have a double aspect, sometimes mild, sometimes terrifying. There is no firm boundary between life and death, and the final goal for man is Tir na n'Og, the Land of the Ever Young, somewhere to the west in the Atlantic.

The 'red branch' cycle of tales is concerned with the Ulaid, whose royal stronghold was Eamhain Macha (Navan Fort, in Northern Ireland), and their great hero CuChulainn. The subjects of the tales are cattle raids and their consequences, described in graphic, colourful and sometimes grotesque scenes. In the best known of these sagas, the 'Tain Bó Cuailnge' ('Cattle Raid of Cooley'), Queen Maeve, dissatisfied with her husband's possessions, plays the role of the evil opponent of the hero, CuChulainn. The third cycle, which is dated after the year 1000, centres on the exploits of Finn MacCool and his war band, the Fianna, which seems to anticipate some of the ideals of the later knightly culture. The theme of tragic love – the story of Diarmaid and Grainne, who can also be compared with Tristan and Isolde – appears in these tales too.

The Folklore Commission began to record the tales of the *shanachies* in 1935, and they were later issued on records and tapes.

Middle period
(1200–1650)

The middle period was the Age of the Bards – Celtic poets who composed and sang songs in praise of their lord or king. The prose literature of this period was mainly devoted to the 'Fenian' cycle, the fourth of the great Irish cycles, fairy-tale stories of adventure, often incorporating ballads.

Late period
(1650–1850)

The characteristic feature of the late period was the oppression of the Irish by the English conquerors, which had a detrimental influence on the development of Irish language and literature. The predominant element in literature was now folk poetry, cherished by country people and craft workers. Many of the poems gave expression to sorrow and the love of nature. Since this poetry flourished particularly in the southern Irish province of Munster, it is also known as 'Munster poetry'.

From the 17th c. onwards the names of individual Irish authors – writing in English – begin to feature in the history of literature. Early on there is Jonathan Swift (▶ Famous People), whose best-known work was *Gulliver's Travels*, written in 1726. Its original version was definitely not a children's book, but a furious satire on contemporary English society.

Typical Irish qualities – wit and humour, delight in telling stories – can be seen in the work of Laurence Sterne (1713–68), scion of an old Irish family, who spent his life as a country clergyman. His principal work is the humorous novel *The Life and Opinions of Tristram Shandy* (1760–7); it is divided into five books in which the action of the story takes second place to the expression of the author's own personality and whimsical fantasy.

Witty comedies were also written by the Anglo-Irish playwright Richard Brinsley Sheridan (1751–1816), best known for *The School for Scandal* (1777).

Oliver Goldsmith (1728–74), known for his novel *The Vicar of Wakefield* (1766), describes in his works the country around Athlone, still known as Goldsmith Country. The son of a poor vicar, as a student at Trinity College, Dublin, Goldsmith wrote ballads for street singers in order to earn a few coins; he would then creep out at night to hear them sung.

Thomas Moore (1779–1852), a talented musician as well as a poet, sought to build a bridge between the world of Celtic traditions and the rather frivolous attitudes of the Anglo-Irish society which he admired by fitting the old sagas to traditional airs in his *Irish Melodies*. With these songs, which were soon popular in English drawing rooms and on the Continent, he won new friends for Ireland and the Irish cause.

Modern period
(since the late
19th c.)

The beginning of the modern period was marked by the establishment of the Gaelic League (1893). The object of the league, whose members included Douglas Hyde, first president of the Irish Republic (1938–45), and the writer George Moore (1852–1933), was the revival of Irish language and literature – in a movement which came to be called the Celtic Renaissance. About the turn of the century Pádraic Pearse (1878–1916), Pádraic Ó Conaire (1882–1928), Peadar Ó Laoire (1839–1929) and others began to produce literary works in the Irish language. In 1899 Lady Augusta Gregory co-founded the Irish National Theatre in Dublin – known from 1904 as the Abbey Theatre – in which plays in both English and Irish were performed. This laid the foundation for an independent theatre culture in Dublin with influence on world literature.

Some of the writers of the modern period, including William Butler Yeats and John Millington Synge (▶ Famous People), concerned themselves with Irish traditions and the problems of Ireland; others, like Oscar Wilde and George Bernard Shaw (▶ Famous People), turned more towards Britain; but even those Irish writers who spent most of their life away from Ireland, such as James Joyce, reflect in their work the mentality and language of their native country.

The dramatist Sean O'Casey (1880–1964), who began by earning his living as a labourer on the railways, joined the Irish national movement at an early age. The Irish struggle for independence is the background both to his six-volume autobiography and to his early plays, such as *The Shadow of a Gunman* (1923), most of which reflects the life of the poor and wretched. In his dramas O'Casey combines comedy and humour with tragic irony. When the Abbey Theatre turned down a new play he offered them in 1928, he left Ireland for good.

Brendan Behan (1923–64) became involved as an adolescent in the activities of the Irish Republican Army and spent several years in British penal establishments. His experiences during this period are described in his autobiographical novel *Borstal Boy* (1958) and his posthumous *Confessions of an Irish Rebel* (1965). The heroes of his plays, with their fierce social criticism, are the outsiders of society (*The Quare Fellow*, 1956). He took two weeks to write *The Hostage* (1959), first in Irish, which depicts the shooting of an English soldier held hostage in a brothel.

The Irish are particularly noted as writers of short stories, mainly concerned with the precise depiction of a particular situation or state of mind, their expressive force resulting from the tension between linguistic precision and the humour of the situation, between pessimism and cheerfulness. The subjects are mostly taken from Irish everyday life. Among particular masters of the genre are Liam O'Flaherty (1897–1984), Sean O'Faoláin (1900–91) and Frank O'Connor (1903–66).

Music

The heyday of Irish music was in the early Middle Ages, the favourite instrument being the harp. In the banqueting hall of the high king, at lesser courts and in the houses of the magnates of the day, the 'three tunes, of laughing, of weeping and of sleep' were played. We know the names of only a few of the most celebrated harpists – many of whom were blind – and of the tunes ascribed to them. Later we hear of itinerant troubadours, who specialised in folk music. More than 200 compositions by Turlough O'Carolan (1670–1738), a blind poet and harpist, have been preserved.

The Irish harp

Since the 17th c. the harp has appeared in the Irish coat of arms. It remains the symbol of the Irish Republic today, and is also to be found on official documents, coins, stamps and soldiers' buttons.

During the centuries of English rule the poverty of the people ruled out any serious musical interest, and most of the Anglo-Irish landlords, preferring an outdoor life, had little time for the arts. Dublin during its 18th c. heyday was the exception, and in 1742 Handel's *Messiah* had its first performance in the city, conducted by the composer.

Nevertheless, the musical talents of the Irish managed to find expression. The instruments used in performing light music or dance music were of the simplest – fiddles, played with great virtuosity; tin whistles, with which they produced unexpectedly strong and harmonious sounds; and goatskin drums (*bhodran*). The Irish pipes (*uilleann*) were a softer-toned variant of the Scottish bagpipes, held under the arm and operated by movements of the elbow. These traditional instruments have been supplemented in more recent times by the concertina, the guitar and the banjo.

Other instruments

Folk groups all over the country use these various instruments in a rich repertoire of Irish and also Scottish, English and American tunes and songs, establishing an international reputation not only in concert halls but also in popular folk clubs.

In the late 18th c. much effort was devoted to collecting the traditional Irish songs, and several volumes of old folk tunes were published. Genuine old Irish folk songs are still sung, in Gaelic and without accompaniment. Building up on such songs and traditional melodies, Sean O'Riada (1931–71) composed important works which opened up new avenues and pointed the way for younger colleagues after his early death.

Folk tunes

Quotations

Samuel Johnson
(1709–84)

He had a kindness for the Irish nation, and thus graciously expressed himself to a gentleman from that country, on the subject of an UNION which artful politicians often have in view, 'Do not make an union with us, Sir. We should unite with you, only to rob you. We should have robbed the Scotch, if they had had any thing of which we could have robbed them'.

James Boswell's *The Life of Samuel Johnson*, 1791

Sir Walter Scott
(1771–1832)

There is perpetual kindness in the Irish cabin – butter-milk, potatoes – a stool is offered or a stone is rolled that your honour may sit down and be out of the smoke, and those who beg everywhere else seem desirous to exercise free hospitality in their own houses. Their natural disposition is turned to gaiety and happiness: while a Scotchman is thinking about the term-day, or if easy on that subject about hell in the next world – while an Englishman is making a little hell in the present, because his muffin is not well roasted – Pat's mind is always turned to fun and ridicule. They are terribly excitable, to be sure, and will murder you on slight suspicion, and find out the next day that it was all a mistake, and that it was not yourself they meant to kill, at all at all.

Diary, November 21st 1825

W M Thackeray
(1811–63)

As there is more rain in this country than in any other, and as, therefore, naturally, the inhabitants should be inured to the weather, and made to despair an inconvenience which they can not avoid, the travelling conveyances are so arranged so that you may get as much practice in being wet as possible.

They call Belfast the Irish Liverpool. If people are for calling names, it would be better to call it the Irish London at once – the chief city of the kingdom at any rate. It looks hearty, thriving and prosperous, as if it has money in its pockets, and roast-beef for dinner: it has no pretensions to fashion, but looks mayhap better in its honest broadcloth than some people in their shabby brocade. The houses are as handsome as at Dublin, with the advantage, that the people seem to live in them.

The Irish Sketch Book, 1843

W S Landor
(1775–1864)

Ireland never was contented
Say you so? You are demented
Ireland was contented when
All could use the sword and pen
And when Tara rose so high
That her turrets split the sky
And about her courts were seen
Liveried angels robed in green
Wearing, by St Patrick's bounty
Emeralds, big as half the county

Ireland never was contented, 1853

Dion Boucicault
(1822–90)

O Paddy, dear, an' did ye hear the news that's going round?
The shamrock is by law forbid to grow on Irish ground!
No more St Patrick's Day we'll keep, his colour can't be seen
For there's a cruel law agin the wearin' o' the Green!
I met wid Napper Tandy, and he took me by the hand,

And he said, How's poor ould Ireland, and how does she stand?
She's the most disthressful country that iver yet was seen,
For they're hanging men an' women there for the wearin' o' the
Green.

The Wearin' o' the Green, street ballad, later added to by Boucicault

I am in Aranmor, sitting over a turf fire, listening to a murmur of Gaelic that is rising from a little public house under my room.

The steamer which comes to Aran sails according to the tide, and it was six o'clock this morning when we left the quay of Galway in a dense shroud of mist.

A low line of shore was visible at first on the right between the movement of the waves and fog, but when we came further it was lost sight of, and nothing could be seen but the mist curling in the rigging, and a small circle of foam.

There were few passengers, a couple of men going out with young pigs tied loosely in sacking, three or four young girls who sat in the cabin with their heads completely twisted in their shawls, and a builder, on his way to repair the pier at Kilronan, who walked up and down and talked with me.

In about three hours Aran came in sight. A dreary rock appeared at first sloping up from the sea into the fog, then, as we drew nearer, a coastguard station and the village.

A little later I was wandering out along the one good roadway of the island, looking over low walls on either side into small flat fields of naked rock. I have seen nothing so desolate. Grey floods of water were sweeping everywhere upon the limestone, making at times a wild torrent of the road, which twined continually over low hills and cavities in the rock or passed between a few small fields of potatoes or grass hidden away in corners that had shelter. Whenever the cloud lifted I could see the edge of the sea below me on the right, and the naked ridge of the island above me on the other side. Occasionally I passed a lonely chapel or schoolhouse, or a line of stone pillars with crosses above them and inscriptions asking a prayer for the soul of the person they commemorated.

I met few people; but here and there a band of tall girls passed me on their way to Kilronan, and called out to me in curious wonder, speaking English with a slight foreign intonation that differed a good deal from the brogue of Galway. The rain and cold seemed to have no influence on their vitality, and as they hurried past me with eager laughter and great talking in Gaelic, they left the great masses of rock more desolate than before.

The Aran Islands, 1907

John Millington
Synge
(1871–1909)

Suggested Routes

In the following suggested routes, places which have a separate entry in the Sights from A to Z section of this guide are shown in **bold** type.

The itineraries are designed to take in the major cities, beauty-spots and features of interest (such as high crosses, round towers) in the countryside. Many of the places described in the guide, however, can be reached only by side roads off the main routes. The map at the end of the book will help in detailed planning.

All of the places mentioned in the guide, whether the subject of a separate entry or not, are included in the index.

1. Dublin to Drogheda and Belfast (ca 95 miles)

From **Dublin** the N1 leads north to Swords, an historic little town with a ruined castle and a round tower. Continuing at some distance from the sea, it reaches the coast at Balbriggan, with its water-sports facilities, and then continues north-west to **Drogheda** on the River Boyne.

A detour can be made to the **Boyne Valley** with the famous Newgrange, Knowth and Dowth prehistoric tombs, by turning left onto the N51 immediately after crossing the Boyne.

Detour

From Drogheda the N1 runs to Dunleer. About halfway there, to the left of the road, lies the monastic site of **Monasterboice**, with its fine high crosses.

Main route

From Dunleer the N1 continues, crossing a number of rivers flowing into Dundalk Bay, to the port of **Dundalk**, only a mile or two short of the Northern Ireland border. Over the border the A1 heads north for **Belfast**. From Newry the A28 goes north-west to **Armagh**, from which the A3 leads north-east to Lisburn, on the main road to Belfast.

2. Dublin to Arklow and Wexford (ca 90 miles)

The coast road south from **Dublin** comes in a few miles to **Dún Laoghaire**, from which there are ferry services to Holyhead (Isle of Anglesey) in Wales. There the N11 turns away from the coast, skirting the promontory of Dalkey, on the south side of Dublin Bay. A side road on the left leads to **Bray**, one of Ireland's leading seaside resorts. The N11 then continues along the east side of the **Wicklow Mountains**, past country of great scenic beauty and tracts of forest, to Ashford (with close by the splendid Mount Usher Gardens), and Rathnew.

From Rathnew the R750 follows the coast to **Wicklow**, continuing to Wicklow Head (lighthouses).

From Rathnew it is possible either to continue on the N11 or to take the coast road (Brittas Bay, Mizen Head) to the seaside resort of **Arklow**, where the Avoca River flows into the sea. A detour can be made from here to the Vale of Avoca, to the north-west.

From Arklow the N11 continues to Gorey and **Enniscorthy**, an attractive town on the River Slaney. The N11 then goes on to **Wexford**, where the Slaney reaches the sea. Wexford can also be reached from Gorey on the R741 and then the R742, which keeps relatively close to the coast.

◀ *The picturesque harbour of Kinsale*

From Wexford various roads continue south to the seaside resort of Rosslare and the ferry port of Rosslare Harbour.

3. Dublin to Waterford and Cork (ca 160 miles)

From **Dublin** the N7 leads south-west to **Naas**, once the seat of the kings of Leinster. South of the town lies Punchestown Racecourse.

From Naas the N9 goes south, crossing the River Liffey at Kilcullen. Beyond this the road passes Moone, with its famous high cross, and Castledermot, with its round tower. It then descends into the Barrow Valley to **Carlow**, an industrial town with a ruined castle, to the east of which lies Browne's Hill Dolmen, Ireland's largest megalithic tomb.

From Carlow the N9 continues south along the right bank of the River Barrow. At Leighlinbridge it crosses the river, and then continues south-west – from Whitehall onwards as the N10 – to **Kilkenny** on the River Nore, one of the most attractive towns in Ireland. From there the N10 – with possible detours to Kilree, which has a round tower and a high cross, and to the Augustinian priory of Kells – and the N9 (beyond Knocktopher) continue to **Waterford** on the River Suir, celebrated for the production of Waterford glass.

Detour

From Waterford visits can be made to the coastal resorts of Dunmore East (R683, R684) and Tramore (R675).

Main route

The main route (N25) continues from Waterford, at some distance from the coast, to **Dungarvan**, **Youghal** – a detour, a short distance before the town, on the R673 to **Ardmore**, with a round tower – and **Cork**, the principal city in the south of Ireland and a major port.

Further to Killarney

It is well worth continuing from Cork to **Killarney** along the N71, part of which runs along the coast. The attractive port town of **Kinsale** makes a good stop and in **Bantry** the manor house of that name and Garinish Island near **Glengarriff** both merit a visit.

4. Dublin to Limerick and Killarney Area (ca 125 miles)

From **Dublin** the N7 proceeds south-west to **Naas** and **Kildare**, Ireland's great horse-breeding centre. East of the town lies the Curragh Racecourse, on which race-meetings are held from spring to autumn. Crossing the River Barrow and the **Grand Canal**, the N7 continues to **Portlaoise**, an important traffic junction in the centre of Ireland. The route then takes you, with the Slieve Bloom Mountains on the right, to **Roscrea**, and from there via Nenagh to **Limerick**, on the Shannon.

Detour

From Limerick the N24 is the route south-east to **Tipperary**, from where the N74 continues east to **Cashel**, at the foot of the famous Rock of Cashel.

Main route

From Limerick the N20 and N21 (beyond Patrickswell) run via **Adare** and Newcastle West to Abbeyfeale, from where the route continues south on the N21 (to Castleisland), the N23 (to Farranfore) and the N22 to **Killarney**, in the centre of the beautiful Killarney lake district, one of the most popular holiday areas in south-west Ireland.

Killarney is a good base from which to drive round the Iveragh Peninsula on a beautiful scenic road, the **Ring of Kerry**, which hugs the coast for most of the way, with superb views. A drive round the **Dingle Peninsula** also provides some wonderful scenery.

5.

Fr...
wa...
N6...
Sh...

So...
wa...
wh...

Fro...
Lou...
the...
  (...
for...
Atl...
ferr...

6. ...
  (...

Fro...

Rou...
Tara...
hol...

...d past the great expanse of **Lough Neagh** to the Northern
...Belfast.

Belfast (ca 60 miles)

...runs inland on the A6 and B74 and then
...ugh the Sperrin Mountains, a hilly and
...aried scenery with the tourist centre of
Magherafelt.
...5, M22) continues to the north of
...tands a well-preserved round
...Belfast, a short way north of
...k and Transport Museum.
...oast north and south of

From Ballybofey a detour can...
Ireland. The N56 leads north...
...owed along the coast, by...
– **Horn Head, Rosguill Pe**...
to the **Inishowen Penin**...
fort.

The main rout...
Bridge, ther...
A5 runs n...
London...
surro...
co...

Navan is an important road junction; just north of
Dunaghmore, stands a round tower. From Navan the
Delvin) continue south-west to **Mullingar**, from
north-west to **Longford** and **Carrick-on-Shannon**.
cabin-cruiser trips on the Shannon. From here
Boyle to **Sligo**, on Sligo Bay, to the east of
Gill. From Sligo the N15 goes north and
over the Barnesmore Gap and throu...
Ballybofey.

Suggested Routes

Main route

Detour

Main route

Connemara landscape

Sights from A to Z

Within each entry in this part of the guide the various buildings and other features of interest are described in a sequence which visitors should find easy to follow whether on foot or by car. Except for one or two places where the arrangement did not seem appropriate, the surroundings of the various towns are described in clockwise order commencing from the north.

It needs to be borne in mind that references to the Blackwater River are not always to the same river. Ireland has large expanses of peat bog, which give the waters of the local streams a dark tinge. Perhaps not surprisingly, therefore, there are three different Irish rivers all called Blackwater. The first forms the border between Northern Ireland and the Irish Republic to the west of Armagh, then turns north-east and flows into Lough Neagh; the second, a left-bank tributary of the Boyne, flows through Lough Ramor north-west of Kells and into the Boyne at Navan; the third and longest of the three rises a short distance north-east of Killarney and flows in an easterly direction past Fermoy and Lismore before turning south through 90° to enter the sea in Youghal Bay.

Note also that in Ireland the term 'cathedral' is often applied to a church that is not in the strict sense an episcopal church.

Achill Island · Oiléan Acaill   B/C 1/2

Republic of Ireland
Province: Connacht
County: Mayo
Population: 3100

Achill Island (Oiléan Acaill) lies off the Irish Republic's western coast, separated from the mainland by the narrow Achill Sound (spanned by a swing bridge). With an area of 55 sq miles it is the largest of Ireland's offshore islands.

Hilly and L-shaped, Achill is almost entirely covered by heath and bog, the only cultivated land being in the valleys and near the coast. The hills on the northern and western sides rise to 2198 ft, dropping down to the sea in a series of magnificent cliffs.

Topography

Sights

The main centre on the island is the village of Achill Sound, situated close to the bridge. There are facilities for bathing and sea angling, and motor boats and sailing craft can be hired.

Achill Sound

Near the south end of the island – around which runs a road known as 'Atlantic Drive' (views) – the ruins of the 15th c. Carrickkildavnet Castle (National Monument) stand on the shores of Achill Sound. Part of a vaulted roof and the remains of an old slipway survive. The castle belonged to Grace O'Malley (➤ Famous People).

Carrickkildavnet Castle

◀ *An Italian-style garden on Garinish Island*

Achill Island – view of Keem Bay

Dugort

On the north coast, about 7 miles north-west of Achill Sound, is Dugort where in the main street stands the house (with light-blue painted window frames and two chimneys) in which the German author Heinrich Böll and his family lived periodically from the 1950s onwards. The cottage, little used in the author's later years, was given a new lease of life in 1992. Now, for several months a year, it is available for use by writers and artists, who also receive a small grant.

Among Dugort's other attractions is a good sandy beach. The surrounding area abounds with remains of cairns and chamber tombs.

Slievemore

The ascent of Slievemore (2169 ft), a shapely quartzite and mica cone, provides extensive views to north and south. On the way up, the deserted village of Slievemore can be seen. Only ruins now remain, the village having been abandoned during the Great Famine in the middle of the 19th c.

Below the hill, accessible only from the sea and in good weather, are the Seal Caves, best seen by taking a boat with an experienced crew from Dugort (2 miles).

Keel

Some 4 miles south-west of Dugort lies Keel, an attractive holiday resort with a sheltered sandy beach, 2 miles long, extending south-east to the foot of Minaun Cliffs which at one point fall 800 ft sheer to the sea. Keel is the centre of the island's fish-processing industry.

Dooagh

With its whitewashed houses and white roofs, Dooagh, 3 miles west of Keel, is the prettiest place on the island.

Keem

There is a particularly picturesque stretch of coastal scenery on the road to Keem (5 miles), which has a beautiful sandy beach (Keem Beach; plentiful parking). In dry weather it is possible to walk across the usually boggy ground to Achill Head at the western end of the island.

From Keem there is another rewarding climb up Croaghaun (2068 ft) further to the west, culminating on the seaward side in a 4-mile line of cliffs (magnificent views out over the Atlantic). **Croaghaun**

The cliff edge should not be approached too closely, the sea having undercut the cliffs in many places.

The pretty little resort of Dooega, 5 miles west of Achill Sound, is a convenient point from which to climb Minaun Mountain (1840 ft) and Minaun Cliffs. **Dooega**

★Adare · Áth Dara   D 3

Republic of Ireland
Province: Munster
County: Limerick
Population: 800

Adare (Áth Dara, ford of the oak tree) lies in the south-west of Ireland on the wooded west bank of the River Maigue, some 9 miles south-west of Limerick on the busy road to Killarney. In the early 18th c. refugees from the Pfalz region of Germany settled in the area between Adare and Rathkeale, which soon became known as 'the Palatine' (the English name for the Pfalz). Germanic customs and traditions survived here until the late 19th c. and German names are still in evidence today.

With its thatched roofs and old grey-walled church, Adare has something of the air of an English village. The picturesque cottages were built in the 19th c. by one of the earls of Dunraven. The 14-arch stone bridge **Village**

Thatched cottages in Adare

affords delightful views of the beautifully planted river banks, with their backdrop of old buildings.

Sights

★Adare Manor

Adare Manor, a neo-Gothic mansion (1832), formerly the Dunraven family seat, was converted into a luxury hotel (and restaurant) some years ago (➤ Practical Information, Hotels).

It stands in a large park, the greater part of which is now a golf course. Anyone nevertheless able to gain access will find, on the banks of the river, the extensive ruins of Desmond Castle (13th c.), a truly romantic sight with its semicircular towers and overgrown walls.

Also in the park are the ruins of a Franciscan friary founded in 1464, with later additions paid for by endowments. Of the friary church, the nave, choir and south transept survive (fine fonts, niches and stalls in the choir), in addition to a beautiful cloister with an old yew tree in the centre, and conventual buildings.

Augustinian friary

Near the bridge over the River Maigue at the eastern end of the village are the restored remains of a 14th c. Augustinian friary which, in the 19th c., became a Protestant church and school. Since 1826 the cloister has been the mausoleum of the earls of Dunraven.

Parish church

The Roman Catholic parish church originally belonged to a Trinitarian abbey founded in the 13th c. The church acquired its present form only in the 19th c.

Surroundings

Croom

5 miles south-east of the town on the N20 lies Croom, with a 12th c. castle restored in the 19th c. In the 18th c. the 'Maigue poets' used to meet together in Croom. West of Croom are the ruins of a 15th c. church (National Monument) and a massive round tower (12th c.), the top part of which is missing.

Monasteranenagh

2½ miles east of Croom are more monastic remains – the ruins of Monasteranenagh Abbey (National Monument), a Cistercian house dating mainly from the 12th c., with some good stone carving.

Rathkeale

The little market town of Rathkeale lies on the River Deel some 7 miles south-west of Adare, on the main road. Nearby stands Castle Matrix (1440), now restored (period furniture and objets d'art). Open Jun.–Sep. Mon., Wed., Thu., Sat., Sun. 2–4.30pm.

Cappagh Castle

Cappagh Castle, about 5 miles west of Adare, is a strongly fortified 70 ft-high keep (15th c.) with 16th c. turrets.

Aran Islands · Oileain Arann   C 2

Republic of Ireland
Province: Connacht
County: Galway
Population: about 1600

The Aran Islands (Oileain Arann) lie in the Atlantic south-west of Galway, at distances of between 25 and 30 miles offshore. There are three principal islands: Inishmore (12 sq miles in area), Inishmaan (3½ sq miles) and Inisheer (2¼ sq miles); also four other tiny uninhabited islets.

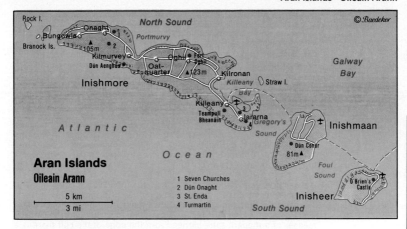

Aran Islands
Oileain Arann

5 km
3 mi

1 Seven Churches
2 Dún Onaght
3 St. Enda
4 Turmartin

Tourism has become increasingly important to the Aran Islands in recent years. While many of the visitors are day trippers, holiday accommodation is also available (bed and breakfast, holiday homes, small guest houses). Despite these new developments, the Aran islanders continue to preserve much of the traditional Irish culture which today has largely disappeared elsewhere; Irish remains the principal spoken tongue. Many books have been written about the islands' tough, staunchly traditional fisherfolk.

Lobster and other fishing is still carried on, providing a second source of income alongside tourism. The island fishermen still use the traditional Irish curragh, a lightweight craft built from tarred canvas stretched over a wicker frame; until relatively recently these also served for transporting people and goods to and from the islands.

Access

The Aran Islands can be reached either by sea or air. Aer Arann flies every day to all three islands from Carnmore, 4 miles north-east of Galway. There are several boats a day to Inishmore from Galway and Rossaveal and, in summer, one boat a day to Inishmore from Doolin. Also in summer there is a ferry service to Inishmaan from Spiddal. Inisheer is most conveniently reached from Doolin or, in summer, from Spiddal.

Topography

The islands, of karstic limestone, are rugged and infertile. By dint of unremitting toil the islanders have built up successive layers of sand and seaweed into small, irregularly shaped fields, which they call 'gardens', sheltered by drystone walls. The rocky coastline falls in terraces to the sea and there are few beaches. The island flora is of particular interest with many rare species continuing to thrive here, as they do also in the Burren.

Souvenirs, clothing

Until quite recently the islanders still wove woollen cloth from which they made their clothing, and wore handmade shoes of hide, without heels, known as *parnpooties*. Still very much in evidence are the very durable hand-knitted white wool (*bainin*) Aran sweaters and the long, coloured, patterned woollen belts called *crios*. These can be bought on the islands as well as throughout mainland Ireland.

Inishmore

Inishmore, some 7½ miles long by 2 miles wide, today has a population of about 900 (compared with twice that number a century ago). Life on the island is centred on the main settlement, Kilronan, to which the ferries also run.

Aran Centre

Housed in the old coastguard station, the Aran Centre informs visitors about the bleak but beautiful islands and their inhabitants. Open daily Jul.–Oct. 10am–7pm.

★★Dún Aenghus

On the edge of the cliffs fringing the south-west coast of Inishmore is the islands' main attraction, the great stone fort of Dún Aenghus, one of the largest prehistoric fortifications in Europe – a huge semicircle of three more-or-less concentric enclosures with a fourth outer ring, almost totally destroyed, on the very brink of sheer cliffs plunging 300 ft to the sea. The innermost enclosure, 150 ft in diameter, is surrounded by a stepped drystone wall (restored at the end of the 19th c.), 20 ft high and 18 ft thick at the base, incorporating various passages and chambers. The middle rampart is surrounded by a defensive ring of thousands of sharp-pointed stones set close together (*chevaux-de-frise*) in the manner of a modern tank barrier. From the edge of the cliff there is a breathtaking glimpse of the surf far below, and splendid views over the sea.

Oghil Fort

Further east is another stone fort, Oghil Fort (National Monument), with two concentric walls and steps leading up to the ramparts.

Kilmurvey

North of Dún Aenghus, at the hamlet of Kilmurvey, are the 9th c. church of St Brecan and Temple MacDuagh, an early church with a choir.

Dún Onaght

On a ridge north-west of Kilmurvey stands Dún Onaght, an almost perfectly circular stone fort.

Killeany

Around Killeany, 2 miles south of Kilronan, are remnants of numerous ecclesiastical buildings. Of particular interest is Tighlagh Eany, an early church with later features, which is all that remains of the monastic settlement of St Enda (Eany). There is a very fine cross shaft with interlace ornamentation and the figure of a horseman in relief. In the vicinity is St Benan's Church (Teampull Bheanáin), one of the smallest churches in the world, measuring only 10½ by 7 ft.

Inishmaan

A steep hill on Inishmaan is the site of another National Monument, Dún Conor, an oval fort with, inside it, a number of stone huts (restored). From the fort there are splendid views. There is also a fine dolmen.

The cottage of the poet and dramatist John Millington Synge who, in his book *The Aran Islands* (1907), first drew attention to the unique character of this delightful little archipelago, has been carefully preserved.

Inisheer

Among the remains on Inisheer are: the medieval tower of O'Brien's Castle, prominently situated on a rocky hill; St Gobnet's Church (Cill Gobnet), a small oratory with features characteristic of early Irish architecture; and the little St Cavan's Church which, every year on June 14th, is cleared of the sand which drifts ceaselessly over it, so that a service can be held. St Cavan's tomb is similarly swept clear of sand for the occasion.

Ardara · Arda Rath   B 3

Republic of Ireland
Province: Ulster
County: Donegal
Population: 650

Ardara (Arda Rath, earth hills) is prettily situated on the little River Owentocher in the most northerly county of Ireland, close to the east shore of Loughros More Bay, an arm of the sea penetrating deep inland.
    The village is noted particularly for the manufacture of homespun tweeds, as well as hosiery and embroidery.

Surroundings

Some 7 miles north-east of Ardara, on the River Owenea, lies Glenties, situated in a wooded region with good fishing in its rivers and loughs. There is a state-owned fish hatchery in the village. Glenties is also known for the manufacture of hosiery and gloves.

Glenties

North-east of Glenties, Aghla Mountain (1933 ft; splendid viewpoint) rises above the long narrow Lough Finn, from the eastern end of which flows the River Finn. The road follows the river for several miles, running along the hillside high above it, with magnificent views.

Aghla Mountain

2 miles south-west of Ardara an unclassified road branches off to the west , winding its way, with sharp bends and steep gradients, through a rugged landscape of bare hills to the Glengesh Pass and on to Glencolumbkille (➤ entry).

Glengesh Pass

To the west of Ardara extends a long narrow peninsula ending in Loughros Point, with fine views.

Loughros Point

The Maghera Caves are accessible at low tide from the north shore of Loughros Beg Bay. Nearby are the Essaranks Falls. Footpaths continue along the coast, with beautiful scenery; also through the Slievetooey hills (1510 ft) to Glencolumbkille.

**Maghera Caves
Essaranks Falls**

North of Ardara the R261 branches west off the N56. Near Kilclooney a massive, highly photogenic dolmen stands in grassy surroundings to the right of the road. (Coming from Adara turn right immediately after the church; the track leads past the bell tower and, after about five minutes, to the very prominent dolmen; ➤ picture, p. 82).

★Kilclooney dolmen

Further on lie the twin holiday villages of Narin and Portnoo, delightfully situated in the shelter of the hills on the south side of Gweebarra Bay. Narin has a fine sandy beach 1½ miles long and an 18-hole golf course. At low tide it is possible to walk (or, more usually, paddle) to the little islet of Inishkeel, with the ruins of an old chapel on the shore. Further west, on Dunmore Head, are two ancient ring-forts from which there are fine views.

**Narin
Portnoo**

1½ miles south of Portnoo, on an island in Lough Doon, stands a massive and well-preserved oval stone fort called The Bawn (signposted).

Lough Doon

The quiet little resort of Rosbeg, 3 miles south of Portnoo, has a sandy beach and there is good fishing for brown trout in the loughs round it.

Rosbeg

Dolmen, Kilclooney

Ardmore · Ard mor   E 4

Republic of Ireland
Province: Munster
County: Waterford
Population: 300

Ardmore (Ard mor, big hill) is an attractive little resort halfway along
the south coast of Ireland. Lying some 2½ miles east of the N25, it offers
a good beach and fine cliffs; the village itself is a mixture of old and
new.

Sights

★Round tower

Ardmore's well-preserved round tower (12th c.; National Monument;
➤ picture, p. 49), one of the last such towers to be built in Ireland, has
four tapering storeys rising to a height of 95 ft and a round-arched doorway set high above the ground. Inside the tower are projecting stones
carved with grotesque heads.

★St Declan's
Church

Adjoining the tower is the ruined St Declan's Church (13th c.; National
Monument). It bears the name of a bishop who founded a monastery
here in the Early Christian period and who is still honoured by an annual
pilgrimage (July 24th). The blind arcading on the west gable incorporates fine Romanesque reliefs, regrettably much weathered. In the upper
tier is a figure of the Archangel Michael weighing souls, while below are
seen Adam and Eve, the Judgement of Solomon and the Adoration of
the Magi. In the choir of the church are two ogham stones.

Built on to the church is St Declan's House, which is believed to contain the saint's tomb (an important station on the annual pilgrimage).

About ½ mile east of the main group of buildings are the ruins of Dysert Church, clearly a church of some size in its day. Nearby is St Declan's Well (restored 1798), a sacred well in which pilgrims used to bathe.

Dysert Church

At the southern end of the beach is an erratic boulder known as St Declan's Stone. It is said that anyone crawling beneath it – an impossible feat, apparently, for those in a state of sin – will be cured of rheumatism.

St Declan's Stone

Surroundings

There are many pleasant walks along the cliffs – to the sea caves at Ardmore Head and Ram Head east and south of the village; to Whiting Bay (west of Ardmore); and to the beautiful Monatray Bay (sandy beach).

Arklow · An Tinbhear Mor   D 5

Republic of Ireland
Province: Leinster
County: Wicklow
Population: 8650

Arklow (An Tinbhear Mor, broad estuary) is situated on the N11, the main road from Dublin to the south. Here the River Avoca, from which the Vale of Avoca takes its name, flows into the Irish Sea. In addition to its good sandy bays, Arklow is a lively small town with boatyards, a fertiliser factory and potteries (guided tours).

Arklow has had an eventful history. There is a tradition that St Patrick landed here. In later centuries the town was much fought over, changing hands several times. The last battle to take place here, during the 1798 Rising, is commemorated by a memorial in front of the Roman Catholic church.

History

The Arklow Maritime Museum is well worth visiting. Beyond the southern beach and golf course lies Arklow Rock, its Well of Our Lady still much venerated today.

Sights

Surroundings

From Arklow the R747 heads north-westwards along the River Avoca. To the right of the road, in a park with rhododendrons and other beautiful shrubs, stands Shelton Abbey, now a government-run school of forestry.

Shelton Abbey

At Woodenbridge the R752 branches off northwards into the lovely Vale of Avoca, a celebrated beauty spot. In spring the valley, fringed with green hills, is white with the blossom of wild cherry trees. In prehistory, copper, lead, zinc and sulphur were all mined here; today too the Vale is becoming increasingly industrialised, as a result of which some parts are no longer as scenic as they used to be.

Vale of Avoca

The principal centre of population in the Vale is the village of Avoca, widely known for its hand-loom weaving. Avoca handweavers welcome visitors and their handmade goods are on sale.

Meeting of the Waters

Some 3 miles further up the valley, Castle Howard looks down from its crag upon the famous 'Meeting of the Waters', where the rivers Avonmore and Avonbeg flow into the Avoca. A good view of the confluence is obtained from the Lion's Bridge.

Avondale Forest Park

Another 2 miles further on lies Avondale Forest Park, an extensive woodland park in which stands the house where the great Irish patriot Charles Stewart Parnell (➤ Famous People) was born. Built by James Wyatt in 1779, the mansion has a lovely interior. Parnell's life is documented on video. Open daily 11am–5.30pm.

Armagh · Ard Macha   B 5

Northern Ireland
Province: Ulster
District: Armagh
Population: 13,000

Armagh (Ard Macha, Macha's hill) is in Northern Ireland, to the south-west of Lough Neagh. Situated at the junction of several main roads, it is the principal town of the district and, as the seat of both a Roman Catholic cardinal and Protestant archbishop, has an important place in the religious life of the province. Textiles and fish processing are mainstays of its economy.

The surrounding area is known as the 'garden of Ulster' on account of its apple orchards and is particularly lovely in May when the trees are in blossom (Apple Blossom Route, signposted, starting and finishing in Armagh).

History

The town takes its name (Macha's hill) from the legendary Queen Macha, who in the 3rd c. BC built a stronghold, now known as Navan Fort (➤ Surroundings, Navan Fort), on a hill 2 miles to the west. Armagh grew in importance in the Early Christian period, St Patrick founding a

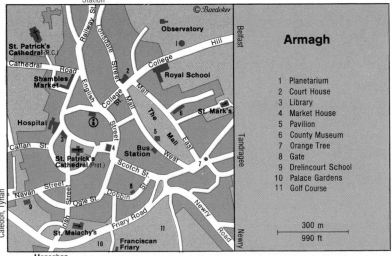

© Baedeker

Armagh

1 Planetarium
2 Court House
3 Library
4 Market House
5 Pavilion
6 County Museum
7 Orange Tree
8 Gate
9 Drelincourt School
10 Palace Gardens
11 Golf Course

300 m
990 ft

monastery and a church here in about 445. The settlement developed into a centre of missionary activity, and the Book of Armagh was written in the monastery. Over the centuries the town has burned down several times and been rebuilt.

Armagh is a friendly little town, many of its buildings being constructed of the pink, yellow or reddish sandstone known as 'Armagh marble', a favourite building material of the architect Francis Johnston (1761–1829), himself a native of Armagh. Johnston designed many public buildings and Georgian town houses along the town's principal thoroughfare, encompassing the elongated green known as The Mall.

Town

Sights

The County Museum occupies a former school house in The Mall dating from the first half of the 19th c. In addition to interesting sections devoted to archaeology and natural and local history, the museum possesses a sizeable library. Also on display are paintings by George Russell (1867–1935) and James Sleator (1889–1950), the latter having painted the portraits of many local dignatories. Open Mon.–Sat. 10am–1pm, 2–5pm.

County Museum

At the north-west end of The Mall stands the Court House, designed by Francis Johnston and built 1805–9.

Court House

From the Court House, College Hill runs north-east, past, on the right, the Royal School, founded in 1608 by James I, to the Armagh Astronomy Centre, where the Observatory, established in 1791, is open to the public. The Centre also incorporates a Planetarium, opened in 1968 (presentations every afternoon except Sunday), and a Hall of Astronomy in which are displayed assorted pieces of astronomical apparatus and a model of a spacecraft.

Observatory

Proceeding south-west from The Mall, and past the fine 18th c. Market House, you reach St Patrick's Protestant Cathedral. It stands on the site of the church founded by St Patrick in the 5th c. The cathedral of the Church of Ireland acquired its present aspect in the course of a 19th c. restoration by Lewis Cottingham. Notable features of the interior are a 10th c. crypt, several monuments (including that of Sir Thomas Molyneux) and a bust of Archbishop Richard Robinson who, in the 18th c., was responsible for so much of what makes Armagh the attractive place it is today. On the cathedral's outer wall can be seen a tablet supposedly marking the grave of the Irish king Brian Boru, killed at the Battle of Clontarf in 1014 and buried here by his own wish.

St Patrick's Protestant Cathedral

Likewise commandingly situated on a hill, in the north-west of the town, is the Roman Catholic St Patrick's Cathedral, a neo-Gothic building (1840–73), the interior decoration of which includes mosaic work by Italian artists.

St Patrick's Roman Catholic Cathedral

To the south of the town, on land once belonging to the old Archbishop's Palace, are the remnants of a Franciscan friary founded in 1266.

Franciscan friary

The former stables of the old Archbishop's Palace now house craft workshops and a café. Horse-drawn carriages can also be hired here.

Palace stables

Surroundings

Navan Fort (Eamhain Macha), 2 miles west of Armagh on the A28, was for centuries the seat of the kings of Ulster. There are graves and earth-

Navan Fort

works and, from the hill, a fine panorama of the surrounding country-side; also a Visitor Centre with information on the fort and its history.

Caledon

9 miles west of Armagh lies the village of Caledon, 2 miles south-west of which stands Caledon House, a Georgian mansion (1779) set in beautiful gardens.

Tynan

At Tynan, south of Caledon, are a number of 12th c. high crosses carved with biblical scenes.

Athlone · Baile Atha Luain   C 4

Republic of Ireland
Province: Leinster
County: Westmeath
Population: 9450

Athlone (Ath Luain, ford of Luan) is situated almost exactly at the geographical centre of Ireland. It lies on the River Shannon which, to the north of the town, flows through Lough Ree and forms the provincial boundary between Leinster and Connacht. Athlone is a busy road and rail intersection and its marina is also a haven for pleasure craft on the Shannon (➤ entry) and Lough Ree. It has developed a number of light industries and is the main shopping and commercial centre for the region. Not far to the east of the town is the powerful Athlone long-wave radio transmitter.

History

This has been an important crossing of the Shannon since time immemorial. By the end of the first millennium AD the river was already spanned by a wooden bridge. In the 13th c. a bridgehead was constructed comprising a castle and riverside defences; again and again in later centuries these were the scene of fierce fighting, being several times razed and rebuilt.

Sights

Athlone Castle

Known also as King John's Castle, Athlone Castle was built in 1210 on the instructions of King John of England. It acquired its present appearance mainly at the beginning of the 19th c. Designated a National Monument in 1970, the castle now houses a Visitor Centre with several exhibition rooms highlighting the history of the town and the flora and fauna of the Shannon region. A small section celebrates the life and work of the distinguished Irish tenor John McCormack (1884–1945), born in Athlone. Open daily Apr.–Sep. 10am–4.30pm.

Church of St Peter and St Paul

The Renaissance-style Church of St Peter and St Paul, close by the bridge, dates from 1937. The tenor John McCormack is one of several well-known figures depicted in the stained glass.

Surroundings

Poets' Country

From Athlone the N55 runs north-eastwards through the so-called Poets' Country of Oliver Goldsmith and John Keegan Casey. Goldsmith grew up in Lissoy .

Bealin

4½ miles east of Athlone, on a byroad near the Athlone radio transmitter, lies the village of Bealin where, on a nearby hill in the grounds of Twyford House, stands a 9th c. high cross (National Monument) carved with hunting scenes, entwined animal figures and other patterns.

Athy · Baile Átha hí   D 5

Republic of Ireland
Province: Leinster
County: Kildare
Population: 4300

Athy (Baile Átha hí, ford of í), the largest town in Co. Kildare, lies south-west of Dublin on the River Barrow, at a point which used to be an important ford. A branch of the Grand Canal (➤ entry) joins the Barrow at this same point.

Sights

White's Castle, built by the earl of Kildare in the 16th c. to protect the bridge across the Barrow, is a massive rectangular structure with corner turrets. The bridge has the unusual name of 'Crom-a-boo', from the war-cry of the Desmonds (an earl of Desmond was appointed governor by the English in 1420).

White's Castle

Half a mile north, on the L18, is the 13th c. Woodstock Castle, likewise built to guard the river crossing. It was severely damaged in 1649.

Woodstock Castle

Downstream from White's Castle stands the Dominican church (1963–5; by John Thompson), built on a pentagonal plan with an ingenious, spherically vaulted roof. Inside are several notable works of art including fine stained glass and Stations of the Cross by George Campbell.

Dominican church

The old Court and Market House, a fine Georgian building (18th c.), is now the fire station.

Court and Market House

Surroundings

4½ miles north-east of Athy, on the N78, is the Motte of Ardskull, a 30 ft high earthwork castle dating from the 12th c.

Motte of Ardskull

Ballitore, 5 miles east of the Motte of Ardskull, was once a Quaker settlement with a famous school. The former Meeting House is now a bookshop and small museum. Another attraction is the Crookstown Historical and Heritage Centre in a restored mid 19th c. mill; the mill wheel still operates. The numerous exhibits illustrate the techniques of corn milling and bread making over the centuries. Open Apr.–Sep. daily 10am–7pm; Oct.–Mar. Sun. 10am–4pm.

Ballitore

Just off the N9 at Moone, south of Ballitore, by a ruined 13th c. church (to the right of the road when coming from Dublin), stands a slender high cross, 17½ ft high, decorated with a series of superb bas reliefs: on the east side Daniel with seven lions, Abraham's sacrifice, Adam and Eve, and the Crucifixion; on the west side the Twelve Apostles, the Crucifixion, the Virgin Mary and St John; on the north side the Miracle of the Loaves and Fishes, the Flight into Egypt, the Three Men in the Fiery Furnace and assorted animals; on the south side further human figures and animals.

★ **Moone high cross**

Baltinglass

At Baltinglass, on the N81 east of Moone, are remains of a 12th c. Cistercian monastery, Valle Salutis (National Monument), the nave and chancel being decorated with stone carvings in a mixture of styles (Irish Romanesque, Cistercian). A section of the cloister has been restored; the tower and east window date from the 19th c. Rising above the village, to the north-east, is Baltinglass Hill (1237 ft) with, on its summit, a large megalithic tomb (Stone Age; National Monument). Around this a hill fort was evidently constructed at a later date (sometime between 500 BC and AD 500?). Stone ramparts are still visible. From the top of the hill there is a superb panorama.

Castledermot

Further interesting ruins are found at Castledermot, 5 miles south of Moone on the N9. They include the remains of an ancient monastery (National Monument) with a Romanesque doorway, a round tower, the upper part of which is medieval, and two granite high crosses embellished with biblical scenes. The relief of David with his harp on the more northerly of the two crosses is of particular interest as one of the few early representations of an Irish harp. On the south side of Castledermot are the ruins of a Franciscan friary (National Monument) founded in the 14th c. and dissolved in the 16th c.

Kilkea Castle

3 miles along the road leading north-west from Castledermot back in the direction of Athy, lies Kilkea Castle, dating from 1180. Considerably altered in the 19th c., it is now a luxury hotel and health farm.

Ballina · Béal an Atha   B 2

Republic of Ireland
Province: Connacht
County: Mayo
Population: 6900

Ballina (Béal an Atha, mouth of the ford) lies in the far north-west of Ireland, in bog country on the banks of the River Moy, at the point where it widens out before entering Killala Bay on the Atlantic coast.

As the largest town in Co. Mayo, Ballina is the market centre for an extensive hinterland. For anglers it makes a good base from which to fish the River Moy and two well-stocked loughs, Conn and Cullin.

Sights

The Roman Catholic cathedral (20th c.) has fine stained glass. Close by are the remains of a 15th c. Augustinian abbey. Near the railway station there is a dolmen (National Monument) marking the grave of four brothers said to have murdered their foster-father, a bishop, in the 6th c.

Surroundings

Inishcrone

Inishcrone (also spelled Enniscrone), a good 9 miles north of Ballina, is a popular holiday resort at the wide mouth of the River Moy in Killala Bay. It has two well-appointed spas offering sulphur and other medicinal baths as well as sea-water baths and saunas.

The remains of Castle Firbis, about 2½ miles north of Inishcrone on the R297, are of interest because the MacFirbis family produced several notable scholars. It was a MacFirbis who compiled the 'Great Book of Lecan', an important early 15th c. genealogy (ca 1416; now in the Royal Irish Academy, Dublin); two other codices were also compiled here.

Foxford

At Foxford, a quick 10 miles south of Ballina on the N57, is the Foxford Woollen Mills Visitor Centre. The River Moy, winding its way through the little town, once provided the water power which drove the spinning mills. Set up in one of the old mill buildings, the Visitor Centre explains the process of wool production in the 19th c. and the present. Open Mon.–Sat. 10am–6pm, Sun. 2–6pm.

From Ballina the R310 runs south before crossing the narrow stretch of water separating Lough Conn, famous for its pike, from Lough Cullin (fine views from the bridge). Fishing in both loughs is free. Pontoon is a popular fishing resort where boats can be hired.

Lough Conn
Lough Cullin
Pontoon

Heading north again from Pontoon, the R315 skirts round the southern and western sides of Lough Conn. Over to the left, rising from the low-lying countryside, is the impressive outline of Nephin Mor (2626 ft). Seen from a distance from the north-east, it has the all the majesty of a sacred mountain.

Nephin Mor

At the north-west end of Lough Conn, on the N59, lies Crossmolina. As well as a peat-fired power station, numerous remains of ring-forts and other ancient structures are to be found in the surrounding area. 6 miles south-east, on a peninsula reaching out into the lough, are the ruins of Errew Abbey (13th c.; National Monument).

Crossmolina

From Crossmolina the R315 continues north to Ballycastle, in an area of outstanding Atlantic coastal scenery. On Downpatrick Head, 4 miles north, the forces of nature have sculpted fantastic shapes in the sandstone cliffs along the shore and the isolated stacks in the sea.

Ballycastle

Céide Fields, located 5 miles west of Ballycastle on the R314, is a Neolithic site extending over 3¼ sq miles. It illustrates how this area would have appeared over 5000 years ago when incomers cleared the forests and laid out pasture. The new arrivals lived in individual farmsteads, each with a long narrow piece of ground separated from its neighbours by walls. Intriguingly, if one of these walls has had to be diverted round an obstacle such as a rock, all the adjacent walls follow suit. To the uninitiated the remains of these walls, exposed from beneath a thick layer of peat, appear less than impressive. However, an illuminating Visitor Centre puts this remarkable discovery into perspective. More prehistoric sites, this time dating from 1500 BC, can be seen near Belderg, 5 miles west. Open mid-Mar.–May, Oct. daily 10am–5pm; Jun.–Sep. daily 9.30am–6.30pm; Nov. daily 10am–4.30pm; the archaeological site itself is accessible at all times.

★★Céide Fields

Returning eastwards from Ballycastle, it is worth taking the minor road along the coast via Rathlackan to Carrowmore, there branching left to the sea at Lackan Bay. The road comes to an end at Kilcummin where the picturesque ruins of a little 7th c. church, with a sacred well and old gravestones, stand in lonely isolation by the shore. Further south the road passes by the remains of **Rathfran Friary** (13th c.; National Monument); surviving from the friary church are the nave, choir and a 15th c. chapel.

Kilcummin

4 miles further south, at Killala, stands a well-preserved round tower 84 ft high, adjoining which is a small 17th c. 'cathedral'. In 1798 a French expeditionary force, having landed in Kilcummin Bay to support the rebellion, held out in Killala for some time against British troops.

Killala

Not far beyond Killala a signposted side road branching off left runs south-eastwards to Moyne Friary, a 15th c. Franciscan friary close to the sea (National Monument). Considerable remains survive, albeit in a state of ruin. Unfortunately there is no access to the land at the moment, but the abbey can be viewed from the distance.

★Moyne Friary

2½ miles south, and well worth a visit, is Rosserk Friary (National

Rosserk Friary

Moyne Abbey

Monument), another 15th c. Franciscan friary of which there are extensive remains (to reach it, continue past Moyne Friary on the same small road in the direction of Ballina, eventually turning left at the signpost). A richly carved doorway leads into the aisleless church with a chapel in the south transept. There are fine windows, a double font (with a carving of a round tower on one of the supports) and a square tower. The conventual buildings also survive.

Ballinasloe · Beal Atha an Sluagh   C 3

Republic of Ireland
Province: Connacht
County: Galway
Population: 6400

Ballinasloe (Béal Átha an Sluagh) lies in the centre of Ireland on the N6 south-west of Lough Ree.

A place of some military importance in earlier times, Ballinasloe is now a busy market town, famous for its horse, cattle and sheep fairs. The great October Fair is the biggest in Ireland. Before the days of motor traction, when cavalry were still a major force in warfare, this particular horse fair could claim to be the largest in Europe.

Ballinasloe is the western terminus of the Grand Canal (➤ entry) although today the final section is no longer navigable.

Sights

The town has a number of handsome 18th c. houses. Above the River Suck rises Ivy Castle (19th c.), erected on the foundations of an earlier stronghold. In Garbally Park on the south-west edge of the town stands a fine late Georgian mansion built of the local limestone (now a school).

Surroundings

5 miles south of Ballinasloe on the R355 are the ruins of an Augustinian monastery, Clontuskert Abbey (National Monument). The west doorway of the church (1471) is notable for its carvings, including the Archangel Michael weighing souls, saints, a pelican and a mermaid with a mirror.

Clontuskert Abbey

From Clontuskert the R355 continues to Laurencetown, beyond which a side road leads to Clonfert, 13 miles south-east of Ballinasloe. The doorway of the 'cathedral' (National Monument), below the massive west tower, is a supreme example of Irish Romanesque sculpture. Above a blind arcade, richly decorated with stylised patterns and inward-sloping columns, rises a gable embellished with a row of five fields and, above them, a panel decorated with a diamond pattern of small triangles embellished by carved human heads alternating with other ornamentation. More heads, alternately bearded and shaven, adorn the arches and other available spaces. The east windows in the choir are among the finest examples of late Romanesque art. The (later) decoration of the interior is also notably fine, especially that of the arches supporting the tower (with figures of angels and a mermaid), the chancel arch, and the 15th c. windows.

★ Clonfert

7 miles west of Ballinasloe, on the R348, stands Kilconnell Friary (National Monument), a former Franciscan friary founded in 1353. The church, with its slender, graceful tower rising above the crossing, and beautifully carved west doorway, is a splendid example of Gothic architecture. In the north wall are two remarkable canopy tombs, the first, to the left of the entrance, embellished with figures of saints displaying foreign, probably French, influence, the other in the choir. By the church are the conventual buildings.

Kilconnell Friary

At Aughrim, 2½ miles south-east of Kilconnell, there is a local museum with material from the Stone Age onwards. The Aughrim Interpretative Centre commemorates a 1691 battle referred to in Irish history as 'Aughrim's great disaster'. Open May–Sep. daily 10am–6pm.

Aughrim

Ballinrobe · Baile an Rodbha   C 2

Republic of Ireland
Province: Connacht
County: Mayo
Population: 1450

Ballinrobe (Baile an Rodbha, town of the River Robe) is situated in the west of Ireland at the point where the N84 crosses the River Robe. To the west of the town is Lough Mask (good fishing) and beyond it the range of hills known as the Partry Mountains, of which the highest is Benwee (2206 ft). Ballinrobe is popular both as an angling centre and as a base from which to explore the surrounding area.

Surroundings

The road from Ballinrobe to Ballintubber (N84) crosses the narrow isthmus between Loughs Mask and Carra. The two are linked by an

Lough Mask Lough Carra

underground stream. A cairn on an islet in the green waters of Lough Carra marks the grave of the writer George Moore (1852–1933).

★Ballintubber Abbey

9 miles north of Ballinrobe, on a by road off to the right of the N84, lies Ballintubber, or Ballintober, Abbey (National Monument), an Augustinian monastery founded in 1216. Despite the devastation wrought by Cromwell's troops in 1653 it has remained a place of active worship ever since. The cruciform church and the cloister were restored in 1963–6. A not usually accessible chapel in the choir contains an elaborate altar tomb with finely carved figures on the pediment.

The abbey lay on the pilgrim route to Ireland's holiest mountain, Croagh Patrick (➤ Louisburgh), glimpsed in the distance through the arches of the cloister.

Lough Mask House

About 6 miles south of Ballinrobe a side road branching off towards the east shore of Lough Mask leads to Lough Mask House and park. In the last quarter of the 19th c. this was the residence of Captain Charles Cunningham Boycott (1832–97), agent of an English landlord, who treated the tenants so badly that, one day in 1880, they resolved to have nothing further to do with him. Eschewing violence, they simply refused to work for him or sell him their produce. Labourers consequently had to be brought in from the northern counties to gather in the potato harvest under military protection, rendering the crop totally unprofitable. This form of passive resistance eventually compelled Boycott to retreat to England, at the same time enriching the English language with a new word – boycott (➤ Famous People, Charles Parnell).

Inishmaine Island

On Inishmaine, a small island in Lough Mask, separated from the park by a narrow strip of water, are the ruins of a small 13th c. Augustinian friary (National Monument). The cruciform church has some good carving (animals, foliage).

Ballybunion · Baile an Bhuinne-aneigh   D 2

Republic of Ireland
Province: Munster
County: Kerry
Population: 1350

Ballybunion (Baile an Bhuinne-aneigh, town of the sapling) is a popular family resort in south-west Ireland. It lies on a west-facing stretch of coast where the Shannon emerges from between the headlands flanking its estuary (Mouth of the Shannon) to disgorge into the Atlantic. With its sea caves, rugged cliffs, coves and seemingly endless fine sandy beaches, Ballybunion offers a wide variety of attractions for seaside holidays in a thoroughly delightful area.

Sights

Caves Footpath

In the cliffs to the north of the town are many caves, some accessible only by boat, others reachable on foot at low water. A 3-mile footpath runs along the top of the cliffs between Doon Cove and Doon Point – both with remains of prehistoric headland forts – and past the old stronghold of Lick Castle.

Knockamore Mountain

To the east of Ballybunion, rising out of the flat surrounding countryside, is Knockamore Mountain (866 ft), from which there are superb views.

Surroundings

From Ballybunion the R551 leads north-east to Ballylongford, at the head of a narrow inlet. On the west side of the inlet stands Carrigafoyle Castle (15th c.; National Monument), with a 85-ft-high keep (lovely views). To the east of the little town are the ruins of the beautiful Franciscan Lisloughtin Friary (15th c.; National Monument). The church has a fine west window and there are remains of conventual buildings.

Ballylongford

5 miles beyond Ballylongford on the R551 lies Tarbert, from where a car ferry crosses the Shannon to Killimer in Co. Clare (➤ Kilkee).
   The Tarbert Bridewell gives an insight into crime and punishment in the 19th c. (wax figures are used to reconstruct scenes in the former court house and adjoining prison, telling the story of Thomas Dillon's conviction and punishment). Open Apr.–Oct. daily 10am–6pm.
   1¼ miles north, on Tarbert Island (connected to the mainland by a causeway), are a lighthouse and old gun emplacement.

Tarbert

Listowel, a busy little town about 9 miles south-east of Ballybunion, is said to have more pubs than houses. It is famous for its Writers' Week, held every year in June. Harvest Festival is another major event in the local calendar, being still combined with a marriage fair (end of September).

Listowel

South of Ballybunion the River Feale flows through a fjord-like estuary, Cashen Bay, to the sea. Here there is a well-known salmon hatchery, Cashen Fishery, which visitors can look round.

Cashen Bay

1¼ miles south, on the site of an old monastic settlement (Rattoo), are a 15th c. church and the excellently preserved 92 ft Rattoo Round Tower (National Monument).

★Rattoo Round Tower

Bantry · Beanntraighe   E 2

Republic of Ireland
Province: Munster
County: Cork
Population: 2900

Bantry (Beanntraighe, descendants of Beann) lies sheltered by surrounding hills in the extreme south-west of Ireland, at the head of the famous and beautiful bay which bears its name. The influence of the Gulf Stream is evident in the climate and vegetation of the area, with tall fuchsia hedges and palms frequent features of the landscape.

Bantry Bay has twice been entered by French fleets – once in 1689, in support of James II, and again in 1796, bringing aid to Irish rebels. Neither expedition was successful. In 1796 the ships could not even put in to land on account of fog and violent storms.

History

Though lively enough, Bantry is not a particularly attractive town, an impression reinforced by the presence on nearby Whiddy Island of the oil terminal, capable of handling supertankers.

Town

★Bantry House

In lovely grounds on the southern outskirts of the town stands Bantry House, a Georgian mansion begun in 1740. In 1771 alterations were carried out by the 1st earl of Bantry, and in 1840 the house was sub-

House and park open daily 9am–6pm

stantially enlarged by the addition of two side wings, creating a long, finely proportioned building. It boasts a valuable collection of works of art from all over Europe (icons, Gobelin tapestries, French furniture) while mosaics from Pompeii embellish the hall.

There is a pretty tearoom, comfortably furnished; in summer teas are also served out of doors.

The park, with Italian-style terraces and statuary, is laid out on the slopes of a hill. From the terraces there are extensive views over Bantry Bay, with its islands and inlets.

Park

Situated opposite Bantry House is the Bantry French Armada Exhibition Centre. In the winter of 1796 a French fleet of 43 vessels carrying 16,000 men was despatched to support the 'United Irishmen' in their resistance against the British. Bad weather prevented all but 16 ships from reaching Bantry Bay, and after only a minor skirmish the French were forced to withdraw. In 1985 the wreck of the French frigate *La Surveillante* was discovered lying in 100 ft of water. There is a 1:6 scale model of the ship in the Armada centre. Open Easter–Sep. daily 10am–6pm.

Bantry French Armada Exhibition Centre

Surroundings

Two roads run through particularly lovely scenery near Bantry, the first north-east over Cousane Gap to Macroom (➤ entry), the second along the coast road to Glengarriff (➤ entry), with magnificent views of the sea and the hills.

Scenic drive

To the north of the town on the Glengarriff road are the Donemare Falls on the River Mealagh. There is good fishing in the river and in Drombrow Lough above it, as well as in Lough Bofinna.

Donemare Falls

Extending south-west of Bantry is the long and scenically magnificent Sheep's Head Peninsula, with good beaches at Kilcrohane and Ahakista on the peninsula's south coast.

Sheep's Head Peninsula

There is a splendid drive round the peninsula to its westerly tip, the Sheep's Head. Between Kilcrohane and Gouladoo the road skirts the foot of Seefin (1116 ft), from which there are splendid views to the north over Bantry Bay and the hills of the Beara peninsula beyond.

Belfast · Béal Feirste   B 5/6

Northern Ireland
Province: Ulster
District: Belfast
Population: 300,000 (conurbation 550,000)

Belfast (Béal Feirste, sandy ford) is situated in the north-east corner of Ireland at the outflow of the River Lagan into Belfast Lough.

The 'capital' of Northern Ireland since 1920, home to almost a third of all the northern Irish, it is an important industrial city and port. On Queen's Island is the famous Harland and Wolff shipyard, established in 1859. One of the largest shipyards in the world, employing 10,000 men, it made its name at the beginning of the last century when it built mainly passenger ships, among them the *Titanic*, launched in 1912. Today oil tankers and freighters have replaced the liners.

◀ *View of Bantry Bay from Bantry House*

History

Belfast already possessed a fort in the early Middle Ages but this was destroyed in 1177. Subsequently a castle was built, control of which was often disputed between the native Irish and their English conquerors. In 1613 the town which had grown up around the castle was granted a charter by James I. The manufacture of linen had long been an important industry in Belfast, and it received a further boost in the latter part of the 17th c. when Huguenots fleeing from France introduced improved industrial methods. The newcomers also contributed to the development of the town's intellectual life and gave it a certain French flair. Following the union with Britain (1800), Belfast became the industrial capital of Ireland. Its splendid 19th c. buildings earned it the soubriquet 'Athens of the North'. In addition to linen manufacture, rope making, shipbuilding and tobacco all contributed to its economic success. The city, however, never really recovered from the period of depression between the two world wars, and unemployment remains extremely high (in some areas 50 per cent of the male working population are without jobs).

City centre

Belfast city centre lies on the west bank of the River Lagan, which is spanned by several bridges within the city boundary. Donegall Square and the adjoining streets, Royal Avenue in particular, constitute the main shopping area, with several large department stores. The university district, with its narrow, quiet, tree-lined streets of small shops, galleries and Victorian houses, is especially attractive.

Northern Ireland conflict

For many years now Belfast has suffered repeatedly from terrorist violence associated with the Northern Ireland conflict. The 'Troubles', as the bloody sectarian dispute over Ulster's continued union with Britain is euphemistically known, exercise a profound influence on the everyday life and economic fortunes of the city. The boundaries between Catholic and Protestant districts away from the city centre are not always as clearly defined as they are in mainly Catholic west Belfast, where barbed wire and walls separate the two communities. Segregation extends to schools, pubs and other areas of social life.

Following the IRA ceasefire on September 1st 1994, security in Belfast was gradually relaxed. Though armoured vehicles still patrol the streets, the police and military presence is considerably reduced. In September 1994 the European Union allocated a budget of 2.4 million ecus for projects intended to bring the Catholic and Protestant communities closer together.

Central Belfast

City Hall

Focal point of the city centre is City Hall (Donegall Square; ➤ picture, p. 100), a huge Renaissance-style palazzo (1898–1906) designed by Sir Brumwell Thomas, with four corner towers and a massive dome. The magnificent Banqueting Hall, 165 ft long, can be visited (guided tours Wed. 10.30am; other tours by arrangement, tel. (028) 90320202).

In front of the building are statues of Queen Victoria and prominent citizens of Belfast, and on the west side a war memorial in a Garden of Remembrance. There is also a sculptural group commemorating the loss in 1912 of the *Titanic*, the ill-fated liner built at Belfast's Harland and Wolff shipyard.

Linenhall Library

On the north side of Donegall Square stands the Linenhall Library (1788), with an exhibition on the history of linen manufacture.

Grand Opera House

Opened in 1895, the Grand Opera House, west of City Hall in Great Victoria Street, was altered and enlarged in 1980 and has about 1000 seats. Lacking a permanent company of its own, it stages touring company productions during the winter season (including opera,

The Grand Opera House

drama, musicals, and ballet). The Grand Opera House also hosts the annual Belfast Festival.

The Crown Liquor Saloon, now a National Trust building, has a quite unique atmosphere with gas lamps, a marble-topped bar and an abundance of mahogany.

Crown Liquor Saloon

On the northern edge of the city centre is St Anne's Cathedral, principal church of the Anglican Church of Ireland, begun in 1898 (the original architect was Sir Thomas Drew). On the west front of the neo-Romanesque basilica are three portals with fine sculptural decoration. The baptismal chapel boasts an unusual mosaic ceiling made of hundreds of thousands of tiny pieces of glass. In the same chapel is the tomb of Lord Carson (d 1935), leader of the Ulster Unionists

St Anne's Cathedral

South-east of the cathedral, close to the River Lagan, stands the Custom House (1854–7), its gable adorned with figures of Britannia, Neptune and Mercury.

Custom House

A short distance away, round the corner in the High Street, stands the Albert Memorial Clock Tower, popularly known as Belfast's Big Ben on account of its likeness to that other famous clock. Erected in 1869, it commemorates Prince Albert, Queen Victoria's consort.

Albert Memorial Clock Tower

South Belfast

Three-quarters of a mile south of Donegall Square, reached by way of Bedford Street, Dublin Road and University Road, are the Tudor-style build-

Queen's University

Belfast · Béal Feirste

Londonderry
Airport
Zoo, Belfast Castle
Ferry Terminal

Harbour Office

Belfast

250 m
750 ft

Bangor
Victoria Park
Parliament House

York St.
Donegall
Corporation St.
Art College

Central Library
St. Anne's Cathedral
Custom House

North St.
Royal Av.
North St.
St.
High
Victoria
St.

Albert Memorial

Queen Elizabeth II Bridge
Queen's Bridge

Technical College
Castle
Street
Ann St.
Ann St.

Old Museum
Technical College
College Square
Linenhall Library
Donegall Place
Donegall Sq.
Street
Chichester
Police

Bus Station
Royal Courts of Justice

Oxford St.
Victoria St.
Victoria St.

Bank
Road

End

Albert
Street
Brigde
Bangor

Church House
City Hall
May
Street
Cattle Market

Bridge
Street

Grosvenor Hall
Opera House
Howard
Street
Arts Council Gallery
Ulster Hall
Group Theatre
BBC

East
Central Station

Leisure Centre

Stewart St.

Bus Station/Airport Terminal

Great Victoria Street
Sandy Row
St. Malachy's
Cromac
St.
McAuley Street

Ormeau Avenue

Gas Works

Ballarat
Street

Embankment

L a g a n

Ravenhill Road

Donegall
Pass
Melville Road
Ulster TV

Ormeau
Road

Dublin, Armagh, Enniskillen
Dublin, Armagh, Enniskillen

Arts Theatre
Botanic Station
Vernon Street
McClure Street

Sports Club

Ormeau
Road

Hatfield St.

Ormeau
Embankment

O r m e a u
P a r k

Road
Ravenhill

Queen's Film Theatre
University Avenue
University
Street
Rugby
Ave.

University Road

Queen's University
Whitla Hall
Bregagh Rd.
Rugby Rd.

Ormeau Bridge
Stranmillis
Embankment

B o t a n i c
Ulster Museum
G a r d e n s

Giant's Ring
Newcastle

© Baedeker

St. Peter's

98

ings of Queen's University (1845–94), an independent institution since 1909. Inside one of the red-brick buildings there is the History Museum.

Immediately south of the university campus lie Belfast's attractively laid out Botanic Gardens. The elegant Palm House was erected in 1850 (gardens open all day; Palm House Mon.–Fri. 10am–5pm, Sat., Sun. 2–5pm).

Botanic Gardens

Also located in the Botanic Gardens is the Ulster Museum. It has a substantial number of exhibits from Celtic and Early Christian times (including swords, harps, and jewellery), as well as a collection of gold and silver items recovered in 1968 from the wreck of the *Girona*, a 16th c. Spanish galleon which foundered off the north Irish coast. The museum art gallery is particularly strong in 17th and 18th c. European painting and Irish art of various periods; it also has collections of Irish glass and silver. Evidence of the scale of Irish emigration over many years, especially to the United States, is provided by the portraits of prominent people of Northern Irish descent, including 10 American presidents. Open Mon.–Fri. 10am–5pm, Sat. 1–5pm, Sun. 2–5pm.

Ulster Museum

North Belfast

The Zoological Gardens are attractively laid out on Cave Hill. Open daily 10am–5pm, in winter until 4.30pm.

Zoological Gardens

Halfway up the hill stands Belfast Castle (1870), for a time the home of the earl of Shaftesbury.

Belfast Castle

From the castle it is a simple matter to reach the top of Cave Hill (1182 ft), volcanic in origin, with a profile said to resemble Napoléon's. In clear weather there are splendid views of the city, Lough Neagh to the west and the Irish Sea coast to the east, with the Isle of Man in the far distance.

Cave Hill

Stormont

6 miles east of the city, at Stormont, stands the imposing classical building erected in 1928–32 to house the Northern Ireland parliament. Occupied today by departments of the Northern Ireland Office, the building was badly damaged by fire in early 1995. The attractive grounds are open to the public though the buildings themselves are not. In front stands a monument to Lord Edward Carson.

Parliament building

Situated in delightful surroundings some 3 miles further north, at Cultra, is the Ulster Folk & Transport Museum. It takes the form of a traditional Irish village complete with village shop, trade premises, school and church, all removed from their original sites and re-erected stone by stone. Open Mon.–Sat. 9.30am–6pm, Sun. noon–6pm, winter to 4pm.

★Ulster Folk & Transport Museum

Surroundings

Along the northern and southern shores of Belfast Lough, the wide bay into which the River Lagan flows, are a series of popular seaside resorts. The coast immediately north of the lough is particularly beautiful.

Belfast Lough

Halfway along the north side of the lough, 7 miles from Belfast, is Carrickfergus which, before being displaced by Belfast, was a considerable port. It is noted for its splendidly preserved Norman castle, one of the finest in Ireland (➤ plan, p.101). Known in medieval times as

★Carrickfergus Castle

Belfast's City Hall

Kragfargys Castle, it stands on a spur of black basalt which was originally completely surrounded by water except on the north side. For some 750 years it was a place of great military importance, strategically sited to control the harbour and Belfast Lough.

Begun by the Norman John de Courcy between 1180 and 1204, the castle was taken by King John in 1210 after a year-long siege. In 1316 it fell to the Scots. In the 16th c. it was renovated and the fortifications strengthened but thereafter it was allowed to decay. In 1760 it was captured by the French – the last time it fell into enemy hands. In the 18th c. it was used as a prison. Later, after the defences were further strengthened, it became a military depot and arsenal, continuing to serve as such until 1928.

The most notable features are the massive keep (small military museum; magnificent Norman hall on the third floor; superb views from the top), the gatehouse with twin towers (in the east tower a chamber known as 'the Chapel' on account of its unusual window), and cannon dating from the 16th to the 19th c.

Open Mon.–Sat. 10am–6pm, Sun. 2–6pm.

Island Magee

From Carrickfergus a particularly lovely section of coast road runs by way of Whitehead, a popular seaside resort, to Island Magee, not in fact an island but a peninsula, 7 miles long and 2 miles wide. A striking feature on the peninsula's east side is a stretch of basalt cliffs, 253 ft high, known as the Gobbins and, containing several caves. There are numerous legends associated with the cliffs and the caves. At the end of the peninsula there is a dolmen.

Larne

Quarries and cement works disfigure the coast road from Whitehead to Larne, a busy industrial town and seaside resort on Larne Lough. Of interest here are the remains of Olderfleet Castle (three-storey keep).

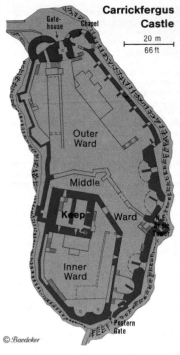

Carrickfergus Castle

20 m
66 ft

Gate-house Chapel

Outer Ward

Middle Ward

Keep Ward N.E. Angle Tower

Inner Ward

Postern Gate

© Baedeker

There are ferry services from Larne to the Scottish mainland (Stranraer and Cairnryan) and across the lough to Island Magee (see above).

From Larne a romantically beautiful stretch of road follows the coast to Cushendun. After passing through the Black Cave Tunnel the road rounds Ballygalley Head with its great basalt crags. Ballygalley is a popular seaside resort with an old castle, now a hotel. From here to Glenarm, a little harbour at the mouth of the River Glenarm, the road is flanked by white limestone cliffs. The next seaside resort is Carnlough, with a small harbour and good sandy beach.

Waterfoot is delightfully situated in a magical spot at the near end of Red Bay on the Antrim coast, lying encircled amphitheatre-like by sandstone cliffs at the mouth of Glenariff, one of the loveliest of the Glens of Antrim extending away to the south-west. A few miles beyond Waterfoot are the little resort of Cushendall and its better - known neighbour Cushendun.

Waterfoot

The road along the south side of Belfast Lough and down the coast also has beautiful scenery and no shortage of attractive little places. Holywood, a suburb of Belfast, has remains of the 12th c. Franciscan friary of Sanctus Boscus (holy wood, hence the name).

Holywood

From here the road continues via Crawfordsburn to Bangor, the most popular of Northern Ireland's seaside resorts, with wide sandy beaches, lovely promenades and plenty of entertainment and sports facilities (and on the debit side an increasing number of unattractive tower blocks). Features of interest include the Castle and Castle Park, and the Abbey Church, on the site of a monastery founded in 555.

Round the coast from Bangor, Copeland Island (bird sanctuary) can be seen out to sea.

Bangor

Further south, at Donaghadee and its colourful port, is the start of the 20-mile-long Ards Peninsula. From Donaghadee a road runs along the Irish Sea coast to Ballywalter (lovely beach), Ballyhalbert and Cloghy, where it turns inland to Portaferry on the peninsula's southern tip.

There is a ferry service between Portaferry and Strangford (see below) on the mainland to the south. There is also a road round to Strangford, the first section of which, on the A20, skirts the west side of the peninsula along the shores of Strangford Lough. After passing through Ardkeen (ruined castle) and Kircubbin, the road comes to Greyabbey, with remains of a Cistercian abbey founded in 1193, one of the best preserved in Ireland. Notable features include the fine Gothic windows and magnificent west doorway.

Ards Peninsula

Newtownards

The road continues, passing Mount Stewart House and Gardens (beautiful park with many dwarf trees), to Newtownards, famous for its linen and a good base from which to explore the coastal scenery and the Mourne Mountains to the south. It has a town hall of 1770 and a ruined Dominican church (1244). The Old Cross in the High Street has been restored several times.

From here there is a fast route back to Belfast (6 miles); alternatively, turn south, heading first for the whiskey-distilling town of Comber, and then on down the west side of Strangford Lough to Downpatrick (21 miles).

★Gardens of Rowallane

Gardening enthusiasts may prefer instead to detour inland to the little town of Saintfield and visit the lovely Rowallane Gardens with their many rare flowers and plants.

Killyleagh

Killyleagh, on the west side of Strangford Lough, was the birthplace of Sir Hans Sloane, founder of the British Museum. Hilltop Castle overlooks the little lakeside resort. The scenery here is particularly beautiful, with the Mourne Mountains shimmering blue in the south-west.

Downpatrick

Downpatrick is the county town of Co. Down. Here in 432 St Patrick (➤ Famous People) began the conversion of Ireland. 2 miles further north is Saul, where he landed, built his first church and is said to have died. Downpatrick Cathedral, the seat of a bishop, was built in 1790 on the remains of an earlier church from which a 17th c. font and a few architectural fragments survive. A granite stone in the churchyard, said to mark St Patrick's grave, dates from only 1900.

Strangford

From Saul a road follows the shore eastwards to Strangford, a Viking settlement beautifully situated at the southern end of Strangford Lough (see above). The strategic importance of this particular area is shown by the fact that there are four 16th c. tower houses in the immediate vicinity; Audley Castle is open to the public.

Ardglass

No fewer than seven castles protected Ardglass, south of Strangford, once an important harbour but now just a fishing village. One of them, Jordan's Castle, has considerable remains, including a square keep. West of the village of Killough on the other side of the bay there is a very fine beach.

St John's Point

At St John's Point begins a magnificent scenic road along probably the most beautiful stretch of coast in Northern Ireland, to Newry (39 miles). It skirts the wide Dundrum Bay, large areas of which are exposed at low tide, until the bay ends at Newcastle.

Dundrum

Dundrum is a picturesque fishing village with good sandy bathing beaches and a tower surrounded by a moat – all that remains of an Anglo-Norman castle.

Newcastle

Newcastle offers all the amenities of a seaside resort, including a golf course. It lies at the western end of Dundrum Bay at the foot of Slieve Donard (2796 ft), the highest of the Mourne Mountains. The climb to the summit takes about 2 hours and is rewarded with magnificent views extending as far as the Scottish coast.

Beyond Newcastle the road begins to ascend, with the sea on the left and the everchanging backdrop of the Mourne Mountains (the home of many rare plants) on the right. It passes through some quiet little fishing and farming villages, including Glas Drummond and Annalong from which a number of summits between 1700 and 2450 ft – including Rocky Mountain and, Slieve Bignian – can be climbed.

Kilkeel

Kilkeel is a favourite resort with fishermen, since there are good catches to be had both from the sea and from the River Kilkeel and nearby Carlingford Lough. Around Kilkeel are a number of prehistoric sites and dolmens.

Beyond Kilkeel, between Greencastle (north) and Greenor (south), Carlingford Lough cuts deep inland, with a road along either shore.
    From Kilkeel another road winds through the Mourne Mountains (steep gradients) to Hilltown.

Carlingford Lough

Hilltown, at the foot of the Mourne Mountains on their north-west side, is a good base from which to climb and walk in the hills, coloured by the hues of their granites and schists.

Hilltown

On the north side of Carlingford Lough, surrounded by woodland (mainly oaks), is Rostrevor, a charming and peaceful little holiday resort ideal for boating, pony-trekking, fishing or walking.

Rostrevor

The port and industrial town of Newry lies on the River Newry and a canal, with the Mourne Mountains to the south-east and the Camlough Mountains to the west. The tower of St Patrick's Church, the first Protestant church in Ireland, dates from 1578. Nearby stands the neo-Gothic Roman Catholic cathedral. Worth visiting in the surroundings are the pretty village of Bessbrook (north-west) and Derrymore House, a thatched 18th c. Georgian manor house.

Newry

The E01 leads north-east from Newry back to Belfast. 9 miles short of the capital the road passes by the trim little town of Hillsborough. Here, in 1650, Colonel Arthur Hill built a fort to secure the road between Dublin and Carrickfergus. It was converted to a splendid mansion in the 18th c. Open Tue.–Sat. 10am–7pm, Sun. 2–7pm, winter to 4pm.

Hillsborough

Belmullet · Béal an Mhuirthead   B 2

Republic of Ireland
Province: Connacht
County: Mayo.
Population: 1000

Belmullet (Béal an Mhuirthead, ford on the sea) is situated in the north-west of Ireland on the narrow isthmus linking the Mullet Peninsula to the mainland. This isolated spot is a good base from which to explore the 15-mile-long peninsula and the country to the north.

Surroundings

The west coast of the Mullet Peninsula, exposed to Atlantic storms, is largely devoid of vegetation; the east side, with numerous little coves, almost completely encloses Blacksod Bay. There are lovely beaches on both sides of the peninsula, particularly at the narrowest point around Elly Bay (east side).

Mullet Peninsula

The peninsula boasts many ancient remains. On Doonamo Point, 5 miles north-west of Belmullet (no signpost), are the remnants of a clifftop fortress with a great rampart 200 ft long and still 18 ft high in places, stretching across the neck of the headland and enclosing three beehive-shape huts and the ruins of a ring-fort.

Doonamo Point

At Fallmore, near the south end of the peninsula, are the ruins of St Dairbhile's Church (National Monument).

Fallmore

Blacksod Point

From Blacksod Point, at the southern tip of the peninsula, there is a fine view across to Achill Island and the tall peak of Slievemore. From the west side, where there used to be a signal station, there are views of the small islands offshore which were inhabited in ancient times and retain various Early Christian remains.

Benwee Head

3 miles south-east of Belmullet the R314 branches off the R313 in a north-easterly direction to Glenamoy from where a delightful detour can be made to Benwee Head (10 miles; road ends at Portacloy, final ¾ mile on foot), rising in sheer and rugged cliffs 843 ft above the sea (magnificent views).

Stags of Broadhaven

North of Portacloy, a group of seven precipitous rock stacks known as the Stags of Broadhaven rise 328 ft from the sea.

Belderg

From Glenamoy the R314 crosses the moors to Belderg, no more than 1¼ miles from the coast with its rugged cliff scenery. Also nearby is the Céide Fields prehistoric site (► Ballina) where extensive remains of an early (1500 BC) settlement and cultivation have been uncovered.

Glinsk

Splendid panoramic views of the entire area can be enjoyed from the Hill of Glinsk (1017 ft), 4 miles to the west. 1¼ miles further north-west is Moista Sound, an inlet enclosed on all sides by cliffs.

Birr · Biorra   C 4

Republic of Ireland
Province: Leinster
County: Offaly
Population: 3700

Birr (Biorra, well springs), a thriving little market town, is situated in the heart of Ireland at the intersection of two main roads (N52, N62) on the western edge of Co. Offaly. Immediately west of the town is the confluence of two good fishing rivers, the Little Brosna and the Camcor.

Town

The town is laid out on a regular plan, with four principal streets meeting in Emmet Square. There are many handsome 17th and 18th c. houses, especially in Oxmanlown Mall and St John's Mall. In St John's Mall there is a monument to the 3rd Earl of Rosse, a famous astronomer.

★Birr Castle Demesne

Park open
daily 9am–6pm

Built in the early 17th c. by Sir Laurence Parsons, Birr Castle was besieged on a number of occasions. In the 18th and 19th c. it was several times altered and enlarged. The magnificent park, laid out along the River Camcor in the mid-18th c., is open to visitors, though the castle itself is not. More than 1000 tree and plant species thrive here, a particular source of pride being the box hedges, over 200 years old and standing 30 ft high. Though well worth a visit whatever the time of year, the park is at its loveliest in spring when the magnolias are in bloom, and again in the autumn when the trees take on autumn hues.

In about 1840 the third earl of Rosse, to whose descendants the castle still belongs, designed and built a giant telescope – for some 80 years the largest in the world – which he set up in the castle grounds. With this telescope he made the first discovery of a spiral galaxy. The objective lens from the telescope is now in the Science Museum in London, but the tube and walls on which the telescope was mounted can be seen in the park. There is a model of the telescope and a small display of optical apparatus and drawings. Temporary exhibitions are mounted in the Exhibition Gallery.

Surroundings

Banagher lies on high ground on the east bank of the Shannon 8 miles north-west of Birr. The gun emplacements constructed by English forces in the 17th c. can still be seen.

Banagher

5 miles east of Banagher stand the imposing ruins of Clonony Castle (16th c.). En route to the castle the road passes Shannon Harbour, at the junction of the Shannon with the Grand Canal (see entries). Old warehouses and a long-established hotel (1806) testify to the former importance of this little haven.

Clonony Castle

Kinnitty is a pretty village at the foot of the Slieve Bloom Mountains east of Birr. From the village an excursion can be made into the delightful little Forelacka Glen.

Kinnitty

Beyond the Clareen crossroads on the road running south-west from Kinnitty, a hawthorn known as St Ciaran's Bush grows in the middle of the roadway. Ciaran, a 5th c. saint, founded a monastery here.

St Ciaran's Bush

A mile or two south stands Leap Castle, a stronghold of the O'Carrolls burned down in 1923 but still impressive as a ruin.

Leap Castle

Blarney · An Bhlarna   E 3

Republic of Ireland
Province: Munster
County: Cork
Population: 2000

Blarney (An Bhlarna, the plain) lies near the south coast of Ireland, 5 miles north-west of the county town, Cork. Numerous souvenir shops and an endless stream of coaches reveal the well-kept village to be an obligatory stop on the itinerary of every round-Ireland tour operator.

Blarney has a long tradition of woollen manufacture which has recently been revived. An old mill complex has been restored and converted into a craft centre (Blarney Woollen Mills).

★Blarney Castle

With walls 18 ft thick and an 82-ft-high tower, the 15th c. castle was once the most impregnable in Munster. Now a picturesque ruin set in a large park, the chief attraction for tourists is the famous Blarney Stone, believed to bestow the gift of eloquence on anyone who kisses it. The origin of this tradition is unknown.

Open Mon.–Sat. 9am–7pm, Sun. 9.30am– 7pm, winter to dusk

How the castle came to enrich the English language with a new word is, on the other hand, well documented. Queen Elizabeth I had instructed her lord deputy in Ireland to bid Cormac MacCarthy of Blarney abandon the traditional system under which the clans elected their own chieftains and accept instead the grant of his lands from the Crown. MacCarthy, while seeming to agree to the proposal, repeatedly put forward plausible excuses for failing to carry it out, causing the Queen to declare in exasperation: 'This is all Blarney; what he says he never means.' Hence the use of 'blarney' to mean fair words intended to deceive without giving offence.

Blarney Castle

Blarney House

Anyone who wants to kiss the Blarney Stone – or observe the contortions of those who try – must first climb up to the battlemented parapet around the top of the tower. There, to succeed in the quest, it is necessary to lean backwards head first over a vent (holding onto a steel frame and gripped firmly by an attendant) in an attempt to kiss the underside of the stone. Many people will find far more to interest them in the magnificent views from the battlements.

Blarney House   Blarney House (completed 1874), in the castle grounds, overlooking the lake, has been carefully restored and has a fine interior. Open Jun. to mid-Sep. Mon.–Sat. noon–6pm.

Rock Close   In the park is a pretty dell known as Rock Close with an assortment of boulders and pieces of rock of interesting shape, as well as a stone circle – not a prehistoric monument but another example of 18th c. landscaping.

Bloody Foreland · Cnoc Fola   A 3

Republic of Ireland
Province: Ulster
County: Donegal

Bloody Foreland (Cnoc Fola) is a broad headland in the far north of Ireland, between Ballyness Bay to the north and Gweedore to the south. It gets its name from the reddish tinge which the rocky coast takes on at sunset. The sea is then bathed in the same reddish hue, and Tory Island, a few miles offshore, assumes a mythical quality, glowing softly in the dusk.

There is a good road encircling the area. This being a part of Ireland where Irish is still commonly spoken, two well-attended summer schools in the language are put on here, at Bunbeg and Gloghanheely.

Sights

To the south-east lies the long, narrow Lough Dunlewy, with good salmon and trout fishing. At the Lakeside Centre (Dunlewy village) the process of woollen manufacture is illustrated and explained – this sheep-rearing area is famous for its tweeds and other woollen goods. Open May–Sep. Mon.–Sat. 11.30am–6.30pm, Sun. noon–7pm.

Dunlewy

North of the lough rises Mount Errigal (2429 ft), the highest in the region, a gleaming white quartzite cone, visible from afar. It has a double summit, with two high points only 30 ft apart linked by a ridge known as One Man Path. The best route up (no mountaineering experience necessary) is from the east via a marked path starting out from the parking place on the R251; allow 1½ to 2 hours. From the top there are magnificent views – northwards towards the wild and lonely Lough Altan with Aglamore (1313 ft) rising sheer from its waters; eastwards towards the glaciated Derryveagh Mountains; southwards towards the rocky Poisoned Glen, so called on account of the spurge which grows there; and westwards over the great expanse of Gweedore and the Atlantic coast beyond.

Mount Errigal

From Bunbeg a boat can be taken to the islands in Gweedore Bay (Innishinny, Gola and others), all with superb rock and cliff scenery. There are beautiful beaches on the mainland coast, including the large Magheraclogher Strand.

Gweedore Bay

Mount Errigal on Bloody Foreland

Muckish Mountain

To the north, in Ballyness Bay, are Gortahork and Falcarragh, from which Muckish Mountain (2166 ft) can be climbed. The ascent is steep but the views from the top are stupendous.

Myrath

Near Falcarragh, in Myrath churchyard, is a large ancient cross hewn from a single block of stone.

Tory Island

Tory Island, lying some distance off the north side of Bloody Foreland, is the largest of the islands in this area. Although inhospitable, it has been inhabited for over 4000 years. Having begun to decline in Elizabethan times, the population today fluctuates around the 200 mark, higher in summer, lower in winter. Highpoint of the islanders' week is the Saturday night *ceili*, a get-together with music and dancing in the island's two villages.

Tory Island's only 'sights' are scant remains of a few buildings, the most interesting being an unusual 55-ft-high round tower of undressed stone (National Monument).

There is no scheduled ferry service to the island (enquire in Bunbeg or Maheraroarty about any sailings). Access depends very much on the weather and rough seas can and often do make crossings to this far-flung outpost of Europe impossible for days on end.

Boyle · Mainistir na Buille   C 3

Republic of Ireland
Province: Connacht
County: Roscommon
Population: 1750

Boyle (Mainistir na Buille, monastery of the pasture river) is situated on the north bank of the River Boyle in the north-west of Ireland, at the foot of the Curlew Hills. The river, which links Lough Gara and Lough Key, is spanned by an old bridge. A market centre, Boyle is one of the principal towns of Co. Roscommon.

★Boyle Abbey

On the north side of the town stand the ruins of Boyle Abbey (National Monument), a Cistercian monastry founded from Mellifont in 1161. Of the cruciform church, now roofless, there survive in a good state of preservation the nave, choir and transepts (fine capitals carved with human figures, animals and foliage); of the conventual buildings only the guest house and kitchen remain. Open mid-Jun. to mid-Sep. daily 9.30am– 6.30pm.

Surroundings

★Lough Key Forest Park

North-east of the town lies forest-fringed Lough Key, with its many bays, promontories and islets and, extending along the southern shore, the Lough Key Forest Park with a very well-equipped campsite, a restaurant, a children's paddling pool, picnic sites, and so on, as well as facilities for rowing, motor-boat hire, fishing and walking. There is also an interesting bog garden. On an island in the lough are the picturesque ruins of an old abbey. An observation tower provides good views over the park. Open daily 10am–7pm.

Strokestown

Strokestown, about 17 miles south-east of Boyle, is a charming little town laid out in 1800 on an axial plan. One of its attractions is a craft centre where traditional Irish crafts continue to be practised (displays and craft shop). Another is the handsome country house belonging to Lord Hartland, situated in a spacious park on the outskirts of the town. The house, which took on its present appearance around 1730, has recently been restored. In 1994 the Famine Museum opened in the old stables; documents, photographs and other exhibits help recount the story of the Great Famine of 1845–9. Strokestown Park House open Jun.–Aug. Tue.–Sun. 10am–5pm.

Just off the R294 at Drumanone (not far from Boyle) is a large chamber tomb, or dolmen, with a massive capstone measuring 15 by 11ft.

Drumanone

West of Lough Gara, at Monasteraden in Co. Sligo, is one of the most celebrated of the many holy wells found in this area, dedicated to St Attracta. It has walls on three sides, on one of which is a relief of the Crucifixion.

Monasteraden

Boyne Valley   C 5

Republic of Ireland
Province: Leinster
County: Meath

At Slane, near the town of Drogheda on the east coast of Ireland, between Dublin and Belfast, the River Boyne begins a broad sweep southwards and then north again. Here in the Boyne Valley there is a large prehistoric burial ground with three great tumuli (south-east of

Entrance to the Newgrange tomb

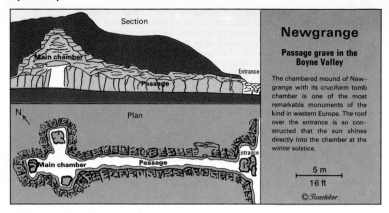

Section

Newgrange

Passage grave in the Boyne Valley

The chambered mound of Newgrange with its cruciform tomb chamber is one of the most remarkable monuments of the kind in western Europe. The roof over the entrance is so constructed that the sun shines directly into the chamber at the winter solstice.

Main chamber

Entrance

Passage

N

Plan

Main chamber   Passage   Entrance

5 m
16 ft

© Baedeker

Slane at Knowth, Newgrange and Dowth, in that order; all National Monuments) dating from around 3000 BC.

★★Newgrange

Open summer daily 10am–6 or 7pm; winter daily 10am–4.30pm

Until 1962 the tumulus at Newgrange lay beneath an earth mound, barely distinguishable from its surroundings; excavation was only completed in the late 1970s. Largest of the three great tumuli, and only to be viewed accompanied by a custodian, it comprises a heart-shape mound of turf and stones some 295 ft in diameter and 36 ft high, surrounded by a kerb of horizontal slabs stabilising the whole. The vertical drystone retaining wall is a reconstruction of the original, based on the results of archaeological research. Around the kerb there was originally a ring of 38 pillar stones, of which twelve survive.

The entrance to the tumulus, on the south-east side, is marked by a threshold stone carved with spiral decoration. It leads into a narrow passageway, 66 ft long, formed from 43 uprights between 5 and 8 ft high and roofed over with massive lintels. At the end of the passage is the main burial chamber with a 20-ft-high vault. Built about 3200 BC, this corbelled dome is so perfect in its construction that it has not only survived for over 5000 years but remains completely watertight even after long spells of wet weather. The structure is so designed that, for a period of about 15 minutes at the winter solstice, the rays of the sun shine directly into the otherwise completely dark chamber through an opening above the entrance. During the tour of the site this effect is reproduced using a source of artificial light. Three side chambers, each containing a shallow basin hollowed out of a stone, open off the main one, making the structure as a whole cruciform in plan. When excavated the stone basins were found to contain remnants of ash and bones. Many of the stones are carved with spirals, lozenges, wave patterns, serpentine designs or zigzags. This decoration from distant prehistory powerfully enhances the effect inside the tomb.

Other sights

Knowth

The tumulus at Knowth is still in the process of excavation. Visitors are admitted to the site but not to the tumulus itself. The mound, 33 ft high and roughly 280 ft across, conceals two passage graves. As at Newgrange, this main mound would have been the burial place of a chieftain and his kin, lesser persons being buried in the 18 smaller tumuli grouped around it. Knowth appears to have been in use as a burial and cult site at various times in prehistory. Open May to mid-Jun., mid-Sep. to Oct. daily 10am–5pm; mid-Jun. to mid-Sep. daily 9.30am–6.30pm.

In the burial mound at Dowth (not open to the public), a 27-ft-long passage leads into one of two principal chambers. Branching off this circular chamber are several side chambers.

Dowth

To the north of Slane rises Slane Hill (492 ft), where in 433 St Patrick is said to have signalled the triumph of Christianity in Ireland by lighting the Paschal fire in defiance of a kingly ban.
  On the hill are the ruins of a Franciscan friary (National Monument) with a 16th c. church and conventual buildings around a cloister (individual rooms with fireplaces, alcoves and aumbries).

Slane Hill

In the grounds of Slane Castle (1¼ miles west of Slane) are the ruins of a Gothic church. The castle itself was extensively damaged in a fire.

Slane Castle

Further up the valley stands Beauparc House (1750) and, lying opposite, the picturesque ruins of Castle Dexter.

Beauparc House

Bray · Bri Cualann   C 5

Republic of Ireland
Province: Leinster
County: Wicklow
Population: 23,000

Bray (Bri Cualann, hill of Cuala) lies a little way south of Dublin in a beautiful, sheltered bay on the Irish Sea, between the Dalkey promontory to the north and Bray Head to the south. It is one of Ireland's largest and oldest seaside resorts, favoured mainly by Dubliners. Bray has excellent sports facilities – tennis, golf courses (9 and 18 holes), swimming, sailing and motor boating.

Bray's centrepiece is the Esplanade, a spacious promenade extending for almost 1¼ miles along the bay (shingle beach), with a bandstand, putting green and other amusements. At the north end is a yacht harbour, to the south Bray Head, rising steeply from the sea to a height of 800 ft. A footpath known as the Great White Way runs from the south end of the Esplanade, past a small ruined 13th c. church, to the summit of the headland (1½ hours there and back). Halfway up, at Eagle's Nest, there is a café. From the top there are fine views over the sea and inland.

Town

Surroundings

2½ miles north-west of Bray stand the ruined 16th c. Rathmichael Church and the stump of a round tower (National Monument). On the south wall of the church are a number of unusual early gravestones and a cross.

Rathmichael

2½ miles west of Bray the River Dargle, which flows through the town to the sea, enters the romantic Glen of the Dargle, a thickly wooded, rocky gorge with a massive, projecting crag known as Lovers' Leap. A narrow path runs alongside the river, and a winding road leads into the upper part of the glen.

River Dargle

To the right of the R761 as it heads south from Bray lies Kilruddery, a fine country mansion (1820) with lovely gardens (open May, Jun., Sep. daily

Kilruddery

1–5pm). The park, with its small twisting canals, laid out in the late 17th c., still retains much of its original character. In the 19th c. a winter garden was added.

Sugar Loaf Mountains

Also to be seen south of Bray are the distinctive outlines of the Sugar Loaf Mountains – Little Sugar Loaf (1106 ft) and Great Sugar Loaf (1628 ft) both afford extensive views.

Greystones

Greystones, 5 miles south of Bray on the R761, is a pleasant resort in wooded countryside, with tennis courts, a golf course (18 holes) and good bathing in the bay; sailing and motor boats can be hired. The Bray Harriers hunt over the surrounding district.

Delgany

1½ miles south-west of Greystones, a little way in from the coast, lies Dalgany, a delightful small village in a wooded setting with an 18-hole golf course. From here an excursion can be made to the Glen of the Downs, a national forest with a nature trail.

Bundoran · Bun Dobhrain   B 3

Republic of Ireland
Province: Ulster
County: Donegal
Population: 1600

Bundoran (Bun Dobhrain, mouth of the Dobhran) is situated high on the Atlantic coast of Ireland, on the N15 from Donegal to Sligo. This popular seaside resort, with excellent facilities for sport and recreation, lies on the south side of Donegal Bay, with Benbulben to the south of the town.

Town

Bundoran's main thoroughfare is lined with hotels and restaurants. The town's principal attraction is its beach of fine sand, with cliffs at either end worn into fantastic shapes by the sea. From here there are any number of delightful walks, one of them north to the cliffs and caves on Aughrus Head, with the Puffing Hole, a funnel-like cavity through which water is ejected with considerable force. Beyond this is Tullan Strand with a cairn, a dolmen and a stone circle.

Surroundings

Ballyshannon

North-east of Bundoran, on the River Erne, which flows out of Lough Erne, is the busy little town of Ballyshannon. On the north-west side of the town is the restored Abbey Mill and close by the ruins of a Cistercian abbey, Assaroe. Also worth visiting is the Donegal Parian China Pottery (on the Bundoran Road). The pottery's wares can be observed in the making as well as purchased. Open Mon.–Fri. 9am–6pm, Sat.–Sun. 10am–8pm.

Kilbarron Castle

3 miles north-west, on the coast, are the ruins of Kilbarron Castle, seat of Michael O'Clery, foremost of the Four Masters (➤ Donegal) who jointly compiled the famous 'Annals' recording the history of Ireland and its leading families from the earliest origins in legend up to their own time in the 17th c.

Lough Melvin

South of Bundoran lies Lough Melvin (coarse fishing) with a very pleasant drive along its south side from the pretty village of Kinlough.

★Burren · Boirinn   C/D 2/3

Republic of Ireland
Province: Munster
County: Clare

The Burren (Boirinn, stony place), or Burren Country, halfway up the
west of Ireland on the south side of Galway Bay, is an extraordinary tract
of karst country – a flat plateau formed from unfolded carboniferous
limestone strata rising in terrace-like steps from the coast.

   When Cromwell's soldiers arrived here, they are said to have com-
plained of 'too few trees to hang anyone, too little water to drown
anyone and too little earth to bury anyone'.

The Burren is a unique place well worth taking the time to explore. It   Topography
offers a landscape of rounded hills of porous grey rock and barren limestone pavements, little streams which seep away into the scarred surface of the land, underground rivers, caves and blowholes, loughs which
are full one day and dry the next, and an exotic mixture of arctic, alpine
and Mediterranean flora vying for a foothold in any crack or cranny
capable of holding the slightest bit of soil.

A waymarked 14-mile footpath known as the Burren Way runs from   Burren Way
Ballyvaughan to Ballynalacken, 2 miles north of Doolin, taking in many
of the more important sights in the Burren.

Through the Burren

For those with cars there is a choice of three routes through the Burren –

Landscape of the Burren

the N67 direct from Ballyvaughan in the north-east to Lisdoonvarna in the south-west; the R480/R476 running more or less eastwards through the interior of the area; and the R477, mostly following the coast and offering an alternative route back to Ballyvaughan from Lisdoonvarna.

Ballyvaughan

Ballyvaughan, a small fishing village, makes an excellent base from which to explore the area.

★Corcomroe Abbey

6½ miles north-east, in a fertile valley signposted just off the N67, are the ruins of Corcomroe Abbey (National Monument), a Cistercian monastery founded in 1180. The church is well preserved (choir, nave, transepts with chapels); the choir has figure carving, fine vaulting and simple but pleasing tombs. Very little remains of the rest of the abbey, dissolved in 1564.

Newton Castle

A few miles south of Ballyvaughan, on the right of the N67, stands the unusually shaped keep of Newtown Castle (circular on a pyramidal base).

After a steep climb the N67, known locally as the 'Corkscrew Road', reaches its highest point (720 ft).

Slieve Elva

To the west rises Slieve Elva (1109 ft), in the vicinity of which are several streams which disappear beneath the ground. Here also is Pollnagollum Cave, the most extensive in Ireland, of which some 7½ miles of passages have so far been explored.

Cahermacnaghten

A few miles before Lisdoonvarna, on the left of the road, stands Cahermacnaghten (National Monument), a stone fort with a wall 100 ft in diameter and the remains of a castle where the O'Davoren family kept alive the study of traditional Irish law until late in the 17th c.

★Ailwee Cave

1¼ miles south of Ballyvaughan the R480 branches off southwards from the Corkscrew Road. A short distance along lies the Ailwee Cave, with many miles of underground passages of which a small, well-laid-out and lit section is open to the public. At the entrance is a Visitor Centre, restaurant and shop, in buildings of local stone successfully blending in with the landscape. Highlights of the guided tour of the cave include impressive stalactitic and stalagmitic formations, an underground river which becomes a raging torrent during periods of heavy rain, and traces left by bears on the cave floor prior to the last ice age (the temperature inside the cave, a steady 10°C, would have made it an ideal place for them to spend the winter). Open mid-Mar. to Nov. daily 10am–5.30pm, Jul.– Aug. to 6.30pm.

★Poulnabrone Dolmen

The R480 continues south through a remote area dotted with ancient remains. On the left of the road (signposted but in any case impossible to miss) stands the Poulnabrone Dolmen, a huge megalithic tomb dating from about 3000 BC.

Caherconnell

A little way off to the right of the R480, at Caherconnell, there is a fine ring-fort.

Carran

The area around Carran, 3 miles east, is particularly rich in remains. A signpost in the village points the way to Temple Cronan (National Monument; 1¼ miles north-east), a small Early Christian church with Romanesque grotesque heads on the exterior.

Cahercommaun

Above a steep-sided valley beyond Carran, in the direction of Killinaboy, stands Cahercommaun (unsignposted; access through private property), a particularly impressive ring-fort with three circuits of stone ramparts.

Leamaneh Castle

At the junction of the R480 with the R476 are the imposing ruins of

Poulnabrone Dolmen

Leamaneh Castle (National Monument), a tower house of 1480 enlarged in 1640 by the addition of a residential wing.

2½ miles east, in Killinaboy, are the ruins of an interesting church (?16th c.) with a well-preserved *sheila-na-gig* over the south doorway, and the stump of a round tower.

Killinaboy

The R476 continues south-east through wooded hills, past the lovely Lough Inchiquin and the ruins of Inchiquin Castle (1459), to Corofin, itself beautifully situated and with excellent trout and coarse fishing in the River Fergus and the local loughs.

Corofin

In the other direction, the R476 leads west from Leamaneh Castle to Kilfenora, which until the 18th c. was the see of a bishop. The west end of the modest 'cathedral' (12th c.; National Monument) is roofed and still used for worship; the roofless choir contains fine 13th and 14th c. gravestones. There are a number of high crosses including, in a field 110 yd to the west, one carved with a Crucifixion and other ornamentation. Finest of all is the Doorty Cross by the west wall of the cathedral, on the east side of which are carved the figures of three bishops and a double-headed bird.

Kilfenora

Situated in Kilfenora is the Burren Display Centre. An audio-visual presentation and small exhibition provide an insight into the geography, flora and fauna of the Burren. Adjoining are a tea-room, shop and information centre. Open mid-Mar. to Oct. daily 10am–5pm, summer to 6 or 7pm.

Burren Display Centre

2 miles north-east of Kilfenora at Ballykinvarga is another ring-fort with remains of huts within a double wall.

Ballykinvarga

115

Kilfenora – cathedral . . .   *. . . with beautiful stonework*

Lisdoonvarna

Lisdoonvarna, 4½ miles north-west of Kilfenora, is Ireland's leading spa, a resort very popular with Irish holidaymakers (tennis, putting course, amusement park). The radioactive springs contain sulphur, magnesium, iron and iodine. The town's Spa Wells Health Centre is open from June to October.

Doolin

About 5 miles west of Lisdoonvarna lies the fishing village of Doolin, with good bathing and fishing. In settled weather several boats a day cross from Doolin Pier to the Aran Islands (➤ entry).

What principally brings tourists flocking to Doolin from far and wide, however, are its pubs where Irish folk music can be heard every evening throughout the summer months.

Starting from Lisdoonvarna there is a delightful coastal drive along the western edge of the Burren. At first the R477 winds its way north-westwards past Ballynalackan Castle (Ballynalackan is one end of the Burren Way; ➤ p. 113) before dropping down to the coast and turning northwards. To seaward lie the Aran Islands and on the landward side the sloping flanks of Slieve Elva with the occasional ruined church or prehistoric fort.

Black Head

From the bare and wind-swept Black Head, at the most northerly point on the coast road, there are extensive views over Galway Bay. Here the road swings south-east along the shores of Ballyvaughan Bay. To the left is Gleninagh Castle (16th c.; National Monument), a four-storey tower house with circular corner turrets. Shortly afterwards the road enters Ballyvaughan.

Cahir · Cathair Dhuin Iascaigh   D 4

Republic of Ireland
Province: Munster
County: Tipperary
Population: 2100

Cahir (Cathair Dhuin Iascaigh, stone fort of the river abounding in fish)
lies on the River Suir in southern Ireland, at the junction of the N8 and
N24. To the west of the town the Galtee Mountains rise to a height of
2954 ft.

There is evidence that the small rocky islet in the Suir was occupied
by a fort as early as the 3rd c. AD.

Sights

Cahir Castle (National Monument), one of the largest in Ireland and frequently used as a setting for films, was constructed in the middle of
the 12th c., though the building seen today dates mainly from the 15th
and 16th c. After an eventful history of destruction and rebuilding, in
recent decades the castle has been extensively restored. It consists of
a massive three-storey keep and great hall and a further hall, with two
spacious wards or courts, all enclosed within strong high outer walls
reinforced by round and rectangular towers. In the living quarters the
furnishings of 500 years ago have been re-created. Open mid-Jun. to
mid-Sep. daily 9am–7.30pm; mid-Sep. to mid-Oct., Apr. to mid-Jun.
daily 10am–6:30pm; mid-Oct to Mar. daily 10am–1pm to 2–4.30pm.

★Cahir Castle

Cahir Castle

Swiss Cottage	In Cahir Park, which runs down to the water's edge, stands the Swiss Cottage, so called because of its resemblance to a Swiss chalet. This little country house was designed in 1810 by the British architect John Nash. The interior was recently restored and the building can be visited. Open May–Sep. daily 10am–6pm; mid-Mar. to Apr., Oct.–Nov. Tue.–Sun. 10am–1pm, 2–4.30pm.
St Paul's Church	Nash also built the Protestant St Paul's Church (1817–20), an early example of the neo-Gothic style.

Surroundings

Motte of Knockgraffon	4 miles north of Cahir is an interesting group of medieval sites (National Monuments): the Motte of Knockgraffon, a 12th c. Anglo-Norman stronghold built to protect a ford over the Suir; the ruins of a 13th c. church and tower; and remains of a 16th c. castle. Nearby is a churchyard with another ruined church.
Ardfinnan	5 miles south of Cahir lies the picturesquely situated village of Ardfinnan, with a 15-arched bridge across the Suir. On the banks of the river are two towers belonging to a castle which was believed impregnable until Cromwell's troops bombarded it with artillery and took it by storm.
Knockmealdown Mountains	The R665 runs south-west from Ardfinnan, passing Castlegrace , a fine ruined castle (?13th c.) just beyond Clogheen, from where the R668 (the 'Vee') winds its way south, with many hairpin bends, through the Knockmealdown Mountains. There are extensive views from Knockmealdown (2658 ft), highest of the hills.
Burncourt Castle	South-west of Cahir, on a minor road branching left off the N8 some 5 miles from the town, is Burncourt Castle (National Monument), the empty shell of an Elizabethan mansion built in 1641–5 and burned down by Cromwell only five years later in 1650.
Glen of Aherlow	North-west of Cahir, between the Galtee Mountains and a parallel wooded ridge of hills to the north, extends the wide Glen of Aherlow, once an important pass between the lowlands of Co. Tipperary and Co. Limerick. Scene of many a battle in the past, the glen later became a refuge for outlaws and the dispossessed. Attractive and fertile, it is good walking country.

Carlow · Ceatharlach   D 5

Republic of Ireland
Province: Leinster
County: Carlow
Population: 12,000

Carlow (Ceatharlach, fourfold lake), county town of Co. Carlow, lies south-west of Dublin on the River Barrow, at the intersection of the N9 and N80. It has a variety of industry, including a sugar-beet factory, flour mills and maltings, but little to interest tourists.

History	Carlow was a strategic Anglo-Norman stronghold. Fortified with a rampart in 1361, it was afterwards frequently besieged, captured and burned down. In the last battle to be fought here, in 1798, 640 Irish rebels were killed. The battle and the fallen are commemorated by a modern Celtic-style high cross in Church Street, where the dead were buried.

Sights

Access to Carlow Castle (National Monument) is from Castle Hill Street. Of the main structure, originally square, there survives only the east side, with two massive round towers at the corners (13th c.). The inner precinct is closed.

Carlow Castle

At the junction of Athy Road and Dublin Road is the handsome neo-classical Court House (1830).

Court House

St Patrick's College (1793) was one of the first Irish seminaries sanctioned by the British.

St Patrick's College

Surroundings

2 miles north-east of Carlow on the Dublin Road (N9) is the beautifully wooded Oak Park, with an 18-hole golf course.

Oak Park

2 miles east of the town, on land belonging to Browne's Hill, a country house built in 1763, is a huge dolmen (National Monument), over 4000 years old and the largest in Ireland. The front end of the capstone, which weighs 100 tons, is carried on three uprights; the collapsed rear end rests on the ground.

★Browne's Hill Dolmen

Continuing east the R725 comes in 7½ miles to the small town of Tullow, a centre for fishing the River Slaney and its tributaries.

Tullow

About 3 miles east of Tullow, in Co. Wicklow, is the ring-fort of Rathgall (National Monument), a hilltop stronghold with three concentric ramparts and ditches, probably built in the early centuries AD as the seat of the kings of southern Leinster. Inside the fort a Bronze Age forge was discovered containing over 400 fragments of clay moulds used to make bronze swords and spear heads. To the north of the fort stands the well-preserved Haroldstown Dolmen (National Monument), with a double capstone borne on ten uprights.

Rathgall

From the R725 a small road (signposted) leads to the ruined Aghowle Church (12th c.). Noteworthy features include the doorway, a simple granite cross and various tombs.

Aghowle Church

South of Carlow the N9 passes through Leighlinbridge, with the ruins of the Black Castle (16th c.; National Monument) on the site of an earlier fortress built in 1180 to protect the River Barrow crossing.

Leighlinbridge

2 miles west is an older village, Old Leighlin, where there was already a monastic community in the 7th c. Still to be seen is a ruined 13th c. church, much altered in the 16th c., with an interesting Gothic doorway leading to the choir, font, stalls and tombs (16th c.).

Old Leighlin

From Leighlinbridge the R705 runs south-east to Muine Bheag (or Bagenalstown), an attractive small town which makes an ideal base for visitors keen on fishing or hunting. In the vicinity are two 13th c. castles, both National Monuments – Ballymoon Castle, an empty shell with walls 8 ft thick and 20 ft high and rectangular towers, and Ballyloughan Castle, the remains of which are notable for the number of fireplaces.

Muine Bheag

Continuing its way towards the southern tip of Co. Carlow, the R705 comes to Borris, which has a 9-hole golf course. Between the town and the river is Borris House.

Borris

Borris is a convenient point from which to explore the Blackstairs

Blackstairs Mountains

Mountains east of the town. Mount Leinster (2576 ft) is the highest of the hills, crowned by a television tower.

St Mullin's

9 miles beyond Borris, at the southernmost point of the triangular county, lies St Mullin's, in the churchyard of which there are Early Christian and medieval remains (National Monuments) – a church with a spiral staircase, an oratory (St James's Chapel), an assortment of other buildings, the stump of a round tower, and a granite high cross. Outside the monastic precinct an Anglo-Norman castle can be seen.

Clonmore

A little to the west of Carlow is the village of Clonmore with an early 13th c. castle of the same name. With its corner towers the castle is typical of its period.

The churchyard, which is cut in two by the road, also contains interesting remains. North of the road stands a beautiful and well-preserved high cross; south of the road there is a fragment of another fine cross (both National Monuments).

Killeshin

Just over a mile further west, in the churchyard at Killeshin (Co. Laois), there is a 12th c. Romanesque church with a doorway notable for its rich sculpture and doorway gable.

From the churchyard there is a lovely view over the low-lying countryside, with the Wicklow Mountains in the distance.

Carrick-on-Shannon · Cara Droma Ruisg   C 3

Republic of Ireland
Province: Connacht
County: Leitrim
Population: 2000

Carrick-on-Shannon (Cara Droma Ruisg, weir of the marshy tract), county town of Co. Leitrim, lies in north central Ireland. It is the starting-point for inland cruising on the Shannon (➤ entry) and the Shannon–Erne Waterway (see below), reopened in 1994.

Town

Carrick-on-Shannon retains few buildings from the past apart from the Court House (1825) and Protestant Church (1827).

Surroundings

Shannon–Erne Waterway

A few miles north of Carrick, the Shannon–Erne Waterway branches off the River Shannon. Closed for more than a century, it was reopened in May 1994 linking two of the most popular recreational inland waterways in Europe, the Shannon and Upper and Lower Lough Erne in Northern Ireland. Opened originally in 1860, the canal was never an economic success; in its first five years only eight boats passed through, and in 1869 it was closed. Following extensive restoration work it now has a minimum depth of 5 ft and is a big attraction for boating enthusiasts. The 48 miles from Carrick to Belturbet (➤ Cavan) can be negotiated by an ordinary cruiser in about 16 hours.

Lough Allen

The R280 runs north via the prettily situated village of Leitrim (from which the county takes its name) to Drumshanbo, an anglers' paradise at the southern end of Lough Allen. Continuing north along the west side of the lough, the road passes through what was once mining country around Arigna.

Fenagh

About 8 miles north-east of Carrick-on-Shannon is Fenagh, with two churches, both National Monuments, on the site of a former monastery. The more southerly of the two has a fine west doorway and east window (14th/15th c.), the other (15th c.) stonework from a pre-Norman building; both have barrel vaults at the west end.

A good 9 miles south-east of Carrick lies Lough Rinn, on the north-east side of which stands Lough Rinn House, set in a delightful park. Unfortunately neither the house nor the gardens are open to the public at present.

Lough Rinn Estate

Carrick-on-Suir · Carraig na Suire　　　　D 4

Republic of Ireland
Province: Munster
Counties: Tipperary and Waterford
Population: 5600

Carrick-on-Suir (Carraig na Suire, rock of the Suir) lies near the south coast of Ireland on the River Suir. Since the river here forms the boundary between Co. Tipperary and Co. Waterford, the town lies in both.

In 1541 Henry VIII of England assumed the title king of Ireland. From then on, particularly in the reign of Elizabeth I, the English sought to consolidate their hold on the country by introducing English landowners. During the 16th and 17th c. these newcomers built numerous fortified Tudor mansions, the finest of which is Ormonde Castle in Carrick-on-Suir.

History

Sights

Ormonde Castle (National Monument), once the seat of the earls Butler of Ormonde, consists of a fortified tower (1450) and a manor house built on to it in 1568. It was actually constructed for Elizabeth I, but the queen seems never to have stayed there. It is a typical Elizabethan mansion with a long gabled front and, inside, a long hall and gallery extending almost the whole length of the building, decorated with stucco likenesses of the queen and members of the Ormonde family.

Ormonde Castle

From the tower there is a magnificent view of the river and the surrounding countryside. Open mid-Jun. to mid-Sep. daily 9.30am–6.30pm.

In the centre of the town, near the medieval bridge, stands the old Tholsel (town hall), originally a town gate, topped by a clock tower.

Tholsel

Surroundings

North of Carrick-on-Suir, on the boundary between Co. Kilkenny and Co. Tipperary, are two villages with notable high crosses, Kilkeeran (5 miles) and Ahenny (6 miles).

Kilkeeran

Of the three crosses in the churchyard at Kilkeeran, the west cross (9th c.) is especially fine. On the east side of the base are eight horsemen, on the other three sides interlace work and geometric patterns. The lower part of the shaft is divided into panels with various patterns, among them intertwined geese-like creatures.

In the churchyard at Ahenny stand two particularly fine crosses (both National Monuments), with figural decoration only on the bases. The more northerly of the two has figures of monks carrying crosses, a headless man on a pony, horsemen and horses, a procession of seven clerics

★Ahenny

carrying crosiers, and assorted animals. The base of the other cross is very badly weathered. The crosses themselves are covered with finely carved geometric designs (spirals, interlace work, rosettes). Because the patterns so resemble those in the Book of Kells, they are assumed to date from the 8th c.

Comeragh Mountains Monavullagh Mountains

South-west of Carrick-on-Suir, the Comeragh and Monavullagh mountains extend towards the sea. This is good climbing country, particularly the area around Lough Coumshingaum, a small tarn in a horseshoe-shaped corrie ringed by cliffs below the highest of the summits (2560 ft).

Cashel · Caiseal Mumhan   D 4

Republic of Ireland
Province: Munster
County: Tipperary
Population: 2400

Cashel (Caisel Mumhan, stone fort of Munster) lies inland in southern Ireland on the N8. Approached through flat countryside along any of the roads converging on the town, the famous Rock of Cashel is a prominent landmark, a steep crag to the north of the town, crowned by a magnificent cluster of ruins.

History

The rock was fortified by the kings of Munster as early as the 4th c. In 450 St Patrick, having baptised King Aengus here, made Cashel a bishop's see; a number of later kings were also bishops. The legendary

Cashel Cathedral

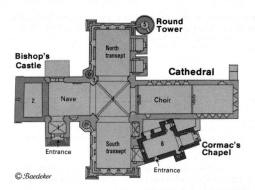

1 Porch
2 Archbishop's Palace
3 Staircases
4 Central tower
5 Round tower
6 Cormac's Chapel

© Baedeker

```
10m
33 ft
```

Brian Boru was crowned here, and in 977 made Cashel his principal seat. An O'Brien later presented the Rock to the Church and soon afterwards, in 1127, Bishop Cormac MacCarthy began the construction of Cormac's Chapel. In 1152 the see became an archbishopric. After the Reformation, Elizabeth I appointed Protestant archbishops. The cathedral, built in the 13th c., was damaged by fire in 1495 and again in 1647. After being restored in 1686 it was abandoned in 1749 and fell into decay. Finally, in 1874, the state assumed responsibility for it and it was declared a National Monument.

★★Rock of Cashel

The Rock of Cashel (National Monument) rises 200 ft above its surroundings. The walled precinct is entered through the Hall of the Vicar's Choral (15th c.), formerly for the use of laymen and minor canons. Today it has been turned into a little museum (upper floor with furniture of the period). St Patrick's Cross is also preserved here, having been removed from its site in front of the cathedral where a replica now stands.

Open daily 9am–7.30pm; winter to 4.30 or 5.30pm

On one side of St Patrick's Cross is a relief of the Crucifixion, on the other one of the saint himself. The base, richly ornamented with geometric designs, may have been the coronation stone of the kings of Munster and stood on the spot where St Patrick baptised King Aengus. Tradition has it that, during the ceremony, the saint accidentally struck the king's foot with his crosier; Aengus made no comment, believing this to be part of the ritual.

St Patrick's Cross

Cormac's Chapel (1127–32), which is enclosed by the choir and south transept of the cathedral, is the most interesting Romanesque church in Ireland. The architecture and sculpture show the influence of German (probably Regensburg) and English masters, while preserving a distinctively Irish character (expressed, for example, in the steeply pitched stone roof and the corbelling of the barrel vault).
The transepts are mini towers. The walls, both external and internal, are relieved by blind arcading and a variety of sculptural decoration. The old main doorway (north doorway: now facing the angle between the choir and south transept) is richly articulated and has a fine tympanum depicting a centaur hunting a lion with a bow and arrow. The chapel contains a 12th c. stone sarcophagus finely carved with Scandinavian-style ornament.

Cormac's Chapel

The cathedral itself, now roofless, still retains something of the grandeur of a medieval cathedral. The choir and transepts are longer than the (unfinished) nave. The transepts retain their Gothic gable ends

Cathedral

123

and their corner turrets. In the angles between nave and transepts, spiral staircases of 127 steps ascend the interior of small circular towers to the massive central tower, with access to roof walks around the nave and the transept. Each is connected to the other, as well as to the round tower (see below), by a series of passageways and flights of steps within the thickness of the walls – perhaps contrived from the point of view of defence. In the north transept are a number of fine tombs, one of them with figures of apostles and saints, including St Thomas à Becket.

In the choir is the tomb of Archbishop Myler MacGrath, who died in 1622 at the age of 100. Having converted to Protestantism, he was for several years both a Protestant archbishop appointed by Elizabeth I and a Roman Catholic one, since it was some time before he was dismissed from office by the Vatican!

| Round tower | The north transept of the cathedral is built against a well-preserved round tower dating from the same period as Cormac's Chapel. It is 92 ft high with a doorway set 12 ft above the ground. |

Bishop's Castle — At the west end of the cathedral stands the Archbishop's Palace, more a fortified castle than a palace, comprising a massive square tower (15th c.) the west wall of which is thick enough to contain a staircase within (no access).

Other Sights

Brú Ború — Near the Rock car park, Comhaltas Ceoltóirí Éireann, an organisation dedicated to the promotion of Irish folk music and art, has opened the Brú Ború Cultural Centre. Each season three plays are produced daily (except Sun. and Mon.) in the adjoining theatre; other events are also arranged. A restaurant, exhibition room and shop selling art and crafts complete the complex. Open Oct.–Mar. Mon.–Sat. 9am–5pm; Apr.–Sep. daily 9am–8pm.

Dominican Friary — The Dominican Friary (National Monument) near the base of the Rock retains a number of handsome windows.

Folk Village — The Folk Village, a few yards further along, re-creates the urban and rural life of the area. Open summer daily 10am–7.30pm.

Cashel Palace — When no longer needing the protection of their castle on the Rock, the Protestant archbishops built a palace in the town. This handsome brick building of 1730 is now the Cashel Palace Hotel, tastefully furnished in 18th c. style (entrance on the north side of Main Street).

Quirke's Castle — Quirke's Castle (in Main Street), a 15th c. tower house, is today also a hotel.

St John's Cathedral — St John's Cathedral (in John Street), is a pleasing neoclassical building (1750–83; tower 1812) erected to replace the cathedral on the Rock, by then falling into disrepair. Set into a wall in the churchyard are a series of fine tomb effigies preserved from Cashel's medieval churches.

Bolton Library — Nearby is the Diocesan library, endowed by Archbishop Bolton in 1741, with a collection of rare prints and maps.

Surroundings

Hore Abbey — West of Cashel lies Hore Abbey (National Monument), a Cistercian monastery founded in 1266, with the ruins of the church and conventual

Hore Abbey with the Rock of Cashel in the background

buildings; the chapter house is well preserved. The central tower of the church was a 15th c. addition.

Castlebar · Caislean an Barraigh   C 2

Republic of Ireland
Province: Connacht
County: Mayo
Population: 6400

Castlebar (Caislean an Barraigh, Barry's castle), county town of Co. Mayo, lies in the north-west of Ireland, at the junction of the N5 and N60. It has a small local airport.

Castlebar is always full of anglers, attracted to the town by the excellent fishing in the loughs to the south – Lough Mallard, Castlebar Lough and Islanddeady Lough.

In 1798 a French and Irish force, having landed near Castlebar, routed a superior British force in an engagement known as 'Castlebar Races'. **History**

The main feature of this little market town, which also has some light industry, is a green called the Mall, lined with lime trees. **Town**

Surroundings

On the N5 3 miles north-east lies Turlough, with an unusually squat **Turlough** round tower (well-preserved; National Monument) in the churchyard. Adjoining it is a ruined 17th c. church.

★Straid

Beyond Turlough, on the Foxford road at Straid, is a ruined abbey church containing fine sculptures and tombstones. One tomb in particular, dating from about 1475, is considered the best example of the flamboyant style in Ireland. The saints depicted on it appear to be having a good chuckle – no one knows why.

Mayo

From Castlebar the N60 runs south-east through the Plain of Mayo, passing by the village of Mayo, with remains of a once-famous abbey founded by St Colman in the 7th c.

Knock

The N60 continues to Claremorris from which the N17 leads north-east to Knock, a place of pilgrimage which attracts more than a million visitors every year. To guarantee them a comfortable journey, an airport suitable for jumbo-jets was opened here in 1986. The new church (1974), dominating the village, can accommodate 6000 people.

Knock's fame goes back to 1879 when 15 local people claimed to have seen the Madonna, accompanied by St Joseph and St John the Evangelist, behind the old parish church. This miraculous appearance, said to have lasted two hours, is commemorated by larger than life-size figures set up on the site there in 1970. The Pope considered Knock important enough to make a personal visit.

Near the church a folk museum was opened in 1987, documenting 19th c. rural life. The principal attraction is the 'museum in a museum' – a thatched cottage complete in every detail. Open May–Oct. daily 10am–6pm, Jul.–Aug. to 7pm.

Ballyhaunis

The R323 runs east from Knock to Ballyhaunis, with remains of a monastery; the church has been restored.

Cavan · An Cabhan   C 4

Republic of Ireland
Province: Ulster
County: Cavan
Population: 3200

Cavan (An Cabhan, hollow place), county town of Co. Cavan, is situated in a pleasant area of lakes and hills close to the border with Northern Ireland. Here the N3 coming from the south-east intersects with the N54/N55, which run north–south.

Town

The town was completely destroyed by British forces in 1690. An old tower marks the site of an abbey, founded in about 1300, around which the original settlement developed.

Cavan crystal

Cavan is noted for its crystal, which visitors can see being made at a local factory. Open Mon.–Fri. 9am–5.30pm, Sun. 2–5pm.

Surroundings

Ballyhaise

5 miles north is Ballyhaise, with a pretty 18th c. market hall and Ballyhaise Castle (1731; by Richard Cassels), now occupied by an agricultural college.

Cootehill
Bellamont Forest

The R188 runs north-east from Cavan to the little town of Cootehill, to the north of which lies Bellamont Forest. Here, on the shores of Dromore

Lough is a fine Palladian mansion, Bellamont House (1729; not open to the public).

At Cohaw, 3 miles south-east of Cootehill on the R192, there is a mega-lithic tomb (National Monument). Excavated in 1949, it has a double entrance court and five chambers. **Cohaw**

The road continues to Shercock, near Lough Sillan (campsite), renowned for its large pike. **Lough Sillan**

8 miles further south, in the extreme east of the province, lies Kingscourt, where rich deposits of gypsum have encouraged the growth of modern industries. The main street has attractive 17th and 18th c. houses. St Mary's Parish Church boasts fine stained-glass windows (1947–8) by Evie Hone. **Kingscourt**

The R165 makes its way west through the hills to the little market town of Bailieborrough, which has a Court House of 1817 and Market House of 1818. **Bailieborrough**

Virginia, 9 miles south of Bailieborrough, was named after the Virgin Queen, Elizabeth I. Prettily situated on the wooded shores of Lough Ramor, it offers a wide range of sports and recreational facilities (9-hole golf course, fishing in Lough Ramor, bathing beach, boat hire). **Virginia**

Jonathan Swift wrote Gulliver's Travels while staying at Cuilcagh House, a mansion belonging to the Sheridan family and situated 1¼ miles north of Virginia. **Cuilcagh House**

To the south of Ballyjamesduff (west of Virginia), on the R194, lies the village of Mount Nugent, with good fishing in Lough Sheelin. **Lough Sheelin**

There is good coarse fishing also in the irregularly shaped Lough Gowna, some 12 miles south of Cavan. It can be reached via Gowna, or direct from Lough Sheelin by driving west. **Lough Gowna**

To the north-west of Cavan, beyond the golf course, Farnham House stands in lovely grounds. **Farnham House**

Further west is Lough Oughter, an intricate maze of inlets and channels through which the River Erne flows. The wooded tracts around the lough have become the Killykeen Forest Park (lovely walks). The ruined Clough Oughter Castle is typical of a 13th c. Irish circular keep. **Lough Oughter**

Not far south of the lough at Cornafean there is a small privately run local museum. **Cornafean**

Kilmore, a mile or two south of Farnham House and the seat of a bishop, boasts a 19th c. Protestant cathedral incorporating a fine late Romanesque doorway. In the churchyard stands the richly decorated tomb of Bishop William Bedell who, in the 17th c., made the first translation of the Bible into Irish. Also in the town is a well-preserved motte and bailey. **Kilmore**

Reached from Cavan by way of Kilmore, Killeshandra lies surrounded by small loughs on the west side of Lough Oughter. It has a church of 1688. **Killeshandra**

Proceeding west from this mini lake district, the R201 comes after 3 miles or so to Drumlane. Here, in an attractive setting between two loughs, stand a round tower and a church (National Monument), both belonging to a former monastery. The church dates from the 13th to 15th c., the tower, still standing 45 ft high, and with carvings of birds (badly weathered), dates from the 12th c. **Drumlane**

Belturbet

The road continues north to Belturbet, near the Northern Ireland border. It is a centre for cruising on the River Erne (good fishing), linked to the Shannon by the Shannon–Erne Waterway (➤ Carrick-on-Shannon).

Ballyconnell

The hilly countryside with its many loughs extends for another 10 or 12 miles west of Belturbet. Ballyconnell is a popular coarse fishing centre with a 17th c. church.

Iron Mountains

From Ballyconnell the R200 climbs steeply up into the Iron Mountains, crossing the Bellavally Gap before descending to Glengevlin at the foot of Cuilcagh Mountain (2070 ft, the highest of the range). Hereabouts are the headwaters of the Shannon which has its source in the Shannon Pot. Good climbing country.

★★Cliffs of Moher · Aillte an Mhothair   D 2

Republic of Ireland
Province: Munster
County: Clare

The Cliffs of Moher (Aillte an Mhothair, cliffs of ruin) rise vertically from the sea on the west coast of Ireland, just south of Galway Bay.

Coastal scenery

Sheer cliffs stretch in an unbroken line for some 5 miles from Hag's Head in the south, where they are 400 ft high, to O'Brien's Tower in the north, where they reach 656 ft. Between these two points the land immediately back from the cliffs forms a roughly level plateau. From the top of the cliffs narrow bands of vegetation can be seen clinging to the cliff face

Cliffs of Moher

while, far below, the surf surges and thunders, ceaselessly pounding the foot of the cliffs and the isolated stacks.

From the car park at the information centre (café) a path leads to a nearby sandstone platform on the cliff edge and to O'Brien's Tower which, particularly on a clear day, affords splendid views seawards and across to the Aran Islands. The viewing tower was built by Sir Cornelius O'Brien in 1835 along with a little tea-room. Tower and information centre open Mar.–Oct. daily 10am–6pm.

O'Brien's Tower

While the magnificent view from O'Brien's Tower usually has to be shared with a host of fellow tourists, it is rare to encounter another soul on the walk to Hag's Head, 3 miles from O'Brien's Tower, at the southern end of the cliffs. The narrow path hugs the cliff edge and care is required in strong winds. The watchtower on Hag's Head dates from the beginning of the 19th c.

Walk to Hag's Head

Surroundings

From the Cliffs of Moher the road leads east to the fishing village of Liscannor, then past the ruins of Kilmacreehy Church (15th c.) and along Liscannor Bay, with its lovely sandy beach, to Lahinch. White houses and a promenade skirting the shore above the breakers give this popular resort an almost Mediterranean air. It has two 18-hole golf courses and a variety of sports and recreational facilities.

Lahinch

2½ miles east of Lahinch is another resort, Ennistymon, situated in a wooded valley where the River Cullenagh cascades down through a rocky gorge. There is good fishing for brown trout (also a horse fair).

Ennistymon

7½ miles south of Lahinch on the N67 a side road branches off to Spanish Point, a rugged promontory on which hundreds of bodies from ships of the Spanish Armada were washed up in 1588. Near the point are a 9-hole golf course and a good sandy beach.

Spanish Point

Clonakilty · Clanna Chaoilte   E 3

Republic of Ireland
Province: Munster
County: Cork
Population: 2700

Clonakilty (Clanna Chaoilte, O'Keelty's clan) lies on the south coast of Ireland in Clonakilty Bay. The head of the bay is almost totally enclosed by the Inchadoney Peninsula. There are good sandy beaches and facilities for water sports and sea angling.

Clonakilty was established in 1614 by the 1st earl of Cork, for occupation by English immigrants. Today it is a small market town in a fertile agricultural area, with an interesting local museum and beautiful park, Kennedy Gardens. The town post office is housed in a former Presbyterian church (1861).

Town

Surroundings

6 miles east, reached via the T71 and R600, lies Timoleague, with an abbey founded in 1240, which in its day was an important religious centre. The present ruins (church with south aisle and transepts, tower,

Timoleague

Timoleague: ruins of the Abbey ... *... and Castle Gardens*

remains of conventual buildings) date from later centuries. Also well worth a visit are Castle Gardens with their huge rhododendron bushes and several varieties of palm.

Courtmacsherry

2½ miles from Timoleague, on the R601, is Courtmacsherry, a fishing village and resort on the south side of a narrow inlet. At the entrance to the village is a plaque commemorating the various tragedies that have occurred in these coastal waters.

Benduff Castle

On the peninsula to the south-west of Clonakilty, near Gastlefreke, are the ruins of Benduff Castle and the remains of a Templars' commandery.

Rosscarbery

Picturesquely situated on a hill by the sea, on the north-west side of Rosscarbery Bay, the little town of Rosscarbery once boasted a 6th c. monastery with a famous school. One or two fragments of it survive near the ancient cathedral (restored in the 17th and 19th c.).

Coppinger's Court

About 2 miles west of Clonakilty stands Coppinger's Court (National Monument), a ruined 17th c. manor house with picturesque turrets, gables and chimneys.

★Drombeg Stone Circle

On a hill just off the road to Glandore (R597) is the Drombeg Stone Circle (National Monument), dating from the Bronze Age (➤ picture, p. 51). During excavation, a cremated body was found in the centre of the ring of 17 upright stones and, a short distance west, the remains of two circular huts. These have been dated to the 2nd–4th c. AD; they were probably used by hunters rather than as dwellings.

Glandore

Glandore is a prettily situated resort with a mild climate and good fishing and bathing.

★★Clonmacnoise · Cluain Mic Nois   C 4

Republic of Ireland
Province: Leinster
County: Offaly

The ancient monastic settlement of Clonmacnoise or Clonmacnois (Cluain Mic Nois, meadow of the son of Nos) is situated in the very heart of Ireland, on high ground above a broad bend of the Shannon. With its many graves scattered among the ruined buildings and high crosses from the Early Christian and medieval periods, the walled monastic precinct resembles a large and lonely churchyard.

A pilgrimage to Clonmacnoise takes place every year on St Ciaran's Day (September 9th), climaxing in an outdoor service conducted before a canopied altar.

Much the pleasantest – if slowest – way of reaching Clonmacnoise is by boat from Athlone (➤ entry).

According to tradition, the monastery was founded in January 545 by St Ciaran, who died in the same year. It developed into the most celebrated religious centre in Ireland and soon acquired the status of a university. As well as the monks working in its scriptoria, who produced valuable manuscripts including the Annals of Tighernach (11th c.) and the Book of the Dun Cow (12th c.), there were also craftsmen making crosiers, reliquaries and other articles. The treasures it contained no doubt attracted the raiders who plundered and burned the monastery several times between 834 and 1204 – first the Vikings, then in the 12th c. the Anglo-Normans, who in 1179 reduced more than 100 buildings to ashes. However, it was only after English troops from Athlone had carried off whatever they could lay their hands on in 1552, and Cromwell's forces had devastated the site again a century later, that the monastery fell into complete ruin. Clonmacnoise has been protected as a National Monument since 1955.

History

Monastic site

The walled enclosure is entered from the car park on the west side. At the entrance is a Visitor Centre in which some gravestones are kept (to avoid further damage being caused by weathering).

The precinct itself is a typical Irish monastic site laid out in a manner very different from monasteries elsewhere in Europe. Several small churches (11th–13th c.) are dotted about the enclosure, between which would have stood numerous wattle and daub huts to house the members of the community.

Open summer, daily 9am–7pm; winter daily 10am–5 or 6.30pm.

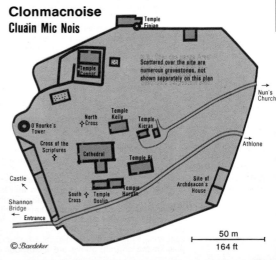

Clonmacnoise
Cluain Mic Nois

Temple Finian

Temple Connor

Scattered over the site are numerous gravestones, not shown separately on this plan

→ Nun's Church

Temple Kelly

North ✛ Cross

Temple Kieran

O'Rourke's Tower

Cross of the Scriptures ✛

Cathedral

Temple Ri

→ Athlone

Castle ↖

South ✛ Cross

Temple Doolin

Temple Hurpan

Site of Archdeacon's House

Shannon Bridge

← Entrance

© Baedeker

50 m
164 ft

The ruins of Clonmacnoise beside the Shannon

Gravestones

To the left of the entrance are some 200 Early Christian gravestones, including some with ogham inscriptions. They are set into the enclosure wall grouped together by age, giving an excellent overview of the different styles from the 8th to the 12th c. Many bear inscriptions incorporating the phrase *or do ...* (a prayer for ...) followed by an Irish name. Many of the slabs are extremely beautiful and very finely worked.

Cathedral

In the centre of the main group of buildings stands the cathedral, incorporating work dating from the 10th to the 15th c. Note especially the figures of St Patrick and two other saints above the north doorway, dating from the Middle Ages. The sacristy is 16th c.

Temple Kieran

To the east of the cathedral is the simple oratory of St Ciaran (Temple Kieran), a tiny 9th c. church probably containing the tomb of the founder.

Other buildings

At the north end of the precinct are the 11th c. Temple Connor, now a Protestant church (closed), and the 12th c. Temple Finian (Temple Finghin) with a 56-ft-high round tower built on to the chancel.

O'Rourke's Tower

A second round tower, 60 ft high, known as O'Rourke's Tower, stands alone on the bank of the Shannon (with a gateway).

Cross of the Scriptures

In front of the cathedral is one of the finest high crosses in Ireland, the Cross of the Scriptures, also known as Flann's Cross after King Flann (877–915) to whom it is dedicated (though the inscription is almost completely illegible). Standing more than 13 ft high, the cross, of soft sandstone, was carved early in the 10th c. On the west face are the Vigil at the Tomb, the Arrest, the Betrayal and, higher up, the Crucifixion. On the east face, King Dermot is depicted helping St Ciaran erect the corner post of the church; above are a number of unidentified figures, and above these, the Last Judgement. On the south face are a bishop and David with his harp, and on the north face another bishop, a man with pan pipes and a falconer. The base of the cross has a hunting scene with horsemen, hunters, chariots and various animals.

To the north of the Cross of the Scriptures is the shaft of another high cross (North Cross) with figures and patterned decoration. A third high cross (South Cross; 9th c.) stands to the south, with a Crucifixion on the west face and panels decorated with intertwined animals and plants.

Other high crosses

To the east of the monastic enclosure, reached by a pathway from Temple Kieran, lies the ruined Nun's Church. The entrance doorway and chancel arch are both well preserved; they are richly ornamented, with a particularly elaborate pattern on the capitals of the chancel arch.

Nun's Church

Clonmacnoise and West Offaly Railway

A small scenic railway, originally built for transporting peat, operates in the summer months from the Bord na Mona Blackwater Works near Shannonbridge, not far from Clonmacnoise. The 40-minute trip to Banagher (4 miles) takes in many places of geological, historical and botanical interest around the Blackwater bog (demonstration of peat cutting).

Operates end of Apr.–Oct. daily 10am–5pm

Clonmel · Cluain Meala   D 4

Republic of Ireland
Province: Munster
County: Tipperary
Population: 12400

Cross of the Scriptures

133

Clonmel (Cluain Meala, honey meadow), county town of Co. Tipperary, lies near Ireland's south coast, in an attractive setting on the north bank of the River Suir. To the south of the town are the Comeragh Mountains. Clonmel is a market town with some industry (principally cider making), in an area with a reputation for horse and dog breeding. Laurence Sterne, author of *Tristram Shandy*, was born in Clonmel in 1713.

In 1815 the first regular passenger service between two Irish towns was instituted here by an Italian immigrant, Charles Bianconi, a picture framer by trade, who, having prospered and become mayor of the town, introduced a horse-drawn vehicle service between Clonmel and Cahir. 'Bianconi Cars' later became established throughout southern Ireland.

Sights

St Mary's Church

Next to the Protestant St Mary's Church (National Monument) are parts of the old rampart walls and three towers. The church, with an octagonal tower, was most recently reconstructed in 1857. Notable features include the tracery of the east window and a number of 16th and 17th c. monuments.

West Gate

Nearby West Gate, a former town gate, closes off O'Connell Street; next to it stands the Roman Catholic church, with a neoclassical façade and good ceiling plasterwork.

Main Guard

The Main Guard, at the other end of the street, is said to have been designed by Wren. It bears the arms of Clonmel and the earls of Ormonde (whose seat this was).

Other sights

In Parnell Street stands the town hall where the civic insignia are on display. Beyond it are the Court House (1800) and, diagonally opposite, the municipal library housing an art gallery and local museum.

Surroundings

Donaghmore

5 miles north, on a side road off the R688, Donaghmore boasts a ruined Romanesque church (National Monument) with a fine doorway and chancel arch.

Fethard

4½ miles further on lies the little town of Fethard, still with an old-world atmosphere. The Protestant church incorporates part of an earlier 15th c. building, while the Roman Catholic church, at the east end of the town, retains enough from an old Augustinian church to give some impression of the original. Parts of the old town walls also survive.

Slievenamon
Comeragh
Mountains

Slievenamon (2330 ft), north-east of Clonmel, and the Comeragh Mountains to the south (highest peak Knockamaffrin, 2439 ft), provide plenty of opportunity for climbing and hill walking.

The Falconry

The Falconry at Anner House, on the north bank of the Suir 2½ miles east of Clonmel, has a collection of birds of prey (demonstrations of falconry).

Gurteen le Poer

Further east, on a hill on the river's heavily wooded south bank, are the lovely grounds of Gurteen le Poer (18th c.).

Cong · Cunga Feichin C 2

Republic of Ireland
Province: Connacht
County: Mayo
Population: 200

The village of Cong (Cunga Feichin, isthmus of Feichin) lies in the far west of Ireland, on the isthmus between Lough Mask to the north and Lough Corrib to the south (good fishing in both loughs), to the north of Galway Bay and close to the county boundary between Mayo and Galway.

The last high king of Ireland, Roderick O'Conor, died in Cong in 1198, having spent the last 15 years of his life here in monastic seclusion.

Cong is a charming little village. In the main street stands a 14th c. stone market cross with inscriptions.

Village

Sights

At the entrance to the village are the ruins of Cong Abbey (12th c.; National Monument), an Augustinian moastery. A finely sculptured doorway and a number of early 13th c. capitals in the cloister (restored), represent striking examples of Irish Romanesque art. Equally interesting is the so-called Anglers' Hut (also restored) on the river bank, from which the monks were able to fish through a hole in the floor.

★Cong Abbey

Cong's processional cross (Cong Cross), made for King Turlough O'Conor in about 1123, is now in the National Museum in Dublin (see entry).

Ashford Castle (hotel)

135

Connemara

Ashford Castle   Near the abbey, in a park on the shores of Lough Corrib (see entry), stands Ashford Castle, which took on its present 19th c. aspect when in the ownership of the Guinness family. In 1939 it became a hotel which today is one of the finest in Ireland.

Surroundings

Lough Mask   Lough Mask and Lough Corrib are linked by underground streams which flow beneath the isthmus separating them. The limestone of the area is pitted with caves.

Kelly's Cave
Pigeon Hole   The most interesting of the caves are Kelly's Cave (National Monument), thought to have been a Bronze Age burial site, and the Pigeon Hole. Access is easy to both (the key to Kelly's Cave is kept in Cong).

Joyce's Country   To the west, beyond the isthmus, lies Joyce's Country, a hilly region traversed by green valleys and lonely roads. It takes its name from a Welsh family who settled here in the 13th c.

Lough Nafooey   A delightful round tour can be made from Cong, through a charming blend of hill, valley and river scenery. From Cong head first for Clonbur and then for Lough Nafooey, with views of the Partry Mountains; after crossing the saddle into the valley of the River Joyce, turn south to follow the L101 along the western tip of Lough Corrib and so back to Cong.

★★Connemara   C 1/2

Republic of Ireland
Province: Connacht
County: Galway

Connemara is the area extending along the heavily indented west coast of Ireland to the north of Galway Bay. It is an area steeped in tradition and in large parts of Connemara Irish is still spoken. Road signs are in Gaelic only.

Topography   With its ranges of hills, bare isolated peaks, valleys with peat-blackened loughs and coastline of sheer cliffs and sandy bays, Connemara is one of the most attractive places in Ireland, appealing alike to tourists, sportsmen and those in search of a quieter, more relaxed kind of holiday.

Clifden

The main centre of population in Connemara is Clifden, a little market town in the extreme west. It lies at the head of Clifden Bay, one of the many narrow, fjord-like inlets which here reach inland in the direction of the Twelve Bens, Connemara's great landmarks further east. The famous Connemara Pony Show with its associated traditional contests and competitions attracts many visitors every August. Below the town the River Owenglin makes its way to the sea in a series of picturesque waterfalls.

Sights   Heading west from the town along Sky Road there are some superb views. The road leads to the abandoned Clifden Castle (1815).
In spring (mid-May) an interesting spectacle can be witnessed at Weir Bridge, to the south of the town. Here during the spawning season vast

Clifden, chief town of Connemara

numbers of salmon can be seen struggling upstream against the fast-flowing current.

Further south still are the remains of the very first transatlantic wireless station, set up here by Guglielmo Marconi (1874–1937), the Italian radio pioneer who, in 1896, came to live in England. Also in the area is a monument to Sir William Alcock (1892–1919) and Arthur Whitten Brown (1886–1948) who, on June 14th–15th 1919, made the first non-stop flight across the Atlantic, taking off from St John's, Newfoundland, and crash-landing here.

Tours in Connemara

The contrasts so typical of the Connemara scenery – whether in the landscape itself or in the natural light and colour – are best appreciated by making several separate excursions.

From Clifden the N59 runs northwards, skirting the coast past little white cottages scattered among stony fields, drystone walls and rocky coves.

At Streamstown, a few miles north of Clifden, the light-coloured Connemara marble is worked. The quarries can be visited. **Streamstown**

A side road branches left to the fishing village of Cleggan (lobsters). On Cleggan Hill (breathtaking views) are the ruins of a 19th c. watchtower. **Cleggan**

From Cleggan a boat can be taken to Inishbofin. The island, today with a population of about 200, was occupied by monks in the 7th c. On it can be seen prehistoric promontory forts, stone houses, and the remains of a barracks built by Cromwell's troops (1652–7) who turned it into a sort **Inishbofin** of internment camp for monks and priests. But the island is also worth visiting for its lovely sandy beaches and rugged cliffs and the scope it offers for sailing and sea angling.

Letterfrack

The N59 proceeds via Moyard to Letterfrack, a community founded in the 19th c. by the Quakers. The mild climate here allows tall fuchsia hedges to flourish.

★Connemara National Park

Letterfrack is the main gateway into the Connemara National Park, with a Visitor Centre in the village. The Visitor Centre has information on the flora, fauna and history of settlement of the 4940–acre park, which can be explored on foot on two shortish waymarked paths or a longer full day's tour. Park open all year round; Visitor Centre, May–Sep. daily 10am–6pm.

Tully Cross Renvyle

From Letterfrack a side road on the left leads to Tully Cross and Renvyle. At the end of the Renvyle Peninsula – lovely coastal scenery of sandy beaches alternating with cliffs – are the remains of a 14th c. castle, a church and a small dolmen.

Kylemore Abbey

The N59, continuing east from Letterfrack, follows the valley of the River Dawros to the loughs at Kylemore, nestling amid hills. This particular area is at its loveliest when the rhododendrons and fuchsias are in bloom. To the left, above the first lough, stands the palatial Kylemore Abbey, built in the 19th c. by a wealthy merchant as a country house but now occupied by Irish Benedictine nuns. Part of the abbey is a girls school and closed to the public; otherwise visitors are welcomed. Open Apr.–Nov. daily 10.30am–6.30pm; restaurant; craft centre.

Killary Harbour

Passing Kylemore Lough and Lough Fee, the road winds its way down to Killary Harbour, a 10-mile-long fjord-like inlet, somewhat gloomy in

Landscape near Kylemore Abbey

shadow but delightful when the sun shines. There was once a British naval base here.

Northwards across the water the beautiful Vale of Delphi can be glimpsed between the Mweelrea Mountains and the Bengorm (2297 ft). This lovely valley got its name when a former lord Sligo called his fishing lodge there Delphi.

Vale of Delphi

The road follows the south side of the inlet to Leenane, a good centre for fishermen and climbers. The Leenane Cultural Centre celebrates the tradition of woollen manufacture for which the area is known. The Centre has its own land on which are kept several breeds of sheep. Open Mar.–Oct. daily 10am–6pm.

Leenane

The River Erriff, flowing through Co. Mayo to its outflow in Killary Harbour, here cascades down the lovely Ashleag Waterfall.

Ashleag Waterfall

From Leenane the R336 cuts directly through the hills southwards to the junction at Maam Cross, following the river as it skirts the edge of the delightful Joyce's Country (➤ Cong).

Maam Cross

Beyond Maam Cross, the R336 continues south through a maze of little loughs to arrive after 6 miles in Screeb, situated on a narrow and irregular arm of the sea which, were it not for the tidemarks along the shore, could easily be mistaken for an inland lough. The tiny fields that are a feature of this area have been painstakingly built up from layer upon layer of seaweed alternating with sand and protected by irregular drystone walls.

Screeb

From Screeb the R340 hugs the shores of Kilkieran Bay to Carna (fishing for sea trout in the bay and for brown trout in nearby loughs).

Carna

On two islets in Lough Skannive are crannogs (lake dwellings built on piles).

Lough Skannive

8 miles further along the coast road (R340, R342), a byroad on the left drops down to Cashel Bay. Cashel is much favoured by anglers.

Cashel

The coast road, regained a little further west, goes on to Roundstone, a community established in the early 19th c. for migrant Scottish fishermen. It is now a holiday resort popular with artists and nature lovers (beautiful shell beaches).

Roundstone

Beyond Roundstone the R341 continues round Ballyconneely Bay to Ballyconneely before branching inland towards Clifden; on the coast 2¼ miles south is an 18-hole golf course.

Ballyconneely

The hinterland of Connemara, with the Twelve Bens (east of Clifden) and the Maamturk Mountains, is lonely and sparsely populated – very different from the coastal strip. Dominating this central part are the Twelve Bens, of which Benbaun (2389 ft) is the highest and the others not much lower. Mosses and lichens colour the steep rock faces, with splashes of purple heather and glistening white quartz from which the mountains are formed.

**The Twelve Bens
Maamturk
Mountains**

Below the Bens on the south side lies Ballynahinch Lough with, on its southern shore, Ballynahinch Castle (now a hotel), an 18th c. mansion built by the Martin family who, during the Great Famine of 1845–9, sold off much of their property to help the poor. On a wooded islet in the lough a ruined castle can be seen.

**Ballynahinch
Lough**

Cork · Corcaigh   E 3

Republic of Ireland
Province: Munster
County: Cork
Population: 136,000

Cork (Corcaigh, marshy place) is the largest city in Ireland apart from
Dublin and Belfast; it has an international airport. Cork lies near the south
coast, at first sight well inland but in fact on an arm of the sea, access to
open waters being through a narrow strait called Passage West.

Along with Limerick, Cork is one of the Irish Republic's biggest industrial centres after Dublin. Industries include brewing and distilling, food
processing, textiles, footwear and chemicals. Several multinational cor-
porations including Ford and Dunlop are represented here. Cork's magnificent harbour has contributed significantly to the economic standing
of the town, particularly the deep-water port at Cobh on the outer harbour from where the produce of the surrounding region, primarily agricultural, is exported.

Cork is also the intellectual capital of southern Ireland, with many cultural institutions including the Cork Literary and Scientific Society,
founded in 1820. It has a college of the National University of Ireland and
two cathedrals, Roman Catholic and Protestant.

History

Cork's history began with the founding of a monastery by St Finbarr
(7th c.) on a small alluvial island in the River Lee, where St Finbarr's
Cathedral now stands. The
monastery and the settlement
which grew up around it flourished in spite of several Danish
raids, and were later incorporated into the fortified base
which the Danes established
there. After the arrival in
Ireland in 1172 of the English
king Henry II, the town was
several times captured, recovered and retaken, being now in
English, now in Irish hands. In
1284 it was surrounded by a
new circuit of walls; in 1378 it
was burned down by the Irish;
in 1495 it was taken by Perkin
Warbeck, the Yorkist pretender
to the English throne; and in
1642 it was captured by Irish
insurgents who were driven
from the city in 1644 and again
in 1649. In 1690 the city walls
were finally pulled down.

During the civil war, in 1920,
two mayors of Cork were killed
and large areas of the city damaged by fire.

Town

The centre of Cork is to all
intents and purposes an island,
sandwiched between two arms
of the River Lee, the North and
South Channels. The river,
spanned by several bridges

within the city, flows into Lough Mahon (as Cork Harbour is also known) at the ferry port.

The quays along the river, with their limestone walls, are lined with trees. The cityscape as a whole, however, is not particularly attractive. Cork's war-torn history has ensured that few historic buildings survive. There are, though, some fine 18th c. buildings, and the central area of the city between the North and South Channels is given architectural character by the churches and other buildings dating from the early 19th c. The main shopping district is the area around St Patrick's Street.

City centre

St Patrick's Bridge, spanning the North Channel, is a convenient starting point for a circuit of Cork city centre. First proceed east along Merchant's Quay to the Custom House on the furthest tip of the island, there doubling back along Lapp's Quay bordering the South Channel to Parnell Bridge, continuing west along South Mall to its junction with the spacious Grand Parade. Where Grand Parade narrows into Corn Market Street, turn right into St Patrick's Street and so back in a wide sweep to St Patrick's Bridge. With some minor detours this walk takes in most of the principal city-centre sights.

City-centre walk

From Lapp's Quay there is a good view across the South Channel to the City Hall, reflected in the waters of the slow-flowing river. Built in the mid-1930s, it has an assembly hall with seating for 2000.

City Hall

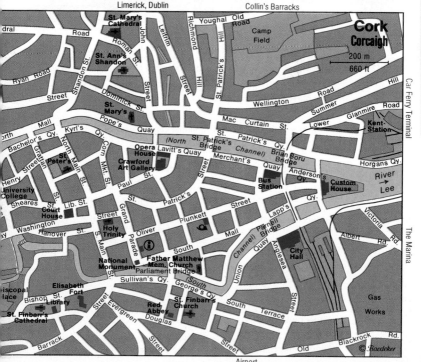

City Hall

St Mary's Church

Father Matthew Memorial Church	Off to the left of South Mall, on the banks of the South Channel which here enters a sharp bend, stands the Father Matthew Memorial Church (Holy Trinity; 1825), a neo-Gothic building designed by G R Pain. It commemorates the 'Apostle of Temperance', Father Matthew (1790–1861), who preached the unpopular doctrine of abstinence and 'made an idea into a crusade'.
St Finbarr's Church	On the far side of the South Channel can be seen St Finbarr's Church, also known as the South Chapel. Built in 1766, it has late 18th c. furnishings; in the interior is a figure of the dead Christ by Hogan.
Red Abbey Tower	A short distance west, almost completely surrounded by later buildings in Abbey Street, is the Red Abbey Tower, one of the few relics of Cork's medieval monasteries. During the siege in 1690, John Churchill, later Duke of Marlborough, is said to have made his headquarters here.
St Finbarr's Cathedral	Further west still rise the prominent spires of St Finbarr's Cathedral (1865–80), in French early Gothic style, with a richly furnished and decorated interior including fine mosaics in the choir. The cathedral's eight bells, cast by Abel Rudhall, are from an earlier church of 1750 on the same site.
Grand Parade	Adorning Grand Parade are the Berwick Fountain and a monument to Irish patriots.
Church of the Holy Trinity	Just to the left, in Washington Street, stands Holy Trinity Church, also known as Christ Church (1720; by Coltsman). Among relics from an earlier building is the tomb of Mayor Ronan and his wife (mid-16th c.).
Court House	Two blocks further along on the north side of Washington Street is the Court House (1832), with a handsome portico.

From Liberty Street continue east to Corn Market Street, with the old market at its southern end. The carefully restored Victorian covered market hall with its arches, fountains and galleries is always a hive of activity with a brisk trade in fruit, vegetables, meat and fish.

Corn Market Street

The Crawford Municipal Art Gallery on Emmet Place, a few hundred yards further east, has a collection of sculpture and modern Irish art. Open Mon.–Sat. 10.30am–5pm.

Crawford Municipal Art Gallery

From Emmet Place a side street leads south to St Patrick's Street, the city's main shopping thoroughfare. Built over an old arm of the River Lee, it runs in a broad arc to St Patrick's Bridge.

St Patrick's Street

Northern district

Across the river to the north stands the Dominican Church of St Mary's (1832–9) with, on the high altar, an image of the Virgin (14th c. Flemish work in ivory).

St Mary's

Just a little to the north of St Mary's is one of the city's landmarks, St Ann's Shandon (1722). Its handsome tower – looking rather like a telescope drawn out in three stages and popularly known as 'the pepperpot' – is of particoloured stone, red sandstone on the north and east sides, grey limestone on the south and west. In the tower hang eight bells cast by Abel Rudhall in 1750, with a celebrated carillon (for a small charge visitors can ring the bells themselves). Although only 120 ft high, because of the church's elevated situation, the tower (very narrow stairway) affords a panorama of the city.

★St Ann's Shandon

View of Cork from St Anne's Shandon

143

St Mary's
Cathedral

A couple of streets further up the hill can be seen the neoclassical St Mary's Cathedral (1808); the interior was renewed in neo-Gothic style in 1820 following a fire.

Collin's Barracks

To the east, in Youghal Old Road, lie Collin's Barracks with, in the chapel, a three-light stained-glass window by Evie Hone (1939; viewing by appointment).

St Patrick's

South of the Barracks, near Lower Glanmire Road, stands the Corinthian-style St Patrick's Church (1836; by G R Pain), unfortunately disfigured by an extension of 1894.

Custom House

From St Patrick's Church cross the Brian Boru Bridge to regain the island. On the right is the large bus station, to the left the Custom House (1814), now the Harbour Master's Office.

Western district

Cork Public
Museum

West of the city centre between the river and Mardyke Walk are sports grounds and Fitzgerald Park with a range of recreational facilities. A handsome Georgian house in the park is home to the Cork Public Museum. The museum covers the history of the region from prehistoric times to the present day. There are also collections of silver, glass and the crochet and lacework for which Cork was famous. Open Mon.–Fri. 11am–1pm, 2–5pm, Sun. 3–5pm.

University College

South of the museum, beyond Western Road and across the South Channel, lies University College (founded 1845), part of the National University of Ireland, with some 4000 students. Many of the neoclassical buildings are well preserved, the Goal Gate (1818) being particularly fine. The Honan Chapel has lovely stained glass by Sarah Purser and Harry Clarke. The college possesses interesting collections including ogham stones and early prints of Cork, which can be viewed by appointment.

Surroundings

Riverstown House

Near the N8 about 4½ miles north-east of the city stands Riverstown House, which acquired its present aspect in the mid-18th c. when it was the residence of the Bishop of Cork. The interior is well worth seeing. Open May–Sep. daily 10am–4pm.

★Fota Island

Fota Island, east of Cork and linked to the city by a bridge, has several attractions, including the Fota Wildlife Park with a variety of waterfowl and many species of animal including giraffes, zebras, antelopes and monkeys; a visit should prove a hit with children. Open Apr.–Oct. Mon.–Sat. 10am–6pm, Sun. 11am–6pm.

Separate from the wildlife park are Fota House and the adjoining grounds (Fota Arboretum). The house with its notable art collection is to be opened to the public after restoration. New varieties of tree are constantly being added to the already extensive collection in the arboretum.

Cobh

Situated south-east of Cork is Great Island, located in the sea and joined to the mainland by bridges. On its south side, 15 miles from Cork, lies Cobh, a relatively modern town and busy deep-water port. Around the harbour, above which Cobh's fine and richly decorated neo-Gothic church stands sentinel, the townscape is particularly picturesque. An additional attraction for tourists is Cobh Heritage Centre, opened in 1993. Housed in an old railway building (1862), it documents the eventful history of the

Grounds of the Fota House   *Cobh with its neo-Gothic church*

town. Open Apr.–Sep. Mon.–Fri. 9.30am–7.30pm, Sat., Sun. 10am–7pm; Nov.–Jan. daily 10am–5pm.

Because of it prime strategic location, the area around Cork Harbour abounds with fortifications from many different periods. There are also many small resorts to which holidaymakers are drawn by the mildness of the climate.   **Cork Harbour**

At the outer end of Passage West stands Monkstown Castle (17th c.; National Monument), now the clubhouse of a 9-hole golf course.   **Monkstown Castle**

The R609 and R612 run south to Carrigaline (8 miles) and then east to Crosshaven, a popular holiday resort with good sandy beaches at the outflow of the River Owenboy into outer Cork Harbour.   **Crosshaven**

Derry

See Londonderry

★Dingle Peninsula   D 1/2

Republic of Ireland
Province: Munster
County: Kerry

The Dingle Peninsula is the most northerly of the hilly promontories which reach out into the Atlantic from the far south-west corner of Ireland. It extends westwards for more than 30 miles, from the low-lying country around Killorglin and Tralee.

This is a predominantly Irish-speaking area (Gaeltacht) where old customs, traditions and crafts continue.

Topography

The highest point of the peninsula, Brandon Mountain (3085 ft), crowns a chain of hills which at Brandon Head plunge almost straight into the sea from a height of 2462 ft. To the west of this range is a rolling coastal plain studded with typical Irish farmsteads and hamlets. Here there are few stone walls; corn is grown in small square fields, and purple-red fuchsia hedges, pale green ferns and black moss add their distinctive colours to the landscape.

Scenic drive

Caherconree

From Tralee (➤ entry) the road runs west along Tralee Bay to Camp. South-east of the village rises Caherconree (2668 ft). Beneath the peak stands a massive prehistoric promontory fort. A path goes up to the fort from a car park on the road from Camp to Aughills.

Inch

At Camp the R559 bears south-west and winds its way up through hilly country. In 5 miles a side road branches off on the left and runs south to Inch, a sheltered seaside resort from which a 3-mile-long ridge of dunes extends into the sea (lovely sandy beach).

Doonsheane

The R559 continues on its way to Dingle, the sea on one side, hills on the other. Just before Dingle turn left and then sharp left again to reach, at Doonsheane, the ancient circular burial ground of Ballintaggart, con-

Inch Beach on Dingle Peninsula

House fronts in Dingle

taining a number of ogham stones (National Monument), some with crosses.

★Dingle

Dingle itself, the chief place on the peninsula and the most westerly town in Europe, lies in a sheltered bay with good beaches surrounded on three sides by hills. It is an excellent centre for sea angling and boating, with other facilities including mini-golf; but, above all, the pretty little port with its brightly painted houses is a good base from which to visit the many ancient sites at the western end of the peninsula.

Milltown

West of Dingle, at the new cemetery in Milltown, is a large standing stone known as the Milestone; nearby are two others, known as 'the Gates of Glory'.

Rahinnane Castle

Continuing west the road comes to Ventry, 2 miles north-west of which, on the Ballyferriter road, are the ruins of Rahinnane Castle (15th c.; National Monument), in a circular enclosure surrounded by a 30-ft-deep moat.

Dunbeg

From Ventry the route follows the peninsula's rocky south coast. About 220 yd to the south on the left-hand side of the road at Fahan, Dunbeg, a fine prehistoric promontory fort (National Monument) with four earthen ramparts and a substantial stone wall, stands directly overlooking the sea. Within the fort are the remains of a house, square within but circular without. An underground passage leads from the innermost part of the fort to the outer defences.

Glanfahan

A few miles further west at Glanfahan can be seen clusters of beehiveshape huts, each cluster enclosed by a wall, making a total of 417 structures, every one built without the use of mortar; also 19 souterrains and 18 standing stones (all National Monuments).

Dingle Peninsula

Slea Head
At the south-western tip of the peninsula is Slea Head. From the narrow road below Mount Eagle there are extensive views.

Blasket Islands
The Blasket Islands can be reached by boat, weather permitting, from the little fishing harbour of Dunquin. Information about the islands is available from the Blasket Centre, also in Dunquin.

The main island of Great Blasket, now a National Historic Park, was inhabited until 1953 when the islanders – said to have been, in the enjoyment of their settled way of life, 'the happiest people on earth' – were moved to the mainland. The abandoned village street can be seen on the hillside; in the centre of the island are the ruins of a church (National Monument) of uncertain age. From the island's highest point (937 ft) there is a view over Blasket Sound to the rugged coast of Kerry. In 1588 one of the ships of the Spanish Armada, the *Santa Maria de la Rosa*, ran aground in Blasket Sound.

4 miles north-west of Great Blasket lies the small island of Inishtooskert, with the ruins of a little church, a well-preserved beehive hut, and three crosses (National Monuments).

Open (Blasket Centre) Easter–Sep. daily 10am–6 or 7pm.

Dun an Oir
From Dunquin the drive continues northwards. After about 2 miles a side road leads left past a beach and a hotel, beyond which turn left again and then first right to arrive at the site of an ancient castle, Dun an Oir (Fort of Gold), today marked only by a monument. Here in 1580, 600 Spanish and Irish soldiers, who had surrendered to the English, were massacred.

Reask
Returning to the main road proceed through Ballyferriter and on to Reask where, amid the remains of a hermitage, stands a notable Early Christian pillar cross decorated with tendril patterns.

★ Gallarus Oratory
The next call is at Gallarus Oratory (National Monument). Shaped like an upturned boat (*gallarus*, curious house), it has walls more than 3 ft thick and so carefully constructed that, even without the use of mortar, the little chapel (measuring only 15 by 10 ft) is still completely weatherproof after 1200 years.

From the chapel's slightly elevated site, the ruins of Gallarus Castle (16th c.; National Monument), a four-storey keep with vaulted rooms, can be seen ½ mile further west.

Kilmalkedar
At the crossroads above Gallarus turn sharp left for Kilmalkedar Church, one of the most important ecclesiastical sites on the peninsula, where a monastery (National Monument) was founded in the 7th c. It preserves a Romanesque church (12th c.) with fine sculpture in the tympanum of the doorway and on the chancel arch. The blind arcading of the interior shows, as indeed does the rest of the church, the influence of Cormac's Chapel at Cashel (➤ entry). In the church is the Alphabet Stone, with ogham and Latin characters side by side. In the churchyard stand an old sundial, a large monolithic cross and another ogham stone. 150 yd away is St Brendan's House (medieval) with, nearby, an oratory (St Brendan's Oratory).

Brandon Mountain
On Brandon Mountain are the remains of another St Brendan's Oratory and a number of stone huts (National Monuments). The ascent, best tackled from Cloghane or Faha, or alternatively from the west (clearly marked paths), is well worth the effort not only for its own sake but also for the magnificent views from the top.

Connor Pass
More superb views can be enjoyed on the exceptionally scenic road from Dingle over the Connor Pass.

Rough Point
With Beenoskee rising high to the right of the road, to the left a long

promontory extends northwards, reaching a good way out to sea. At its
landward end is Castlegregory, a quiet little resort situated between
Lough Gill and Tralee Bay. From here it is a further 4½ miles to Rough
Point at the tip of the promontory, off which lies a group of small islands.

Donegal · Dún na nGall   B 3

Republic of Ireland
Province: Ulster
County: Donegal
Population: 2200

Donegal (Dún na nGall, fortress of the foreigners), county town of Co.
Donegal, is situated well north on Ireland's west coast, at a point where
the River Eske flows into Donegal Bay and where the N56 meets up with
the N15.

Originally a Celtic settlement, the town owes its present aspect to the   Town
English who, early in the 17th c., laid it out on a regular plan around a
market square, appropriately called the Diamond, around which the life
of this busy little town revolves. The obelisk in the market square was
erected as a memorial to the Four Masters (see below, Donegal Abbey).

Sights

On the rocky bank of the River Eske only a short distance from the   Donegal Castle
market place stands the imposing ruin of Donegal Castle (National

Donegal Abbey

Monument), principal seat of the O'Donnells, princes of Tir Chonaill. Falling into English hands in 1607, the large square keep (1505) was altered by the insertion of windows. At the same time a splendid carved fireplace embellished with coats of arms was added to the main floor, and in 1610 a manor house (now in process of restoration) was built on to the tower.

Donegal Abbey

Picturesquely situated at the mouth of the River Eske are the remains of Donegal Abbey (National Monument), a 15th c. Franciscan monastery where the Four Masters, Michael O'Clery and his three assistants, compiled their celebrated annals (Annals of the Four Masters), a monumental work of Irish history. (Coming from Ballyshannon, take the side road branching left at the entrance to the town.)

Donegal Craft Village

Also well worth a visit is the Donegal Craft Village, a collection of arts and crafts workshops grouped around a courtyard on the outskirts of the town on the Ballyshannon road.

Surroundings

Lough Eske

5 miles north-east of the town lies Lough Eske, offering good fishing. A road runs round the lough, from the north end of which a detour can be made to a waterfall 2 miles further north, up a valley.

Blue Stack Mountains

The valley climbs higher into the Blue Stack Mountains and to a beautiful little tarn, Lough Belshade, in a corrie with steep sides.

Lough Derg

3 miles south of Donegal, the R232 branches left off the N15 to Pettigo, from where the R233 leads north through desolate countryside to Lough Derg. In the lough lies Station Island, known in the Middle Ages as St Patrick's Purgatory and the destination every year of large numbers of pilgrims (➤ p. 20). The churches and pilgrim hospices on the island can be seen from the shores of the lough. During the pilgrimage season (June to August), only pilgrims are allowed onto the island.

In pagan times a cave on Station Island was believed to be the entrance to the underworld; the island became known as St Patrick's Purgatory when a journeying medieval knight claimed to have seen the fires of purgatory in the cave.

The pilgrims who make what has been called 'the hardest pilgrimage in Christendom' are today almost exclusively Irish. They spend three days on the island performing the various penances prescribed – mainly vigils and fasting.

Rossnowlagh

12 miles south of Donegal at Rossnowlagh, a holiday resort on the Atlantic coast with a lovely sandy beach, is a modern Franciscan friary which also houses the Donegal Historical Society Museum. Its collection of Stone Age and Bronze Age material includes a finely wrought sword found in the course of building work in the neighbouring town of Ballyshannon. Open daily 9am–6.30pm.

Mountcharles

Mountcharles, a village on a steep hillside 4½ miles west of Donegal (N56), enjoys splendid views; there is good fishing in Eany Water.

Drogheda · Droichead Atha   C 5

Republic of Ireland
Province: Leinster
County: Louth
Population: 24,000

Drogheda (Droichead Átha, bridge over the ford) is situated on the north-east coast of Ireland on the River Boyne, at the point where it is crossed by the N1 and shortly before its outflow into the Irish Sea. With its port and various industries – cement works, steel works, breweries – it is a considerable economic centre.

In 911 Vikings captured the little town, standing on the site of an earlier settlement at a ford over the Boyne. They developed it into a well-defended stronghold. Later, Anglo-Normans built a bridge and fortified the settlements on both sides of the river. In the 14th and 15th c. Drogheda was one of the four principal towns of Ireland, with the right of minting coins and, from 1465, a university. Parliament met there several times up until the 17th c. In 1649 the town was taken by Cromwell's forces, and in 1690, following the Battle of the Boyne, it surrendered to William of Orange's army.

History

Sights

Drogheda had originally 10 gates of which only St Lawrence's Gate (13th c.; National Monument) survives. It has two massive crenellated round towers connected by a loopholed wall and a vaulted arch with barrel-vaulting at street level, all enclosing a low entrance passage.

St Lawrence's Gate

At the other end of St Lawrence's Street, on the left, is the old Tholsel (town hall), a domed building now occupied by a bank.

Tholsel

To the right, on the corner of St Peter's Street and William Street, stands the handsome St Peter's Church (1748 by Francis Johnston; Church of Ireland), the interior of which has fine rococo stucco work.

St Peter's Protestant Church

St Lawrence's Gate, Drogheda

St Peter's Catholic Church

The Roman Catholic St Peter's Church, on the right-hand side of West Street, the continuation of St Lawrence's Street, was erected as a memorial to Oliver Plunkett, Archbishop of Armagh, executed at Tyburn in London in 1681. His embalmed head is kept in a reliquary in the neo-Gothic church.

Millmount Fort

Millmount Fort (National Monument), on the south side of the river, beyond the bridge at the end of Shop Street, was built on top of a passage grave similar to the one at Newgrange in the Boyne Valley (➤ entry). Fortified in the 12th c. it continued in use as a fortification until 1800. Some of the rooms now house a museum documenting the town's history. A fine view of Drogheda is obtained from the fort.

Railway viaduct

Downstream, the river is spanned by the Boyne Viaduct, a splendid example of mid-19th c. railway engineering.

Surroundings

Baltray

4 miles north-east of Drogheda, at Baltray, there is a championship golf course; also good bathing from a sandy beach 3 miles long.

Termonfeckin

2 miles further north, Termonfeckin boasts a three-storey tower house (15th c.; National Monument) which has a fine spiral staircase and an unusual vaulted roof, the latter constructed in exactly the same fashion as the vault at Newgrange, over 4000 years older. Beside St Feckin's Church stands a richly decorated high cross (10th c.; National Monument) with, on the east side, a Crucifixion, on the west side Christ in Glory, and on the other two sides geometric designs and interlace patterns.

Clogherhead

2½ miles beyond Termonfeckin lies the village of Clogherhead and, on the north side of Clogher Head itself, the little harbour of Port Oriel, with lovely sandy beaches.

Dunleer

At Dunleer, 9 miles north-west of Clogherhead, is the Rathgory Transport Museum; fine collection of veteran and vintage cars. Open Sat., Sun. 2–6pm.

Maiden Tower

To the east of Drogheda, at Mornington, on the Boyne estuary, stands a lighthouse from the Elizabethan period, called the Maiden Tower (a reference to the Virgin Queen).

Bettystown Laytown

South-east of Drogheda, in Co. Meath, are the seaside resorts of Bettystown (18-hole golf course) and Laytown. Each have 6-mile-long beaches.

Gormanston

Further south, on the N1, Gormanston, a mansion of 1786, is now occupied by the Franciscans. The park on the east side is well laid out with walks and has a 'tea-house' of clipped yew hedges.

Fourknocks

Inland, between the R108 and R152, can be seen the important prehistoric site of Fourknocks (1800–1500 BC; National Monument), consisting of a large passage grave and two smaller burial mounds. The large grave has a number of inscribed stones, including one which depicts a face, drawn with a few simple strokes – the clearest representation of a human face surviving from Irish prehistory.

Duleek

5 miles south-west of Drogheda, on the River Nanny (good fishing), lies Duleek where, on land belonging to the priory (National Monument), are the ruins of a church and a high cross. The church contains a number of fine monuments and carvings of saints, a Crucifixion, angels and coats

of arms. The rather squat cross (probably 10th c.) has a Crucifixion, various figures, ornamentation and symbols of the Evangelists. The Dowdall Cross (1601; National Monument), standing by the roadside, shows Continental influence; it is decorated with figures of saints and a coat of arms.

3 miles south of Duleek stands Athcarne Castle, a fortified Elizabethan manor house (1587).

Athcarne Castle

At Tullyallen, 2½ miles north-west of Drogheda on the R168 (signposted to Collon), a side road leads left to Mellifont. Here, on the River Mattoch, are the ruins of Mellifont Abbey (National Monument), once an important Cistercian monastery, founded in 1142 and built with the help of monks from France. By 1272 it had become the mother house of 42 other monasteries. After the dissolution of the monasteries (1535) it was converted into a fortified manor house. Only a few remains of the original building have been preserved – to the north a castle-like gatehouse with a massive tower, the fine crypt of the church, part of the two-storey, octagonal well house, or lavabo, in the cloister (arches reconstructed) and the fine vaulted chapter house (14th c.) in which a variety of architectural fragments are now displayed. Part of the floor of the chapter house has been laid with glazed tiles from the church. Stumps of walls and marks on the ground show that the abbey was laid out in the manner of Clairvaux. Open May to mid-Jun., mid-Sep. to Oct. daily 10am–5pm; mid-Jun. to mid-Sep. daily 9.30am–6.30pm.

★Mellifont Abbey

Drumcliffe · Droim Chliabh   B 3

Republic of Ireland
Province: Connacht
County: Sligo

The village of Drumcliffe (Droim Chliabh, back of the baskets) lies on the deep bay of the same name in north-west Ireland, just to the north of Sligo. St Columba founded a monastery here in 574, the last abbot of which died in 1503.

Sights

The grandfather of W B Yeats (➤ Famous People) was for many years the parish priest here, and the great Irish poet is buried in the churchyard. His gravestone bears the inscription which he himself composed:

Yeats' Grave

Cast a cold eye
On life, on death.
Horseman, pass by!

On the path leading up to the church is a high cross (ca 1000; National Monument) with, on its east side, Adam and Eve, Cain and Abel, Daniel in the Lions' Den and Christ in Glory, and on the west side the Presentation in the Temple, two figures and the Crucifixion; the cross is further decorated with fabulous beasts and interlace ornament.

★High cross

Surroundings

To the north of the village, Benbulben (1697 ft), a flat-topped hill with steeply scarped sides furrowed by gullies, rises abruptly out of the plain. This extraordinary table mountain features prominently in Irish legend.

Benbulben

Drumcliffe · Droim Chliabh

Here Queen Maeve and the Ulster hero CuChulainn fought for possession of a herd of giant cattle, and here Diarmaid bled to death after his struggle with the great mountain boar of Benbulben. The slopes of the hill were also the scene of a historical event, the 'Battle of the Books' at Cuildrevne in 561, which led to St Columba's departure from Ireland. The hill, which forms part of the Dartry Mountains, is of interest to geologists and botanists. Those not deterred by the lack of a path will be rewarded by extensive views from the top over the surrounding low ground and westward to the Atlantic.

Glencar Lough

From Drumcliffe a delightful excursion can be made to Glencar Lough, a few miles east of the village. At the east end of the lough is a lovely waterfall in a setting of dense greenery.

Lissadell House

4 miles north-west of Drumcliffe, in a park, is Lissadell House, built in 1834 for the grandfather of the sisters Constance and Eva Gore-Booth. Constance (1884–1927), later Countess Markiewicz, afterwards became involved in nationalist politics in Dublin and took part in the 1916 Easter Rising. Her sister Eva was a writer. Yeats, who wrote a poem about Constance, stayed in the house on several occasions. Open Jun. to mid-Sep. Mon.–Sat. 10.30am–noon, 2–4.30pm.

Pigeon Holes

South-west of Lissadell a small peninsula reaches out into Drumcliffe Bay. On it, at the fishing village of Raghly, are the Pigeon Holes – two holes in the rock into which the sea is driven with tremendous force by way of subterranean channels. Also in this area are the picturesque ruins of Ardtermon Castle (17th c.).

Inishmurray

5 miles north of Drumcliffe, on the N15, lies Grange, from where a side road runs west to Streedagh. There a boat can be hired to cross to the island of Inishmurray (which can also be reached from Mullaghmore, see below). The island, 4½ miles west of Streedagh, was still inhabited in the last century. On it is an excellently preserved Early Christian monastic settlement (National Monument) founded by St Molaise in the early 6th c. and abandoned 300 years later after being raided and plundered. The monastery buildings were used by the island's later inhabitants and were thus preserved. The remains give an excellent impression of what such a settlement was like. A ring wall between 10 and 15 ft high and of similar thickness at the base, with five entrances, surrounds an oval precinct measuring 180 by 135 ft, divided into four enclosures of differing sizes. Within the precinct are the Men's Church, the little Oratory of Teach Molaise, the Church of the Fire, a beehive hut and altar-like structures of masonry. On one of these are the famous five Curse Stones, round speckled stones which are believed to be effective in putting a curse on an enemy. All round the island are various memorial stones and station chapels, which were visited by pilgrims in a prescribed sequence. From St Patrick's memorial, at the eastern tip of the island, there is a fine view of the mainland.

★Creevykeel

5 miles north of Grange, near the village of Cliffoney, is the Creevykeel Court Cairn (National Monument), one of the finest in Ireland. A wedge-shape stone wall encloses an open court, beyond which are a double-chambered gallery, two further chambers and the remains of yet another. The site is thought to be about 4500 years old.

Mullaghmore

From Cliffoney a minor road leads on to the Mullaghmore Peninsula, with a sheltered sandy beach, a small harbour and good sea angling. The hotel arranges trips to the island of Inishmurray (see above).

Dublin · Baile Atha Cliath/Dubhlinn   C 5

Republic of Ireland
Province: Leinster
County: Dublin
Population: 1.1 million (including suburbs)

Dublin (Baile Atha Cliath, town of the hurdle ford, or Dubhlinn, dark pool) lies in the broad sweep of Dublin Bay, between the rocky promontory of Howth to the north and the headland of Dalkey to the south.

Capital of the Irish Republic, Dublin is the undisputed economic and cultural centre of the country as well as its political centre. Almost a third of the population of the Republic live here.

Dublin is a city of startling social contrasts. Strolling through the fashionable residential districts on the south bank of the Liffey, or through the elegant shopping quarters, it seems almost inconceivable that large areas, especially north of the Liffey, should be so dreary and run down (but not so surprising, perhaps, given that the unemployment rate exceeds 20 per cent). The proportion of young people on drugs is relatively high, and beggars are a not uncommon sight on Dublin's streets. Despite this, most Dubliners and most visitors to the city are bewitched by Dublin's charm; it is a warm-hearted place yet one where individuality is almost a passion.

The oldest Irish name for the city, and the one still generally used, Baile Atha Cliath, refers to the ancient ford across the Liffey at this point. St Patrick is believed to have visited Dublin in 448 and converted many of the inhabitants. Subsequently a Christian community grew up around the ford; then in 840 the first Danes appeared, occupying the town and establishing a fortified base from which to conduct both raids and trade. In 988 the Irish king Mael Sechnaill II captured the town, and in 1014 the high king of Ireland, Brian Boru, broke the power of the Danes by his victory at nearby Clontarf (now a suburb of the city). It was not until 1170, however, that the Danes were finally driven out by the Anglo-Normans. Two years later Henry II came to Dublin to receive the homage of the Irish chieftains. The town now became the capital of the area over which the English held sway, known as the Pale (from palisade), the security of which relied upon the Anglo-Norman castles. During the conflicts of the 15th and 16th c., the Dubliners generally aligned themselves with forces opposed to the English Crown. But in the 17th c. they sided with the Royalists against Cromwell (who captured the town in 1649) and later with James II against William of Orange.

In the 18th c. Dublin prospered and the population rose from 65,000 to 200,000. A Wide Street Commission and Paving Board were set up and there was a great boom in building both by the public authorities and the more affluent among Dublin's citizenry.

At the beginning of the 19th c. a brief interlude of independence was brought to an end by political union with Great Britain. There followed a period of repression and resistance: in 1844 the lord mayor of Dublin, Daniel O'Connell, was imprisoned for 'incitement to discontent', and a few years later the leaders of the Land League movement, among them Charles Stewart Parnell (► Famous People), were thrown into Kilmainham Gaol. Political assassinations took place, carried out by a secret society, and separatist agitation grew.

In 1916 the Easter Rising occurred in Dublin and the General Post Office and other public buildings were occupied by the rebels. In 1919, on the initiative of Sinn Fein (we ourselves), an independent parliament met in the Mansion House, presided over by Eamon de Valera. On May

Christ Church Cathedral, Dublin ►

25th 1921, during the civil war, the Custom House was set on fire. In spite of the ratification of the treaty of January 1922 establishing the Irish Free State, domestic conflict persisted in Dublin until 1927. It was not until 1931 that most of the public buildings were finally restored. Throughout the second world war the Irish Republic remained neutral, though in 1940 a number of German bombs were dropped on Dublin as the result of an error.

In the decades immediately following the second world war, Dublin was largely allowed to stagnate. Only in very recent times has a programme of regeneration been put in place, with entire districts of the city earmarked for redevelopment, a process that is still continuing (the most recent example being Temple Bar). Tax and other incentives are used to encourage people back into the centre, and a lavish public relations exercise has been launched in an attempt to improve the city's image – 1988 was chosen (somewhat arbitrarily, it has to be said) for celebration of the thousandth anniversary of Dublin's foundation, and in 1991 Dublin was named European City of Culture.

The River Liffey splits the city into a northern and a southern half before reaching its outflow into the harbour. Much of the inner city lies on the right bank, bounded to the south by a number of fine parks, with a smaller but nevertheless significant nucleus on the north bank. The two are linked by several bridges, of which the most important is O'Connell Bridge. Further upstream, the Father Matthew Bridge crosses the Liffey at the same point as the original ford. | ★City

As well as the domes and neoclassical façades of its numerous 18th and early 19th c. public buildings, fitting tribute to the skill of men such as Sir Edward Lovett Pearce, Richard Cassels, Thomas Cooley, James Gandon and Francis Johnston, the architectural face of Dublin owes much to the numerous private houses of the same period, their plain but elegant style bestowing a pleasing unity on street after street. Unfortunately many have already disappeared, demolished in a wave of uncontrolled property speculation to make way for offices. This destruction has largely been halted in recent years, not least as a result of opposition by citizens' action groups.

A number of tourist trails are signposted in the city centre (brochure available from tourist offices). Street names in Dublin are in English and Irish. In many older streets the houses are still numbered consecutively, up one side and down the other. Note also that the appellation 'Place' or 'Square' is not confined to squares as such but may refer to a street. | Tourist trails

Although, apart from the two cathedrals, few Dublin buildings are older than the 18th c., the city's handsome Georgian streets and squares, its public buildings, museums and libraries, offer a wealth of interesting sights. They can best be appreciated by following a number of separate walks. | City walks

City centre – south-east

O'Connell Bridge, which spans the Liffey (here 138 ft wide) in the centre of the city, makes a good starting point for a sightseeing walk. Built in 1792–4, it was widened in 1880. It is one of 10 bridges crossing the river in the inner-city area. | O'Connell Bridge

From the south end of Connell Bridge, Westmoreland Street leads south to College Green and the substantial building of the Bank of Ireland. Originally designed (1729; by Sir Edward Lovett Pearce) to house the Irish parliament, in 1802, following the Act of Union, it was sold to the | ★Bank of Ireland

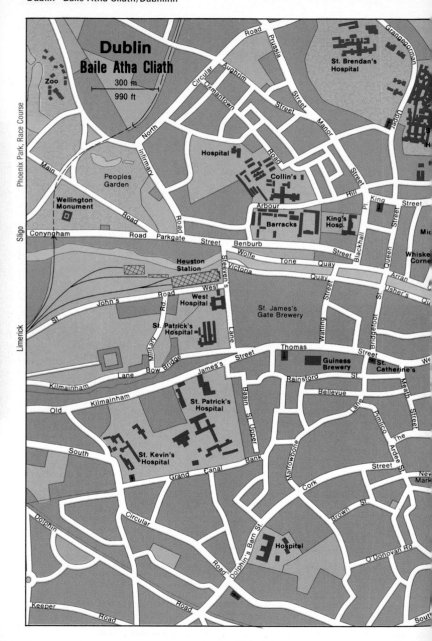

anic Gardens

Belfast
Airport
Belfast

Mountjoy
Square

Art
Gallery

Nat. Wax
Museum

Writer's
Museum

Rotunda
Hospital

King's
Inns

Theatre

Dept. of
Education

St. Mary's
Pro-Cathedral

Conno
Station

Inner Dock

Bus
Station

George's
Dock

Mary
St. Mary's

Custom
House

Abbey
Theatre

Custom
House

Quay

Abbey

O'Connell
Bridge

Eden

River

Liffey →

Four
Courts

Burgh

Quay

City
Quay

Ormond
Gratton
Br.

Aston

Station

Hanover

Quay

D'Olier St.

Townsend

Street

TEMPLE BAR

Bank of
Ireland

Pearse

en's
Dublinia

Christ
Church
Cathedral

Dame Street

City Hall

College
Green

Pearse
Station

The Castle

Trinity
College

St.
Andrew

Powerscourt
House

Nassau

Street

Civic
Museum

St.
Ann's

National
Library

National
Gallery

Theatre

National
Museum

N. H.
Mus.

King St.

St.
Patrick's
Cathedral

Stephen's
Green Shopping
Centre

Mansion
House

Leinster
House

Merrion
Square

College

Marsh's
Library

Library

St. Stephen's
Green

Number
Twenty
Nine

Newman
House

Fitzwilliam
Square

University
College

Shaw
House

Adelaide

Road

Wilton

Terrace

© Baedeker

Dun Laoghaire

Jewish Museum

Cork, Waterford, Wexford

159

Bank of Ireland

bank. The elegant curved façade with its classical orders and sculptural groups – the result of alterations carried out at different times – ranks as one of Dublin's finest.

The imposing banking hall, converted from the old Commons' Chamber, can be seen during banking hours. Groups of visitors may also

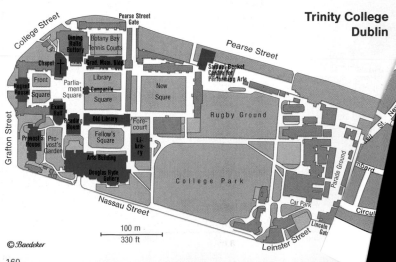

Trinity College Dublin

College Street

Pearse Street Gate

Pearse Street

Dining Halls Buttery

Botany Bay Tennis Courts

Chapel

Grad. Mem. Bldg.

Samuel Beckett Centre for Performing Arts

Regent House

Front Square

Parliament Square

Library

Campanile

New Squre

Exam Hall

Reading Room

Old Library

Rugby Ground

Fellow's Square

Forecourt

Provost's House

Provost's Garden

Library

Arts Building

Grafton Street

Douglas Hyde Gallery

College Park

Car Park

Nassau Street

Parade Ground

Lincoln Gate

100 m
330 ft

Leinster Street

© Baedeker

160

make arrangements to view the former Lords' Chamber, which has a coffered ceiling and fine chandelier.

Situated opposite the Bank of Ireland is the main entrance to Trinity College, in spacious park-like grounds which are open to the public. ★Trinity College

Until 1793 membership of the university, founded by Elizabeth I in 1592 (1591 is often cited, the date of foundation, March 3rd 1591, becoming March 13th 1592 on adoption of the Gregorian calendar in 1751), was confined to Protestants. Even after that Roman Catholics were still excluded from holding fellowships and scholarships until 1873. In 1903 women were admitted to take degrees for the first time. Alumni of Trinity College have included Samuel Beckett, Edmund Burke, Robert Emmet, Oliver Goldsmith, Jonathan Swift, J M Synge and Oscar Wilde (► Famous people). It now has about 6000 students.

Until well into the 17th c. the university was housed in makeshift wooden buildings. The oldest-surviving range, the red-brick 'Rubrics', now in use as student accommodation, were erected in 1690. In front of the college's 300-ft main façade stand statues of Oliver Goldsmith and Edmund Burke by Henry Foley (1863 and 1865 respectively).

After the noisy traffic of College Green the entrance court of Trinity College is a haven of peace. To the left is the Chapel (open, since 1973, to any Christian denomination having a chaplain to the university), and on the right the Examinations Hall (1779–91; originally a theatre), both designed by Sir William Chambers. Beyond the Chapel is the Dining Hall (1743 by Richard Cassels), hung with portraits of notable members of the university. Ahead, in the centre of Library Square, can be seen the Campanile (1853) with, nearby, a sculpture by Henry Moore.

For tourists the most interesting building on the campus is the ★★**Old Library** (1712–32). As a copyright library (since 1801) it is entitled to

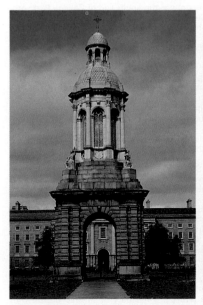

Trinity College: Campanile

National Gallery

receive, as of right, a copy of every book published in Ireland and Great Britain. It now has a collection of some 5000 manuscripts and 2 million printed books. Among its treasures are manuscripts, incunabula and early printed books, the most famous of which, the 8th c. Book of Kells, is displayed on the ground floor in the so-called Colonnades. This superbly illuminated manuscript of the four Gospels consists of 680 richly decorated pages, one of which is open to view each day. The illumination on the opening page of each Gospel and of each individual chapter is particularly elaborate (➤ Baedeker Special, p. 58). Other especially valuable treasures include The Book of Durrow (7th c.), the Book of Dimma (8th c.) and the Book of Armagh (9th c.).

From the ground floor a handsome staircase by Cassels leads up to the Long Room, 200 ft in length, with a timber barrel-vaulted roof. As well as marble busts of famous members of the university, it contains an Irish harp, one of the oldest instruments of its kind.

Open Mon.–Sat. 9.30am–5.30pm, Sun. noon–5pm.

Accommodated in the Arts Building on the campus is a special tourist attraction called the **Dublin Experience**, a multi-media presentation on the history of the city. Showings May–Sep. daily 10am–5pm, starting on the hour.

In the same building is the **Douglas Hyde Gallery** which mounts periodic exhibitions of Irish contemporary art.

On the north side of the campus stands the **Samuel Beckett Centre for Performing Arts**, chiefly used by drama students.

St Andrew's Church	East of Trinity College, in Westland Row, is St Andrew's Church, a handsome neoclassical building (1832–7).
National Library	Leaving the campus via the gate at the south end of College Park, proceed south down Kildare Street where a gateway on the left gives access to an important group of buildings. The National Library (1890), to the left of the entrance, has collections of early printed books (notably 17th c. Irish literature), old maps and topographical works, as well as a newspaper archive.
★★National Museum	To the right of the entrance stands the National Museum housing a rich collection of Irish artefacts from prehistoric times to the end of the Middle Ages.

The entrance rotunda (bookshop; special exhibitions) leads into the Great Hall with a display of Irish gold work. Items of especial value are displayed in the Treasury and include in particular: 11th and 12th c. crosiers; the Ardagh Chalice (early 8th c.), silver with gilt ornament, gold filigree handles; among the processional crosses, the Cross of Cong (1123), of oak with silver and gilt bronze animal ornament; among a number of shrines, that of St Patrick's Bell (12th c.), decorated with silver gilt, gold filigree and ornamental stones; and various reliquaries, among them the Breac Maod Hóg reliquary (11th c.) with a depiction of the dress of the period.

Also in the Great Hall is an exhibition under the title 'Dublin 1000', with finds from the Viking period uncovered during excavation of a building site on Wood Quay (since filled in and over-built with office blocks). Elsewhere on the ground floor is a room devoted to 'The Road to Independence', an exhibition and video presentation illustrating Irish history between 1900 and 1921. In the gallery of the Great Hall are exhibits spanning a period of more than 7000 years (ca 6000 BC to AD 1800), among which two in particular stand out: the Tara Brooch (early 8th c.), of gilded bronze inlaid with silver, copper and enamelwork; and the Moylough Belt Shrine (8th c.), a reliquary of silvered bronze with enamel ornament, designed to be attached to a belt. Other rooms on the

upper floor contain metalwork, glass and ceramics, porcelain and textiles. The cabinets of Irish silver and the collection of musical instruments are of special note.
Open Tue.–Sat. 10am–5pm, Sun. 2–5pm.

To the rear of the Library and Museum, set back from the street (entrance in Merrion Street), stands Leinster House, home of the Republic of Ireland Parliament and seat of the Dáil Éireann (House of Representatives) and Seanad Éireann (Senate). This sober and dignified building (1745 by Richard Cassels) was originally the town house of the dukes of Leinster. Guided tours can be provided when there are no sittings (Sat. 10.30–12.45pm, 1.30–4.45pm).

Leinster House

Adjoining Leinster House to the north is the Natural History Museum, which has a large collection displaying the fauna of Ireland (including skeletons of prehistoric animals). It also houses the Blashka Collection (glass models of marine creatures). Open Tue.–Sat. 10am–5pm, Sun. 2–5pm.

Natural History Museum

Also with its entrance on Merrion Street is the National Gallery. First opened in 1864, it has since been extended, most recently in 1968.

★National Gallery

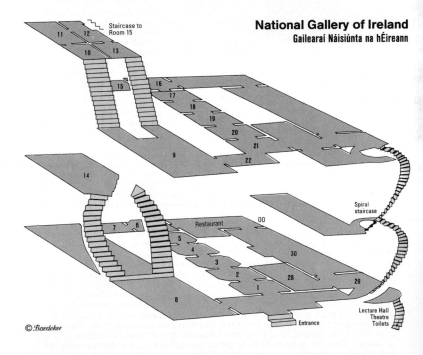

National Gallery of Ireland
Gailearaí Náisiúnta na hÉireann

1–5 Irish and British schools
6 Jack B. Yeats
7 Bookstall
8 Shaw Room (Portraits)
9–13 Italian school
14 Temporary exhibitions
15 German and Flemish schools
16 British school
18 Rembrandt and his circle
19 French school
20–21 Spanish school
22 Vestibule
28 In process of rearrangement
30 French school

© Baedeker

163

Ulysses – a literary Baedeker

Bronze plaque in the road surface

June 16th is a kind of holiday in Dublin – it is 'Bloomsday'. Hundreds of people, alone or in small groups, can be seen walking through the city centre. They pause in front of many a crossing and building and search thoughtfully in their books as they look around them. The 800-page tome they are referring to is a travel guide. Not the usual kind of travel guide – this one is a novel! A literary masterpiece of the 20th c. It is the novel *Ulysses* by the Irish author James Joyce (1882–1941), one of the most important writers of the last century. *Ulysses* describes the events of a particular day – June 16th 1904, from eight in the morning to about three the next morning – in the lives of three of Dublin's inhabitants, the advertising agent Leopold Bloom, his wife Molly and the teacher and writer Stephen Dedalus. In his novel (first edition Paris 1922; it did not appear in the UK and the US until 1933 and 1936 respectively owing to its 'treatment of sexual matters in the everyday language of the lower classes'), Joyce describes in so much detail the route taken that day through the Irish capital by Bloom and Dedalus that it can still be followed today. *Ulysses* is, if you like, 'a literary Baedeker' (Frank Delaney). While writing his major work Joyce remarked to a friend: 'I want to paint such a complete picture of Dublin that if this town were to disappear in an earthquake it could be rebuilt according to this book.'

Since June 16th 1954, when four Dubliners first celebrated this day upon which Leopold Bloom walked around Dublin, 'Bloomsday' has become a hit with visitors. Joyce's followers focus mainly on the eighth chapter of the novel; it begins in Middle Abbey Street and ends in Kildare Street. Bronze plaques set into the pavement mark the route and refer to the corresponding page numbers of the English standard edition. (Further information can be found on the *Ulysses Map of Dublin*, published by the tourist board.)

Ulysses consists of 18 episodes. The first three centre around the writer and teacher Stephen Dedalus: he has breakfast with friends in the Martello tower (➤ p. 188) in Dublin Bay, then teaches in the school, where he has a talk with the headmaster, and goes for a walk along the beach alone, deep in conversation with himself. Leopold Bloom, a modern Everyman, advertising agent by profession, first appears in the fourth episode. First breakfast with his wife Molly, followed by his daily odyssey through Dublin: the post office, a church service, the public baths, the cemetery (to a funeral), the newpaper offices, a pub, a restaurant and the library. In the library Bloom and Dedalus catch a brief glimpse of each other. Then the Ormond restaurant, Barney Kiernan's pub, the Dublin Strand. In the women's hospital Bloom visits a relative who is in labour. Then he goes to Bella Cohen's brothel with some companions. He and Dedalus leave the brothel together, slowly developing a liking for each other. They stop off in a coaching inn before going to Bloom's flat at 7 Eccles Street. When Dedalus goes home, Bloom lies down to sleep beside Molly. The 18 episodes have their parallel in the 24 verses of Homer's *Odyssey*: Bloom wandering the streets of Dublin compares with Odysseus' travels around the Greek islands.

Traditional narrative techniques are brilliantly laid open to question in this novel. It is an epic, a chronicle, a drama, a report, an essay and a character novel rolled into one. The action in its traditional sense is the backcloth. *Ulysses* is one of the first novels to be influenced by Freud's deep psychological observations. The 20 or so hours from the everyday life of these three Dubliners – their actions, encounters with other Dubliners, their thoughts, wishes and dreams – are not so much descriptions as reflections (streams of consciousness). The chief formal devices include inner monologues, chains of association, changing narrative perspective, interrupted chronology and occasional ungrammatical syntax; all of which do not make the novel easy to read. With this new form of linguistic expression, in particular the stream of consciousness style of narrative technique which he developed, James Joyce had a decisive influence on the 20th c. novel.

In past decades Dublin, which has been untouched by wars and natural catastrophes, has none the less undergone radical topographical changes. Many streets and alleys have lost their original form, houses have been demolished or are ready for demolition. Only the larger streets have survived but not as Joyce described them. Even Leopold Bloom's house, 7 Eccles Street, one of the most famous streets in English literature, no longer exists. Other properties have been completely altered. In this regard *Ulysses* dramatically highlights the changes that have taken place in the city during the 20th c.

As with so many other settings in the novel, the pubs have disappeared too: Barney Kiernan's, where the 'cyclops banquet' takes place, Burke's, where the pair get drunk before going on to the brothel, and the coaching inn of the Eumaeus episode, which Bloom and Dedalus visit after the brothel. But a hint of the Dublin of James Joyce is still there: in the dark alleys by the quay; in the streets which lead down to the river; behind Trinity College; in the houses with the canopies in Grafton Street; and in the National Library.

The site where the first chapter of the novel, 'Telemachus', begins – Martello Tower in Sandycove (a suburb of Dun Laoghaire) – has been preserved. Joyce himself once lived in this tower; today it is the Joyce Museum. A visit to Glasnevin cemetery ('Hades') is interesting – Joyce's parents are buried here, as are the Irish heroes Daniel O'Connell and Charles Stewart Parnell. In Duke Street the Bailey, which used to be frequented by Bloom, is one of the smartest pubs in Dublin today; to Joyce fans it is the 'Burton' of the 'Laestrigonian episode'. For fear of court proceedings because of the unappetising scenes of gluttony, Joyce did not use the pub's real name. In the hallway of the Bailey is the original door of 7 Eccles Street. The house itself had to give way to new building a few years ago. Opposite the Bailey is the pub Davy Byrne's where Bloom, hungry but sickened by Bailey's, comes for a gorgonzola sandwich. This snack is only available on the menu on Bloomsday. A small cheap souvenir of the official or personal Bloomsday can be purchased at the late 19th c. chemist's Sweny (Lincoln Place). Here Joyce fans, like Leopold Bloom on June 16th 1904, always come to buy a piece of lemon soap.

National Gallery: Apple Gathering *(Osborne) and* A Connemara Girl *(Burke)*

There are several rooms devoted to representative works by Irish painters including George Barrett, James Barry, Burke, Francis Danby, Nathaniel Hone the Elder, Nathaniel Hone the Younger, Robert Hunter, James Latham, James Arthur O'Connor, Walter Osborne, Thomas Roberts, Patrick Tuohy, Jack Butler Yeats (brother of the poet W B Yeats) and John Butler Yeats (the poet's father). In addition there is a broad collection of works by non-Irish artists: American (John Singer Sargent, Gilbert Stuart, Benjamin West, James McNeill Whistler); English (John Constable, Thomas Gainsborough, William Hogarth, Thomas Lawrence, William Turner); Flemish (Gerard David, Anthony van–Dyke, Jacob Jordaens, Peter-Paul Rubens, Jan van Scorel, David Teniers the Younger); French (Camille Corot, Edgar Degas, Eugène Delacroix, Claude Monet, Alfred Sisley); Italian (Fra Angelico, Giovanni Bellini, Michelangelo, Tintoretto, Titian, Paolo Veronese); and Dutch (Peter Claesz, Jan van Goyen, Pieter de Hooch, Jan Steen, Rembrandt van Rijn, Salomon and Jacob van Ruisdael, Emanuel de Witte). While the collection of Spanish paintings is relatively small, it includes works by such major artists as Francisco de Goya, El Greco, Bartolomé Esteban Murillo and Francisco de Zurbarán. German painting is represented by Lucas Cranach the Elder and Wolf Huber.

Today, the large number of portraits belonging to the National Gallery (of, among others, Brendan Behan, Sir Roger Casement, Eamon de Valera and James Joyce) are mostly on display in Malahide Castle (➤ p. 183). However a few can be seen in the Gallery's Shaw Room, so named in honour of George Bernard Shaw (1856–1950) who bequeathed a third of his estate to the gallery in recognition of its contribution to his own early development. The gallery also possesses a collection of 31 watercolours by Turner which, under the terms of the bequest, can only be put on public display during the month of January, to protect them from overexposure to light. At other times of the year they can be seen by arrangement.

Distributed throughout the rooms are sculptures from the 16th c. to the present day, among them works by Auguste Rodin and Aristide Maillol.

On the ground floor are a bookstall and restaurant, and in the basement a library and lecture theatre.

Open Mon.–Sat. 10am–5.30pm, Thu. to 8.30pm, Sun. 2–5pm.

To the south-west of the National Gallery lies Merrion Square, surrounded on three sides by handsome Georgian houses. Previous residents have included Oscar Wilde's parents, and Daniel O'Connell and W B Yeats. On the west side of the square is the Rutland Fountain (1791). **★Merrion Square**

No. 29, one of the fine Georgian houses in Lower Fitzwilliam Street, at the south-east corner of Merrion Square, has been turned into a museum. The house is furnished exactly as it was at the end of the 18th c. when Olive Beatty, a widow, moved in with her three children. Open Tue.–Sat. 10am–5pm, Sun. 2–5pm. **No. 29**

Fitzwilliam Street runs south to Fitzwilliam Square (ca 1825), the best-preserved Georgian square in Dublin with the additional attraction of a view of the Wicklow Mountains in the distance to the south-west. **Fitzwilliam Square**

Return northwards up Pembroke Street and left into Baggot Street, then turn left again into Ely Place, a cul-de-sac of elegant Georgian houses of about 1770. The finest is Ely House (No. 8), with a handsome staircase and fine stucco ceilings; it is now the headquarters of a charity, the Knights of St Columbanus. **Ely Place**

Opposite Ely House, Hume Street leads into the east side of St Stephen's Green, a 20-acre park laid out in 1880 at Sir Arthur Guinness's expense. **St Stephen's Green**

St Stephen's Green Shopping Centre: exterior and interior

It has flower beds, ponds and a variety of monuments, including a fountain (*The Three Fates*) by Joseph Wackerle, a gift from the German people in gratitude for Irish help in relieving distress following the second world war. The park is a popular place of recreation; in July and August there are concerts of Irish music.

Concealed behind a highly ornate Victorian façade is the modern St Stephen's Green Shopping Centre, opened in 1989. On the west side of the park can be seen the Royal College of Surgeons (1806), and on the south side the Department of Foreign Affairs (No. 80), formerly the residence of Lord Iveagh, with a large garden. Also on the south side is the neo-Byzantine University Church (1854).

Newman House
: Another pair of buildings on the south side of St Stephen's Green (Nos. 85 and 86) are known as Newman House. They are owned by University College and have recently been thoroughly restored. These houses are especially renowned for their stucco work. No. 85 was built in 1738 for Captain Hugh Montgomery; No. 86 was designed by Robert West in 1765. The buildings commemorate John Henry Newman, the first rector of the Catholic University, precursor of Dublin's University College. Open Jun.–Sep. Tue.–Fri. 10am–4.30pm, Sat. 2–4.30pm, Sun. 11am–4.30pm.

University College
: A short distance south of St Stephen's Green are the former buildings of University College itself. This, like the colleges at Cork and Galway, is part of the National University of Ireland, an institution which makes a speciality of the study and preservation of the Irish language. Following rapid expansion in the mid-1960s the college moved to a spacious new campus at Belfield, 3 miles south-east on the N11, now with some interesting modern buildings. Only the Faculties of Medicine and Architecture remain in the original buildings here in Earlsfort Terrace.

Shaw House
: From Earlsfort Terrace a detour can be made to Synge Street, two or three blocks further south-west. No. 33 Synge Street was the birthplace in 1856 of George Bernard Shaw. Following extensive restoration the house once again appears at it would have done in the latter half of the 19th c. when it was the home of the Shaw family. Open May–Sep. Mon.–Sat. 10am–5pm, Sun. 2–6pm.

Jewish Museum
: In 1990 a small Jewish museum was opened in conjunction with a newly restored synagogue, in Walworth Road, at the south end of Synge Street. Open May–Sep. Tue., Thu., Sun. 11am–3.30pm; Oct.–Apr. Sun. 10.30am–2.30pm.

Mansion House
Royal Irish Academy
: In Dawson Street, to the north of St Stephen's Green, is the Mansion House (1705), official residence, since 1715, of Dublin's lord mayor (with the Round Room, 1821, by John Semple); also the Royal Irish Academy, the library of which contains a priceless collection of manuscripts of the 6th to the 17th c., including the Cathach, a psalter written by St Columba. Visitors normally only see facsimiles; the originals can be viewed by special arrangement. Open Mon.–Fri. 9.30am–5.30pm; closed during the second half of August.

St Ann's Church
: Also in Dawson Street stands St Ann's Church (1720 by Isaac Wills), with a mid-19th c. neo-Romanesque façade and good woodwork in the interior.

Grafton Street
: From Dawson Street, St Ann's Street runs west to Grafton Street, one of the city's principal shopping thoroughfares (pedestrianised). Not to be missed is a visit to Browne & Thomas, a superior traditional department store. A respite from shopping can be enjoyed at **Bewley's Oriental Café** (78 Grafton Street), a favourite rendezvous for Dubliners. With its dark wooden furniture, marble-topped tables and striking windows by Irish

artist Harry Clarke, it preserves an authentic coffee-house atmosphere. The part of the café known as 'Bewley's Museum' is usually somewhat less noisy than the ground floor.

An alleyway near Bewley's Café leads to Powerscourt House, an imposing mansion (1771–4) built by Robert Mack for viscount Powerscourt, now converted into an elegant department store and offices (Powerscourt Town House Centre; ➤ picture, p. 310). Around the attractive covered courtyard are cafés, upmarket shops and galleries. Note the fine stucco work adorning the staircase, hall and individual shops.

★Powerscourt House

A few doors along is the Civic Museum, in a building of 1765–71 originally occupied by the Society of Artists. Among the numerous exhibits on display are old street plans and models of Dublin. Open Tue.–Sat. 10am–6pm, Sun. 11am–2pm.

Civic Museum

Inner city – south-west

A short distance west from O'Connell Bridge lies the district known as Temple Bar, between the south bank of the Liffey and Dame Street. Originally earmarked for redevelopment as the site of a new central bus station, this Old City area with its Georgian houses and cobbled streets, once populated by craftsmen, tradespeople, artists and writers, was thankfully reprieved and the decision taken to renovate it while preserving its historic character. Many of the houses in its narrow lanes and alleyways (some of which are now pedestrianised) have already been restored. Others have been converted into small shops, studios, pubs and restaurants. Street art thrives and Temple Bar is gradually rediscovering itself as an artists' quarter.

Temple Bar

Of iron construction, the elegant Halfpenny Bridge spanning the Liffey to

Halfpenny Bridge

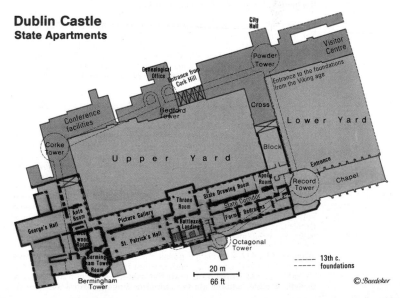

Dublin Castle
State Apartments

City Hall

Visitor Centre

Powder Tower

Genealogical Office

Entrance from Cork Hill

Entrance to the foundations from the Viking age

Bedford Tower

Cross

Conference facilities

Corke Tower

Lower Yard

Block

Upper Yard

Entrance

Record Tower

Chapel

Apollo Room

Throne Room

State Drawing Room

State Corridor

Ante Room

Picture Gallery

Battleaxe Landing

(Former) Bedrooms

George's Hall

Wedgewood Room

St. Patrick's Hall

Octagonal Tower

Bermingham Tower Room

Bermingham Tower

20 m
66 ft

----- 13th c.
----- foundations

© Baedeker

Dublin Castle: Throne Room

the north of Temple Bar was built in 1816 and paid for by tolls – hence the name (officially it is called Liffey Bridge).

City Hall

The City Hall stands in Dame Street at the south-west corner of Temple Bar. Formerly the Royal Exchange (1769–79 by Thomas Cooley), the imposing domed building is now the headquarters of Dublin Corporation. The entrance hall is adorned with statues of local notables. Among documents in the archives are several royal charters, the earliest of which, dated 1172, grants the territory of Dublin to the city of Bristol.

★Dublin Castle

Beyond the City Hall stands Dublin Castle, the main entrance of which is on Cork Hill. The hill now occupied by the Upper Yard was probably the site of a Celtic and later a Danish fort (foundations dating from the Viking and Anglo-Norman periods have been preserved). In 1204 King John began the construction of a castle (completed in 1226) of which little survives, and then much altered, in the present building, the greater part of which dates from the 18th and 19th c. From the reign of Elizabeth I to the establishment of the Irish Free State in 1921, Dublin Castle was the official residence of the viceroy and seat of British administration.

At the east end of the Upper Yard a passage leads through into the Lower Yard. To the right is the Record Tower, one of the four old corner towers, well preserved with almost 16 ft thick walls, which gives some impression of what the medieval castle must have been like. The neo-Gothic Chapel (1807–14) is notable for its unusual external decoration of over a hundred limestone heads of famous Irishmen.

When not in use for official purposes, the **State Apartments** are shown to visitors in the course of a conducted tour lasting about half an hour (entrance across Upper Yard from the castle's main entrance in Cork Street). Notable features are the colourful Donegal and Killybegs carpets, the chandeliers of Waterford glass and the pavement of green Connemara marble in the entrance hall. The conducted tour takes in the following rooms: St Patrick's Hall, with a painted ceiling (1778) and the banners of the Knights of St Patrick; the blue Wedgwood Room with pictures by Angelica Kauffmann (1740–1807); the picture gallery with portraits of viceroys; the Throne Room, richly decorated in gold (1740), with an 18th c. throne; the long State Drawing Room with its original furniture; and the Apollo Room or Music Room, with a ceiling of 1746. After viewing the State Apartments visitors are shown the remains of the medieval fortifications (entrance by the Powder Tower). Open Mon.–Fri. 10am–12.15pm, 2–5pm, Sat., Sun. 2–5pm.

From the castle a narrow street, Castle Street, runs west. By Nos. 7 and 8 is the entrance to the little St Werburgh's Church (1759), with a beautiful interior which can be seen by appointment (tel. (01) 720673).

St Werburgh's Church

Castle Street leads into Christchurch Place, in which stands one of Dublin's two principal churches, Christ Church Cathedral (➤ picture, p. 156), the cathedral of the Anglican dioceses of Dublin and Glendalough. In its present form it is the result of a major reconstruction in 1871–8; of the original 13th c. church there remain the crypt, which extends under the whole length of the nave, a doorway in the south transept and perhaps parts of the transepts. Enough remains, however, including some sculpture, to give an impression of the magnificence of the old church. The crypt contains numerous architectural fragments of different periods and 17th c. statues of Charles II and James II. In the nave is a fine recumbent tomb effigy of a knight, identified as Richard Strongbow, earl of Pembroke, with, to the side, a small half-length figure incorrectly described as 'Strongbow's Son'. Other monuments in the choir include the tomb of a 13th c. bishop. Open daily 10am–6.30pm.

Christ Church Cathedral

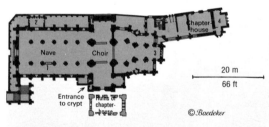

Christ Church Cathedral

20 m
66 ft

1 Tomb of Strongbow
2 Baptistery
3 Lady Chapel
4 Library

© Baedeker

The former Synod Hall, linked to the cathedral by a bridge, now houses a multi-media presentation called 'Dublinia'. Here the history of Dublin is portrayed, from the coming of the Anglo-Normans (1170) up to the dissolution of the monasteries (1535). About an hour should be allowed for viewing the exhibition, which by means of displays, an informative video presentation and numerous exhibits including a scale model of the city, tools and art work, illustrates this phase of Dublin's history. Open May–Oct. Mon.–Sat. 9am–5pm, Sun. 10am–4pm.

Dublinia

Christ Church Cathedral continued to exercise a leading role through the vicissitudes of Irish history down the centuries. This was despite the fact that, in the 13th c., another church, only ¼ mile away to the south, was also elevated to cathedral status, which status it has retained, in defiance of all subsequent changes, to this day. St Patrick' Cathedral, 305 ft long, is the largest church in Ireland, and like Christ Church, Anglican by denomination. Open Mon.–Fri. 8.30am–6.15pm, Sat. to 5pm, Sun. to 4.30pm.
  At the time of its foundation in the 11th c., the church stood on a marshy site outside the town walls. Like Christ Church Cathedral, it too

★St Patrick's Cathedral

has suffered from overrestoration (1864–9). The massive tower at the north-west corner dates from the end of the 14th c., the steeple from 1739.

The church is entered from the south side. The tall interior in severe early Gothic style creates an impressive effect. It contains numerous monuments and tombs. At the second pier to the right of the entrance are the tombs of Jonathan Swift (1667–1745) and his 'Stella' (Esther Johnson, 1681–1728) with bronze tablets. To the left of the nearby door is a bust of Swift, with an epitaph which he himself composed: 'He lies where furious indignation can no longer rend his heart.' Swift was Dean of St Patrick's for 35 years.

Other notable monuments include: to the right of the baptismal chapel (old font) the Boyle Monument (1631) commemorating the earl of Cork, with a number of coloured figures, including a child who is believed to be Richard Boyle – in adulthood the celebrated physicist; on the north wall, opposite the entrance, the monument of Turlough O'Carolan (1670–1738), last of the Irish bards; on the north wall of the choir, a marble effigy of Archbishop Fulk de Saundfort (d 1271); on the south wall of the Lady Chapel an effigy of Archbishop Tregury (d 1471); on the south wall of the choir, four brasses, the finest of which are those of Dean Sutton (d 1528) and Dean Fyche (d 1539); and at the south-west corner of the south transept, the typical 18th c. monument of Lady Doneraile (1780).

The choir was, from 1783 to 1869, the chapel of the Order of the Knights of St Patrick, whose banners, swords and helmets can be seen above the stalls.

In the little park near the cathedral, twelve tablets let into the wall commemorate Irish writers.

St Patrick's Cathedral

St. Patrick's Cathedral

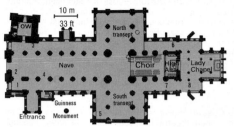

© Baedeker

1 Baptistery
2 Boyle Monument
3 Monument of Turlough O'Carolan
4 Tombs of Swift and Hester Johnson ("Stella")
5 Monument of Lady Doneraile
6 Effigy of Archbishop Fulk de Saundfort
7 Brasses of Dean Sutton, Dean Fyche, etc.
8 Effigy of Archbishop Tregury

To the right of St Patrick's an alley runs in a curve to Marsh's Library, the city's oldest public library, founded by Archbishop Marsh and built in 1701 by Sir William Robinson. The façades were renewed in 1863–9 but the attractive interior has been preserved practically unchanged, including the three 'cages' in which readers of rare books were obliged to work under the eye of the custodian. Open Mon., Wed.–Fri. 10am–12.45pm and 2–5pm, Sat. 10.30am–12.45pm.

Marsh's Library

Returning along Patrick Street and Nicholas Street to Christ Church, and turning left into High Street, St Audoen's, Dublin's only surviving medieval church (Protestant; National Monument) can be seen on the right. Of the original structure there remain the 13th c. nave in which services are still held, the choir and the south aisle (both roofless) and two chapels. In the porch are the Portlester Monument (1496) and a number of gravestones.

St Audoen's Church

High Street continues by way of Cornmarket into Thomas Street West. On the left is the massive façade of St Catherine's Church (1769 by John Smyth) in front of which Robert Emmet, who had led a rising against the British, was hanged in 1803.

St Catherine's Church

Some 550 yd further west lies the expansive site of the St James's Gate Brewery, better known as Guinness's, where 60 per cent of the beer drunk in Ireland is brewed (➤ Baedeker Special, p. 324). The brewery, founded by Arthur Guinness in 1759 and located here since 1761, prospered in spite of competition from imported English beers. In the early 19th c. Napoléon's Continental empire brought economic problems, as did the catastrophic famine of the 1840s; but in spite of this Guinness's grew to become Ireland's largest brewery, and by 1870 the largest in the world. Exports likewise continued to grow. The first Guinness brewery outside Ireland was established in London in 1936, and there are now breweries as far afield as Nigeria, Ghana, the Cameroons and Malaysia. The Dublin brewery exports 40 per cent of its total production.

Guinness's Brewery

In the brewery's Visitor Centre (Guinness Hop Store, Crane Street), the individual stages in the brewing process can be followed; the Transport Museum shows how beer was transported in past centuries. After an informative film about the company and the brewing business, visitors are invited to sample the famous beer. Open Mon.–Fri. 10am–4pm.

Inner city – north

★Custom House

Downstream of O'Connell Bridge, east of Eden Quay and the unsightly railway bridge (1889), stands the Custom House, a magnificent building designed by James Gandon (1743–1823), an English architect of Huguenot descent who was responsible for many buildings in Dublin. After the building had been completely burned out in 1921 during the civil war, the exterior was restored from the original plans. The long façade with its Doric portico, and the 125-ft domed tower surmounting it, are best seen from the opposite side of the river. Most of the fine statues and sculpture are by the Dubliner Edward Smyth. Though less magnificent than the main façade, the north front is also of notable quality.

Abbey Theatre

To the west of the Custom House is the new Abbey Theatre (1966 by Michael Scott); the main theatre has 638 seats, the small Peacock Theatre 157 seats. It is built on the site of the old Abbey Theatre, burned down in 1951, the first directors of which were W B Yeats and Lady Gregory. Plays are staged in Irish as well as in English.

Tyrone House

Proceeding north along Marlborough Street, Tyrone House (1741 by Richard Cassels) is found on the right. Now occupied by the Department of Education, it has a handsome staircase and good stucco work by Francini.

St Mary's
Pro-Cathedral

Facing stands St Mary's Pro-Cathedral, Dublin's principal Roman Catholic church, built in 1816–25 on the model of the Temple of Theseus in Athens. The high altar was the work of Peter Turnerelli. Masses are also said here in Italian and Spanish.

Custom House by the River Liffey

View of O'Connell Street from O'Connell Bridge

Parallel to Marlborough Street, two streets further west, is O'Connell Street, Dublin's main north–south artery. Originally a residential street, it lost many fine old buildings during the fighting of 1916–22 and is now a commercial thoroughfare, with cinemas and restaurants.

O'Connell Street

Along the middle of the street are a series of statues of Irish patriots, including Daniel O'Connell (near O'Connell Bridge) and Charles Stewart Parnell (► Famous People, in both cases), as well as the 'Apostle of Temperance', Father Matthew. Not long ago a sculpture of the river goddess Anna Livia was set up near the main post office – and immediately dubbed 'the floozie in the jacuzzi' by Irish wits.

On the west side of the street stands the imposing **General Post Office** (1815–17 by Francis Johnston), which in 1916 became the headquarters of the rebels under the leadership of Patrick Pearse and James Connolly. The Irish freedom fighters are commemorated by a monument (*Death of CuChulainn*) in the main hall.

Immediately past the Post Office, Henry Street leads west off O'Connell Street. A little way along it is Moore Street, where fruit and vegetable stalls create a colourful picture.

Moore Street

From Upper O'Connell Street, turn right into Parnell Street, then left along Gardiner Street to reach Mountjoy Square (1792–1808), a once-fashionable and elegant square which has come down in the world but is now gradually being renovated.

Mountjoy Square

From the north-west corner Gardiner's Place leads into Denmark Street, on the right-hand side of which is Belvedere House (1785 by Michael Stapleton), a dignified building with a fine interior. Since 1841

Belvedere House

175

Fruit and vegetable market in Moore Street

it has been a Jesuit school, James Joyce being its most celebrated pupil.

Parnell Square

Denmark Street opens onto Parnell Square, part of which is occupied by a Garden of Remembrance, laid out in 1966, with a sculpture by Oisin Kelly – *Lir's Children* (1970). The garden is dedicated to all who gave their lives for Irish independence. The most interesting of the buildings around Parnell Square are the Gate Theatre (founded in 1928 in part of the old Assembly Rooms), the Rotunda (now the Ambassador Cinema) and Richard Cassels' Rotunda Hospital, the main building of which, linked to the wings by colonnades, is topped by a domed tower. A lovely staircase leads up to the chapel, which has a fine stucco ceiling with numerous figures in strong relief.

Municipal Gallery of Modern Art

On Parnell Square North stands Charlemont House (1762 by the English architect Sir William Chambers; a columned hall added in 1930), since 1927 occupied by the Hugh Lane Municipal Gallery of Modern Art, founded in 1908. Hugh Lane, after whom the gallery is named, was a prominent member of Irish artistic and literary circles early in the last century. He was also an art collector who quickly developed an interest in Impressionism and later artistic movements. He accumulated an outstanding collection (including works by Camille Corot, Edgar Degas, Juan Gris, Edouard Manet, Claude Monet, Pablo Picasso, Camille Pissaro and Auguste Renoir). At the time of his death Lane had loaned the collection to the Tate Gallery in London, but in his will he left it to the City of Dublin. After protracted argument the collection was divided, the two halves being rotated on a five-yearly basis between Dublin and London. Open Tue.–Fri. 9.30am–6pm, Sat. 9.30–5pm, Sun. 11am–5pm.

Dublin Writers' Museum

In 1991 the Dublin Writers' Museum was opened in two 18th c. houses (Nos. 18 and 19) situated next to the art gallery. No. 18 honours the great

Irish writers, including Jonathan Swift, Oscar Wilde, W B Yeats, George Bernard Shaw and James Joyce – manuscripts, first editions, letters, photographs and writing implements are on display; the adjacent building serves as a meeting place for contemporary writers and for exhibiting and conducting readings from their work. There are also temporary exhibitions, a bookshop and a café. Open Apr.–Sep. Tue.–Sat. 10am–5pm, Sun. 1–5pm, Jun.–Aug. also Mon. 10am–5pm; Oct.–Mar. Fri., Sat. 10am–5pm, Sun. 1–5pm.

To the west of Parnell Square, in Granby Row, can be found the National Wax Museum, with wax figures of Irish politicians (Charles Stewart Parnell, Douglas Hyde, Eamon de Valera), actors and writers (James Joyce), and prominent international personalities (Ronald Reagan, Pope John Paul II). Open Mon.–Sat. 10am–5.30pm, Sun. 1–5.30pm.

National Wax Museum

From Granby Row turn left into Upper Dorset Street (which, as the N1, is the main road to the airport), then along its continuation, Bolton Street, to Henrietta Street, a cul-de-sac on the right. Away at the far end, raised on a tall base, are Dublin's Inns of Court, the King's Inns (1795 by James Gandon; the two wings on the west front are later additions), home to the ruling body of the Irish legal profession, with a fine dining hall (sculpture by Edward Smyth) and large library.

King's Inns

Continuing down Bolton Street, branch left into Capel Street, off to the left of which in Mary Street stands St Mary's Church (1702), Dublin's oldest Protestant church, with rich carving on the organ loft and galleries. In 1966 the Church authorities made a present of the churchyard to the city of Dublin for a memorial garden dedicated to Wolfe Tone, leader of the United Irishmen.

St Mary's Church

Capel Street descends to the Liffey at Gratton Bridge. About ¼ mile upstream, on Inns Quay, is an architectural masterpiece by James Gandon – the Four Courts, seat of the Irish High Court. Built between 1786 and 1802, it incorporated an older building (1776–84 by Thomas Cooley). After being badly damaged by gunfire during the civil war in 1922, it was restored in 1931 with only minor alterations. The 456-ft façade overlooking the river, embellished with a fine Corinthian portico, is capped by a great domed rotunda, a prominent Dublin landmark. The central hall beneath the dome gave access to the four courts from which the building takes its name – the Exchequer, Common Pleas, King's Bench and Chancery Courts.

★Four Courts

West of the Four Courts, in Church Street, is St Michan's Church (1095; much restored) in the crypt of which can be seen a number of mummified bodies which, because of the tannic acid in the air, have not decayed. Of rather greater interest is the carving on the gallery depicting 17 musical instruments. Handel is reputed to have played the church organ, built in 1724. Open Mon.–Fri. 10am–12.45pm, 2–4.45pm, Sat. 10am–12.45pm.

St Michan's Church

In Bow Street, parallel to Church Street, the Whiskey Corner Visitor Centre occupies a former storehouse of the Jameson Distillery, which closed in 1972. A film illustrates the 1000-year history of Irish whiskey; afterwards visitors have an opportunity to sample the product. Open May–Oct. Mon.–Fri. 11am–3.30pm.

Whiskey Corner

Half a mile further west, in Blackhall Place, can be seen the King's Hospital, also known as the Bluecoat School. The school was founded in 1669 but the present handsome building (by Thomas Ivory) dates only from the last quarter of the 18th c.; the dome was added in 1894. The interior has fine stucco work and carving.

King's Hospital

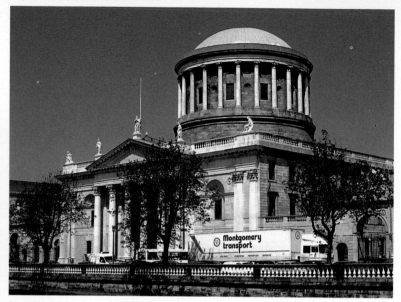

Four Courts, on the bank of the Liffey

Collin's Barracks   Immediately west of the school are the extensive Collin's Barracks (18th c.).

Outer districts – north

★Phoenix Park   From Collin's Barracks, Parkgate Street leads west to Phoenix Park. This vast public park (1996 acres) owes its name, not to the phoenix on a column set up in 1747 by the viceroy, Lord Chesterfield, who established the park, but to the Irish name of a nearby spring, Fionn Uisage (clear water). In that part of the park north of Main Road are the People's Garden; the Zoological Gardens (open Mon.–Sat. 9.30am–6pm, Sun. 11am–6pm), noted for their success in breeding lions; a polo ground; the former viceregal lodge and now official residence of the president of the Irish Republic (1751–4 by Nathaniel Clements); and the former Apostolic Nunciature, now a visitor centre. South of the road stands the Wellington Monument (1817 by Sir Robert Smirke), a huge obelisk 200 ft high which makes an eye-catching landmark for visitors coming from the city, with beyond it various sports grounds, the US ambassador's residence and, at the far west end, the Ordnance Survey Office. At the north end of the park is the Phoenix Park Race Course.

Glasnevin Cemetery   Leaving the park by either of the two northern exits – Cabra Gate or Ashtown Gate – proceed east along Navan Road and Cabra Road before turning north up Phibsborough Road to the Glasnevin or Prospect Cemetery, an extensive burial ground in which are situated the graves of David O'Connell, Charles Stewart Parnell, Sir Roger Casement and many other Irish patriots.

Botanic Gardens   North-east of the cemetery, bounded by the River Tolka, are the 50-acre Botanic Gardens. The wrought-iron Palm House was built in 1842–50 by

Richard Turner. Open summer Mon.–Sat. 9am–6pm., Sun. 11am–6pm; winter Mon.–Sat. 10am–4.30pm, Sun. 11am–4.30pm.

From the Botanic Gardens, follow the River Tolka east to Fairview Park, laid out on land reclaimed from the sea adjoining the harbour.

Fairview Park

North of the park, in the Marino district, reached via Malahide Road, stands the Marino Casino (1765–71; National Monument), a summer residence built by William Chambers for the earl of Charlemont, with sumptuously appointed rooms and a handsome staircase. In the basement are extensive domestic offices beneath a terrace flanked by four lions.

Casino Marino

From Fairview Park Clontarf Road and its continuations skirt the north side of Dublin Bay to Howth, picturesquely spread over the slopes of a rocky promontory of quartzite and schist. The older part of the town lies on the north-east side of the peninsula. Here there is a large fishing and leisure-craft harbour, from which a boat can be taken to Ireland's Eye, a rocky islet 1¼ mile offshore, with a little church and a Martello tower.

★Howth

Above Howth harbour are the ruins of St Mary's Collegiate Church (14th–15th c.; National Monument), with two aisles of differing length. In the south aisle can be seen the handsome tomb of the Lawrence family (ca 1470).

West of the church is the 15th c. Howth Castle, a battlemented stronghold of irregular plan, much restored. The lovely park is open to the public though the castle itself is not. Part of the park belongs to a golf club; elsewhere there is a French-style garden (18th c.) with 30 ft-high beech hedges and a profusion of rhododendrons, and a Transport Museum where old vehicles (tractors, double-decker buses, trams) are displayed.

The highest point on the peninsula (best reached from 'The Summit',

Landscape on the Howth Peninsula

Howth: harbour with fishing boats ...   *... and yachts*

a district at the eastern end) is Ben of Howth (568 ft), on which can be seen a burial mound; from the top there is a fine panorama.

There is an attractive cliff walk along the east and south sides of Howth Peninsula, passing the Baily Lighthouse (1814), a short distance off the path at the south-eastern tip of the peninsula, and St Fintan's Chapel (?9th c.). The view over the expanse of Dublin Bay to Dún Laoghaire (➤ entry) is magnificent.

Outer districts – south

Ballsbridge

Either side of the River Dodder in south-east Dublin lies the residential district of Ballsbridge, where dignified early 19th c. houses are dispersed among parks and sports grounds. At the junction of Shelbourne Road and Pembroke Road are the United States Embassy, a circular building of 1964, and a number of new hotels.

Royal Dublin Society

East of the bridge (1791) over the Dodder, to the right of Merrion Road, are the Royal Dublin Society Showgrounds. This extensive open site with its carefully tended turf, low white fences and handsome buildings, is the venue for the Dublin Horse Show, which takes place every year in August. The huge show, with more than 2000 horses and a full programme of races, displays, trials, prize-giving ceremonies and auctions, attracts visitors and buyers from far and wide. The show is a major event in the city's social calendar, with dances in the big hotels.

A Spring Show is also held, in conjunction with a trade fair, at the beginning of May, devoted to stock breeding, agricultural produce and machinery. While nowadays mainly concerned with agricultural science and stock breeding, the Royal Dublin Society also has a cultural programme of concerts and lectures on subjects of more general interest, as well as a library of over 150,000 volumes for use by its members.

550 yd further south, Shrewsbury Road branches right off Merrion Road. Here, at No. 20, is the Chester Beatty Library and Gallery of Oriental Art, founded by an American who settled in Dublin in 1953. Among the principal treasures in this valuable collection are: in the Garden Library, French books of hours of the 14th and 15th c. and a prayer book which belonged to Philip II of Spain; in the New Gallery, works of Far Eastern art, including Chinese cups of rhinoceros horn (11th c.) and Japanese coloured woodcuts, Islamic prints, Sanskrit manuscripts (12th–13th c.), Indian miniatures, Babylonian clay tablets (2500–2300 BC) and numerous texts in all the Near Eastern languages. The items on show in the New Gallery are changed from time to time, there being insufficient space to display the whole collection. Open Tue.–Fri. 10am–5pm, Sat. 2–5pm; conducted tours Wed., Sat. 2.30pm.

Chester Beatty Library and Gallery of Oriental Art

Merrion Road continues south-eastwards to Merrion Strand and along the shores of Dublin Bay to Dun Laoghaire (➤ entry).

Merrion Strand

Situated in the Donnybrook district beyond the River Dodder is the national radio and television station, with a tall transmission tower. This was the site of the famous Donnybrook Fair, established by King John in 1204 and suppressed in 1855.

Donnybrook

A mile further south, at 20 Palmerston Park, is the Museum of Childhood, with a collection of dolls from 1730 to 1940, as well as rocking horses and other toys. Open Jul.–Aug. daily 2–5.30pm; Sep., Nov.–Jun. Sun. 2–5.30pm.

Museum of Childhood

South-west lies the Rathfarnham district, with a castle of the same name (National Monument). This stately mansion dating from 1593 is being restored. The restored former stables have been turned into workshops for traditional crafts. Open (guided tours only) Jun.–Oct. daily 10am–5 or 6pm.

Rathfarnham

In the Drimnagh district north-west of Rathfarnham stands Drimnagh Castle (15th c.), with a well-preserved moat and outer ward. The castle itself is incorporated into a later building occupied by the Christian Brothers. Formerly lying outside the town, the castle was built to deter cattle thieves.

Drimnagh

Further along Nass Road in the direction of the city, north of the Grand Canal, extends the Kilmainham district. Here, between Emmet Road and Inchicore Road, is Kilmainham Gaol (1792) in which up until 1924 numerous Irish patriots were imprisoned and many were executed. In the entrance archway is a carving of intertwined serpents and chains, a sinister foretaste of the atmosphere within. Since 1960 the prison has been restored and is now a museum commemorating the patriots who were confined here. The cells in which the executed died can be visited and numerous exhibits give a grim insight into the darker side of Irish history. Open May–Sep. daily 10am–6pm; Oct.–Apr. Wed.–Fri. 1–4pm, Sun. 1–6pm.

Kilmainham Gaol

Continue towards the city along Kilmainham Lane, then turn left into Military Road to arrive at the main entrance to the Royal Hospital, which today houses the Irish Museum of Modern Art. The building was erected between 1680 and 1687 by order of Charles II as a hospital 'for maimed and infirm soldiers'. In the 1980s no expense was spared in restoring Sir William Robinson's neoclassical building (Franco-Dutch style; the tower dates from 1701), those who worked on it winning international acclaim. The Great Hall, with many portraits of kings and viceroys, is now used

★Irish Museum of Modern Art (Royal Hospital)

for concerts, banquets and conferences. Of particular interest in the chapel are the wood carving and the baroque stucco ceiling (a copy of the original that was destroyed in 1902). Some rooms have been furnished in their original style while others have been enlarged to provide exhibition space for the Irish Museum of Modern Art, which moved into its fine new premises in 1991. It would be hard to imagine a grander setting for its collection of 20th c. Irish and international art. Open Tue.–Sat. 10am–5.30pm, Sun. noon–5.30pm.

Surroundings – north

Santry

Heading north from Dublin the N1 passes through Santry where St Papan's Church (1709) boasts a 14th c. font, a reredos of 1709 and a fine pulpit.

Swords

Swords, 4 miles further on, is a historic small town with the ruins of Swords Castle (13th–15th c.; National Monument). The castle, pentagonal in plan, was the seat of the archbishops of Dublin. It retains a chapel, the gatehouse and towers. Adjacent to the village church stand a 74-ft round tower (entrance and roof modern) and the tower (14th c.) of a former monastic church.

Newbridge House

Continuing north on the N1, turn off after 2 miles onto the R126 for Donabate where, in 1992, Newbridge House together with its surrounding park and farm, were transformed into a museum portraying rural life in Ireland in the 18th c. Open to the public are Newbridge House itself, built in the mid-18th c., various workshops and estate workers' cottages, and the adjoining farm complete with livestock and 18th c. implements. Open Tue.–Fri. 11am–5pm, Sat. 11am–6pm, Sun. 2–6pm.

Lusk

Rejoin the N1, soon forking right on the R127 to Lusk. It too boasts a round tower (National Monument), all that remains of a 9th c. monastery suppressed by the Anglo-Normans. The square tower seen nearby belongs to a later structure. The church (1847) contains a number of good medieval tombs.

Lambay Island

On the coast to the east of Lusk lies the village of Rush, a bulb-growing centre from where a boat can be taken to Lambay Island. In the 8th c. the island was the scene of one of the first Viking incursions; fortifications dating from about 1550 still survive. The rocky islet (of porphyry; highest point 427 ft) is now a bird sanctuary; it can be visited only with the permission of the owner, Lord Revelstoke.

Skerries

From Lusk the R127 runs north-east past the ruined church (15th c.; National Monument) and castle of Baldongan, to Skerries (good sandy beach, 18-hole golf course). Just offshore are three little islets: St Patrick's Island, with a ruined church; Colt Island; and Shenick's Island (reached by foot at low water) with a Martello tower.

Ardgillan Demesne

North of Skerries on the Balbriggan road (R127) lies the Ardgillan Demesne, a restored country house standing in a large park. Garden open daily 10am–dusk; house open Apr.–Oct. Tue.–Sun. 2.30–5.30pm; Nov.–Mar. Sun. only.

Balbriggan

Balbriggan is a quiet seaside resort on the River Delvin, with lovely beaches and a 9-hole golf course.

Surroundings – north-east

Portmarnock

From the city's north-eastern suburbs, or alternatively from Howth, the

Beach at Portmarnock

R106 can be followed to the little resort of Portmarnock, with its beautiful 2-mile Velvet Strand and well-known championship golf course.

Situated about 1¼ mile west of Portmarnock is St Doulagh's Church (13th c.), with its original stone roof, a chapel and a battlemented tower (15th c.). Cells in the tower, above the chapel and in the crypt suggest that this may have been a hermitage.

★St Doulagh's Church

In a field 110 yd north-east there is a well, in a octagonal well house with a stone roof.

From Portmarnock the R106 skirts the coast to Malahide, a popular little seaside resort. South-west of the town, in lovely gardens, stands Malahide Castle, which from the 13th c. to 1975 was owned and occupied by the Talbot family and now belongs to the city of Dublin. Much rebuilt and altered over time, it shows a variety of architectural styles – medieval, Georgian and modern. The Great Hall with its oak panelling is the only one in Ireland to have retained its medieval aspect.

★Malahide Castle

The castle now houses the National Portrait Gallery, a branch of the National Gallery in Dublin (➤ p. 163). The pictures in the collection are of interest both on account of the artists represented (among them William Hogarth and Sir Joshua Reynolds) and also their subjects (Anne Boleyn, Robert Dudley, James Gandon, Jonathan Swift, Daniel O'Connell). Open Jun.–Oct. Mon.–Fri. 10am–5pm, Sat. 11am–6pm, Sun. 2–6pm; Nov.–May Sat., Sun. 2–5pm.

Another attraction, in the park of Malahide Castle, is the Fry Model Railway. It is the work of an Irishman, Cyril Fry, who spent many years creating the railway to a scale of 1:43; in its originality and detail it surpasses most others. Open Apr.–Oct. Mon.–Thu. 10am–5pm, Sat. 11am–6pm, Sun. 2–6pm.

Malahide Castle

Surroundings – south

See Dun Laoghaire

Surroundings – west

Clondalkin

2½ miles north-west of Tallaght on the R113 lies Clondalkin, a monastic settlement founded by St Mochua in the 7th c., of which nothing remains but an 84-ft round tower (National Monument), with its original roof and an external staircase (18th c.); in the churchyard are two granite crosses and a font (all National Monuments).

Lucan

The N4 follows the course of the Liffey through the suburb of Chapelizod to Lucan, once a much-frequented spa. To the west stands Lucan House (1776), with beautiful interiors by James Wyatt, Michael Stapleton and Angelica Kauffmann.

Finglas

Finglas, on the north-west outskirts of Dublin on the N2, has a ruined medieval church and a 12th c. high cross in the churchyard. On a hill 2 miles west can be seen Dunsink Observatory which, from 1782 to 1921, was the observatory of Trinity College, Dublin (➤ p. 161).

★Dunsoghly Castle

3 miles north of Finglas, to the right of the N2, stands Dunsoghly Castle (15th c.; National Monument) which, unusually among Irish castles, still retains its original oak roof. It is a square tower with rectangular corner turrets; far-ranging views can be enjoyed from the parapet walks. The roof structure provided the model for the reconstruction of Bunratty Castle (➤ Ennis). To the south of the castle are the remains of a small chapel (1573).

Dundalk · Dún Dealgan   B 5

Republic of Ireland
Province: Leinster
County: Louth
Population: 29,000

Dundalk (Dún Dealgan, Delga's fort) lies on the east coast of Ireland near the Northern Ireland border, where Dundalk Bay forms a sheltered harbour. With a variety of industry (engineering, printing, tobacco, footwear) the town has a busy and prosperous air.

In the 10th c. the Irish inhabitants of the area were attacked by Viking raiders and a naval battle was fought in the bay. The town was fortified in 1185. In 1253, and again in 1315, it was burned down. Thereafter for 300 years it was a cornerstone in the defence of the English Pale (the territory in the east of Ireland under English control). In 1690 it was taken by William of Orange and in 1724 its fortifications were pulled down.

History

In the centre of the town, in Crowe Street (near the bus station), are two handsome 19th c. buildings, the Court House and Town Hall. Further east, in Seatown Place, can be seen an old windmill, a massive seven-storey structure. On the main street leading north stands St Nicholas's Church (18th c. with an older tower). St Patrick's Cathedral, built in 1848, is modelled on King's College Chapel, Cambridge. A short distance east is a newly opened museum which documents Dundalk and its history.

Sights

Surroundings

2 miles north-east of the town a side road (R173) branches off the N1 and runs east into the Cooley Peninsula, an attractive hilly promontory between Dundalk Bay and Carlingford Lough, an arm of the sea.

Cooley Peninsula

A little way along the R173, at Ballymascanlon, stands Proleek Dolmen (National Monument; in the grounds of the Ballymascanlon Hotel). It has a capstone weighing some 40 tons carried on only three uprights. Tradition has it that anyone who can throw a pebble onto the capstone without it rolling off will have their wish fulfilled.

★Proleek Dolmen

On the north-east side of the peninsula lies the historic small town of Carlingford, dominated by the massive King John's Castle (13th c.; National Monument) on a crag above the harbour. Nearby can be seen the Tholsel, an old gate tower in which the elders of the town used to meet. In a little street off the Square is the old Mint (National Monument), a 15th c. fortified tower house with curious window carvings. Taffee's Castle opposite the railway station has a large square keep (16th c.) with a fine spiral staircase. Carlingford Forest, west of the town, is excellent walking country; one road leads up to an observation point from which there is a fine panorama of Carlingford and the coastal scenery.

Carlingford

On the coast south of Dundalk is the little resort of Blackrock with an 18-hole golf course, tennis courts and facilities for water sports. There is trout and salmon fishing in the River Fane.

Blackrock

3 miles further south, in the graveyard at Dromiskin, just off the N1, are a 56-ft round tower and a high cross, both dating from the early years of a monastery established here in the 6th c. Adjoining is a 13th c. church. All are National Monuments. There are a number of well-preserved castles within a few miles' radius.

Dromiskin

Castlebellingham   At Castlebellingham, 1¼ miles south of Dromiskin, Bellingham Castle stands in a beautiful setting on the River Glyde. It has been renovated and is now a hotel (handsome yew hedges).

Ardee   15 miles south-west of Dundalk on the N52 the little town of Ardee lies on the River Dee, with a 9-hole golf course and good fishing. It has two castles – Hatch's Castle and Ardee Castle, a square keep which now houses a small museum. St Mary's Protestant Church, which incorporates parts of an older building, has a carved font.

Louth   Louth, now just a village, to the north of Ardee, was at one time a place of such importance that it gave its name to the county. St Mochta's House (National Monument) is a vaulted two-storey oratory (12th c.) with a stone roof. Nearby are the ruins of a 14th c. church.

Inniskeen   At Inniskeen, 5 miles north of Louth, a redundant church now houses a museum of local history, one section of which is devoted to the former Great Northern Railway, which passed through the town. On the site of an old monastery is the stump of a round tower (National Monument).

Castletown Castle   To the east on the N53, almost within the Dundalk suburbs, rises a 60-ft-high earthwork said to be the birthplace of the legendary hero CuChulainn. The site is now occupied by a building of 1780; fine views.

A short distance away is Castletown Castle (15th c.), a four-storey structure with flanking towers.

Castleroche   4½ miles north-west of Dundalk are the ruins of Castleroche (13th c.; National Monument), a triangular enclosure with towers; it is particularly impressive when seen from the plain.

Dungarvan · Dun Garbhan   D 4

Republic of Ireland
Province: Munster
County: Waterford
Population: 6600

Dungarvan (Dun Garbhan, Garvan's fort) lies halfway along the south coast of Ireland in a sheltered bay at the mouth of the River Colligan. North of the town are the Comeragh and Monavullagh Mountains, rising to a height of 2560 ft. The town is the administrative centre of Co. Waterford (with the exception of the city of Waterford itself), and is also a busy market centre, with leather-processing works.

Sights   The town extends on both sides of the River Colligan, which is spanned by a bridge of 1815 with a 74 ft arch. On the right bank of the river are the ruins of Dungarvan Castle (built in 1185 and subsequently much altered), a massive circular keep surrounded by walls. Nearby in the 17th c. Old Market House, a small municipal museum has been established. In the churchyard of St Mary's Church can be seen the Holed Gable, a peculiar structure with a number of circular openings, the function of which is unknown.

In Abbeyside, on the left bank of the river, is a tower which belonged to a 13th c. Augustinian abbey and now serves as the belfry of the adjoining church. Nearby stands a curious shell house.

Surroundings

Clonea   Off the R676 to the east of Dungarvan, on the far side of the bay, lies

Clonea, a popular little seaside resort with a good sandy beach, a 9-hole golf course and two campsites.

South of the town (ferry service) the Cunnigar Peninsula also has good beaches. There is a pleasant walk by way of Ring – with an Irish language school – and the little, old-world fishing village of Ballynagaul to Helvick Head (which can also be reached on the R674), with fine views of Dungarvan Harbour and the hills to the north.

Cunnigar Peninsula

The region south of Dungarvan Harbour, between the N25 and the sea, is the only area on the east coast where Irish is still predominantly spoken.

2½ miles west of Dungarvan, on the N72, is a monument to the celebrated greyhound Master McGrath, three times winner of the Waterloo Cup and defeated only once in 37 races.

Greyhound Monument

The Touraneena Heritage Centre, about 9 miles north of Dungarvan on the R672, comprises a farmhouse furnished as it would have been at the close of the 19th c. together with an old smithy. Open daily 10am–8pm.

Touraneena Heritage Centre

Dun Laoghaire   C 5

Republic of Ireland
Province: Leinster
County: Dublin
Population: 54,000

Dun Laoghaire (pronounced Dunleary, Leary's fort) lies at the south end of the wide sweep of Dublin Bay, below the north-eastern foothills of the

House fronts in Dun Laoghaire

187

Wicklow Mountains. At the beginning of the 19th c. it was still a small fishing village, called at that time Kingstown following a visit by King George IV in 1821. In 1921 it reassumed its original name. Today Dun Laoghaire is an attractive suburb of Dublin, a seaside resort and residential town much favoured by prosperous Dubliners, and an important port, terminus of the car ferry services to and from Britain (Holyhead). It is also Ireland's premier yachting centre, with the headquarters of almost all the country's major yacht clubs.

Town

Dun Laoghaire's elegant residential suburbs extend eastwards into the hills. The town's commercial life, on the other hand, is concentrated in the streets around the harbour.

Sights

Harbour

At the time of its construction (1817–21) the large harbour was a masterpiece of civil engineering. Its east pier is a popular promenade, with concerts in summer. The somewhat quieter west pier attracts mainly anglers.

National Maritime Museum

A deconsecrated seafarers' church a little to the south of the harbour now houses the National Maritime Museum. A comprehensive collection of model ships, paintings, photographs and documents provide a tribute to Ireland's seafaring tradition. Open May–Sep. Tue.–Sun. 2.30–5.30pm.

Joyce's Tower

A minor road leads from the harbour, skirting the bathing beach, to Joyce's Tower, situated on a rocky promontory with an extensive view over Dublin Bay. It was one of the Martello towers built during the Napoleonic Wars to keep a watch for possible invasion. In 1904 James Joyce lived for some time in the tower, and he describes it in *Ulysses*. It now houses a museum containing original manuscripts and rare editions of Joyce's work as well as personal mementoes. Open Apr.–Oct. Mon.–Sat. 10am–1pm, 2–5pm, Sun. 2.30–6pm; other times by arrangement with the tourist office.

Surroundings

Monkstown Blackrock

Along the coast to the north of the town, extending into the suburbs of Dublin, are the residential districts of Monkstown and Blackrock. Monkstown has a 19th c. church with towers like chess pawns. Blackrock has very popular sea-water swimming-baths.

Dalkey

To the south, now continuous with Dun Laoghaire, is the historic little town of Dalkey, another residential area favoured by affluent people from the capital. In Main Street stand two relics of the town's medieval defences, Archbold's Castle (16th c.; National Monument) and another structure which is now the town hall.

Dalkey Island

Just off the coast lies a small islet, Dalkey Island, with the remains of an old church (National Monument) and a Martello tower. From Sorrento Terrace and Sorrento Park, on the town's south beach, there are magnificent views. The old granite quarries are a good practice ground for rock-climbers.

Killiney

To the south of Sorrento Point stretches Killiney Bay, with the seaside resort of Killiney. The slopes of the hills are studded, almost Mediterranean-like, with villas of different periods set in well-groomed gardens, while beyond the railway line, which here follows the coast, the beach is rocky. The mid-19th c. Ayesha Castle and grounds in Victoria

Road can be visited by arrangement (tel. (01) 2852323). There are some lovely walks in Killiney Hill Park. The highest point, marked by an obelisk dating from 1741, affords superb views of the surrounding hills and the sea.

To the west of Killiney, just off the R117, is the village of Kilternan. On a nearby hill can be seen the impressive Kilternan Dolmen (ca 2000 BC; National Monument), with a capstone 6 ft thick borne on ten orthostats.

Kilternan Dolmen

On the R117 a short distance north of Kilternan are Fernhill Gardens with old trees, a rock garden and a water garden. The park is privately owned.

Fernhill Gardens

Ennis · Inis   D 3

Republic of Ireland
Province: Munster
County: Clare
Population: 6200

Ennis (Inis, river meadow), county town of Co. Clare and an important road and rail junction (N18, N68), is situated in the west of Ireland on the River Fergus.
  Shannon International Airport is only 15 miles away. With its extensive hinterland and its light industries, Ennis is a market town and commercial centre of considerable importance.

The River Fergus flows in broad curves through the town which, with its narrow winding streets, has retained something of its medieval aspect.

Town

Quin Abbey, near Ennis

Sights

At the end of Abbey Street stands Ennis Friary, a Franciscan friary founded in 1241 which in the mid-14th c. was a flourishing community with 375 friars and 600 students. The church dates from the original foundation but has been much altered. It has some very fine sculpture, including a figure of St Francis with the stigmata (on the south-west side of the tower), the MacMahon monument of about 1475 (on the south wall), a royal tomb with scenes from the Passion and a small representation of the Scourging, with the 'cock-in-the-pot' (for an explanation of the legend, see Kilkenny: St Canice's Cathedral). Open Jun.-Sep. daily 9.30am–6.30pm.

Ennis Friary

Near the abbey, in Harmony Row, is the De Valera Museum and Library, with material on Ennis and the surrounding area and the history of Ireland. Among the exhibits is the fountain pen with which Eamon de Valera and Neville Chamberlain signed the 1938 treaty under which Britain gave up its naval bases in Ireland. Open Mon.–Wed., Fri. 11am–1pm, 2.15–5.30pm, 7–9pm, Thu. 11am–1pm, 2.15–5.30pm.

De Valera Museum and Library

Surroundings

6 miles south-east of Ennis on the R469 is Quin, with Quin Friary (1402; National Monument), the well-preserved ruins of a Franciscan friary built on the foundations of an earlier castle, the bastions of which can still be seen. The church has tombstones of the 15th to 19th c. and a well-preserved cloister.
On the other side of the little river stands the 13th c. St Finghin's Church (National Monument); the tower is a later addition.

★Quin Friary

2½ miles further south-east on the R469 lies Knappogue Castle, a tower house dating from 1467, restored in 15th c. style, with furniture of the period (open May–Oct. daily 9.30am–5.30pm). In summer medieval-style banquets are held in the 19th c. annex.

Knappogue Castle

A further 1¼ mile along the R469, a small road to the left leads to an estate signposted Craggaunowen Project. In the mid-1960s this land was acquired by John Hunt, an art collector, who restored the 16th c. Craggaunowen Castle and around it created an impressive open-air museum. Open mid-Mar. to Oct. daily 10am–6pm.
The castle itself contains a small collection of medieval religious art from the Hunt Collection (➤ Limerick, p. 241), mostly Continental in origin. The gatekeeper's lodge, to the left of the castle entrance, has been turned into a chapel (notable 15th c. bronze cross).
In the grounds are reconstructions of some of the earliest types of man-made structure in Ireland, including a crannog (Bronze Age pile dwelling) in a small lough and a stone ring-fort, both with huts and implements of the period. Displayed in a specially built glass shed is the leather boat in which some young people re-enacted the medieval voyages of St Brendan (➤ Famous People).

★Craggaunowen Project

The R462 goes south to Sixmilebridge, a pretty little village with a delightful 18th c. mansion, Mount Jevers (1736), which has been described as a 'Georgian doll's house'. From here a minor road runs south-west to the village of Bunratty.

Sixmilebridge

◀ *The high cross of Dysert O'Dea, near Ennis*

Craggaunowen Project: reconstructions of prehistoric dwellings

★★Bunratty Castle and Folk Park

Bunratty Castle and Folk Park are one of Ireland's principal tourist attractions. Following an eventful history of destruction and rebuilding, the 15th c. castle was acquired in 1954 by viscount Gort and magnificently restored; it and the surrounding park are now managed as a non-profit-making foundation by Shannon Free Airport Development Ltd. The Great Hall and Banqueting Hall, Chapel and residential apartments are furnished with an outstanding collection of pieces from the late Middle Ages and early Renaissance. Medieval-style banquets are laid on for holidaymakers in the banqueting hall. Basement shop. Open daily 9.30am–5pm; Jun.–Aug. park open until 7pm.

Bunratty Folk Park, to the rear of the castle, is an interesting open-air museum with numerous cottages, shops and workshops, such as were found all over Ireland in the late 19th c. In the centre of the park a whole village street has been reconstructed.

Cratloe

At Cratloe, a short distance east of Bunratty, is a 17th c. mansion, Cratloe Woods House. Open Jun. to mid-Sep. Mon.–Sat. 2–6pm.

Ballycasey Workshops

Leather goods, jewellery, woollens and can be seen in the making as well as purchased at the Ballycasey Workshops (open Mon.–Fri. 10am–6pm), about 4 miles west of Bunratty on the approach road to Shannon Airport.

Shannon International Airport

Being only 7 miles from Shannon International Airport, Bunratty naturally attracts large numbers of tourists. The airport, the most westerly in Europe, opened in 1945 and boasted the world's first duty-free shop. Shannon having long since lost its importance as a staging post for transatlantic flights, a development company,

Shannon Free Airport Development Ltd, has instead succeeded in attracting a range of industries here (including precision tools, electronic equipment and industrial diamonds). The town of Shannon has a population of 7000.

On the way north from Shannon Airport to Ennis, the N18 passes through Newmarket on Fergus, a small market town and commercial centre. A little to the north, Dromoland Castle, built in about 1830, stands resplendent in extensive grounds. The castle is now a luxury hotel and golf course but the lovely park remains open to the public.

Newmarket on Fergus

Nearer to Ennis the road crosses the River Fergus at Clarecastle, with the ruined castle from which the village, and possibly the county of Clare too, takes its name.

Clarecastle

Almost a mile further north on the N18 are the ruins of Clare Abbey (National Monument), founded in the 12th c. and extended at various times up until the 15th c.

Clare Abbey

3 miles south-west of Ennis on the N68, in a beautiful setting on a lough, are the remains of Killone Abbey (12th c.; National Monument), one of Ireland's few nunneries.

Killone Abbey

Having followed the N85 north-westwards from Ennis to Fountain Cross, turn north onto the R476, arriving after 4 miles at Dysert O'Dea (National Monument). Dysert O'Dea Castle (1480) has been extensively restored and now houses a small archaeological museum. Open May–Sep. daily 10am–7pm.
  The castle is the start of a history trail (accessible at all times) taking in a series of historical and archaeological remains in the near vicinity,

★Dysert O'Dea

Dysert O'Dea Castle ...

... and the Romanesque church doorway

193

the most interesting of which are a church, a round tower and a high cross. The church seen today dates from the late 17th c., when it was reconstructed more or less in its original form (12th–13th c.). It has a fine Romanesque doorway carved with beautiful geometric designs, foliage and beak-head masks. At the north-west corner of the church stands the stump of a round tower, still 40 ft high, and in a field to the east is a high cross (➤ picture, 190), with an unusual figure of the crucified Christ, fully clothed, on the east side; the other sides are divided into panels with a variety of geometric patterns, human figures and interlace with animals.

Enniscorthy · Inis Corthaidh   D 5

Republic of Ireland
Province: Leinster
County: Wexford
Population: 5000

Enniscorthy (Inis Coirthaidh, rock island) lies in the south-east corner of Ireland on the main road from Dublin to Wexford. The town is built on the west side of the River Slaney, both banks of which rise sharply above the river. The Slaney is navigable up to this point and carries considerable traffic between Enniscorthy and Wexford (about 15 miles south).

Sights

Enniscorthy Castle

The town developed as a market and distribution centre around Enniscorthy Castle (1586; National Monument), a rectangular keep with corner towers. Now restored, it houses the Wexford County Museum with finds from prehistory onwards and documents relating to local crafts. Open Jun.–Sep. Mon.–Sat. 10am–1pm, 2–6pm, Sun. 2–5.30pm; Oct.–May daily 2–5.30pm.

St Aidan's Cathedral

St Aidan's Cathedral, commandingly situated above the river, is a neo-Gothic church by Augustus Pugin (1840).

Vinegar Hill

There are fine views from Vinegar Hill (east of the town), where there are also remains of a windmill (National Monument).

Surroundings

Ferns

Ferns, about 8 miles north of Enniscorthy on the N11, was once the county's episcopal see. The road crosses the site of an old abbey (National Monument), with three churches and other buildings. The present Protestant church incorporates some work from an earlier building; in the churchyard are a number of high crosses. Ferns Castle (National Monument) is a large rectangular keep with circular towers; in one of the towers there is a beautiful vaulted 13th c. chapel.

Gorey
Courtown

Further north-east, still on the N11, lies Gorey, once with an important cattle market. Courtown, on the coast near by (R742), is a popular family seaside resort with lovely sandy beaches and an 18-hole golf course.

Blackstairs Mountains

The Blackstairs Mountains to the west of Enniscorthy provide plenty of scope for hill walking and climbing.

Enniskerry · Ath na Scairbhe   C 5

Republic of Ireland
Province: Leinster
County: Wicklow
Population: 1200

Enniskerry (Ath na Scairbhe, bumpy ford), one of the prettiest villages in
Ireland, lies south-east of Dublin to the west of Bray, in a hollow in the
foothills of the Wicklow Mountains.

Enniskerry is a good base for walking in the hills and for a visit to
nearby Powerscourt.

★★Powerscourt Gardens

About ½ mile south of the village is the entrance to the demesne of
Powerscourt, with gardens and a landscaped park which are among the
most beautiful in Ireland. The gardens were completed in 1875, the culmination of 30 years' work.

Open mid-March
to Oct. daily
9.30am–5.30pm

The house, the centrepiece of the grounds, was once an imposing
granite mansion (1731 by Richard Cassels), approached along a mile-
long avenue of beeches. Today only the façade still stands, the middle
part of the building having been gutted by fire in 1974. From the house,
situated on a rise, the gardens extend down the slope, with terraces,
statuary, tessellated pavements, an ornamental lake and fine wrought-
iron work. In the grounds are plantations of exotic trees, beds of rhododendrons and other flowering shrubs, also an Italian and a Japanese
garden and a deer park. From various viewpoints there are magnificent

Powercourt Gardens: only the façade of the mansion remains

prospects of the surrounding hills – Great Sugar Loaf, 1631 ft; Kippure, 2430 ft.

Powerscourt
Waterfall

An hour's walk away lies the celebrated Powerscourt Waterfall, the highest in Ireland, formed by the River Dargle tumbling over a 400-ft cliff into the valley below. At its most impressive after a rainy spell, the waterfall can be visited all year round. Open summer daily 9.30am–7pm; winter 10.30am to dusk; waymarked footpath from Powerscourt Gardens.

Glencree River

About 2 miles upstream the Glencree River joins the Dargle, flowing down from Glendoo Mountain through a lovely valley. A delightful road ascends the valley to a group of 18th c. buildings known today as St Kevin's, originally a barracks erected by the British for the protection of the Military Road.

Surroundings

The Scalp

About 2 miles north of Enniskerry the Dublin road passes through the Scalp, a steep gorge littered with granite boulders hewn from the hills by glaciers during the last ice age.

Fanad Peninsula   A 4

Republic of Ireland
Province: Ulster
County: Donegal

Situated in the far north of Ireland and of Co. Donegal, the Fanad Peninsula extends northwards for some 12 miles between the narrow fjord-like inlet of Mulroy Bay to the west and Lough Swilly, the broad estuary of the River Swilly, to the east. An area of spectacular cliff and coastal scenery, the peninsula terminates in Fanad Head.

Circuit

Milford

From Letterkenny (➤ entry) the R245 runs north to Milford, a fishing centre at the head of Mulroy Bay. The village has a modern church. Near by is a waterfall known as the Grey Mare's Tail. There is good fishing in Lough Fern and other small loughs in the neighbourhood.

Kerrykeel

From Milford the R245 makes its way north along the east side of Mulroy Bay. Just before Kerrykeel (also spelt Carrowkeel) is a dolmen with a massive capstone measuring 6 by 12 ft. Kerrykeel lies at the foot of the Knockalla Mountains, known hereabouts as the 'Devil's Backbone'.

Fanad Head

The R245 and its continuation lead to Fanad Head at the northern tip of the peninsula (fine views). The return is down the west side of Lough Swilly.

Portsalon

Beyond Portsalon, which has a picturesque little harbour and an 18-hole golf course, are a group of spectacular tunnels in the cliffs, known as the Seven Arches, up to 300 ft long, 20 ft wide and 30 ft high; also the Great Arch of Doagh Beg.

The Knockalla Mountains, which can be seen ahead, fall steeply to the loughside. On the slopes is a 19th c. gun emplacement built for defence against a possible French invasion.

Knockalla Mountains

The R247 leads past Otway golf course (9 holes) to Rathmullan, an attractive seaside resort with a sandy beach. At Rathmullan are the ruins of a Carmelite friary (15th c.; National Monument), the church of which a 17th c. bishop converted into his residence. Near the harbour a gun emplacement known as the Battery, built at the beginning of the 19th c. in anticipation of a French invasion, has been turned into a Visitor Centre devoted in particular to the 'Flight of the Earls'. It was from Rathmullan in 1607 that the earls of Tyrone and Tyrconnell fled to France accompanied by a band of friends and supporters. Afterwards their vast estates in Ireland were confiscated and resettled by the English and Scots. Open May–Sep. Mon.–Sat. 10am–6pm, Sun. 12.30–6pm.

Rathmullan

Fermoy · Mainistir Fhear Muighe   D 3

Republic of Ireland
Province: Munster
County: Cork
Population: 3100

The little market town of Fermoy (Mainistir Fhear Muighe, abbey of the plainsmen) lies inland from the south coast of Ireland between spurs of the Knockmealdown and Nagles mountains. A major cattle auction is held here.

This is excellent salmon-and-trout fishing country, and angling competitions take place regularly in the area. There is also good coarse fishing; the Blackwater is the only river in Ireland where roach are found.

Castle Hyde, a late Georgian house on the banks of the Blackwater in the west of the town, was the ancestral home of Douglas Hyde, president of the Irish Republic from 1938 to 1945.

Sights

Surroundings

10 miles north on the N8 lies Mitchelstown, a small country town with a creamery producing butter and cheese. An 18th c. planned town, it grew further in the 19th c. Buildings of interest include an attractive group of almshouses (1780) known as Kingston College.

Mitchelstown

Located 7 miles north-east in Co. Tipperary is the extensive limestone cave system known as the Mitchelstown Caves. Desmond's Cave was the refuge of a 16th c. earl of Desmond who had a large price put on his head. The New Cave, discovered in 1833, contains fine stalactitic and stalagmitic formations; 390 ft long and 40 ft high, it is believed to be the largest cave in the British Isles. Open summer only, daily 9am–6pm.

Mitchelstown Caves

Labbamolaga, in hill country 5½ miles north-west of Mitchelstown on the R665, has ruins of a modest Early Christian church (National Monument).

Labbamolaga Church

4½ miles south-east of Fermoy lies Castlelyons where there are the remains of a 15th c. priory (National Monument) comprising a church with a beautiful west doorway and a tower and other buildings.

Castlelyons

A few miles east, on a crag above the River Bride, stands a 14th c. tower house, Gonna Castle (National Monument).

Anne's Grove Gardens

Driving west from Fermoy on the N72, branch off northwards in Castletownroche to arrive after another 2 miles at Anne's Grove Gardens, a delightful park with many exotic trees and flowers on the banks of the River Awbeg. Open Apr.–Sep. Mon.–Sat. 10am–5pm, Sun. 1–6pm.

Killavullen

Continue in the direction of Mallow, passing the village of Killavullen. Not far to the west on a cliff above the Blackwater stands the ancestral home of the Hennessy family, whose cognac, distilled in France, is renowned the world over.

Mallow

Mallow, an important sugar-refining centre, lies 30 km west of Fermoy in the wooded valley of the Blackwater, a river well stocked with fish. In the 18th and 19th c. the town was a much-frequented spa, but it retains only a little of the atmosphere of those days. It has a number of notable buildings: the Court House, the Market House, a picturesque clock tower and some good 18th c. dwellings; also one or two relics of its fashionable heyday – the old Spa House, the racecourse and three gushing springs in Fermoy Road. At the south-east end of the town are the ruins of Mallow Castle (16th c.; National Monument), with a small museum.

Ballybeg Abbey Buttevant

In close proximity to one another on the N20 north of Mallow are Ballybeg Abbey (13th c.; National Monument), with a fine dovecot, and, in the little town of Buttevant, the ruined church of a Franciscan friary (13th c.; National Monument) with a handsome choir and a crypt built beneath on a steep river bank.

Kilcolman Castle

A short distance north-east are the ruins of Kilcolman Castle, in which the poet Edmund Spenser (1552–99) lived for 13 years.

Kanturk

The small market town of Kanturk, 12 miles west of Mallow, boasts a massive early 17th c. fortified house (National Monument) which belonged to the MacCarthys. When news of the scale of the project reached England an order to suspend work was issued. The castle was never finished.

Liscarroll Castle

9 miles north-east of Kanturk are the ruins of Liscarroll Castle (National Monument), a handsome tower house built in the 13th c. but later much altered; it is surrounded by a walled outer ward with defensive towers.

Tullylease

North of Kanturk on the R579 at Tullylease are the ruins of a 13th–15th c. monastery (National Monument). It has a number of Early Christian gravestones built into the walls, including one in particular on the east end of the church embellished with fine ornament in the style of the 8th c. Book of Lindisfarne and a Latin inscription.

Labbacallee Cairn

North-west of Fermoy on the R512 can be seen Labbacallee Cairn (National Monument), an unusually large Neolithic wedge-shape tomb with a rectangular main chamber and a smaller chamber to the rear.

Glanworth

A short distance further on, at Glanworth, the River Funshion is spanned by an ancient 13-arched bridge. In the surrounding area are a number of ruined castles along the river.

Galway · Gaillimh   C 2

Republic of Ireland
Province: Connacht
County: Galway
Population: 47,000

Galway (Gaillimh) is picturesquely situated at the north-east end of
Galway Bay, at the point where the short tidal River Corrib, coming
from Lough Corrib, disgorges its abundant flow of water into the
Atlantic.

Galway is the see of the diocese of Co. Galway, and has a university
(part of the National University of Ireland), in which much of the teaching is in Irish (summer courses for visitors in July and August). Irish culture and language are also promoted by Taebhdhearc na Gaillimhe, an
Irish language theatre.

In the last two decades Galway has experienced a 40 per cent increase
in population with a corresponding economic and cultural upsurge and
an increase in tourism. Although Galway itself has no really outstanding
features, it is an excellent centre for exploring the west of Ireland.

There is a regular ferry service from the harbour to the Aran Islands
(➤ entry), the terminal being at the east end of the harbour at the end of
Lough Atalia Road. There are likewise regular air services to the islands
from Carnmore Airport, some 5½ miles to the east.

There has been a settlement on this site from earliest times. After the   History
building of a castle in 1124 and its capture by Richard de Burgo in 1232,
Galway rapidly developed into a flourishing Anglo-Norman town. The
'14 tribes of Galway' – aristocratic merchant families – transformed the
town into a kind of urban outpost, maintaining the English connection in
defiance of all Irish assaults (the Irish in fact were barred from entering
the town). Galway was destroyed by a great fire in 1473 but was soon
rebuilt. Trade with the countries of western Europe, particularly Spain,
brought wealth and prosperity. During the 16th and 17th c. there was a
celebrated grammar school here which is said at one time to have had

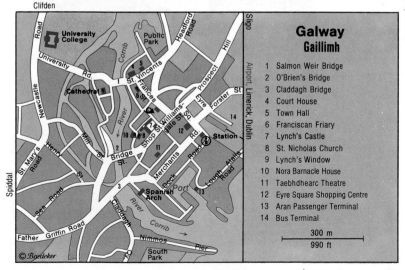

Galway
Gaillimh

1 Salmon Weir Bridge
2 O'Brien's Bridge
3 Claddagh Bridge
4 Court House
5 Town Hall
6 Franciscan Friary
7 Lynch's Castle
8 St. Nicholas Church
9 Lynch's Window
10 Nora Barnacle House
11 Taebhdhearc Theatre
12 Eyre Square Shopping Centre
13 Aran Passenger Terminal
14 Bus Terminal

300 m
990 ft

© Baedeker

199

1200 pupils. In the 17th c. the town supported the Irish cause and suffered widespread destruction at the hands of Cromwell's forces; in 1691 it was further damaged when it fell to William of Orange's army.

Town

The central area of Galway lies on the east bank of the River Corrib, and although few old buildings have survived, the narrow winding streets still have a certain atmosphere. The walls of a number of houses have stones with coats of arms carved on them, relics of Galway's heyday.

For centuries Galway had active trading relations with Spain and has retained something of this Spanish influence – manifested architecturally, for instance, by houses built around an open courtyard.

Sights

Eyre Square
Kennedy Park

The centre of Eyre Square has been landscaped as a memorial to US president John F Kennedy, who was of Irish descent. On its north-west side stands Browne's Gateway, the doorway of an old patrician mansion which has been re-erected here. Also in the square is a striking monument to the Irish language poet Pádraic O'Conaire (1882–1923), seen seated on a rock.

Eyre Square
Shopping Centre

Situated west of Eyre Square is the eponymous modern shopping centre which, with its cafés, has become a popular meeting place. Part of the old town wall has been restored and incorporated into the complex (see picture below).

★Lynch's Castle

Eyre Square leads to Williamsgate Street, one of the town's main shopping thoroughfares, and to Lynch's Castle (16th c.; National Monument).

Eyre Square Shopping Centre

Lynch's Castle

Today occupied by a bank, the tall grey building with coats of arms on the exterior was considerably altered during restoration in the 1960s. The castle was formerly the residence of the Lynches, an aristocratic family several of whom became mayors of Galway. It was while holding that office that one of the Lynches condemned his own son to death for the murder of a young visiting Spaniard. When no one else proved willing, he carried out the sentence with his own hands – so giving rise to the expression 'lynch law'.

A black marble tablet on the wall of the old prison in Market Street marks the spot (**Lynch's Window**) where the execution is said to have taken place.

St Nicholas's Church (National Monument), also in Market Street, was built in the 14th c. and, although later much altered, has retained the aspect of a medieval parish church. Notable features are the west front, the gargoyles (rare in Ireland) and, in the interior, a number of tombs and a reader's desk.

★St Nicholas's Church

A short distance from the church (in Bowling Green) stands the house of James Joyce's wife, Nora Barnacle, where the writer often stayed. On Wednesdays in summer, literary evenings are held here. Open Mon.–Sat. 10am–5pm.

Nora Barnacle House

Further upstream the River Corrib is spanned by the Salmon Weir Bridge (1818). In spring (mid-May) countless salmon can be seen making their way up river to the expanse of Lough Corrib (➤ entry), a journey of only 4 miles from the sea.

Salmon Weir Bridge

Strong tidal currents are experienced in the river here, with a powerful flow downstream on the ebb and an equally powerful flow upstream when the tide turns.

The cathedral (St Nicholas and the Assumption), on the right bank, was consecrated in 1965. One of the largest churches in Ireland (300 ft long by 155 ft wide), it occupies the site of a prison in which many Irish patriots were confined. Building costs were met almost entirely by public subscription. There are good mosaics in the side chapels.

Cathedral

Of the town's three bridges the middle one, O'Brien's Bridge, is the oldest, its existence being first recorded in 1342.

O'Brien's Bridge
Claddagh Bridge

The Claddagh Bridge (a swing bridge) at the south end of the town, takes its name from an old fishermen's quarter on the right bank of the Corrib, occupied for centuries by a fishermen's guild but now replaced by modern buildings. Today the only reminder of the guild is the traditional 'Claddagh ring', in the form of two hands clasping a heart. Worn as an amulet, it was handed down from mother to daughter.

On the east side of the Corrib, below Claddagh Bridge, is the old town gate known as the Spanish Arch (1594), leading to Spanish Parade, once the favourite promenade of Spanish merchants. The arch now houses the Galway City Museum, with material on the history of Galway, and old weapons found in Galway Bay. Open summer daily 10am–5pm.

Spanish Arch
City Museum

Surroundings

North-east of Galway on the N17, Claregalway has the ruins of a Franciscan friary (National Monument) founded in 1290 and enlarged in the 15th c. On a tombstone in the church there is a representation of a primitive plough.

Claregalway

From Carnmore proceed to Oranmore and from there south on the N18 to Clarinbridge, a pretty little village where excellent local oysters and shellfish can be sampled.

Clarinbridge

Glencolumbkille · Gleann Cholaim Cille

Kilcolgan

1¼ mile south of Clarinbridge, at Kilcolgan, the N67 branches off to the right, leading after ¾ mile to the ruins of Drumacoo Church (National Monument), with finely carved windows and doorway; also notable is St Surney's Well, a holy well.

Dunguaire Castle

10 miles further south-west on the N67 stands Dunguaire Castle, a 16th c. tower house complete with furnishings and open to visitors. In the evenings medieval banquets are held in the hall.

Salthill

Situated immediately west of Galway, and today continuous with it, is Salthill (Irish name Bothar na Tra, shore road), a seaside resort on the north side of Galway Bay. Though its rather basic hotels, bingo halls and amusement arcades will not appeal to everyone, it does have a lovely seafront promenade above a broad sandy beach from where there are extensive views of the hills of Clare, the Burren and the Aran Islands.

Spiddal

The R336 follows the coast to Barna and Spiddal, a pretty little resort with good fishing. Irish crafts flourish in the Spiddal Craft Centre with demonstrations and a range of goods on sale. Open May–Oct. Mon.–Sat. 9am–5.30pm, Sun. 1–6pm.

Glencolumbkille · Gleann Cholaim Cille   B 3

Republic of Ireland
Province: Ulster
County: Donegal
Population: 250

Dunguaire Castle

Countryside around Glencolumbkille: beautiful scenery and a lovely beach

Glencolumbkille (Gleann Cholaim Cille, St Columba's glen) is a picturesque holiday resort in the far north of Ireland, at the most westerly point of Co. Donegal. It lies in a valley opening into Glen Bay on the Atlantic, with a sandy beach and magnificent cliff scenery in the surrounding area.

The area around Glencolumbkille is one of the Irish-speaking parts of Donegal. Here St Columcille (Columba) lived in solitude and meditated. Another tradition has it that Bonnie Prince Charlie, last in the line of Stuart pretenders, spent some time here when fleeing from the British.

In the middle of the 20th c., when Glencolumbkille was in danger of dying through lack of employment, Father James McDyer set up a co-operative to maximise agricultural potential and market local handmade art and crafts. The undertaking proved successful. Thatched cottages were built for holiday letting and a Folk Museum established to attract day trippers.

Pilgrimage

Every year on June 9th (St Columba's Day) a pilgrimage takes place here, the route – a circuit of some 3 miles on the hillsides around the village – being marked by a series of stone slabs and pillars inscribed with crosses and geometric designs; the largest of these stones can be seen beside the church. Pilgrims complete either three or seven full circles, from time to time adding a stone to the heaps accumulating around the stations. The pilgrimage must be completed before sunrise.

Sights

Folk Museum

The open-air museum (open Apr.–Sep. Mon.–Sat. 10am–6pm, Sun. noon–6pm) at the west end of the village consists of four thatched cottages furnished with folk items dating from 1700 to 1900, together with

Folk Museum in Glencolumbkille

a 19th c. schoolhouse. There is also a shop selling local products and a tea room serving homemade cakes. This entire project, too, was the brainchild of Father James McDyer.

Surroundings

Malinmore

South-west of Glencolumbkille lies Malinmore, a pretty little resort with a bay and picturesque cliffs. Nearby, at Cloghanmore, is a Bronze Age court cairn (National Monument).

Rathlin O'Birne

There is good fishing in the coastal waters extending out to the island of Rathlin O'Birne, which has a number of historic sites (6th c.) and a lighthouse.

★★Glendalough · Gleann da Locha   C/D 5

Republic of Ireland
Province: Leinster
County: Wicklow

The celebrated monastic settlement of Glendalough (Gleann da Locha, glen of the two lakes) lies a little way inland from the Irish Sea coast some 25 miles south of Dublin. On summer weekends it tends to be crowded with day trippers; weekdays are generally quieter.

Turn off the R755 – running south from Bray through the hills to Arklow – at Laragh, into a wooded valley opening out to the west. After about a mile Glendalough comes into view, famous both for its monastic remains and for its scenery. Grouped around the two lakes from which the village takes its name are the impressive, and for the most part well preserved, remains of a religious centre that was once among the most influential in Ireland.

Enclosed by hills of varying height between 2130 and 2460 ft, the valley of the River Glenealo, which narrows sharply further upstream, offers plenty of scope for walking and climbing. The valley cuts through the Glendalough Forest Park in the Wicklow Mountains (➤ entry).

Topography

St Kevin first took up his abode in this remote valley as a hermit seeking solitude. His piety and learning attracted so many disciples, however, that he founded a monastery. When in 618 he died at an advanced age, Glendalough's period of greatness was only just beginning; after his time the Glendalough school is said to have had more than a thousand students. The annals tell of Viking raids and, in the 12th c., a number of damaging fires. In 1163 an abbot of Glendalough, Laurence O'Toole, was appointed archbishop of Dublin. In 1214 the Anglo-Normans made the monastery subject to the see of Dublin; then, after a fire in 1398, it steadily declined. In 1875–80 the buildings were restored and have been meticulously maintained ever since.

History

Monastic settlement

The opening times given refer to the Visitor Centre, the monastic site itself being open at all times. Car parks are provided at the Visitor Centre and between the Upper and Lower lakes. By far the best plan is to see the video presentation at the Centre first, then start the tour of the site at the Upper Lake, the real heart of the complex. A delightful path known as the Green Road then leads from the Upper Lake to the remains of the monastic settlement near the Visitor Centre.

Open daily 9.30am–5pm, 6.30pm in summer

Exhibits in the Visitor Centre include a model of the site as well as various gravestones, carved stones and other masonry. Of special interest is a 12th c. high cross (Market Cross) with a Crucifixion, the figure of an abbot and interlace ornament; this may once have stood on the pilgrim route to Glendalough.

Visitor Centre

Accessible only by boat, the little rectangular Teampull na Skellig (Church on the Rock) stands on a quarried platform by the lakeside. The oldest fragment of the partly restored church dates from the late 7th c.

Teampull na Skellig

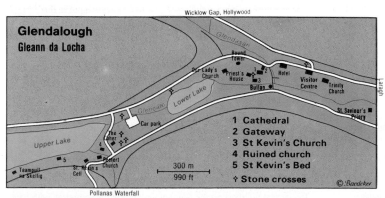

Wicklow Gap, Hollywood

Glendalough
Gleann da Locha

Glendasan

Round Tower

Our Lady's Church

Priest's House

Hotel

Visitor Centre

Trinity Church

Laragh

Bullan

Lower Lake

Glenealo

St. Saviour's Priory

Car park

The Caher

Upper Lake

Reefert Church

St. Kevin's Cell

Teampull na Skellig

300 m

990 ft

1 **Cathedral**
2 **Gateway**
3 **St Kevin's Church**
4 **Ruined church**
5 **St Kevin's Bed**
✟ **Stone crosses**

© Baedeker

Pollanas Waterfall

205

Glendalough Round Tower *St Kevin's Church*

St Kevin's Bed	About 220 yd further east is a cavity in the cliff known as St Kevin's Bed (or hermitage), in all probability a Bronze Age burial place.
St Kevin's Cell	Easier to reach is St Kevin's Cell, the beehive hut in which the saint is said to have lived.
Reefert Church	By a small bridge are remains (nave, chancel) of Reefert Church (11th c.); the projecting stones at the corners supported the rafters.
The Caher	Between the Upper and Lower Lake, to the right of the car park, stand an ancient stone fort (the Caher) and three stone crosses (probably boundary stones originally but afterwards stations on the pilgrimage circuit).
Gateway	The main group of monastic buildings lie further downstream near the Visitor Centre. Access to the precinct dating from the heyday of the monastery was through an entrance gateway.
Round tower	Near the gate stands the exceptionally well-preserved round tower, 102 ft high and 16 ft in diameter at the base. It is still very much as it was when first built, apart from the roof which was reconstructed using the old stones. The doorway is more than 10 ft from the ground.
St Mary's Church	West of the round tower is the granite St Mary's Church (10th c.), venerated up until the 18th c. as St Kevin's burial place.
Priest's House	Beyond this is the Priest's House, a 12th c. Irish Romanesque building with an interesting carving of much earlier date on the lintel of the doorway.
Cathedral	The largest building on the Glendalough site is the cathedral, with nave,

chancel and sacristy (11th and 12th c.). It had cathedral status until the beginning of the 13th c.

Perhaps the most remarkable of all the buildings at Glendalough, however, is St Kevin's Church, traditionally – though mistakenly – known as St Kevin's Kitchen on account of its chimney-like belfry. This building of hard mica schist with a steeply pitched roof dates from the 11th/12th c. It houses a small number of stone carvings discovered on the site.

St Kevin's Church

Trinity Church (11th/12th c.), on the right of the Laragh road, still has its original granite chancel arch.

Trinity Church

Further to the east, on the far side of the river, stands the most recent complex of buildings, St Saviour's Priory (12th c.; reconstructed about 1875). Some fine Romanesque carvings on the chancel arch and windows and some conventual buildings are the only original work to survive.

St Saviour's Priory

Glengarriff · Gleann Garb   E 2

Republic of Ireland
Province: Munster
County: Cork
Population: 150

Glengarriff (Gleann Garb, rugged glen) lies in the far south-west of Ireland at the mouth of a 6-mile-long valley where the River Glengarriff flows into Bantry Bay. The village is wholly given over to tourism, a large

View of Glengarriff and some of its islands

amount of holiday accommodation being provided in private houses. Day trippers come mainly to visit Garinish Island offshore or to do a circuit of the Ring of Beara.

Village

Glengarriff's location makes it particularly attractive as a destination. In the favourable climate of the region, bathed in the warm moist air of the Gulf Stream, a mantle of vegetation of almost tropical luxuriance – fuchsias, yews, hollies and arbutus – garbs the rocky hillsides reaching down to the sea.

★★Garinish Island – Ilnacullin

Open Mon.–Sat.
10am–4.30pm,
Sun. 1–5pm

Of the many little islands in the bay the one most worth visiting is Garinish (Ilnacullin; ➤ picture, p. 74), which lies offshore to the east of the R572. Small boats run regularly to the island from Glengarriff, a 15-minute crossing during which seals are often seen basking on the rocks. The gardens, with their magnolias, rhododendrons, camellias and many exotic trees, were only laid out between 1910 and 1920. The oldest building on the island is the Martello tower, dating from Napoleonic times; the others, blending beautifully with the landscaping, were erected only when the gardens were first established.

Among the best-known personalities to visit Garinish was George Bernard Shaw (➤ Famous People). In 1923 he spent several months in a house (not open to the public) on the island writing the greater part of *Saint Joan*.

★Ring of Beara

Glengarriff is a good base from which to explore the peninsula jutting out westwards into the Atlantic. Though not nearly so well known as the Ring of Kerry (➤ entry), this 84-mile drive offers no less spectacular scenery. Strung across the interior of the peninsula are the Caha and Slieve Miskish mountains which reach heights of between 1313 and 2297 ft.

Castletownbere

The R572, skirting the shores of Bantry Bay with the Caha Mountains on one side and the sea on the other, loops around Adrigole Harbour before resuming its westward course to Castletownbere.

About 2 miles south-west of Castletownbere stand the ruins of Dunboy Castle. The present building, constructed at the turn of the 20th c. in remarkable a mixture of styles, was erected over the remnants of a castle destroyed in 1602. The view is magnificent.

Bere Island

Offshore can be seen the striking silhouette of Bere Island where today there is a sailing school.

Dursey Island

Off the western tip of the peninsula lies Dursey Island, separated from the mainland by Dursey Sound. Only a dozen people live on the island (access by cable car for those of strong nerve).

Eyeries

North of Castletownbere the R571 crosses a saddle in the Slieve Miskish Mountains to the well-kept little village of Eyeries.

At Ballycrovane, a little to the east, a huge ogham stone (National Monument) can be seen from the road. Situated on private land, it stands 17 ft high and looks almost like a piece of modern sculpture.

Derreen Garden

Beyond Eyeries the road continues north-east to Lauragh in Co. Kerry where the beautiful Derreen Gardens can be visited. Mossy paths lead through woods, past lush rhododendrons, eucalyptus and bamboo groves with superb views of the sea. Open Apr.–Sep. daily 11am–6pm.

From Lauragh a road crosses the Healy Pass (1066 ft) to Adrigole and thence back to Glengarriff.

Gort · Gort Iase Guaire C 3

Republic of Ireland
Province: Connacht
County: Galway
Population: 1100

Gort (Gort Iase Guaire, Guaire's field by the shore) lies in the far west of Ireland to the south of Galway Bay. It attracts visitors mainly on account of the many features of interest in the surrounding area.

The little town is neatly laid out around a large central market place, with two early 19th c. churches.   Town

Surroundings

On the north side of the town, to the west of the N18, lies Coole Park,   **Coole Park**
former home of the author Lady Gregory (1852–1932) where once the cream of Irish writers and poets were entertained. Destroyed in 1941, nothing now remains except a magnificent avenue of cedars and a copper beech bearing the initials of many Irish literati (George Bernard Shaw, Yeats, O'Casey and others). The estate is now a national forest and deer park.

Yeats' Thoor Ballylee

Kilmacduagh Round Tower

Coole Park Interpretative Centre has information on the flora and fauna of the region as well as a collection of portraits of Lady Gregory and her literary associates. Open Apr.–Sep. daily 9.30am–6.30pm; park open at all times.

★ Thoor Ballylee

On the banks of a stream about 4½ miles north of Gort stands Thoor Ballylee, a four-storey 16th c. tower house purchased and restored by W B Yeats (➤ Famous People) who lived in it from 1921 to 1929. His period of residence is commemorated by a stone tablet with some lines of verse by him. The tower has been carefully restored and now appears as it did during Yeats' lifetime. It contains a museum of Yeats memorabilia including first editions of his works. Open Apr.–Sep. daily 10am–6pm.

Lough Cutra

South-east of Gort lies Lough Cutra. The River Beagh flows out of the lough, after which – like other rivers in this limestone region – it disappears below ground several times only to reappear again. The lough itself is highly picturesque, with a number of small wooded islets on which there are the ruins of churches and a castle. Commandingly situated on the shore of the lough is Lough Cutra Castle (1810 by John Nash), complete with tower and battlements. The castle is not open to the public.

★ Kilmacduagh

South-west of Gort on the R460 are the ruins of Kilmacduagh (National Monument), a monastic site with several churches and a round tower. The round tower, 112 ft high, is excellently preserved, but leans about 2 ft from perpendicular; the entrance is 25 ft above the ground. Beside it is the cathedral (12th–15th c.) with nave, chancel and transepts; in the north transept are rustic representations of the Crucifixion. To the right of the cathedral stands St John's Church (12th c.), and adjoining it a fortress-like 13th c. building, probably the abbot's lodging. At the north-west corner of the precinct is O'Heyne's Church (13th c.), with a fine chancel arch; close by are the remains of another small church. On the other side of the road, opposite the cathedral, is St Mary's Church (12th c.). The entire site, set in green meadowland on the shores of a lough with the Burren Hills in the background, is exceedingly picturesque.

Grand Canal   C 3–4

Republic of Ireland
Length: 80 miles

The Grand Canal links Dublin Bay to the Shannon (➤ entry), following a fairly direct westerly course from Dublin (➤ entry), by way of Naas and Tullamore (see entries) to Shannon Harbour. Differences of height are overcome by a total of 52 locks.

History

Construction of the canal began in 1756. Soon afterwards the project was taken over by a Dublin company and by 1777 had been carried forward as far as the River Mortell, one of the purposes of this section being to improve the city's water supply. Two years later the completed section was opened to navigation. In 1785 the Barrow Line, a branch canal from Robertstown to Athy, was brought into use. In 1804 the whole canal was completed and the first barges began to ply between Dublin and Shannon Harbour. Thereafter, until the middle of the 19th c., various other branch canals were constructed to towns lying near the main canal. With the coming of the railways the economic importance of the canal declined; this continued in the 20th c. until, by about 1960, commercial traffic on the branch canals had ceased altogether.

Pleasure craft

The Grand Canal is now used mainly by pleasure craft, subject to the following maximum dimensions: overall length 60 ft, beam 13 ft, draught 4 ft, air draught 9 ft. Every craft must bear a name or a number. The maximum permitted speed is 3 mph. Vessels must keep to the right, with overtaking on the left. Locks can only be worked during daylight hours. Hire craft are available at various places along the canal.

Horn Head · Corran Binne   A 4

Republic of Ireland
Province: Ulster
County: Donegal

Horn Head (Corran Binne, hollow in the hills) is the northernmost extremity of a peninsula jutting into the Atlantic in the far north of Ireland. It is reached by way of the N56.
    The best starting point for excursions to Horn Head and the surrounding area is Dunfanaghy, with an 18-hole golf course and the little harbour of Port-na-Blagh nearby. 1¼ miles further east, on a sheltered bay, lies Marble Hill. All these places have beautiful sandy beaches.

From Dunfanaghy there is a delightful walk along the west coast of the peninsula to Horn Head. The headland rises straight from the sea to a height of about 600 ft, with views northward over the boundless ocean, broken only by numerous islands and promontories, and inland to splendid ranges of hills, with Muckish Mountain and Errigal Mountain as backdrops. Horn Head is well known for its seabird colonies
    It is also possible to drive to the tip of the peninsula. The best view of the cliffs is obtained from Traghlisk Point on the east side.

Topography

Landscape on Horn Head

211

Surroundings

Ards
South-east of the village of Marble Hill, on the Ards Peninsula, which sticks out into the bay of Sheep Haven, is a Capuchin friary. The grounds and parkland can be visited on application to the fathers.

Doe Castle
To the south of the friary, beautifully situated on a promontory, are the ruins of Doe Castle (16th c.; National Monument), a four-storey keep surrounded by defensive walls and towers. Chieftains from many leading Donegal families are interred in the burial ground.

Creeslough
6 miles south of Dunfanaghy lies Creeslough, with a picturesque bridge over the Duntally River, a waterfall and St Michael's Church, a fine modern building (1971 by Liam McCormick and Partners).

Inishowen Peninsula · Inis Eoghain   A 4/5

Republic of Ireland
Province: Ulster
County: Donegal

The Inishowen Peninsula (Inis Eoghain, Eoghain's island) is the northernmost part of Ireland; its most northerly point is Malin Head.
  To the west of the peninsula Lough Swilly, a broad arm of the sea, cuts deep inland; to the east lies the great and almost land-locked expanse of Lough Foyle with Northern Ireland beyond. Malin Head, at the extreme north-western tip, looks out across open ocean. A 100-mile-long signposted route, the Inis Eoghain 100, makes a circuit of the peninsula.

Buncrana

The principal settlement on the peninsula is Buncrana (population 4000), a popular seaside resort on the east side of Lough Swilly, with a 3-mile-long beach, Lisfannon Strand. In recent years a greater range of entertainment and leisure facilities has become available to holidaymakers, the majority of whom come from Northern Ireland. Buncrana and the surrounding area have a tradition of textile manufacture; today 2000 jobs are provided by the American textile firm Fruit of the Loom (factory shop).

O'Doherty's Keep
Beautifully situated on the lough is O'Doherty's Keep, a well-preserved but architecturally undistinguished stronghold (14th–17th c.; National Monument).

Buncrana Castle
Beyond the bridge stands Buncrana Castle (1716 by Vaughan), a handsome mansion with a beautiful interior, unfortunately falling into a state of disrepair.

Vintage Car and
Carriage Museum
The nearby Vintage Car and Carriage Musuem has a collection of vintage cars, carriages and Victorian bicycles. Open summer daily 10am–8pm.

Tullyarvan Mill
Tullyarvan Mill, built in the 19th c., stands at the edge of Buncrana on the road to Dunree Head. It has been carefully restored and now houses a small textile museum and museum shop. Open Apr.–Sep. Mon.–Sat. 10am–6pm, Sun. noon–6pm.

Circuit of the peninsula

Setting out from Buncrana, start by taking the byroad going north-west to Dunree Head. At Fort Dunree (4 miles) there is a military museum with a video presentation covering the history of the fort and area. Open Apr.–Sep. Tue.–Sat. 10am–6pm, Sun. noon–6pm.

Dunree Head

Continue over the Gap of Mamore, a breathtakingly steep pass with gradients of up to 30 per cent. The magnificence of the scenery is best appreciated when, as in this case, crossing from the south.

Gap of Mamore

At the most northerly point on this stretch of road lies Dunaff Head (superb cliffs, much frequented by rock climbers, and exceptional views).

Dunaff Head

Rejoining the R238 at Clonmany continue to Ballyliffin with its 2-mile-long beach, Pollan Strand. Picturesquely situated on the northern tip of the Doagh Peninsula are the ruins of Carrickabrahey Castle.

Ballyliffin

Next stop is Carndonagh, a little town with shirt-making factories and a distillery. Opposite the church stand three Early Christian pillars (all National Monuments), of which the most noteworthy is the 7th c. St Patrick's Cross, one of the earliest in Ireland. The cruciform motif is only hinted at in the arrangement of the Celtic interlace decoration; in the lower half is the figure of a man with extended arms, flanked by smaller figures; the reverse has more interlace work and a human figure. On either side of the cross are smaller stones with reliefs of David with his harp, a bird, a man with two bells, and other devices. More monuments can be seen in the churchyard at the rear.

Carndonagh

3 miles north of Carndonagh the road reaches Malin. Here the R242 branches off left past the handsome Malin Hall (1758) to Malin Head (magnificent cliff scenery).
1¼ miles west of the point is Hell's Hole, a narrow cleft through which the incoming tide surges with awesome force.

Malin Head

From Malin Head a long succession of cliffs up to 790 ft high stretch south-east to Glengad Head.

Glengad Head

Continue south to Culdaff, a fishing centre (sea trout), and then a further 2 miles south again to Clonca where there is a ruined church, a fine but badly weathered high cross with a representation of the Miracle of the Loaves and Fishes, as well as two male figures and geometric designs, and a finely carved tombstone (all National Monuments).

Culdaff
Clonca

At Carrowmore there is a group of high crosses (National Monuments).

Carrowmore

The R238 proceeds next to Moville, a popular resort on Lough Foyle and once a departure point for ships crossing the Atlantic.

Moville

2½ miles to the north-east lies Greencastle, with the ruins of a large castle (1305; National Monument). Nearby is a Martello tower (1810), now a hotel.

Greencastle

From Greencastle continue north-east on the R241 for 2½ miles to Inishowen Head from which another range of superb cliffs (with views across to the Northern Ireland coast) extends north-westward. The cliff scenery and the delightful valley of Glenagiveny attract many visitors.

Inishowen Head

To complete the circuit of the peninsula, follow the R238 along the shores of Lough Foyle to Muff (border crossing to Londonderry; ➤ entry). There head west on the R239 to rejoin the R238 south of Burnfoot.

Muff

St Aengus Church

Further south of Burnfoot, at the intersection of the R238 with the N13, is a notable modern church by MacCormick and Madden. Dedicated to St Aengus, the circular building with its band of windows and curving roof canopy surmounted by a pyramidal glass spire, may well have been influenced by the Grianán of Aileach (see below), only 2½ miles away to the south.

★Grianán of Aileach

Grianán of Aileach (Grianán, sun palace) is an Early Christian circular stone fort surrounded by three concentric earth ramparts, commandingly situated on a 790-ft hill. The windowless outer wall, constructed without mortar, stands 17 ft high and is 13 ft thick at the base; it encloses a grassy area 79 ft in diameter, entered via a low doorway. The wall is terraced on the inside, with steps leading up to each level; within the thickness of the wall are a series of small chambers and passages. The precise period of construction of the fort, which from the 5th to the 12th c. was the seat of the kings of Ulster, is unknown. It was extensively restored in 1874–8. From the walls of the fort there are breathtaking views over the the surrounding countryside and loughs.

Fahan

4½ miles north-west, at Fahan on the shores of Lough Swilly, an ancient cross slab (8th c.) stands in a former monastic churchyard adjoining the modern church. Two crudely carved figures flank the cross which itself is of elaborate interlace work; on one of the edges is a Greek inscription, something of a rarity in Ireland.

Kells · Ceanannus Mor   C 5

Republic of Ireland
Province: Leinster
County: Meath
Population: 2600

Kells (Ceanannus Mor, great residence) lies in the wooded valley of the Blackwater 25 miles inland from the Irish Sea coast, at the intersection of the N3 and N52.
The name Kells is primarily associated with the celebrated Book of Kells, a magnificently illuminated manuscript of the four Gospels now in the library of Trinity College, Dublin (► Dublin; Baedeker Special, p. 58). A facsimile can be seen in St Columba's Church, a modern building in the centre of town.

History

A monastic settlement was established at Kells by St Columba in the 6th c.; in the 9th c. monks from Iona sought refuge here after been driven from the Scottish island by Viking raids. In later centuries the settlement was several times plundered and subsequently restored. The town was fortified by the Anglo-Normans and maintained its importance until the dissolution of the monasteries in 1535.

Sights

Round tower

In the upper cemetery (in the town centre) stands a 100-ft round tower (10th c.; National Monument) with five windows at the top; the original roof is missing.

★South Cross

Nearby is the South Cross or Cross of St Patrick and St Columba (National Monument), probably erected in the 9th c. It has a wealth of sculptured ornament: on the base a train of chariots, animals and interlace; on the south face in ascending order the Fall, Cain and Abel and the Three Men in the Fiery Furnace, then Daniel in the Lions'

Kells: South Cross and ...   *... St Colomba's House*

Den, the Sacrifice of Isaac (left), Paul and Anthony in the Wilderness (right) and higher up David with his harp and the Miracle of the Loaves and Fishes; on the west face the Crucifixion and Christ as Judge. Other details include a representation of David killing the lion and the bear and a number of panels with interlace ornament and fabulous beasts.

Some 33 yd away can be seen the stump of a very large cross (National Monument) on the east side of which are unusual representations of the Baptism of Christ in the River Jordan (two rivers flowing together), the ?Marriage in Cana, the ?Presentation in the Temple, David with his harp and the ?Entry into Jerusalem; and on the west side Adam and Eve, Noah's Ark, among others. An unfinished cross beside the church gives an insight into the sculptor's method of working.

Other high
crosses

North-westwards, beyond the churchyard walls, stands St Columba's House (National Monument; bear left on leaving the churchyard), an oratory with a steeply pitched stone roof (probably 10th c.). The interior measures 24 by 21ft, the walls, more than 4 ft thick, inclining inwards to meet at the ridge. There is an upper chamber (entered via a steep ladder), the wall of which forms the roof. The original entrance was over 6 ft above the ground.

★St Columba's
House

The Market Cross (National Monument) in Cross Street (National Monument), in the centre of the town, is of considerably later date than the high crosses referred to above. An inscription states that it was erected in 1688, though modelled on a much earlier 9th c. one.

Market Cross

Surroundings

Headford

The estate of Headford, on the north-east side of the town, has a handsome Georgian manor house (1770), now occupied by a school.

Slieve na Calliagh

12½ miles west of Kells (R168 and R154) lies Slieve na Calliagh (witch's hill). The burial ground of Loughcrew scattered over two adjacent summits (access from a car park on the road between Drumone and Millbrook) includes some 30 Neolithic chambered cairns, only a few with their chambers intact. Cairn T, in the eastern group, is perhaps the most interesting; 120 ft in diameter, it has a large main chamber with side chambers and many stones with inscribed ornament.

A walk in the hills is rewarded with superb views of the fertile countryside of Meath some 985 ft below.

Hill of Loyd

From Kells the N3 runs north-west towards Virginia (➤ Cavan Surroundings). To the left just outside the town, on the Hill of Loyd, is a memorial tower of 1791 (delightful views).

St Ciarán's Church

2½ miles further along, on the bank of the Blackwater, are the ruins of St Ciarán's Church, with three simple high crosses (National Monuments), an Early Christian gravestone and a holy well.

Kenmare · An Neidin   E 2

Republic of Ireland
Province: Munster
County: Kerry
Population: 1200

Colourful houses in Kenmare

Kenmare (An Neidin, little nest), a friendly little seaside resort at the south-western tip of Ireland, lies at the outflow of the River Roughty into the long inlet known as the Kenmare River.

The town is noted for its high-quality lace, and also for its excellent woollen goods. The principal source of income, however, is tourism.

Despite the obvious influence of tourism, Kenmare, a planned town founded in 1775, still retains considerable charm. Its two main streets form a cross, the upper arms of which enclose a pleasant green. Not far to the west on the banks of the River Finnihy is Druids' Circle, a ring of 15 standing stones, 49 ft in diameter, with a dolmen in the centre.

Town

Surroundings

Kenmare makes a good base from which to set out round the Ring of Kerry (➤ entry), the exceptionally scenic circuit of the Iveragh Peninsula.

Ring of Kerry

Not quite so well known, and perhaps a little less spectacular – though highly rewarding all the same – is the drive round the Ring of Beara, circling the peninsula of that name south of Kenmare (➤ Glengarriff).

Ring of Beara

Kildare · Cill Dara   C 5

Republic of Ireland
Province: Leinster
County: Kildare
Population: 4000

Kildare (Cill Dara, church of the oak) lies in a slightly elevated situation in the east of Ireland, on the Dublin–Limerick road (N7). St Brigid of Kildare (453–521), who like St Patrick is patron saint of Ireland, founded a famous double monastery here. It had both monks and nuns and was headed jointly by a bishop abbot and an abbess. The nuns tended St Brigid's 'fire', a perpetual flame which was finally extinguished only at the dissolution of the monastery.

Today Kildare is the centre of Ireland's bloodstock and horse-racing industry.

Sights

The town's past glories are recalled by St Brigid's Cathedral (1223), which has undergone several restorations, most recently in 1875–96. It contains a number of medieval monuments, notably the tomb of one of the Fitzgeralds of Lackagh (d 1575).

St Brigid's Cathedral

In the churchyard stands a fine round tower, 105 ft high, probably one of the last to be erected in Ireland; it can be climbed without difficulty. The roof is modern.

Round tower

Tully, on the south-eastern outskirts of Kildare, is the home of the Irish National Stud, which can be visited along with the notable Japanese Gardens (open mid-Feb. to mid-Nov. daily 9.30am–6pm). The Visitor Centre, opened in 1993, leads first to the gardens, established using plants specially imported for the purpose. The gardens take the form of a 'Path of Life', each of the 20 'stations' representing a stage in man's journey from the cradle to the grave. The final station is the 'Gate to Eternity' – through which visitors pass only to find themselves unmis-

★★Irish National Stud
Japanese Gardens

takably earthbound in the National Stud, which has produced many famous racehorses.

The stud was established in about 1900 by a Scot, William Hall-Walker, whose breeding methods were eccentric to say the least. Stallions and mares were paired according to their zodiacal signs, and a horoscope was drawn up for every foal. If the omens were not good, the foal was sold. For all this, Hall-Walker became a successful breeder. In 1915 he presented his stud to the British government; in 1943 it was handed over to the Irish government.

Walking round the grounds visitors can see some valuable breeding stallions and in spring and summer the mares and their foals at pasture. The saddler and smith can also be watched at work. Another attraction here is the Irish Horse Museum, covering the history of the horse from the Bronze Age to the present day. Among the many exhibits on display is the skeleton of Arkle, one of the most celebrated of Irish racehorses.

The Curragh

East of the National Stud lies the world-famous racecourse known as 'the Curragh', surrounded by a vast stretch of fine grassland from which it takes its name. The Irish Derby (so called after the 12th Earl of Derby) is run here every year at the end of June/beginning of July.

Surroundings

Hill of Allen

On the Hill of Allen, 5 miles north of the town on the R415, there once stood a castle belonging to the kings of Leinster. The site is now occupied by a tower (1859) with Latin inscriptions; extensive views.

Old Kilcullen

At the eastern edge of the Curragh, on the River Liffey (bridge of 1319), is the little town of Kilcullen, 2 miles south of which lies Old Kilcullen.

The famous racecourse 'the Curragh'

Once a walled town with seven gates, Old Kilcullen comprises the remains of a monastery (National Monument) founded by St Patrick, with a fragment of a 9th c. high cross on which are representations of David and the lion (north side), Samson with the lion (west side), bishops, other unidentified figures, and interlace ornament. A second cross shaft is badly weathered. Nearby are the remains of a round tower and a Romanesque church (12th c.).

Between Kilcullen and Old Kilcullen, on the west side of the N78, stands **Dún Ailinne** the hill fort of Dún Ailinne, once a stronghold of the kings of Leinster. Its 15-ft-high walls enclose an area 450 ft in diameter. Most unusually, the circular ditch is inside rather than outside the walls. The site remained occupied from the Bronze Age until about 1800.

Monasterevin, 7 miles west of Kildare, is a historic little market town **Monasterevin** with handsome late 19th c. houses.
   Moore Abbey, an elegant 18th c. house on the site of a monastery, is now a home for the mentally ill. North of Monasterevin the Grand Canal (➤ entry) crosses over the River Barrow by means of an aqueduct.

Kilkee · Cill Chaoidhe   D 2

Republic of Ireland
Province: Munster
County: Clare
Population: 1400

The attractive family holiday resort of Kilkee (Cill Chaoidhe, church of St Caoidhe), is situated on a crescent-shape bay on the west coast of Ireland, its long sandy beach protected from the Atlantic by the Duggerna Rocks. Along the beach to the west, past some impressive rock formations, stands Lookout Hill, from which vantage point, 200 ft above the sea, beautiful far-reaching views are obtained in clear weather (care required on the edge of the cliffs).

Surroundings

South-east of Kilkee (N67) lies the little market town of Kilrush, with a **Kilrush** harbour (Kilrush Creek Marina) 2 miles further south on the estuary of the Shannon. Recently enlarged and modernised, the harbour offers good moorings and other facilities for pleasure craft (boats available for charter).
   The Heritage Centre in the Town Hall takes as its theme 'Kilrush in Landlord Times'. Open Mon.–Sat. 11am–6pm, Sun. 2–6pm.

From Kilrush it is possible once again to go by pedestrian ferry to **Scattery Island** Scattery Island (information from the Scattery Island Centre, Merchants Quay, Kilrush) with the ruins of a 6th c. monastery (National Monument) founded by St Senan. Barely ½ sq mile, the island was inhabited until 1978, since when the village has fallen into decay. The round tower, one of the tallest in Ireland (115 ft), can be seen from some way off; it is unusual in having the entrance at ground level. To the east is the 'cathedral', to the north a 12th c. Romanesque church and to the south-east an early church with medieval additions. The monastery, a place of great importance in the 14th and 15th c., was destroyed in the reign of Elizabeth I.
   The island is the focus of several seafaring superstitions. For their maiden voyage newly built craft would be sailed around the island 'with

the sun'. And pebbles from Scattery carried in a ship were believed to protect it from shipwreck.

Killimer

The N67 comes to an abrupt end at Killimer, 5 miles south-east of Kilrush. Here a car ferry crosses the Shannon estuary to Tarbert (► Ballybunion), thus saving, on a north–south journey, a detour of some 55 miles around the estuaries of the Fergus and the Shannon (hourly departures).

Fooagh Point

Another very pleasant drive from Kilkee follows a minor road south-west along the coast to Fooagh – once a small spa with a chalybeate spring – and Fooagh Point, with a holy well and magnificent rock scenery (tunnels, caves, cliffs).

Carrigaholt

Above the harbour at Carrigaholt, across on the other (south) side of the peninsula, are the fine ruins of a tall, slender tower house (15th c.; National Monument) within a well-preserved enclosure; the turret facing towards the pier is modern. There is an Irish-language college in the village.

Loop Head

A delightful road then runs west from Carrigaholt to Kilbaha, beyond which lies Loop Head (lighthouse). Just off the point stands an isolated stack known as Diarmaid's and Grainne's Rock. The views are breathtaking.

★★Kilkenny · Cill Chainnigh   D 4

Republic of Ireland
Province: Leinster
County: Kilkenny
Population: 10,000

Kilkenny (Cill Chainnigh, Canice's church) is situated in the south-east of Ireland on the banks of the peat-brown River Nore. The town enjoys a degree of prosperity, reflecting not only the presence of several small industrial firms, but also its role as a market for local agriculture and as a focus for tourism. The Kilkenny Design Centre, dedicated to improving the quality of design and packaging of Irish products, has an excellent reputation throughout Ireland, as a consequence of which it attracts craftsmen and artists who settle in the town.

History

A church was built here in the 6th c. by St Canice. In the early Middle Ages it was the seat of the kings of Ossory, later passing into the hands of the Ormondes. During the 14th c. a number of parliaments met in Kilkenny, including the one in 1366 which approved the infamous Statute of Kilkenny. This made it high treason for an Anglo-Norman (i.e. an Englishman settled in Ireland) to marry an Irishwoman, adopt Irish customs, speak Irish or wear Irish dress, while at the same time prohibiting Irish people from living in a walled town. Although rigorously enforced, the statute failed in its object of preventing the assimilation of Anglo-Normans and Irish. From 1642 to 1648 the town was the seat of the Confederation of Kilkenny, an independent Irish parliament which brought together both the old Irish and the Anglo-Irish Catholics; later, however, the confederation split into two camps and the Anglo-Irish allied themselves with the English. In 1650 Cromwell took the town, the Irish garrison being permitted to march out with full honours.

Town

Kilkenny is considered by many to be second only to Dublin in its attraction for visitors. Its narrow winding streets lend it an atmosphere of old-world charm; its handsome Georgian terraces give it a certain elegance.

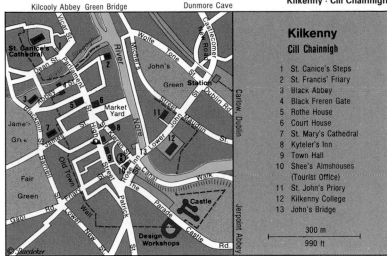

Kilcooly Abbey Green Bridge   Dunmore Cave

Kilkenny

Cill Chainnigh

1 St. Canice's Steps
2 St. Francis' Friary
3 Black Abbey
4 Black Freren Gate
5 Rothe House
6 Court House
7 St. Mary's Cathedral
8 Kyteler's Inn
9 Town Hall
10 Shee's Almshouses
    (Tourist Office)
11 St. John's Priory
12 Kilkenny College
13 John's Bridge

300 m
990 ft

Kells, Waterford

Recent decades have seen a comprehensive programme of restoration of the historic architecture, as a result of which the whole of Kilkenny once again presents a medieval aspect.

From time immemorial the town has been divided into three districts or wards – Irishtown, with the cathedral as its central landmark; High Town to the south, dominated by Kilkenny Castle; and, on the other bank of the River Nore, the eastern district, with St John's Priory.

Irishtown

At the north end of the town, just off Vicar Street, stands St Canice's Cathedral, one of the finest in Ireland. Built on the site of an earlier church, it was begun about 1251 and completed in 1280. The massive squat tower (14th c.) and exterior walls of the aisles, transepts and clerestory are all topped by crenellations. In spite of much restoration (most recently in 1863–4) the interior has retained its spacious character.

★St Canice's Cathedral

It contains many fine monuments, including the tombs of Henry de Ponto (1285; the oldest of the tombs) and of Edmund Purcell (1549), both in the north aisle. The Purcell tomb has a carving on a theme frequently found in Irish sculpture – a cock crowing on the edge of a cooking pot. This is a representation of the old Irish legend that, following Christ's Resurrection, a servant carried the news to the high priest's kitchen. The cook scoffed at the story – as unlikely, he said, as that the notion that the cock cooking in the pot would come to life again: whereupon the cock jumped out of the pot and crowed.

In the choir are the tombs of Bishop de Ledrede (d 1360) and Bishop Rothe; in the south transept the tomb of the 8th earl of Ormonde and his wife (1539); and in the south aisle the tombs of viscount Mountgarrett (in armour), Bishop Walsh (1585) and a lady in old Irish dress. In the north transept is St Ciarán's Chair, of black marble, and in the nave a 12th c. font.

By the south transept stands a 100-ft round tower with numerous windows; the roof is not original. From the top (very steep and narrow staircase) there are fine views of the city and the surrounding area.

Round tower

221

St Canice's Cathedral

St Canice's Steps · From the cathedral St Canice's Steps (1614) lead down to Dean Street.

High Town

St Francis' Friary · Parliament Street, running south, crosses the little River Bregagh, the boundary between Irishtown and High Town. Just to the left, on ground belonging to Smithwick's Brewery (guided tours and beer tasting; summer Mon.–Fri. 3pm), are the ruins of St Francis' Friary (National Monument), founded in about 1232 and extended in 1321 when the seven-light east window was inserted. The slender tower has fine sculpture.

Black Freren Gate · Continue southwards down Parliament Street to Abbey Street where, to the right, can be seen one of the old gates of the town defences, Black Freren Gate.

Black Abbey Church · A little further to the west stands Black Abbey Church, once the church of a Dominican friary founded in 1225. The church has recently been completely restored; the south transept is essentially 14th c. and the tower 15th c. Notable features of the interior include a medieval alabaster carving of the Trinity and a crudely carved oak figure of St Dominic.

★Rothe House · On returning to Parliament Street, the next building to catch the eye is Rothe House, an Elizabethan-style merchant's house built between 1594 and 1610 with two adjacent inner courtyards (restored 1966). It is now occupied by the City and County Museum. Open Apr.–Oct. Mon.–Sat. 10.30am–5pm, Sun. 3–5pm; Nov.–Mar. Sat., Sun. 3–5pm.

The Court House on the opposite side of the street dates from the 19th c. It was built on the remains of the 13th c. Grace's Castle.

Court House

Higher up to the right can be seen St Mary's Cathedral (1843), with a 200-ft tower.

St Mary's
Cathedral

The oldest building in the town is Kyteler's Inn (in St Kieran Street), today restored with a period interior. Still an inn, it is said that in the 14th c. a woman called Alice Kyteler lived here. Surviving four husbands, suspicion fell on her and she was condemned as a witch. She herself fled to safety, but a culprit was needed so her elderly servant perished at the stake instead.

Kyteler's Inn

In High Street, the southward continuation of Parliament Street, stands the Tholsel (1761), now the Town Hall, in which the civic insignia and muniments (dating back to 1230) are preserved. The building was completely restored in 1987 following a fire.

Town Hall

South-east of the Town Hall, in a lane between High Street and St Kieran Street, is St Mary's Hall, originally a parish church (?13th c.) but now a community centre. It contains a number of monuments from the old church, notably the tomb of Richard Rothe (d 1637) and, in the churchyard, a monument with figures of Faith, Hope and Charity and the Twelve Apostles.

St Mary's Hall

Not far from St Mary's Hall, in Rose Inn Street, are Shee's Almshouses. Founded in 1582 by Sir Richard Shee as a hospital for the poor, they remained in use as almhouses until 1895. Following comprehensive restoration the building now accommodates the tourist office and City Scope Exhibition, the latter illustrating Kilkenny in the 17th c. Open May–Sep. Mon.–Sat. 9am–6pm, Sun. 11am–5pm; Oct.–Apr. Tue.–Sat. 9am–12.45pm and 2–5pm.

Shee's
Almshouses

On the east side of the Parade stands Kilkenny Castle, begun by William Marshal in the 13th c. and over the years much altered and enlarged, especially in the 17th c. by the 1st duke of Ormonde, and in the 19th c. (picture-gallery wing). From 1391 to 1931 the castle was the principal seat of the Butler family. Finely situated on a bank above the river, and surrounded by gardens, the castle is open to the public.
    Some of the former state rooms have been restored, the Victorian Great Hall being particularly charming. Open Jun.–Sep. daily 10am–7pm; Apr., May daily 10.30am–5pm; Oct.–Mar. Tue.–Sun. 11am–12.45pm, 2–5pm.

★Kilkenny Castle

Across on the other side of the Parade are the Butler family's former stables, now occupied by the Kilkenny Design Centre. A wide range of quality Irish products (textiles, jewellery, glass, ceramics, among other items) are on sale and craftsmen can be seen at work. Their designs are used throughout Ireland, a striking feature being the employment by many artists of Celtic motifs as seen, for instance, in illuminated manuscripts such as the Book of Kells. Open daily 9am–6pm.

★Kilkenny Design
Centre

Eastern district

From the busy junction by Shee's Almshouses, John's Bridge crosses the river to the eastern district. In Lower John Street is Kilkenny College, a handsome Georgian building of 1782 and successor to St John's College (founded 1666), which counted Jonathan Swift and George Berkeley among its pupils. It is being converted for use as the County Hall.

Kilkenny College

Across the street stands St John's Priory (13th c.; National Monument).

St John's Priory

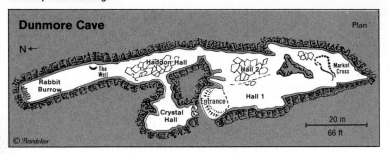

Of the church there survives only the chancel, with beautiful windows and stonework; the Lady Chapel is still used for worship.

Surroundings

★Dunmore Cave

Dunmore Cave (National Monument), 6 miles north of Kilkenny, is reached by taking a side road branching off the N78 (Note: on many maps the cave is incorrectly shown further south near the N77).

A little above the entrance to the cave a Visitor Centre has been constructed. On display are items excavated from the cave (bones, coins, primitive tools), many of which date from the 10th c. In 928, 40 people fleeing from raiding Vikings took refuge in the cave but were discovered and cruelly slaughtered. Among the most impressive formations in the cave is a stalagmite over 19 ft high known as the 'Market Cross'. Open mid-Mar. to mid-Jun. Tue.–Sun. 10am–5pm; mid-Jun. to mid-Sep. daily 10am–7pm; mid-Sep. to mid-Mar. Sat., Sun. 10am–5pm.

Ballyragget

The N77 leads north to Ballyragget where the ruins of Ormonde Castle (15th–16th c.) can be seen – a keep surrounded by walls and four round towers. One particular countess of Ormonde was renowned for her courage in leading her soldiers into battle.

Clara Castle

4½ miles east of Kilkenny, reached on a minor road branching left off the N10, stands the privately owned Clara Castle (15th c.), an unusually well-preserved six-storey tower house which still has its original oak beams, giving an excellent impression of the character of a fortified dwelling of the period. Among the features of particular interest are the forecourt, a passage with a 'murder hole' (a hole in the roof through which intruders could be pelted with missiles), a fine fireplace, and a secret room.

Gowran

A mile further on, the R702 branches right to Gowran, with a fine old parish church (ca 1275; National Monument) the tower of which (14th or 15th c.) has been incorporated into the present 19th c. building standing on the site of the original choir. The interior has a fine pointed arcade of black marble; good sculpture and monuments (14th–17th c.).

Thomastown

11 miles south of Kilkenny, reached on the N9 from Gowran or the R700 direct from Kilkenny, lies Thomastown, with a ruined 13th c. church (National Monument) and, in the Roman Catholic parish church, a high altar from Jerpoint Abbey (see below).

Kilfane

The village church at Kilfane, on the N9 north of Thomastown, is noteworthy for its larger-than-life effigy of Sir Thomas de Cantwell on his tomb (13th c.; National Monument).

From Kilfane a minor road runs east to join the R703 leading to Graiguenamanagh, a small town on the River Barrow (good fishing), with the ruins of a Cistercian monastery, Duiske Abbey (National Monument). In the churchyard, on the south side of the chancel, are two small granite high crosses with carvings of biblical scenes and abstract ornament.

5 miles south-east of Thomastown on the wooded banks of the River Nore, here spanned by a graceful 18th c. bridge, lies Inistioge, with the remains of an Augustinian abbey founded in 1210. The nave, Lady Chapel and tower of the church still survive. The tower, of which the lower part is square and the upper part octagonal, is now a mausoleum.

From Inistioge, Brandon Hill (1677 ft) can be easily climbed. On the summit are a cairn and a stone circle; fine views of the Barrow and Nore valleys.

About 2 miles south-west of Thomastown stands Jerpoint Abbey (National Monument), one of the finest ruined monasteries in Ireland. The abbey, founded in 1158, was occupied by the Cistercians from 1180 until its dissolution in 1540. Open mid-Jun. to Sep. daily 9.30am–6.30pm; May to mid-Jun. and the first half of Oct. Tue.–Sun. 10am–5pm.

The layout shows Cistercian influence. The church, with nave and aisles, transepts and an altar niche, is flanked to the south by the (restored) cloister round which are grouped the conventual buildings. Of these only the sacristy, chapter house and day rooms on the east side have been preserved. Above the crossing, as the rule of the order

Jerpoint Abbey

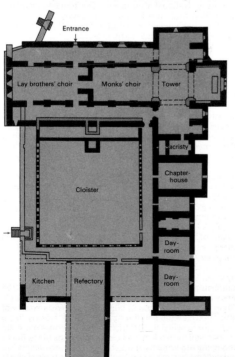

Jerpoint Abbey is one of the most impressive monastic ruins in Ireland. It was founded in the 12th c., probably by Donal, Lord of Ossory.

Originally a Benedictine house, the abbey passed into the hands of the Cistercians in 1180. It was much influenced by the French Abbey of Clairvaux, the most famous monastic house in the West.

The most notable features of the architecture are the cloister and the tower (both 15th c.). There is an abundance, unusual in a Cistercian house, of fine sculpture.

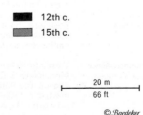

■ 12th c.

■ 15th c.

20 m
66 ft

© Baedeker

required, rises a handsome 15th c. tower (closed for fear of collapse). The nave is divided in roughly equal proportions into the monks' choir and lay brothers' choir.

The church has many fine monuments, including the tombs of Bishop O'Dulany of Ossory (d 1202), Katerine Poher and Robert Walsh (d 1501; by Rory O'Tunney) and two 13th c. knights. Note the rows of figures known as 'weepers' on the tombs.

The arcading in the cloister is embellished with a fine set of carved figures forming what has been described as 'a late Gothic picture-book'. They were the work of Rory O'Tunney, of whom nothing is known except that he came from a renowned family of sculptors and is believed to have been active between 1501 and 1552.

Kells

6 miles west of Thomastown, at Kells – not to be confused with the former monastery of that name in the north of the Irish Republic – are extensive remnants of a fortified Augustinian priory (National Monument) founded in 1193. The surviving buildings, dating from the 14th and 15th c., present an exceedingly impressive group of medieval remains. The church, with nave, transepts, chancel and Lady Chapel, has a tower above the crossing and two further towers, one of which was probably the prior's lodging. On the south side of the church are remains of conventual buildings, laid out around a courtyard and protected by a wall with two towers; further south again is a spacious outer court enclosed by a wall with five towers.

Kilree

2 miles south of Kells, on a narrow byroad, lies Kilree, with the remains of yet another monastery (National Monument). The remains include a roofless round tower 95 ft high; a ruined church (good 17th c. monument in the choir); and a badly weathered high cross (?9th c.) with representations of biblical scenes and geometric designs.

Callan

6 miles south-west of Kilkenny on the N76 is Callan, a busy little market town which was strongly fortified in the Middle Ages and has retained a number of old buildings. Of the 15th c. Augustinian priory (National Monument) only the church, a long rectangular building with a central tower, survives; fine carved choir stalls. In the town centre are the ruins of St Mary's Church (16th c.; National Monument), with fine details. The choir (restored), which is still used for worship, contains an old font. In the nave are a number of good monuments (16th and 17th c.), including that of John Tobyn, by Rory O'Tunney. Elsewhere Rice House has been carefully restored to convey an impression of a typical farmhouse of the late 18th c.

Killamery

At Killamery, 5 miles south of Callan, on the border of Co. Tipperary, there is a 9th c. high cross (National Monument). The decoration, unfortunately badly weathered, includes a chariot procession, a hunting scene, David with his harp, and other biblical themes, together with geometric and animal ornament.

Freshford

Freshford, north-west of Kilkenny on the R693, has a church of 1730 (National Monument) with a lovely Romanesque doorway from an earlier church incorporated in the west front.

★Kilcooly Abbey

West from Kilkenny in Co. Tipperary lie the ruins of Kilcooly Abbey (National Monument), a Cistercian monastery founded from Jerpoint in 1182 (see above). The entrance lies on the west side of the precinct. The church, erected in 1445–70 on the site of an earlier building, contains a wealth of sculpture. The screen between the south transept and the sacristy has a whole series of reliefs – the Crucifixion, St Christopher, a bishop, a mermaid with a hand mirror, followed by two fish, and the coat of arms of the Butler family. Notable among the monuments in the choir is the tomb of Piers Fitz Oge Butler, adorned with the knight's recumbent effigy and panels of saints and Fathers of the Church as weepers. Rory O'Tunney, who carved this tomb about 1526, was also responsible for the monuments of William Cantwell and Margaret Butler and of John Cantwell and Elicia Stouk. In front of the altar is the gravestone of Abbot Philip (d 1463). One rather unusual feature is a pair of stone seats set against the piers at the end of the nave.

Among the remains of the conventual buildings is a corbel-vaulted circular dovecot.

Killaloe · Cill Dalua   D 3

Republic of Ireland
Province: Munster
County: Clare
Population: 1000

The village of Killaloe (Cill Dalua, Dalua's church) lies inland in the southwest of Ireland, at the point where the Shannon, emerging from the elongated Lough Derg, threads a course between the Arra Mountains and Slieve Bernagh out into the Plain of Limerick.

Killaloe is a good centre for water sports and a popular stop for cabin cruisers.

Sights

St Flannan's Cathedral, built in 1185, occupies the site of an earlier church and incorporates its Romanesque doorway. Beside it is an interesting stone shaft with matching inscriptions in ogham script and Viking runes – a rarity in Ireland – which, translated, mean: 'A blessing on Thorgrim, who made this stone.'

St Flannan's Cathedral

Elsewhere within the cathedral precinct is St Flannan's Oratory (12th c.; National Monument), a small Romanesque church with a beautiful doorway and a well-preserved stone roof.

St Flannan's Oratory

Also of interest is St Molua's Oratory (?11th c.; National Monument), transferred here in 1929 from an island in the Shannon due to be submerged by the rising waters of a hydroelectric scheme. Re-erected on a site near the Roman Catholic parish church, the little chapel has a nave and stone-roofed chancel.

St Molua's Oratory

Surroundings

To the north of the town extends Lough Derg, a long straggling lough with the boundary between Co. Clare and Co. Tipperary running down the middle. A beautiful road, the R463, skirts the west side of the lough, passing the large fort of Beal Boru, from which King Brian Boru took his title.

Lough Derg

Continue for 8 miles to Tuamgraney, which boasts the oldest church in Ireland still in regular use (parts of it dating from the 10th/11th c.). The East Clare Heritage Centre provides information about the region and arranges excursions to Holy Island offshore. Open summer Mon.–Fri. 9am–5pm, Sat. 9am–1pm.

Tuamgraney

The most convenient access to Holy Island, also known as Inishcealtra, is from the Mountshannon Angler Centre (boats at the landing stage). In the 7th c. St Caimin founded a monastery on the island, which was still being visited by pilgrims and penitents at the end of the 17th c. It is now a peaceful and charming little spot, with five churches, an 80-ft round tower, a hermit's cell and a churchyard with numerous crosses.

Holy Island

Killarney · Cill Airne   D 2

Republic of Ireland
Province: Munster
County: Kerry
Population: 9000

Killarney (Cill Airne, church of the sloe) is situated close to the coast in the south-west corner of Ireland. Nearby lie the well-known Killarney Lakes. Killarney itself has few outstanding sights, but the lake district to the south and east, known as the 'Killarney Area', makes it a popular holiday destination. Its tourist tradition goes back to the 19th c. when it particularly appealed to prosperous English travellers. Today the town offers accommodation for around 6000 visitors; crowds of day trippers swell the numbers during the peak season.

Sights

St Mary's
Cathedral

The Roman Catholic St Mary's Cathedral, a building by Pugin, in the neo-Gothic style, was erected in 1846–55.

Kerry Poets
Monument

Opposite the Franciscan church (1860) near to the railway station, stands a monument to the 'four Kerry poets' of the 17th and 18th c.: Pierce Ferrifer (d 1653), Geoffrey O'Donoughue (d 1677), Aodhagan O'Rahilly (d 1728) and Eoghan Ruadh O'Sullivan (d 1784).

National Museum
of Irish Transport

In East Avenue Road, leading to the bus station, is the National Museum of Irish Transport (open daily 10am–6pm). As well as a collection of vin-

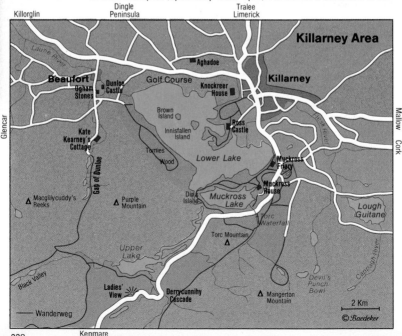

In the Killarney lake district

tage vehicles including a 1907 'Silver Stream', designed by an Irishman, and the 1910 Wolseley Siddeley in which W B Yeats toured the area, there are old bicycles and motorcycles and a workshop of the 1930s.

★★Killarney Area

Visitors to the Killarney Lakes have a choice between exploring the area independently or taking advantage of the sightseeing tours organised by local agencies. The most popular are packages including a trip in a jaunting car (pony and trap), on pony and by boat. One such – very much the standard tour – is as follows: by jaunting car from Killarney round the north side of the Lower Lake to Kate Kearney's Cottage; from there by pony, in a jaunting car or on foot over the Gap of Dunloe and down to the Upper Lake; by boat from the south end of the lake by way of Muckross Lake to Ross Castle; finally back to Killarney by jaunting car. Bicycles are another option (several bicycle-hire firms in Killarney).

The lakes, of varying sizes, around Killarney lie in a breathtakingly beautiful landscape of mountains and hills, the legacy of glaciation. The largest of the lakes, the Lower Lake, also known as Lough Leane, lies immediately south-east of Killarney, separated from the smaller Muckross Lake, or Middle Lake, by a narrow isthmus. A long narrow channel links these two lakes to the Upper Lake, the smallest of the three. 4 miles away to the east is Lough Guitane. To the south, where the hills rise to 2700 ft, are numerous smaller lakes, mostly just hill tarns. Due to the mild oceanic climate, the shores of all the lakes have a dense covering of woodland – including oak, arbutus, bamboos and giant ferns. In early summer the roads are bordered by banks of tall foxgloves and the hillsides covered in brightly coloured rhododendron bushes.

Topography

Killarney · Cill Airne

Killarney National Park

Some 23 sq miles of the Killarney Area has been designated a National Park. Included are the Lower Lake, Muckross Lake and the Upper Lake together with their shores. The heart of the National Park is the Bourne Vincent Memorial Park around Muckross House. This park was presented to the Irish nation in 1932 by the Bourne family and Senator Vincent of California. Various waymarked paths criss-cross the entire area.

Knockreer House

A few minutes' walk westwards from the centre of Killarney stands Knockreer House, surrounded by lovely gardens.

Ross Castle

Ross Castle, 1½ miles south-west of the town, is a ruined 14th c. castle. The 16th c. tower house, enclosed by a wall with round corner towers, has been preserved. There was an old prophecy that the castle would only fall to an attack from the water. Taking advantage of this, in 1652 Cromwell's General Ludlow had a large vessel brought up and launched in the Lower Lake, whereupon the defenders, anticipating fulfilment of the prophecy, promptly surrendered. Open Apr. daily 11am–6pm; May, Sep. daily 9am–6pm; Jun.–Aug. daily 9am–6.30pm; Oct. daily 9am–5pm.

Innisfallen

From the pier at Ross Castle visitors can be rowed out to the peaceful little island of Innisfallen, with the remains of a monastery (National Monument). Here, at the beginning of the 13th c., were written the Annals of Innisfallen, now in the Bodleian Library in Oxford. On the north-east side of the island is a small 12th c. church of red sandstone. Innisfallen still retains the old native woodland of Ireland – rowan, ash, yew and holly.

★Muckross Friary

3 miles south of Killarney in a lovely woodland setting, lies Muckross Friary (15th c.; National Monument), one of the best-preserved

Muckross House

The lower lake at Aghadoe

Franciscan friaries in Ireland. The church, with a massive central tower, contains a number of tombs. The very beautiful cloister has arcading in different architectural styles, while in the centre grows a huge yew (a tree frequently found in monasteries since its wood is ideal for carving). Three flights of steps lead to the domestic quarters on the upper floor.

About ¾ mile south, in a park with magnificent beds of rhododendrons, stands Muckross House, built in 1843. Some of the rooms with their Victorian furniture are open to the public, including those occupied by Queen Victoria when she stayed here in 1861. In the basement are several workshops (smithy, weaving room, pottery and saddlery) where visitors can watch craftsmen at work.

Muckross House

In one wing of the house is the National Park Visitor Centre (video presentation). Open daily 9am–5pm, to 7pm in summer.

Another attraction in the neighbourhood of Muckross House is the National Park's recently established Kerry Country Life Experience, providing an insight into rural life here in the 1930s. Three typical Kerry farmhouses together with outbuildings have been reconstructed complete with furniture and equipment. The adjoining land is farmed using the methods of the time. Open daily 10am–5pm.

Kerry Country Life Experience

Further along the north side of Muckross Lake, which has curiously shaped limestone rock formations, lies Brickeen Bridge leading to Dinis Island. Here boats can be hired for trips on the three lakes. The track continues round Muckross Lake to the N71, running between the lake and Torc Mountain (1740 ft).

Dinis Island

Away to the east of Torc Mountain the River Torc, flowing down from a small clear tarn known as the Devil's Punch Bowl, plunges over a succession of sandstone cliffs 60 ft high to form the beautiful Torc Cascade.

Devil's Punch Bowl

231

Mangerton Mountain	A path passing the Devil's Punch Bowl leads to the top of Mangerton Mountain (2714 ft), from the summit of which there are breathtaking views, both near and distant, of hills, lakes, valleys and arms of the sea – at their most impressive when scurrying clouds cast their shadows and showers of rain are gusting by.
Derrycunnihy	The N71, continuing south-west flanked by rocky hillsides, skirts the shores of the Upper Lake before climbing towards Derrycunnihy, a place of enchanting beauty where a waterfall dashes down over rocks in a delightful sylvan setting. To the north-east the old road to Killarney traverses a wildly beautiful valley.
★Ladies' View	The Kenmare road climbs higher still to one of the finest vantage points in the district, Ladies' View, so called after Queen Victoria and her ladies-in-waiting stopped here to admire the prospect more than a century ago (➤ picture, p. 11). From the Upper Lake it is possible to return to Ross Castle by boat, along a narrow tree-lined waterway past the 'Eagle's Nest' and Dinis Island.
Aghadoe	3 miles from Killarney, on high ground to the right of the R562, stand Aghadoe Church and round tower (National Monument), formerly belonging to a monastery. Built into the south wall of the church is an ogham stone. To the south-west of the church are the ruins of a circular keep (13th c.; National Monument) in a rectangular walled enclosure encircled by a moat. From the hill above there are panoramic ★views of the lakes and their islands against a backdrop of mountains – the twin summits known as the Paps (2248 ft) to the south-east, Mangerton Mountain to the south, and Carrantuohill (3360 ft) to the south-west.
Ogham stones	Continuing to the village of Beaufort, turn south through the village in the direction of the Gap of Dunloe. By the roadside stand a group of ogham stones, discovered in 1833 (➤ picture, p. 52).
Gap of Dunloe	The walk (gravelled track) over the Gap of Dunloe west of the Lower Lake promises more delightful impressions of the landscape. The Gap, a wild and rocky defile, separates Macgillycuddy's Reeks (➤ entry) to the west from Purple Mountain (2689 ft) and its northern spurs to the east. It can be reached by car from the R562 skirting the north end of the Lower Lake. There is parking at Kate Kearney's Cottage. If the 2½ mile walk to the top does not appeal, a pony or jaunting car can be hired instead. The route ascends past five small lakes fed by a swift mountain stream, the highest being Serpent Lake into which St Patrick is said to have consigned all the snakes he expelled from Ireland (and indeed none are to be found here). The steep walls of the gorge, scarred by glacial action, produce an excellent echo. From the Head of the Gap (784 ft) there are superb views of the surrounding hills, valleys and lakes, the greens, yellows and browns of the vegetation flecked with the red of sandstone.
Tomies Wood	Another extremely pleasant walk is through Tomies Wood, a round walk of roughly 4½ miles. As a rule, fewer people are encountered here on the west side of the Lower Lake – though the views of the lake scenery are second to none.

Killybegs · Na Cealla Beaga   B 3

Republic of Ireland
Province: Ulster

Slieve League: the highest cliffs in Europe➤

County: Donegal
Population: 1600

Killybegs (Na Cealla Beaga, the little churches) is an important fishing
port on the south coast of Donegal in north-west Ireland. It lies on a
natural harbour formed by an inlet of Donegal Bay. Fish processing and
sailmaking are established industries. The arrival of the fishing fleet and
the unloading of the catch are a sight not to be missed. Killybegs also
produces the famous Donegal hand-tufted carpets which can be found
gracing Buckingham Palace and aboard Cunard liners. There are guided
tours of the workshops.

Surroundings

Dunkineely

5 miles east of Killybegs on the N56 lies Dunkineely, from where a road
runs past a ruined castle and along a narrow tongue of land jutting 5
miles into the sea, to St John's Point (excellent fishing and fine beaches).

Kilcar

Kilcar, a picturesque village to the west of Killybegs, is a centre of the
Donegal hand-woven tweed industry. South of the village, on Muckross
Head, are cliffs and caves which can be reached on foot at low tide.

Carrick

Carrick, 2½ miles further on and a little way inland, is situated just
upstream of the outflow of the River Glen into the very attractive Teelin
Bay.

★Slieve League

From Carrick a detour can be made via Teelin to Slieve League, where
the sea cliffs are the highest in Europe (1936 ft). Passing through Teelin,
continue for another 2 miles south-west to Bunglass Point, where the
narrow road ends in a car park a few steps from the cliffs.
   Here there is a choice between simply enjoying the view or proceeding further on foot. Those sufficiently nimble and with a good head for
heights may wish to continue beyond Bunglass Point to the summit of
Slieve League, negotiating en route the 2½-mile ridge walk known as
One Man's Path, with precipitous slopes on either side. Though not
marked, the route is easily followed in the open terrain. Less adventur-
ous walkers can gain the summit by an alternative route – Old Man's
Path – signposted from Teelin village. Allow 1½–2 hours to the top and
back. Both routes are arduous despite a mere 1300 ft of ascent, and
neither should be attempted without stout footwear.

★Kinsale · Ceann Saile   E 3

Republic of Ireland
Province: Munster
County: Cork
Population: 2000

Kinsale (Ceann Saile, tide head) lies on the south coast of Ireland overlooking the broad estuary of the River Bandon. It is a favourite destination for trippers and holidaymakers. There is still some fishing from
the harbour, mainly for mackerel; also a well-equipped marina. Kinsale's
popularity with yachtsmen of many nationalities has led to the appearance of several good restaurants and wine bars.

History

In 1602 Kinsale became an English town from which the Irish were
barred as residents until the end of the 18th c. It was once an important
naval base. In 1601 a Spanish fleet landed a force of several thousand
men with the purpose of supporting the Irish against the English; when

the Irish were defeated the Spaniards surrendered. It was this English victory which prompted the 'Flight of the Earls' and confirmed Ireland's position as a dependency of England.

William Penn, founder of Pennsylvania, was a native of Kinsale.

Kinsale still retains something of its 18th c. charm. Many of its older buildings have been well restored. The gaily painted houses and narrow streets give the town something of a Mediterranean air.

Town

The best views of the town are gained from Compass Hill (south-west of the town centre) or from the road leading to Charles Fort (➤ picture, p. 68).

Sights

Kinsale's most notable building is St Multose's Church, originally 12th c. but several times rebuilt and today the parish church (➤ picture, p. 236). The sturdy north-west tower has a Romanesque doorway. Above the west door is a 15th c. statue of St Multose, credited with founding a monastery here. Inside the church is an interesting collection of tombstones (17th c.) and a fine medieval font.

St Multose's Church

Desmond Castle, in Cork Street, a 15th or 16th c. tower house (National Monument), was used for a period at the beginning of the 19th c. to hold French prisoners of war – hence its other name, the 'French Prison'.

French Prison

Kinsale Regional Museum is housed in the pretty Court House of 1706. In it can be seen several of the black-hooded cloaks that were once the

Kinsale Museum

In the centre of Kinsale ...   *... the Court House*

St Multose's Church in Kinsale

traditional dress of the women of the district. Open summer Mon.–Fri. 11am–1pm, 3–5pm.

Surroundings

Charles Fort
Summer Cove, 2 miles south of the town on the east side of the inlet, is the site of the well-preserved star-shaped Charles Fort (1677), the walls of which still stand 40 ft high. At the south-west corner there is a lighthouse and inside the fort ruins of a 19th c. barracks (guided tours; caution needed when visiting the outworks). The opposite side of the inlet is similarly fortified (James Fort).

Oyster Haven
2 miles east of Kinsale lies another inlet, Oyster Haven, with good bathing and, on the east side, the imposing ruins of Mount Long Castle (1631).

Ballinspittle
The R600 runs south-west from Kinsale to the village of Ballinspittle, above which stands the Ballycateen ring-fort, with three deep ditches and an overall diameter of 400 ft.

Old Head of Kinsale
5 miles south of Ballinspittle, the Old Head of Kinsale juts well out to sea, with a ruined castle and a lighthouse amid superb cliff scenery.

Garrettstown
Garrettstown, west of the promontory, is a quiet little holiday resort with a sheltered bay. Neither Coolmain Castle nor Kilbrittain Castle (north-west) are open to the public.

Bandon
Beyond Kilbrittain the R603 continues to Bandon (on the N71; 9-hole golf course and good trout fishing). The town was established in 1608 to

house English settlers. Kilbrogan Parish Church (1610) was one of the first Protestant churches in Ireland.

Letterkenny · Leitir Ceanainn   B 4

Republic of Ireland
Province: Ulster
County: Donegal
Population: 7000

Letterkenny (Leitir Ceanainn, hillside of the O'Cannons), county town of Co. Donegal, lies on rising ground above the River Swilly in the far north of Ireland, overlooking the outflow of the river into Lough Swilly, a 25-mile inlet opening off the Atlantic.

Although Letterkenny has few notable features, it is a good base from which to explore northern Donegal.

Sights

The principal landmark of Letterkenny, a long straggling town on the slopes of the O'Cannon Hills, is the 215-ft spire of St Eunan's Cathedral (1901); the church is finely decorated with Celtic motifs and stained glass by Harry Clarke and Michael Healy.

St Eunan's
Cathedral

Occupying a restored mid-19th c. poorhouse used latterly as local authority offices, the County Museum documents the history, geology and archaeology of Donegal as well as Donegal life in times past. Open Tue.–Sat. 11am–1pm, 2–5pm.

County Museum

Surroundings

From Letterkenny the R245 runs north-east to Rathmelton (8 miles), a friendly little anglers' centre with an attractive harbour flanked by fine Georgian houses. The 17th c. Old Meeting House serves both as an exhibition hall and library. Open Jul.–Aug. daily 9am–5pm.

Rathmelton

Kilmacrenan, another angling centre, this time on the N56 7 miles north of Letterkenny, once boasted a monastery founded by St Columba. Only the ruins of a 15th c. Franciscan friary and an old parish church survive today.

Kilmacrenan

2 miles west is the Rock of Doom, a large flat-topped block of stone on which the O'Donnell princes were crowned. It is well worth clambering up for the sake of the extensive view of the surrounding moorland. At the foot of the rock is the Holy Well, visited by pilgrims on account of its supposed healing powers.

A side road leads from Kilmacrenan to Church Hill, 10 miles north-west of Letterkenny, reached from there on the R251. A mile west of the village, by Gartan Lough, stands Glebe House, belonging to the English painter and art collector Derek Hill and worth visiting on account of its superb furnishings. The adjoining stables house the Glebe Gallery, not only displaying landscapes and portraits by Hill himself but also a considerable collection of modern painting (including works by Degas, Renoir, Picasso and J B Yeats) and contemporary British and Irish art. Open Jun.–Sep. Mon.–Thu., Sat., Sun. 11am–6.30pm.

Church Hill
★Glebe Gallery

The Colmcille Heritage Centre in Gartan is devoted to the life, work and times of St Columba the Elder (also known as St Columcille; ➤ Facts and

Gartan

Figures, Religion). Situated not far to the west of Church Hill, Gartan was Columba's birthplace. Open May–beginning of Oct. Mon.–Sat. 10.30am–6.30pm, Sun. 1–6.30pm.

★Glenveagh National Park

West of Gartan Lough stretches the Glenveag National Park. The entrance and Visitor Centre are on the northern shore of Lough Beagh, reached via the R251. The 38 sq mile park, an area of impressive mountain and moorland scenery surrounding Lough Beagh, was established in 1986.

Private cars are not allowed into the park: a shuttle bus runs to Glenveagh Castle, 2 miles from the entrance. This neo-Gothic building, dating from 1870 has lovely grounds with a Mediterranean aspect. The kitchen garden is particularly attractive. Open Easter–Oct. daily 10am–6.30pm, closed Fri. in Oct.

Glenveagh Castle

Limerick · Luimneach   D 3

Republic of Ireland
Province: Munster
County: Limerick
Population: 75,000

Limerick (Luimneach, barren spot), the Irish Republic's third-largest city, lies on the River Shannon in the south-west of the country, at the point where the river begins to open out into its estuary. This was the most westerly point at which the river could be forded and round it, at the junction of busy traffic routes, a considerable town grew up. A number of main roads and railway lines meet here, and Shannon Airport is only 15 miles away.

Economy

Limerick has a harbour, not particularly large but very busy. The arrival in recent years of various modern industries (optics, electronics, medicinal drugs) has increased the standing of the town. The mainstays of the economy, however, are flour milling, tobacco, off-the-peg clothing, cement and steel cables. Even so, unemployment tends to be high in Limerick and the standard of living low.

History

In the 9th c. the Vikings established a base at this 'barren spot' from which they could plunder the interior of the country. They were driven out by the celebrated Irish king Brian Boru, after which possession of the town passed back and forth between the Irish and the Anglo-Normans. In 1210 King John ordered a bridge and a castle to be built. In later centuries the town grew in size and maintained its allegiance to the English Crown. During the 17th c. it was several times besieged and captured. The last occasion was in 1691, the 'year of the broken treaty', when, after a valiant defence, 10,000 Irish troops were allowed to march out with full military honours. Under the treaty, signed by William of Orange himself, the Irish nobility were also granted safe passage, but the British Parliament, objecting to the clauses guaranteeing religious freedom, refused to ratify it. The Irish troops thereupon went to France and took service in the army of Louis XIV; in the course of the next 50 years hundreds of thousands of Irishmen followed their example, entering the service of France and of Spain. During the 18th c. the town expanded south-westwards along the banks of the Shannon.

Many people assume that the limerick, a five-line verse with a comic-satirical message, originated in the town of Limerick. In fact its origin is uncertain; evidence points to its having its roots in England. The specific use of the word 'limerick', however, is often traced to a popular 19th c. Irish song recounting, in numerous verses, the adventures of Irish townspeople. The following is an example of a limerick:

There was a young lady of Wilts,
Who walked up to Scotland on stilts;
When they said it was shocking
To show so much stocking,
She answered, 'Well, what about kilts?'

Town

First impressions are of a not especially attractive town; in particular, parts of English Town, the older district north of the confluence of the Abbey River and the Shannon, appear very run down. South of the Abbey River lies Irish Town, the medieval town centre, and south of that Newtown Pery; dating from the 18th c., this has a distinctly more prosperous air. Today Newtown Pery is the commercial and financial quarter, through which runs O'Connell Street, Limerick's principal thoroughfare. Here and in Mallow Street, which branches off it, there are some attractive Georgian houses.

English Town

Treaty Stone

Cross the Shannon by Sarsfield Bridge (1824–35) and turn right along Clancy's Strand, with a fine view of the city, to reach Thomond Bridge, on the site of the original Shannon bridge built on the orders of King John. At the end of the bridge is the Treaty Stone on which the 1691 treaty is said to have been signed.

Thomond Bridge on the Shannon, Limerick

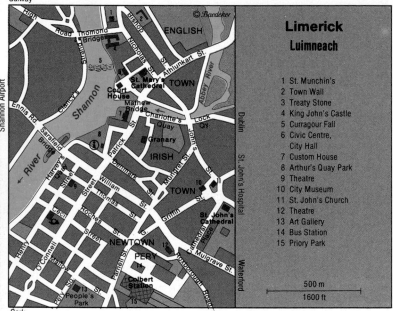

Cork

Limerick

Luimneach

1 St. Munchin's
2 Town Wall
3 Treaty Stone
4 King John's Castle
5 Curragour Fall
6 Civic Centre,
   City Hall
7 Custom House
8 Arthur's Quay Park
9 Theatre
10 City Museum
11 St. John's Church
12 Theatre
13 Art Gallery
14 Bus Station
15 Priory Park

500 m

1600 ft

King John's Castle	On the opposite bank, rising imposingly above the Shannon, stands King John's Castle (13th c.; National Monument), a pentagonal fortress with a main block, three round corner towers, a bastion and a twin-towered gatehouse (disfigured by 18th c. additions). It has recently been restored. Parts of the complex are now an interpretative centre with reconstructions of scenes from Irish history and the history of the town, a video presentation, and information on the excavation of early medieval houses, defensive works and siege tunnels. Open mid-Apr. to Oct. daily 9.30am–5.30pm; Nov. to mid-Apr. Sat., Sun. noon–5.30pm.
St Mary's Cathedral	Turning right at the end of Castle Street, follow Nicholas Street southwards to St Mary's Cathedral, which retains much 15th c. work (west doorway 12th c.). The oak choir stalls, a rarity in Ireland, with misericords carved with fabulous creatures, date from 1489. There are a number of notable monuments. From the 120-ft tower fine views may be enjoyed.
Court House	Not far west, in St Augustine's Place, stands the handsome Court House (1764).

Irish Town

Custom House	To the south, beyond Mathew Bridge spanning the Abbey River, is the Custom House (1769), today an art gallery.
The Granary	The restored Granary in Michael Street, centrepiece of a recently established conservation area, now accommodates the municipal archives and a library.

At the eastern end of Irish Town can be seen St John's Roman Catholic Cathedral (1856–94), boasting the tallest tower in Ireland (275 ft).

St John's Cathedral

Adjacent to the cathedral is St John's Square, once an elegant 18th c. residential quarter and now a protected area.

St John's Square

The Limerick City Museum occupies one of the restored buildings in St John's Square. Open Tue.–Sat. 10am–1pm, 2.15–5pm.

City Museum

Newtown Pery

Newtown Pery, the district south-west of Irish Town, came into being with the expansion of the city in the 18th c. Through it runs O'Connell Street, Limerick's main thoroughfare, almost a mile long, and today the heart of the city. At the end of the street stands the O'Connell Monument commemorating Daniel O'Connell, who in 1829 won emancipation for Irish Catholics.

O'Connell Street

Mallow Street is celebrated for its handsome Georgian houses with brightly painted front doors. The easternmost section of the street borders the People's Park in which is situated the Limerick Art Gallery (modern Irish painters).

Mallow Street

Plassey

3 miles east of the city centre at Plassey (N7) are the National Institute for Higher Education (NIHE) and a museum, the latter housing part of the Hunt Collection, principally medieval church art from continental Europe and Bronze Age and Early Christian finds from Ireland. Other parts of the Hunt Collection are displayed at Craggaunowen Castle (➤ Ennis). Open May–Sep. daily 9.30am–5.30pm.

★Hunt Collection

Surroundings

In the village of Murroe, a good 12 miles east of Limerick at the foot of the Slievefelim Mountains, is Glenstal Benedictine Abbey, founded in 1927. Visitors are welcome at the extensive complex. High points are the terraced garden going back to the 17th c. and the abbey's modern church (1953). Open Mon.–Sat. 9am–noon, 2–6pm, Sun. 11am–noon, 2–6pm.

Murroe

15 miles south of Limerick, at Holycross on the crescent-shape Lough Gur, there is an exceptional prehistoric site (National Monument). When in the 19th c. the lough was partially drained, evidence was uncovered of occupation since Neolithic times. Numerous finds can be seen in the interpretative centre beside the lough, where models, drawings and an audio-visual presentation provide detailed information on what is known as the Lough Gur Stone Age Centre. Open mid-May to Sep. daily 10am–6pm.

★**Lough Gur Stone Age Centre**

Highlights on the tour of the site include: No. 4, a wedge-shaped passage grave (ca 2000 BC); No. 7, a stone fort (8th c.); No. 8, an oval stone fort (Early Christian period); No. 12, a Neolithic burial place surrounded by a double earthwork, with a menhir in the centre; No. 16, a burial mound with a circle of standing stones (ca 1500 BC); No. 17, a fine double stone circle with an earth rampart and ditch (age uncertain); No. 22, a small stone circle formed from large slabs; No. 23, a crannog (originally an artificial islet but now high and dry); No. 28, an imposing stone circle (ca 2000 BC), a cult site with an entrance of almost monumental proportions. There are in addition two medieval buildings, Bourchier's Castle

(16th c.) and Black Castle (14th c.), and also the ruined New Church (17th c.).

Hospital

Heading south from Lough Gur in the direction of Kilmallock, a detour can be made eastwards to Hospital where the church (National Monument), originally belonging to an establishment of the Knights Hospitallers founded in 1215, contains three very interesting tombs, all with effigies.

Kilmallock

Kilmallock, 21 miles south of Limerick on the R512, is a historic little country town. The Collegiate Church of St Peter and St Paul (15th c.; National Monument) incorporates 13th c. elements (round tower) and contains fine monuments. King's Castle (14th c.; National Monument) and Blossom's Gate in Emmet Street testify to the importance of the town in the Middle Ages. The Civic Museum has a model of Kilmallock (1600) and a small collection illustrating life in the area in the 19th and 20th c. (open daily Sun.–Fri. 1.30–5pm).

To the north of the town are the ruins of a Dominican friary (13th–15th c.; National Monument); the church has some good stonework, a fine five-light west window, and interesting monuments in the chancel. The 87-ft tower is borne on excpeptionally narrow arches.

Kilfinane

6 miles south-east of Kilmallock lies the little market town of Kilfinane, at the foot of the Ballyhoura Mountains. Its most striking feature is an unusually large motte surrounded by three earth ramparts. It is 130 ft high with a diameter of 50 ft at the base and 20 ft at the top. From the summit there is a magnificent view of the Golden Vale.

Glenosheen

In Glenosheen, a beautiful side valley south-west of Kilfinane, stands Castle Oliver, a 19th c. building complete with battlements, towers and bastions, approached along two avenues with curious lodges at the gates. Near the castle is one of the follies built to provide employment in times of famine. Castle Oliver is said to have been the birthplace of Marie Gilbert, better known as Lola Montez, mistress of King Ludwig of Bavaria.

Newcastle West

From Kilmallock the R518 and R520 lead westwards to Newcastle West, 20 miles south-west of Limerick, a busy market town with the ruins of a 12th c. Templar castle.

Glenquin Castle

Glenquin Castle (15th c.; National Monument), is a well-preserved six-storey tower house situated 5 miles south of Newcastle West.

Mungret

2½ miles west of Limerick on the N69 lie the ruins of Mungret Abbey (National Monument), once an influential monastic school; three of the abbey's original six churches are preserved.

Carrigogunnell Castle

4 miles further west stands Carrigogunnell Castle (National Monument), prominently situated on a volcanic crag. An imposing structure with two towers (15th and 16th c.), it is in a poor state of preservation. From the castle there are fine views of the Shannon and surrounding area.

Kildimo

Kildimo boasts the remains of a small Templar church (13th c.) and a parish church of 1705.

On a hill beyond Kildimo is the little **Killulta Church** (12th c.; National Monument) with an unusual triangular window.

Kilcornan

Kilcornan is the starting point for walks in Curraghchase Forest Park, where there are ruins of an 18th c. mansion, Curraghchase House.

Replicas of major Irish monuments are a feature of the Celtic Park and Gardens. There is also a rose garden, and children especially will delight in the many animals – horses, sheep, deer – and domestic fowl. Open May–Oct. daily 9am–7pm.

Askeaton lies on the banks of the River Deel. On a rocky islet near the bridge stand the ruins of Desmond Castle (15th c.; National Monument), a tower house with a banqueting hall measuring 30 by 90 ft, with fine windows, blind arcading and vaulting.

On the east side of the river are the well-preserved remains of a Franciscan friary (15th c.; National Monument): a church with handsome windows; a cloister with 12 marble arches and a figure of St Francis; and a refectory and other conventual buildings.

Foynes, 7 miles beyond Askeaton, is a little port picturesquely situated on the estuary of the Shannon. From the mid-1930s until the end of the second world war, this tiny isolated place was the terminal for the only passenger air service to and from North America. The GPA Foynes Flying Boat Museum tells the amazing story. On view are the first terminal building, the signal and weather station, and photographs of the first flying boats used on the Atlantic crossing. Open Apr.–Oct. daily 10am–6pm.

From Knockpatrick Hill (565 ft), south of the town, there are extensive views over the Shannon estuary. On the summit of the hill are a ruined church and a holy well.

8 miles west, beautifully situated on the banks of the Shannon (here 1¼ miles wide), lies the village of Glin. Above the harbour rises Hamilton's Tower (19th c.). Outside the town stands Glin Castle, a ruined tower house on the estate of the Knights of Glin, who have been established here in uninterrupted succession for 700 years. The present house, originally Georgian (1780) but remodelled in the neo-Gothic style in 1820 has handsome rooms with good stucco ceilings (staircase, hall, library). It is furnished in period style (Irish, 18th c.) with family portraits of the 18th to 20th c. Open May daily 10am–noon, 2–4pm; otherwise by arrangement, tel. (068) 34173.

Lismore · Lios Mor Mochuda   D 4

Republic of Ireland
Province: Munster
County: Waterford
Population: 900

Lismore (Lios Mor Mochuda, Mochuda's great hill fort) lies near the south coast of Ireland on the wide Blackwater, a good fishing river spanned at this point by a handsome stone bridge (1775). North of the town the Knockmealdown Mountains rise to heights of up to 2560 ft. As early as the 7th c. there was a monastery here, renowned for its learning, where in the 9th c. King Alfred is said to have studied.

Sights

Lismore Castle, splendidly situated on a tall crag, probably occupies the site of the monastery. Erected in the 12th c., it survived the upheavals of later centuries and in 1602 came into the hands of Richard Boyle, later 1st earl of Cork, whose son Robert Boyle (1627–91) became the celebrated scientist who formulated Boyle's Law. The castle, which was much enlarged in the 19th c., now belongs to the duke of Devonshire. The gardens, but not the house, can be visited. Open mid-May to mid-Sep. Mon.–Fri. 1.45–4.45pm.

St Carthage's Cathedral	St Carthage's Cathedral (17th c.; National Monument), built by Richard Boyle, incorporates parts of an earlier 13th c. church (chancel arch, windows in south transept). The elaborate MacGrath tomb (1557) has representations of the Crucifixion, an Ecce Homo, and various saints and apostles. Built into the west wall of the nave are a number of early gravestones. The slender and graceful spire was the work of George Richard Pain (1827).
Lismore Heritage Centre	The history of the town is vividly portrayed in a multi-media presentation at the Lismore Heritage Centre. Open Jun.–Aug. Mon.–Fri. 10am–8pm, Sat. 10am–6pm, Sun. 2–6pm; Sep., Oct. Mon.–Sat. 10am–5.30pm, Sun. 2–5pm.

Surroundings

Cappoquin	4½ miles east of Lismore lies the little town of Cappoquin, charmingly situated on the Blackwater at the point where the river turns sharply south. There is good fishing in the Blackwater and its tributaries. Below Cappoquin the river is tidal.
Mount Melleray Abbey	Mount Melleray Abbey, in the hills some 4½ miles north of Cappoquin, is a Trappist monastery built in 1833. It has a guest house in which visitors are accommodated.
Affane	Sir Walter Raleigh (1552–1618), credited with having introduced tobacco and the potato into Ireland, is said to have planted the first cherry tree in the British Isles at Affane, a village graced by a handsome Georgian mansion a mile or so south of Cappoquin.
Villierstown	At Villierstown, south of Affane, is the Dromana Gate, a curious Indian-style gateway.
Ballyduff	5 miles west of Lismore lies Ballyduff, with Ballyduff Castle, a fortified manor house of 1628.
Ballysaggartmore Towers	Ballysaggartmore Towers stands in pleasant wooded surroundings near Ballyduff. Close by is the elaborate Gothic entrance to Ballysaggartmore Castle (the house was never completed due to lack of funds).

Londonderry (Derry) · Doire   A/B 4

Northern Ireland
Province: Ulster
District: Londonderry
Population: 70,000

Londonderry, or Derry (Doire, oakwood), Northern Ireland's second-largest city, lies on the River Foyle just above its outflow into Lough Foyle. It is an important port and industrial town known for its chemical and textile industries, engineering and ceramics.

The partition of Ireland in 1921 cut off Londonderry from much of its natural hinterland. Even so, because of the openness of the border, there has always been a high degree of economic interchange. Many living in the north of the Irish Republic take advantage of the choice of shopping and lower prices Londonderry offers.

History	A monastery was founded here by Columba the Elder in 546. Later the monastery and the settlement which had grown up around it were several times attacked and destroyed by the Vikings. In 1613, following the

'colonisation' of Ulster by James I, when mainly English and Scots Protestants were settled in Derry under the auspices of London's wealthy merchant guilds, the town and county were declared a 'London settlement' and renamed Londonderry. The massive town walls date from this time. When the partition of Ireland took place in 1921, Derry became a frontier town. In recent years it has been one of the main flashpoints for the sectarian violence associated with the conflict between Catholics and Protestants in Northern Ireland.

The political conflict has left its mark on the city. Protestants and Catholics live for the most part segregated, the Protestant districts, protected by elaborate security measures, lying mainly east of the River Foyle. The majority of Catholics live in Bogside, which has recently been redeveloped, and on the Creggan estates.

Town

In the walled Old Town a programme of reconstruction and restoration has been carried out in recent times. One such project is Craft Village, a gallery of shops in a reconstruction of a Derry street at the turn of the century. Shipquay Street, Magazine Street and Bishop Street all have a number of Georgian houses.

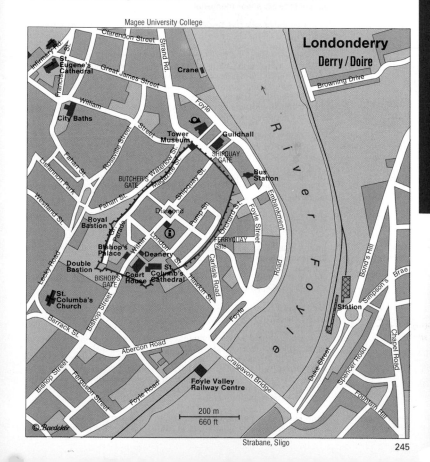

Sights

★Walls

Londonderry's Old Town is surrounded by the best-preserved town walls in the United Kingdom, still, apart from the addition of three gates of later date, very much as they were in 1618. There is a pleasant walk circling the town on the walls; the best view of the town is from the Walker Monument on the Royal Bastion. The four original gateways giving admittance to the old town are Butcher's Gate, Shipquay Gate, Ferryquay Gate and Bishop's Gate, the finest of the four.

Tower Museum

One of the towers houses a museum documenting the history of Derry from the very earliest times. Open Tue.–Sat. 10am–5pm., later in summer.

Diamond

Still in accord with the medieval street plan, Derry's four principal streets, one from each of the original four gates, meet in the central square, known since the 17th c. as the Diamond. The town hall formerly stood here, but after being destroyed during one of the many sieges of the town, it was moved to another site. The principal feature of the square today is a war memorial.

Court House

In the south of the Old Town in Bishop Street stands the neoclassical Court House (19th c.).

St Columb's Cathedral

Immediately east of the Court House is St Columb's Protestant Cathedral, built in the 17th c. and Gothicised in the 19th c. The roof is borne on brackets carved with the heads of 16 bishops of Derry. Eight of the 13 bells in the bell tower date from the 17th c. Incorporated in the bishop's throne is the seat of Bishop Bramhall, who consecrated the cathedral in 1633. The chapter house contains documents on the history of the town, as well as the locks and keys of the four old town gates.

St Columba's Church

To the south-west, outside the walls, is St Columba's Anglican Church, a 19th c. neo-Gothic building occupying the site of an older church. Nearby is St Columb's Stone, at which the saint is said to have prayed.

Guildhall

The neo-Gothic Guildhall (1912), outside the walls, to the north, has a collection of items relating to Irish history (guided tours by arrangement, tel. (028) 365151).

Magee University College

From the Guildhall, Strand Road runs north to Magee University College (1865), the grounds of which extend to the banks of the Foyle.

Foyle Valley Railway Centre

On the west bank of the River Foyle, near the splendid double-decked Craigavon Bridge (1933; 400 yd long), is the Foyle Valley Railway Centre, a museum documenting the history of the region's railways. Visitors can enjoy a short trip in a 1934 diesel locomotive. Open Jun.–Aug. Tue.–Sat. 10am–5pm; Sep.–May Sun. 2–6pm.

Surroundings

Limavady

From the east bank of the Foyle the A2 runs by way of two charming villages, Eglington and Ballykelly, to Limavady (18 miles), an old town in the valley of the River Roe. Less than a mile from Limavady is the Roe Valley Country Park, offering walks, canoeing, fishing and an opportunity to visit old watermills once used in linen manufacture. (Further information from the Visitor Centre; open daily 9am–5pm, summer to 9pm; park open at all times.)

Downhill Castle Mussenden Temple

From Limavady the A2 describes an arc northward to Downhill on the coast. Here, superbly situated on the cliff edge near the ruined Downhill

Castle, stands the Mussenden Temple, erected in 1783 to house a private library.

Continue inland to Coleraine, one of the oldest English settlements in the area. This busy little town on the navigable River Bann is famous for its salmon, distilleries and linen manufacture.

Coleraine

From Coleraine the road heads north again along the coast, coming in 6 miles to Portstewart, with lovely sandy beaches and a picturesque harbour. There is also good bathing at Portrush, 4 miles further east. Offshore lie the Skerry Islands.

Portstewart

On the way to the Giant's Causeway the road passes Dunluce Castle (14th c.; altered several times in the 16th and 17th c.), perched on a rocky islet linked to the mainland by a bridge. Open Apr.–Sep. Mon.–Sat. 10am–7pm, Sun. 2–7pm; Oct–Mar. Tue.–Sat. 10am–4pm, Sun. 2–4pm.

Dunluce Castle

Bushmills boasts the oldest whiskey distillery in the world still in production. Irish monks are said to have been producing 'the water of life' here as early as the 13th c., long before the first distiller's licence was granted by James I in 1608. Unlike other Irish producers who use unmalted barley for their pot-still whiskeys, Bushmills follows the method used in Scotland for distilling single malts. The tour of the distillery ends with an opportunity to sample the resulting light, smoky-tasting whiskey.

Bushmills Distillery

About 8 miles from Bushmills lies the Giant's Causeway, one of the most extraordinary natural phenomena in Northern Ireland or indeed in the world, a rock formation of volcanic origin consisting of an estimated

★★Giant's Causeway

Dunluce Castle   *Carrick-a-rede Rope Bridge*

247

The Giant's Causeway

40,000 prismatic basalt columns of varying sizes and heights. There is a Visitor Centre at the approach to the Causeway (open daily 10am–7pm, winter to 4pm; film presentation; small museum), the Causeway itself being a 10-minute walk away (good path; shuttle service). Some of the columnar formations have been given fanciful names – the Lady's Fan, the Giant's Organ, the Horseshoe, and so on. The most impressive, reached by way of the Shepherd's Path, is the Amphitheatre, with columns up to 80 ft high and numerous blocks of smaller columns like so many giant seats.

According to legend, the Causeway was the work of the giant Finn McCool. Falling in love with a giantess from the island of Staffa (in the Hebrides), he began to build the Causeway as a means of bringing her to Ulster.

For an alternative route back to the Visitor Centre (30 minutes), go on past the basalt columns and take the first path climbing upwards beyond them. Another option is to continue even further along the coast, on a path which leads to several more unusual rock formations before again doubling back to the Visitor Centre (a circuit of some 4 miles in all).

Carrick-a-rede Rope Bridge

13 miles along the coast lies Ballintoy where, during the salmon season (May to September), a 60-ft-wide chasm east of the village is spanned by the Carrick-a-rede Rope Bridge (15-minute walk from the car park at the Larrybane Visitor Centre). Intended principally for use by salmon fishermen, the bridge has become a considerable tourist attraction, a test of nerves for those daring enough to set foot on the swaying structure.

Ballycastle

Ballycastle, 6 miles beyond Ballintoy, is a picturesque little fishing village in wooded surroundings.

Rathlin Island

Weather permitting, a boat runs from Ballintoy to Rathlin Island, 6 miles offshore. In earlier times this still inhabited island was used as a base by Vikings.

The road from Ballycastle to Cushendall past the famous Glens of Antrim is one of the most beautiful stretches of coast road in Ireland. At Cushendall either continue down the coast to Belfast (47 miles; ➤ entry) or alternatively head inland through the delightful Glenarriff (A43) and afterwards on lovely country roads via Kilrea and Dungiven back to Londonderry.

★Antrim Coast

Longford · Longphort C 4

Republic of Ireland
Province: Leinster
County: Longford
Population: 4000

Longford (Longphort, fortress), county town of Co. Longford, lies in the centre of Ireland north-east of Lough Ree.
    The town offers a wide range of leisure activities – golf, tennis, fishing, shooting, horse and greyhound racing.

A prominent landmark in the town is the dome of St Mel's Cathedral (1840–93), a neo-Renaissance building by Joseph Keane. Longford takes its name from a fortress of the O'Farrels of which no trace now remains. The present castle dates from 1627.

Sights

Surroundings

4 miles north-east of Longford, on the R194, stands Carriglass Manor, a private house dating from 1837. A costume museum has been established in the stables. Open mid-Jun. to early Sep. Mon., Thu.–Sat. 1–5.30pm, Sun. 2–6pm.

Carriglass Manor

The R194 continues east to Granard, a good place for fishing. Situated close by is a large motte (12th c.; National Monument), possibly the largest of its kind in Ireland. It is topped – though bearing no obvious connection – by a statue of St Patrick, erected in 1932.

Granard

About 2½ miles east, beginning at Lough Kinale and extending 6 miles north-west to Lough Gowna, is part of the Black Pig's Dyke, a long series of earthworks built to protect a network of interconnecting routes. Cutting obliquely across the northern part of Ireland, the individual sections have been dated to between 300 BC and AD 300. At this particular point the dyke is up to 20 ft high and 30 ft thick at the base, with a ditch on either side.

Black Pig's Dyke

About 8 miles south-west of Granard (7½ miles south-east of Longford) lies Edgeworthstown. Edgeworthstown House was the birthplace of the celebrated novelist Maria Edgeworth (1767–1849), whose works depict the social conditions of her time. The house is now an old people's home and is not open to the public.

Edgeworthstown

En route from Edgeworthstown to Ballymahon on the N55 heading south-west, a short detour can be made (right, on a minor road) to Ardagh, with St Mel's Church (National Monument), said to have been founded by St Patrick.

Ardagh

Ballymahon is charmingly situated on the River Inny; good fishing.

Ballymahon

Lough Ree

From Ballymahon the R392 runs north-west to Lanesborough on the Shannon which here flows into Lough Ree. There is good trout fishing in both the river and the lough; in summer boats can be hired. Lanesborough is a popular halt for cruising boats on the Shannon (➤ entry). Near the town, on the east bank of the river, there is a peat-fired power station.

Inchcleraun

On Inchcleraun, an island in Lough Ree, some 6 miles south of Lanesborough, are the ruins of an early monastery (National Monument), including the remains of five churches and other buildings.

★Lough Corrib   C 2

Republic of Ireland
Province: Connacht
County: Galway

Lough Corrib, north of Galway Bay in the west of Ireland, is nearly 30 miles in length but at some points no more than a few hundred yards wide.

The lough is linked with Lough Mask just to the north by underground streams. The River Corrib, flowing out from its southern end, has barely left the lough before reaching the sea. In summer, excursion boats ply between Galway in the south and Cong in the north. The lough is dotted with numerous islands – said to number 365 in all. They are best seen from a viewpoint on high ground.

Topography

The scenery of Lough Corrib is strikingly beautiful. Round the lough's green shores, with their clumps of trees and expanses of pastureland, lie countless little bays, promontories and peninsulas, reaching out to tiny islets forming almost a continuation of the land. The countryside east of Lough Corrib is low lying, while to the west rise hills; in the distance to the north are the mountains of Connemara.

Tour of Lough Corrib

While it is possible to drive right round Lough Corrib, with the exception of a short stretch at the north end of the lough, the road runs at some distance from its shores. These can only be reached by access roads.

Moycullen

From Galway (➤ entry) the N59 goes north-west to Moycullen (8 miles), a good fishing centre.

Aughnanure Castle

Continue past Ross Lake to where Aughnanure Castle (1500; National Monument) stands proudly on a rocky islet. The castle, a six-storey tower house within an inner and an outer ward with round towers, has been restored. Open mid-Jun. to mid-Sep. daily 10am–6pm.

Oughterard

Oughterard, a few miles further on, often dubbed 'the Gateway to Connemara', is a pleasant small town in a lovely setting on the River Owenriff. A well-known fishing centre, it is amply supplied with restaurants and accommodation and a good base from which to pursue other activities (9-hole golf course).

Inchagoill

From Oughterard a boat can be taken to the picturesque island of Inchagoill, with the remains of two churches (both National Monuments). The smaller of the two dates from the 5th c.; the other (12th c.; restored) is a good example of Irish Romanesque architecture.

A narrow road running north along the shore of the lough is a dead end; to continue round the lake, rejoin the N59.

Cornamona

From the junction at Maam Cross (➤ Connemara) the R336 leads north to Maam Bridge. Here the L101 branches off eastwards to Cornamona, a fishing centre in a beautiful location which is also a good base for walking and climbing in the Connemara mountains further west and the hills of Joyce's Country.

Castle Kirke

From Cornamona a visit can be made to the impressive ruins of Castle Kirke, also known as Hen's Castle (12th c.; National Monument). A large tower enclosed by curtain walls, it takes up virtually the whole of the islet on which it stands.

Clonbur

Skirting the lough for much of the way, the road continues for another 5 miles to Clonbur on the isthmus between Lough Mask and Lough Corrib (fine view of Mount Gable to the west).

★Ross Abbey

Passing through Cong (➤ entry), head south on the R346 and R334 to the substantial and exceptionally interesting ruins of Ross Abbey (National Monument), to which, in the little market town of Headford, a signposted road branches off. Also known as Ross Errilly, the abbey, a Franciscan friary founded in 1351, stayed occupied until 1753. Most of the surviving remains, including the tower and the double south transept, date from the 16th c. The cloister has beautiful arcading. To the north of it is an inner court surrounded by conventual buildings, among which are a kitchen with a tank for fish, a bakery complete with oven, and a refectory with readers' alcoves. Altogether this is one of the best-preserved ruins of a Franciscan friary in Ireland.

Ross Abbey
Ross Errilly

Kitchen

Bakery

Larder

Inner court

Refectory

Cloister

Sacristy

Nave

Choir

Transept Transept Chapel

The ruins of Ross Abbey (Ross Errilly) lies only a mile or two from the eastern shores of beautiful Lough Corrib.

The abbey was founded about 1351, probably by Raymond de Burgo. Soon afterwards it was occupied by Franciscans, who remained here until 1753.

Over the centuries the abbey was much altered and rebuilt, particularly in the 15th c. The striking tower was built in 1498.

The cloister with its beautiful arcading is the architectural gem of this little abbey.

50 m
165 ft

© Baedeker

251

Annaghdown

5 miles south of Headford a narrow road goes off on the right to Annaghdown, with the ruins of Annaghdown Abbey (National Monument). There are some remains of 12th c. work, but the principal church ('cathedral') and the conventual buildings are 15th c.

★Lough Erne   B 4

Northern Ireland
Province: Ulster

The extensive and much-broken-up lake system comprising Lough Erne lies in the far west of Northern Ireland, its northern end being close to the border with the Irish Republic and a short distance inland from Donegal Bay. The lough, some 20 miles long and up to 6 miles wide, is a paradise for angling and water sports. In summer motor launches ply the lake and house boats can be hired. The Shannon–Erne Waterway, opened in 1994, connects Lough Erne to the Shannon (➤ Carrick-on-Shannon).

Topography

The lake, the northern part of which is called Lower Lough Erne and the southern part Upper Lough Erne, is considered the most beautiful in Ireland. Upper Lough Erne is a maze of bays and inlets, its southern half being studded with numerous small islands.

Enniskillen

The chief town in the area is the busy resort of Enniskillen, situated between the Upper and Lower loughs, on the River Erne which links the two.

Enniskillen Castle

Of interest in the town is St Macartan's Protestant Cathedral (17th–18th c.), in which the banners of Enniskillen's famous royal regiments hang. Enniskillen Castle (National Monument) now houses a military museum (uniforms, arms). Open May–Sep. Mon., Sat., Sun. 2–5pm, Tue.–Fri. 10am–5pm; Oct.–Apr. Mon. 2–5pm, Tue.–Fri. 10am–1pm, 2–5pm.

Sights

Portora Royal School, founded by James I in the early 17th c., claims Oscar Wilde and Samuel Beckett among its former pupils.

About 1¼ miles south-east of Enniskillen stands Castle Coole, a magnificent 18th c. mansion by James Wyatt. Open Jun.–Aug. Fri.–Wed. 2–6pm; May and Sep. Sat. and Sun. 2–6pm.

Castle Coole

Just north of Enniskillen, at the southern end of Lower Lough Erne, lies Devenish Island, with the remains of a monastery founded in the 6th c. by St Molaise, including an impressive and perfectly preserved round tower standing more than 82 ft high. Parts of St Mary's Abbey and the Great Church (12th c.) also survive together with a particularly fine 6-ft-high cross. In summer there is a regular boat service to the island from Trory, 3 miles north of Enniskillen.

Devenish Island

Tour of Lower Lough Erne

Leave Enniskillen – not on the A46, which keeps close to the lough, but on the B81 heading north-west at some distance from it – to Monea, with the ruins of an early 17th c. castle (accessible at any time). The church has a mid-15th c. window from the church on Devenish Island (➤ above).

Monea

Passing Derrygonnelly, follow the road down again to the shores of the lough. Tully Castle, about 3 miles north of Derrygonnelly, is well worth a visit. Though little remains of the fortified castle (17th c.), the gardens of the same period are very fine. Open Tue.–Sat. 10am–4pm, Sun. 2–4pm, summer to 7pm.

Tully Castle

Further on, the road skirts, on the left, Lough Navar Forest, where there are a number of small loughs. A side road leads to a viewpoint 985 ft above Lough Erne.

Lough Navar Forest

Continue on the A46 to the small town of Belleek (porcelain manufacture), on the border between Northern Ireland and the Irish Republic.

From here a road runs west to Ballyshannon (➤ Bundoran). Instead bear sharp right across the River Erne – flowing out of Lough Erne to eventually disgorge into Donegal Bay – and follow the A47 along the north side of the lough. Beyond the Castle Caldwell Forest Reserve (with the ruins of Castle Caldwell on a promontory in the lough), the road branches; ignoring the left-hand fork leading to Pettigo in the Irish Republic, bear right, still on the A47, across a bridge onto the long, narrow Boa Island.

Belleek

From the east end of Boa Island proceed round the foot of the lough to Kesh, where a worthwhile detour can be made north-east to Omagh, at the junction of the Rivers Drumragh and Camowen. This is a good base for salmon fishing and for walks in the Sperrin Mountains to the north.

Omagh

Just off the A5 about 4 miles north of Omagh is the Ulster American Folk Park, an extensive open-air museum recreating life in Ireland during the period of mass emigration in the 18th and 19th c., in addition to the emigration itself (replica of an emigrant ship), and the emigrants' new life in America. Further graphic illustration of the problems of Irish emigration is presented on video in the Visitor Centre at the park entrance. In the 18th c. alone, 250,000 people left Ulster for an uncertain future in the New World. Open Easter to mid-Sep. Mon.–Sat.

★Ulster American Folk Park

11am–6.30pm, Sun. 11.30am–7pm; mid-Sep. to Easter Mon.–Fri. 10.30am–5pm.

Ulster History Park

The Ulster History Park, another open-air museum, is situated on the B48 6 miles north of Omagh. It illustrates by means of reconstructed dwellings, the history of settlement from the Stone Age to the end of the 17th c. Open Easter–Sep. Mon.–Sat. 11am–6pm, Sun. 1–7pm; Oct.–Easter Mon.–Fri. 11am–5pm.

Castle Archdale Forest

Resuming the circuit of Lower Lough Erne, fork right off the A35 beyond Kesh to follow the B82 along the shores of the lough. After passing a number of marinas, the road comes to Castle Archdale Forest, with a ruined 18th c. mansion of the same name.

From here a boat can be taken to White Island, another of the lough's many delightful little islands, with the remains of a Romanesque church.

Soon afterwards the B82 rejoins the main road further south (now the A32) leading back to Enniskillen.

Tour of Upper Lough Erne

Heading south-west from Enniskillen on the A4, branch left shortly onto the A509 to reach, after 5 miles, the popular holiday resort of Bellanaleck (boat hire). Continue to Derrylin, just beyond which take the B127 left across a narrow isthmus in the lough to the fishing centre of Lisnaskea, with the ruins of Balfour Castle. The A509, meanwhile, keeps straight on to Cavan (➤ entry) in the Irish Republic, becoming the N3 south of the border. The hill above Lisnaskea provides extensive views of Upper Lough Erne's deeply indented shoreline. From Lisnaskea proceed north again on the A34 and A4 (or the slightly shorter B514 closer to the lough), returning by way of Castle Coole (➤ above) to Enniskillen.

Florence Court

Another delightful excursion from Enniskillen is the drive south-west, at first on the A4 and A32 and then on a side road to the right, to Florence Court, one of the first mansions to be built in the area. The gardens still look much as they did when the house was erected at the end of the 18th c. House open Jun.-Aug. Mon., Wed.–Sun. noon–6pm; park daily 10am to an hour before dusk.

Marble Arch Caves

Further along the same side road lie the Marble Arch Caves, on the northern slopes of the Cuticagh Mountains. This limestone cave complex, of which a 766 yd section can be visited, features several underground lakes and waterfalls as well as dripstone formations. The guided tour begins with a short subterranean boat trip, passing some impressive stalactites and stalagmites. Open mid-Mar. to Oct. 11am–4.30pm.

Lough Neagh   B 5

Northern Ireland
Province: Ulster

Lough Neagh, at 150 sq miles the largest lake in the British Isles, is situated just to the west of Belfast. It is drained by the River Bann, which flows out at its northern end. The lough is 18 miles long and 11 miles wide, with a greatest depth of 40 ft. Its waters, sustaining an abundance of fish, are fed by 10 tributary streams.

No road or footpath runs close to the shores of the lough, which are low-lying, covered in thick vegetation and in some places marshy. Only gradually are leisure facilities being created – the marinas at Oxford Island and Ballyronan, for example.

Antrim

The town of Antrim, from which the magnificent stretch of coast further to the north-east takes its name (➤ Londonderry, Surroundings), lies at the outflow of Six Mile Water into the lough. Antrim Castle (1622) was several times burned down and rebuilt. The castle gardens were laid out by Le Nôtre, designer of the gardens of Versailles. A mile north-east of the town, in the grounds of Steeple House, stands an excellently preserved round tower, 89 ft high.

Loughrea · Baile Locha Riach   C 3

Republic of Ireland
Province: Connacht
County: Galway
Population: 3400

The thriving little town of Loughrea (Baile Locha Riach, town on the grey lough), episcopal seat of the bishop of Clonfert, lies in the west of Ireland, at the junction of the N6 and N66 a few miles inland from Galway Bay.

St Brendan's Cathedral, externally a modest and unassuming church, is notable for a magnificent sequence of stained-glass windows which, taken together, illustrate the evolution of Irish stained glass in the 20th c. (work by A E Childe, Michael Healy, Evie Hone and Sarah Purser and others). The church has other fine examples of modern art, including a series of Stations of the Cross.

St Brendan's Cathedral

Surroundings

4 miles north of the town, on the R350 near Bullaun, stands the Turoe Stone (3rd c.; National Monument), an oval granite block 3 ft high with, on the rounded upper half, curvilinear relief ornament in a style characteristic of the late European Iron Age; this is separated from the otherwise undecorated lower part by a band of meander pattern. The stone formerly stood close to a nearby ring wall and doubtless served some ritual purpose.

★Turoe Stone

South-east of Loughrea, a road at first running along the shores of the eponymous lough, leads to Carrowkeel. Here turn left via Duniry to Pallas with its imposing 16th c. castle (National Monument), a well-preserved tower house in an enclosure. The curtain walls with their parapet walks and towers are largely undamaged.

Pallas

20 miles south-east of Loughrea, at the north end of Lough Derg where the Shannon enters the lough, lies Portumna, with a 9-hole golf course, good fishing and facilities for sailing and rowing (new marina). On the outskirts of the town, in the fine Portumna Forest Park, is Portumna Castle (1618; National Monument), a large fortified mansion with corner towers; also the ruins of a Dominican friary (National Monument) comprising a church with a splendid east window and various conventual buildings.

Portumna

The R349 and then R348 head north-west from Loughrea through an area which becomes steadily more stony and barren, arriving in 11 miles at Athenry, a little town which was a place of some consequence until the end of the 16th c. and has retained many medieval buildings. Athenry Castle (1235–50; National Monument) is a ruined hall block

Athenry

within the remains of curtain walls with two corner towers. The Dominican friary (National Monument), founded in 1241 and in subsequent centuries much altered and several times destroyed, is represented by a ruined church containing a number of funerary monuments. The Market Cross, of which only the base and the top part survive, has reliefs of the Crucifixion and the Virgin and Child (15th c.). The remains of the medieval town walls (probably early 14th c.) show the extent of the old town; the tower-like north gate is well preserved.

Louisburgh · Cluain Cearban   C 2

Republic of Ireland
Province: Connacht
County: Mayo
Population: 300

Louisburgh (Cluain Cearban, Kerwan's meadow) is a fishing village and holiday resort in the north-west of Ireland, on the south side of Clew Bay. The village is beautifully situated in a coastal plain with good fishing rivers, bounded by Croagh Patrick to the east and the Mweelrea Mountains (2576 ft) to the south and fringed on the seaward side by cliffs and sandy beaches. North-east of the village, a promontory called Old Head, from which there are fine views, extends into the wide bay.

Granuaile Centre

Opened in 1994, Louisburgh's Granuaile Centre commemorates the life and exploits of Grace O'Malley (► below, Clare Island), 'Granuaile' being Irish for Grace. Documents and models of castles and ships complement a video film telling the story of this legendary female pirate. Open Jun.–Aug. daily 10am–5pm; May, Sep., Oct. Mon.–Fri. 10am– 5pm.

Surroundings

★Croagh Patrick

To the east of Louisburgh, Croagh Patrick (2471 ft), Ireland's holy mountain, rises abruptly from the plain. It can be climbed from Murrisk (parking on the R335). A small road leads first to the white statue of St Patrick, from where the continuing stony track is clearly seen. The final climb is up a steep slope covered with quartzite scree (strong footwear essential). The ascent is strenuous and takes a good 2 hours, being rewarded by ever more extensive views. From the top the prospect extends northwards over Clew Bay, studded with little islands, to the hills of the Curraun Peninsula and as far north as Nephin – a view which is at its finest at sunset – and southwards across the Mweelrea Mountains to the Twelve Bens of Connemara.

There is a great pilgrimage to Croagh Patrick on the last Sunday in July, commemorating the 40 days of penance which the saint is said to have spent here in the year 441. In the chapel on the flat top of the hill a service is held for the pilgrims, many of whom shed their footwear to complete the final stage of the journey barefoot; the discarded shoes can be seen lying along the wayside.

Doo Lough

South of Louisburgh the R335 ascends gradually to Doo Lough, enclosed on either side by steep rock walls. The loughs here offer good salmon and trout fishing, while the beauty of the valley itself is reflected in its name, 'Vale of Delphi' (► Connemara).

Killeen

A minor road runs south-west from Louisburgh to the River Carrownisky (trout and salmon fishing) and Killeen, an isolated little village with good beaches.

Off the coast to the north-west lies hilly Clare Island, today a quiet holiday retreat but in the 16th c. the domain of the legendary Grace O'Malley
(➤ Famous People), by whom the castle beside the small harbour
(National Monument) is said to have been built. The island, which has a
population of 140 can be reached by boat from Roonagh Quay, 4 miles
west of Louisburgh (no regular service). About 1½ miles south-west of
the harbour stand the ruins of St Bridget's Church (ca 1500; National
Monument). In the choir are medieval frescos with an extraordinary min-
gling of human figures and animals, the meaning of which is unknown;
the only scene which can be understood is a figure of the Archangel
Michael weighing souls. On the south side of the island, commandingly
situated on the cliffs, is a promontory fort.

Macgillycuddy's Reeks · Na Cruacha Dubha   D/E 2

Republic of Ireland
Province: Munster
County: Kerry

Pronounced 'Maclicuddis Reeks', Macgillycuddy's Reeks (Na Cruacha
Dubha, the black mountains) lie on the Iveragh Peninsula (➤ Ring of
Kerry) in the south-west corner of Ireland.
   Among these ancient red sandstone hills, partly wooded, partly bare,
are Ireland's highest peaks, Carrantuohill (3414 ft), Beenkeragh (3262 ft)
and Caher (3150 ft). They offer good climbing, and from the two highest
peaks there are views over Dingle Bay to the north-west, the Killarney
Lakes and the south Kerry hills. No less fine are the nearer views of the
gorges, green valleys and little lakes glittering far below.

Macgillycuddy's Reeks near Killarney

Carrantuohill

The youth hostel on the northern slopes of Macgillycuddy's Reeks, or the car park a mile or so from it on the Glencar road, both make good starting points for excursions into the mountains.

Ascent

The first part of the climb, following a wide path through Hag's Glen, is quite delightful and presents no problems even for less experienced walkers. It takes about an hour and a half to reach Lough Callee, a mountain tarn in a lovely setting at the head of Hag's Glen. From there allow a further 2 hours to the summit. This second part of the climb involves negotiating the 'Devil's Ladder', the name a pointer to its being only for the more experienced.

Alternative route

Carrantuohill can also be climbed from the west by a route starting from Lough Acoose, a picturesque tarn nestling between spurs of the main mountain. This ascent too is only for more seasoned hill walkers.

Macroom · Maghcromtha   E 3

Republic of Ireland
Province: Munster
County: Cork
Population: 2500

Macroom (Maghcromtha, sloping valley) lies on the River Sullane, to the west of Cork in south-west Ireland. It is a busy little town, a market centre for the surrounding area.

The gatehouse of Macroom Castle

In the Square are a number of Georgian houses and the charming Market House. Also of note are the ruins of Macroom Castle (gutted by fire in 1922) with a massive gatehouse. The church is 19th c., by G R Pain.

Surroundings

The roads east (to Cork) and west from Macroom are noted scenic routes. The R618 follows a winding course eastwards by way of Carrighadrohid Castle, situated on an island, to Dripsey, well known for its woollen mills.

From the N22 running south-east along the west side of Carrighadrohid Reservoir, a side road branching off to the right after 12 miles leads to Kilcrea, with the well-preserved remains of a Franciscan abbey (15th c.; National Monument) in a delightful setting on the banks of the River Bridge. The remains include the church, with a fine sacristy and bell tower, and conventual buildings. There is also the keep of an old castle.

12 miles south of Macroom, beyond a hilly area on the R588 (N22 out of Macroom, then almost immediately right onto the R584 and finally the R585 eastbound), lies Kinneigh. Here, on the site of an early monastery, stands an unusual round tower (National Monument), 65 ft high, the lower 18 ft being hexagonal.

The R584, branching west off the N22 just south of Macroom, leads to Inchigeelagh, a resort popular with fishermen and artists. It is picturesquely situated at the east end of Lough Allua, a long narrow lough famous for its white water lilies.

Near the west end of Lough Allua is the hamlet of Ballingeary, from which the road climbs to the celebrated Pass of Keimaneigh. Here it runs for almost a mile between sheer rock faces, relieved by ferns and flowering plants clinging to crevices in the cliffs.

Just before the head of the pass, a narrow road branches off on the right to Gougane Barra Forest Park and Lough Gougane Barra. This dark and lonely lough, surrounded on three sides by high hills, is the source of the River Lee, which falls in cascades down the rocky hillside and in times of heavy rain fills the whole valley with the sound of rushing water. In late autumn a pilgrimage takes place here to the site of a monastery founded in the 7th c. by St Finbar, on a little island in the lough connected to the shore by a causeway. There are remains of old buildings and a modern neo-Romanesque church.

From Macroom the N22 continues north-westwards up the valley of the River Sullane, past Carrigaphooca Castle (15th c.; National Monument), to the pilgrimage centre of Ballyvourney. Of the monastery founded by St Gobnat in the 7th c. there remain a circular building with an inner diameter of 20 ft and walls 5 ft thick, a well and the saint's grave.

Monaghan · Muineachan   B 5

Republic of Ireland
Province: Ulster
County: Monaghan
Population: 6200

Monaghan (Muineachan, little hills), county town and agricultural centre of Co. Monaghan, lies in the north of the Irish Republic near the border with Northern Ireland, at the junction of the N2, N12 and N54. The Ulster Canal – which, though today in a state of neglect, links Belfast in Northern Ireland to the Atlantic coast of Ireland – runs through the town.

There was a settlement here as early as the 9th c., but the present town dates from the 18th and 19th c.

Sights

Near the neo-Gothic parish church of St Patrick stands the fine Court House (1829), now occupied by the County Museum and its attached small art gallery (open Tue.–Sat. 11am–1pm, 2–5pm). Gracing the Market Place is the small and elegant neoclassical Market House (1792), while in Old Cross Square are the Old Infirmary (1768) and nearby Market Cross (1714). On the south side of the town stands the neo-Gothic St Macartan's Cathedral, its slender spire a local landmark.

Surroundings

Glaslough

7 miles north of Monaghan on the R185 lies the pretty little village of Glaslough, on the eastern edge of which extend the grounds of Leslie Castle. Dating in its present form from the second half of the 19th c., and still owned by the Leslie family, it can be visited by arrangement (guided tours). It is also possible to stay overnight in one of the rooms and/or participate in dinner evenings (bookings, tel. (047) 88109).

Castleblayney
Lough Muckno

Near Castleblayney, 14 miles south-east of Monaghan on the N2, is Lough Muckno, the largest and loveliest of the Monaghan lakes. Like other loughs in the area, it offers good fishing.

Carrickmacross

12 miles further south on the N2 is Carrickmacross, with a convent producing high-quality lace.

Clones

Clones, 13 miles south-west of Monaghan on the Northern Ireland border, boasts the remains of a very early monastery founded by St Tigernach.

Handmade Clones lace is also still made here and samples of this superlative handwork are displayed in the Clones Lace Gallery. Open Tue.–Sat. 10am–6pm.

In the Diamond, the main square, stands a 15-ft high cross (10th c., restored; National Monument) with, on the west side, representations of Adam and Eve, Cain and Abel, Daniel in the Lion's Den and the Arrest of Christ, and on the east side the Adoration of the Magi, the ?Twelve Apostles, the Last Supper and the Crucifixion.

In an ancient graveyard are a 75-ft round tower and a tomb in the shape of a house, with notable finials (National Monument). In another graveyard nearby is a ruined 12th c. church known as 'the Abbey' (National Monument). In both graveyards are a number of unusual 17th and 18th c. gravestones.

Monasterboice · Mainistir Buithe   C 5

Republic of Ireland
Province: Leinster
County: Louth

Monasterboice (Mainistir Bulthe, St Buithe's Abbey), an early monastic site celebrated for its crosses, lies near the Irish Sea coast, on the R168 6 miles north-west of Drogheda.

St Buithe, a little-known saint, founded a monastery here in about the year 500. In 1097 the round tower was gutted by fire, destroying the monastic library. The monastery survived only until the beginning of the 12th c.

Monastic site

Within the old graveyard are the remains of two churches, a round tower and three high crosses (all National Monuments), together with two early gravestones and a sundial.

The ruins of the two churches are of no special interest. The round tower stands 108 ft high even though the top section is missing. The entrance, 6 ft above the ground, is now reached by a fixed staircase (closed to the public for reasons of safety).

The most impressive feature, standing near the entrance to the graveyard, is the South Cross or Muireadach's Cross, one of the finest high crosses in Ireland, which takes its name from a donor mentioned in an inscription on the west side. At first it was thought that this was Muireadach II, who died in 922; recent research, however, has established that the cross probably existed in the first half of the 9th c. Accordingly it could have been commissioned by the first abbot of that name, who died at Monasterboice in 844.

The monolith, standing 16 ft 9 inches high, has reliefs on all four sides which are remarkable both for their form and their execution. A variety of scenes are represented in square panels on the shaft. On the east side are Adam and Eve, Cain and Abel, ?David and Goliath, ?Moses striking water from the rock, the Adoration of the Magi, Christ as Judge surrounded by good and bad souls, and the Archangel Michael weighing

Muireadach's Cross   *Tall Cross*

souls; on the church-shaped summit of the cross is the meeting of St Paul and St Anthony in the desert. On the west side can be seen the ?Arrest of Christ, ?Doubting Thomas, ?Christ with St Peter and St Paul, the Crucifixion, and an unidentified scene. On the north side are St Paul and St Anthony again, the Scourging, the Hand of God, and interlace ornament, and on the south side the Flight into Egypt, Pontius Pilate and more interlace ornament. On the base appear hunting scenes, animals, interlace ornament and meander patterns.

★Tall Cross

As its name implies, the Tall or West Cross is unusually high (21 ft), in addition to being richly decorated. Not all the 22 scenes represented can be identified. On the east side are David killing the lion, the Sacrifice of Isaac, the Three Young Men in the Fiery Furnace, the Arrest of Christ, the Ascension, and St Michael with the Devil. On the west side are the Vigil at the Tomb, the Baptism, the Mocking of Christ, the Kiss of Judas and the Crucifixion. The base has ornamental patterns.

North Cross

Of the North Cross, on the edge of the graveyard, only the upper part and a section of the original shaft survive. The old sundial, enclosed by a railing, is a decorated granite block over 6 ft high; its age has not yet been determined.

Mullingar · Muileann gCearr   C 4

Republic of Ireland
Province: Leinster
County: Westmeath
Population: 8000

Mullingar (Muileanng gCearr, Carr's mill), county town of Co. Westmeath and market centre for this largely agricultural area (mainly stock farming), lies on the River Brosna in north-eastern central Ireland, at the junction of three railway lines and the intersection of two major roads (the N4 and N52). The town is almost completely encircled by the Royal Canal. Mullingar lies between two large loughs, Lough Owel to the north and Lough Ennell to the south. There is fishing for brown trout in both loughs and in the River Brosna in this popular recreational area.

Sights

Cathedral of
Christ the King

The town is dominated by the Roman Catholic Cathedral of Christ the King (1936–9) with its 140-ft twin towers. Attached to the church is an ecclesiastical museum.

Town Hall
Court House

Both the Town Hall and the Court House are handsome 18th c. buildings.

Mullingar pewter

Pewter, produced in Mullingar for centuries, underwent a revival in the mid-1970s; many of the pewter items made today are based on old patterns. The factory can be visited, the craftsmen watched at their work, and the finished articles purchased.

Surroundings

Multyfarnham

North of Mullingar on the N4, between Lough Owel and Lough Derravaragh, lies Multyfarnham, with a modern Franciscan college built on the site of a 14th c. monastery, of which the church, with a fine tower, has been restored. In the grounds of the college are life-size Stations of the Cross.

The R394 runs north from Mullingar past several small loughs to Castlepollard. En route, 7 miles from Mullingar at Crookedwood, are the ruins of Taghmon Church (15th c.; National Monument) and a four-storey tower house. Both the church and the tower house have vaulted roofs.

At Castlepollard stands Tullynally Castle, still the family seat of the Pakenhams, created earls of Longford in 1655. A charming 18th c. mansion, much altered in the 19th c., Tullynally has associations with the duke of Wellington and the 18th c. novelist Maria Edgeworth (➤ Longford).

The house is set in an attractive park bordering the banks of Lough Derravaragh. Open: park all year; house mid-Jul. to mid-Aug. daily 2–6pm, otherwise by arrangement, tel. (044) 61159.

2½ miles east of Castlepollard, between two hills, lies Fore, an ancient settlement where St Fechin founded a monastery in the 7th c. The monastic church (ca 900; National Monument) has been preserved and in the churchyard are a high cross and a tower house known as the Anchorite's Cell, with a 19th c. mausoleum built onto it. The original monastery was superseded in the 13th c. by a Benedictine priory; its fortress-like ruins (National Monument) lie ¼ mile away. They consist of a church, two tower houses, part of a cloister, domestic buildings and a circular dovecot. Not far distant, in the fields, are two gates (National Monuments), relics of old town walls.

Belvedere House and Gardens are situated on the N52 a short distance south of Mullingar. The name reflects the lovely view of Lough Ennell enjoyed from the mid-18th c. mansion. Park open Apr.–Sep. daily noon–6pm.

15 miles south of Mullingar on the N6 lies Tyrrellspass, an 18th c. planned village of well-built houses laid out in a crescent round the village green. The village won an award in the 1976 European Architectural Heritage Year. On the green is an unusual memorial to those who died in the struggle for Irish independence – it shows in stone three children of different ages on their way to school.

Kilbeggan lies on the N6 4 miles west of Tyrrellspass. Here Locke's Distillery, first licensed in 1757, is worth a visit. When its doors closed for the last time in 1954, an industrial museum was planned for the site. In 1987 it was taken over by the Cooley Distillery, whose whiskey continues to be matured here in traditional fashion in wooden barrels. A winery has recently been added to the museum so that now, on a tour of the distillery, the secrets of producing Irish sherry are divulged along with those of pot-still whiskey. Open Apr.–Oct. daily 9am–6pm, Sun. from 10am; Nov.–Mar. daily 10am–4.30pm, Sun. to 6pm.

Naas · Nas na Ri   C 5

Republic of Ireland
Province: Leinster
County: Kildare
Population: 8500

Naas (Nas na Ri, assembly place of the kings), county town of Co. Kildare, lies 21 miles south-west of Dublin on the N7. In early times Naas was the seat of the kings of Leinster, the site of whose stronghold was the North Mote (a motte situated in the north of the town). Fortified by the Anglo-Normans – the remains of one of whose castles are now incorporated in the rectory of the Protestant church – the town was sacked in the 14th c.

Naas is now a thriving industrial town on the edge of the Curragh (➤ Kildare), a celebrated horse-breeding area. 2½ miles south on the R411 is Punchestown Racecourse (➤ below), famous for its steeplechases.

Surroundings

Clane

7 miles north of Naas lies Clane; with a Jesuit school, Clongowes Wood College, opened in 1814. The old chapel is a good example of neoclassical architecture; the new one has fine stained glass by Evie Hone and Michael Healy.

Maynooth

8 miles north-east of Clane, on the Royal Canal, is Maynooth, a little town best known for its seminary, St Patrick's College, now part of the National University of Ireland. It was established with British approval in 1795, on the site of an earlier college, to enable Roman Catholic priests to be trained in Ireland. It is now the largest seminary for priests in Ireland and in the British Isles, and in recent years has also admitted laymen and women. The handsome college buildings, grouped round lawned courts, are mostly 19th c. They include a church and a small museum with artefacts and works of art illustrating the history of the Church in Ireland and its missionary activity. Adjacent to the college gates can be seen the remains of Maynooth Castle (13th–17th c.; National Monument) – a large keep, a gatehouse and part of the curtain walls.

At the east end of the main street stands Carton House, a classical mansion of 1739 by Richard Cassels (not open to the public).

Leixlip

Leixlip (a name of Danish origin meaning salmon leap) is situated on the N4 4½ miles east of Maynooth. Leixlip Castle dominates the town, which in recent years has become a dormitory town of Dublin.

On private land a mile south-west of the town stands the 'Wonderful Barn', a five-storey conical structure of brick and stone built in 1743 for Lady Connolly of Castletown . Each storey has a vaulted ceiling and a circular hole in the floor through which goods stored in the barn could be hauled up and down. A spiral staircase winds up round the outside of the building.

★Castletown House

South-west of Leixlip, on the Liffey, lies the village of Celbridge, 2½ miles upstream from which is Castletown House, a spacious and architecturally important mansion built by the Italian architect Alessandro Galilei in 1722 for the Irish parliamentarian William Connolly. It consists of a finely proportioned three-storey central block, approached up a broad flight of steps, with side wings connected to it by quadrant colonnades. The interior has superb stucco decoration; the main staircase and the Pompeian Gallery are particularly fine. The house is today the headquarters of the Irish Georgian Society, dedicated to preserving as much

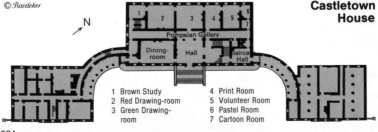

© *Baedeker*

N

Castletown House

Pompeian Gallery

Dining-room | Hall | Staircase Hall

1 Brown Study
2 Red Drawing-room
3 Green Drawing-room

4 Print Room
5 Volunteer Room
6 Pastel Room
7 Cartoon Room

as possible of Ireland's Georgian heritage. Open Apr.–Sep. Mon.–Fri.
10am–6pm, Sat. 11am–6pm, Sun. 2–6pm; Oct.–Mar. Mon.–Fri.
10am–5pm, Sun. 2–5pm.

Straffan, 4 miles south-west of Celbridge, boasts a railway museum with   **Straffan**
a collection of rare models. Open Jun.–Aug. daily 11.30am–5.30pm;
Sep.–May Sun. 11.30am–5.30pm.

From Maynooth the N4/R402 runs west to Johnstown, with a large   **Carburry**
19th c. mansion, and Carbury, with the extensive remains, commandingly situated on a hill, of Carbury Castle (14th–16th c.), an imposing pile
with chimneys and towers.
   Less than a mile to the north, also on a hill, are the remains of Carrick
Castle (14th c.) and a 13th c. church.

North-east of Naas, at Kilteel, are the ruins of a fine Romanesque church   **Kilteel**
and a castle (National Monument). The church (12th c.) has a richly decorated chancel arch, with figures of Adam and Eve, David and Goliath,
Samson with the lion, an acrobat, a man with a drinking horn and an
abbot with his crosier.

3 miles south-east of Naas is Punchestown where, near the racecourse,   **Punchestown**
on the Woolpack Road (the medieval road from Dublin to Kilkenny),
stands the Lone Stone of Punchestown (National Monument), a huge
tapering granite monolith 23 ft high. When it toppled over in 1931, a
Bronze Age burial was discovered at its foot.

A mile south-west of Naas on the N7 are the massive remains of   **Jigginstown**
Jigginstown House (National Monument), begun by the earl of Strafford   **House**
in 1633 as a summer residence for himself and for the entertainment of
Charles I, but left unfinished after Strafford's execution in 1641. It was
one of the first houses to be built entirely in red brick and with a frontage
of 374 ft would have been one of the largest mansions in Ireland. As
seen at present the most notable features are the vaulted basement and
a series of handsome rooms on the ground floor.

9 miles north-west of Naas the R409 reaches Robertstown. Here, at the   **Robertstown**
highest point on the Grand Canal (➤ entry), is the old Canal Hotel, built
in 1801 for the convenience of water-borne passengers. The canal
frontages of the village and the hotel have been restored to their early
19th c. appearance.

Navan · An Uaimh   C 5

Republic of Ireland
Province: Leinster
County: Meath
Population: 5000

Navan (An Uaimh, the cave) is situated in undulating country north-west
of Dublin, at the junction of the River Boyne and the Blackwater. The
largest town in Co. Meath, it is a busy market centre and an important
road intersection.

The Roman Catholic church (1836) has a fine carved figure of Christ   Sights
Crucified (1792) by Edward Smyth. West of the town is a large medieval
motte, which is a favourite viewpoint.

Surroundings

Donaghmore

A mile north-east of the town on the N51, at Donaghmore, is the site of an early monastery, with a well-preserved round tower and a church (National Monument). St Patrick is said to have founded his first monastery in Ireland here. The tower (?10th c.) has a round-headed doorway 12 ft above the ground with a relief of the Crucifixion above it and a human mask on either side of the architrave. The church is 15th c. There are Early Christian gravestones in the churchyard.

On a hill to the east stands Dunmoe Castle (National Monument): two sides of an originally rectangular structure (16th c.) with round towers at the corners.

Bective

A little more than half a mile beyond the village of Bective, south of Navan on the R161, a path leads off left to the ruins of Bective Abbey (12th c.; National Monument), a Cistercian house founded from Mellifont (► Drogheda). Of the original buildings there remain only the chapter house and some parts of the church. In the 15th c. the monastery was fortified, and from this period date the beautiful cloister, the tower and the great hall (refectory?).

Rathmore

Rathmore, 7½ miles west of Navan on the N51, has a ruined 15th c. church (National Monument). The nave and chancel are flanked by towers, while the outside of the handsome east window has figure decoration. The interior has fine carvings in the apse, on a number of tombs and on a font. On the north side of the church is a cross (1519) with reliefs of St Lawrence, St Patrick and an abbess.

Hill of Ward

Further along the N51 just before Athboy, the Hill of Ward (384 ft; National Monument), an ancient cult site and meeting place, is on the left.

New Ross · Ros Mhic Treoin   D 5

Republic of Ireland
Province: Leinster
County: Wexford
Population: 5500

New Ross (Ros Mhic Treoin, wood of Treann's son) lies in the south-east corner of Ireland on the steep east bank of the River Barrow. A market centre for the fertile surrounding area, its chief attraction for tourists are the excursions by boat on the Barrow and Nore rivers.

Town

New Ross is one of the oldest towns in Co. Wexford; its narrow winding streets – some of them stepped and only for pedestrians – still retain something of a medieval atmosphere. The broad river is busy with small boats.

Sights

St Mary's Church

Of the original St Mary's Church (early 13th c.; National Monument) only the chancel and transepts survive. The nave was pulled down in the 19th c. to make way for a large new parish church. Notable features are the three fine Gothic windows in the choir and a number of medieval tombs.

Tholsel

The Tholsel (town hall), built between 1749 and 1804, is a handsome neoclassical building with a cupola-topped bell tower.

Surroundings

A few miles south of New Ross, on the R733, lies the 620-acre John F Kennedy Memorial Forest Park, opened in 1968 with funds provided by Americans of Irish descent. The assassinated president's great-grandfather came from the village of Dunganstown not far to the west. 4500 different types of tree and shrub are found in the park, including 500 varieties of rhododendron and 150 of azalea. There is a good panorama from Slieve Coilte, a hill in the park accessible by car. In the Visitor Centre, in addition to a video presentation, there is a permanent exhibition documenting the flora of the park (open May–Aug. daily 10am–8pm; Apr., Sep. to 6.30pm; Oct.–Mar. to 5pm).

Kennedy Memorial Forest Park

4½ miles further south on the R733 are the imposing remains of Dunbrody Abbey (National Monument), a 12th c. Cistercian monastery. The church, in austere Cistercian style, has a chancel, transepts, nave and crossing tower (15th c.). The surviving conventual buildings include the library and chapter house on the east side and the refectory and kitchen on the south side.

★Dunbrody Abbey

Still further to the south, at Arthurstown, stands Ballyhack Castle (15th c.; National Monument), a fine five-storey tower with vaulted rooms, situated at some distance from the road on the banks of the Barrow. The castle has been restored and can be visited (open Jul.–Aug. daily 10am–7pm; Mar.–Jun., Sep. Wed.–Sun. noon–6pm). From Ballyhack there is a pedestrian ferry across the broad estuary of the Barrow to Passage East.

Ballyhack

Turning off the R733 beyond Arthurstown, follow a byroad south to the little fishing village of Duncannon, with a good sandy beach and an old fort of the same name on a rocky promontory guarding the entrance to the estuary.

Duncannon

The road continues to Hook Head, at the tip of a long narrow peninsula. On the east side of the peninsula stands Slade Castle (15th–17th c.; National Monument), picturesquely situated beside a small fishing harbour. The 56-ft tower is battlemented, as are the lower parts of the castle.

Slade Castle

The lighthouse on the south tip of the peninsula, Hook Head, rests on a 700-year-old circular keep.

Hook Head

2 miles back northwards along the road, at Templetown, a right-hand fork leads to Fethard-on-Sea, which has good sandy beaches. Not far to the south is Baginbun Head where in 1169 the Anglo-Normans first landed in Ireland.

Fethard-on-Sea

4½ miles north of Fethard the R733 and R734 intersect. A little to the east of the crossroads, a signposted access road branches off on the right to the ruins of Tintern Abbey (11th and 15th c.; National Monument), a Cistercian monastery. In the 16th c. the tower and chancel of the church were converted into a dwelling. The entire complex has now been restored.

Tintern Abbey

Portlaoise · Port Laoise   C 4

Republic of Ireland
Province: Leinster
County: Laois
Population: 4000

Pronounced 'Portleesh', Portlaoise (Port Laoise, fort of Laois) lies in south-east central Ireland on the railway line from Dublin to Cork. It is an important road intersection where the N7, N8 and N80 meet.

Town

The town was destroyed in the 17th c. and no buildings of that period remain. The Court House and the town gate are both early 19th c.

Surroundings

Emo Court

At Emo, a village about 8 miles north-east of Portlaoise, stands Emo Court, a late 18th c. mansion by James Gandon set in a lovely park. With yew-lined avenues, extensive lawns and rare trees and shrubs, it is a perfect place to walk. Park open daily 10am–6pm; house by appointment only, tel. (0502) 26110.

Rock of
Dunamase

From Portlaoise the N80 runs east, passing in about 3 miles the Rock of Dunamase, an imposing crag 200 ft high with the ruins of a large and forbidding 10th–17th c. castle comprising a rectangular tower, a gate-house, bastioned and turreted curtain walls and a moat. Fine panoramic views.

Timahoe

Timahoe, 7½ miles south-east of Portlaoise, boasts a well-preserved round tower (12th c.; National Monument) nearly 100 ft high.

Abbeyleix

8 miles south-west of Timahoe, along minor roads, lies Abbeyleix, an attractive little planned village laid out in the 18th c. on the site of an old monastery by the then viscount de Vesci. The de Vesci mansion, Abbeyleix House (1773), stands in a park laid out at the beginning of the 19th c. Open Easter– Sep. daily 2.30–6.30pm.

Ballinakill

The Heywood Gardens near Ballinakill, about 3 miles south of Abbeyleix, are also worth a visit. Until 1993 the park was in the care of the Salesians but is now owned by the state. Open daily.

Slieve Bloom
Mountains

To the west of Portlaoise the Slieve Bloom Mountains rise to 1700 ft, with beautiful valleys which are best reached from Mountrath along delightful minor roads.

Mountmellick

7 miles north-west of Portlaoise is Mountmellick, almost completely encircled by the River Owenass. Here in 1677 the Quakers opened their first school in Ireland; and at Rosenallis, 4½ miles north-west at the foot of the Slieve Bloom Mountains, they established their first large ceme-tery. At Mountmellick, and also to the north of Portlaoise, are found countless drumlins – whale-backed mounds of glacial deposits.

★★Ring of Kerry   D/E 1/2

Republic of Ireland
Province: Munster
County: Kerry

Iveragh Peninsula

The Iveragh Peninsula is the largest of the peninsulas of Kerry, jutting into the Atlantic in the south-west corner of Ireland. It is bounded to the south by the estuary of the Kenmare River, to the west by the Atlantic and to the north by Dingle Bay. At the east end of the peninsula Macgillicuddy's Reeks (➤ entry) rise above the Killarney Lakes.

A scenic road, the famous Ring of Kerry, encircles the peninsula, keep-ing close to the coastline for most of the way. Starting from Kenmare at the south-east corner of peninsula, the route runs west on the N70 to

Waterville, then north and east to Killorglin; from there it follows the R562 inland to Killarney before returning to Kenmare on the N71. The total distance is 100 miles, to which the detour to Valentia Island in the north-west corner of the peninsula adds at least another 25 miles. In suitable weather the Ring of Kerry is a road of extraordinary scenic beauty; it is not really possible, therefore, to do it justice in a day. It should also be remembered that at the height of the season traffic can be very heavy.

So as not to be trailing the whole way behind a tourist coach, it is best to start from Kenmare (the coaches set off from Killorglin).

Tour of the Ring of Kerry

From Kenmare (➤ entry) the N70 proceeds west along the north side of the inlet known as the Kenmare River. On the right can be seen the foothills of Macgillicuddy's Reeks (➤ entry).

Kenmare

Templenoe's church dates from 1816. Further on, by the ruins of Dromare Castle, there is a viewpoint and car park.

Templenoe

In 4 miles the valley of the Blackwater opens up on the right, the river plunging down to the sea in a deep gorge. A footpath leads down from the road through dense, almost tropical vegetation.

A delightful little road climbs up through the valley and over a 850 ft pass to Glencar and Lough Caragh.

River Blackwater

Next along the coast comes Tahilla (sea and freshwater angling), and beyond that Parknasilla, a beautifully situated resort blessed with a climate that is mild throughout the year, in which palms, pines, bamboo and jasmine flourish.

Tahilla
Parknasilla

Pastoral scene on the Ring of Kerry

Sneem

The road now loops inland to Sneem, a fishing centre on a narrow inlet. The Protestant church (16th c., much altered) has an unusual weather-vane in the form of a salmon. There is good walking and climbing in hills to the north and west rising to 2166 ft.

★ Staigue Fort

At Castlecove, about 8 miles west of Sneem, an extremely narrow road branches right off the N70 to arrive in a little over 2½ miles at a large stone fort, situated on a hill between two valleys. This is Staigue Fort (National Monument), of unknown date, a circular structure of drystone walling, 90 ft in diameter and over 16 ft high, surrounded by a ditch. The walls are 13 ft thick with stairways on the inward side and small chambers in the thickness of the wall.

Caherdaniel

The N70 continues for some distance close to the sea, here with many small islands, before turning inland to Caherdaniel (trout fishing, swimming, surfing), near which is a small stone fort similar to Staigue (➤ above).

★ Derrynane National Historic Park

South-west of Caherdaniel stretches the Derrynane National Historic Park. Nature trails with explanatory panels conduct the visitor through the dunes, which border a long sandy beach. The tiny Abbey Island offshore can be reached at low tide. Within the grounds stands a fine mansion where the 'Great Liberator' Daniel O'Connell (1775–1847) lived. The building now houses a museum. Open May–Sep. Mon.–Sat. 9am–6pm, Sun. 11am–7pm; Apr.–Oct. Tue.–Sun. 2–5pm. The park itself is always open.

Lough Currane

The N70 now climbs to the Coomakista Gap (690 ft), from which there are magnificent views, afterwards descending again to Ballinskelligs Bay. To the right, in a beautiful setting, lies Lough Currane. On Church

Staigue Fort

Island in this freshwater lough are a destroyed 12th c. church (National Monument) with a Romanesque doorway, remains of monks' dwellings and a number of gravestones with Christian symbols. From a narrow road that follows the south side of Lough Currane can be seen the ruins of a castle which has been engulfed by the lough. On the west side of the lough are the horseshoe-shape stone fort of Beenbane and the ruins of a thick-walled beehive hut (both National Monuments).

Waterville (An Coirean, the little whirlpool) lies a good 40 miles west of Kenmare on the narrow strip of land between Lough Currane and Ballinskelligs Bay. The abundance of fish in the local rivers and loughs and in the sea makes this a popular centre for both freshwater and sea fishing.

 From Waterville two lonely, scenic minor roads, which later unite, traverse the mountainous centre of the Iveragh Peninsula before dropping down to to Killorglin (➤ below). The more southerly of the two passes a number of loughs, well stocked with fish.

Waterville

To the west of Waterville there are good beaches on Ballinskelligs Bay. Across the bay is the village of Ballinskelligs itself.

Ballinskelligs

Some distance north of Waterville a road branches left off the N70 to Portmagee. Here another delightful but narrow road runs south to the Coomanaspig Pass (1080 ft) from where there are splendid views of the bays and bird-colonised islands along the Atlantic.

Coomanaspig Pass

Also at Portmagee a bridge (1970) crosses the narrow strait to Valentia Island. This bare rocky island offers excellent opportunities for sea fishing. From Bray Head (788 ft), at the western extremity, there are

Valentia Island

Valentia Island: starting point for the boats to the Skellig Experience

271

magnificent views of the Atlantic cliffs. At its eastern end is Knights Town from which there is a pedestrian and car ferry to the mainland.

★Skellig Experience

The Skellig Experience (near the bridge) is a recent tourist attraction on Valentia Island. The Visitor Centre (open Apr.–Sep. 10am–7pm) has a wealth of information about the Skellig Islands (➤ entry) and about the life and work of the monks who lived there from the 6th to the 13th c. Another exhibition is devoted to the seabirds and underwater world of the islands. From Valentia Island comfortably equipped boats make regular excursions around the Skelligs, which tower above the water like the summits of sunken mountains. In 1987 the little group of islands was designated a bird sanctuary and landing is no longer permitted. Sailings depend on the weather so enquire beforehand (tel. (0667) 6306).

Cahirciveen

Next stop along the Ring of Kerry is Cahirciveen, at the foot of Bentee Mountain (1227 ft). Facing Cahirciveen across the broad Valentia River are the ruins of Ballycarbery Castle (15th c.). To the north-east of the castle, reached via a side road off to the left of the N70, are two good stone ring-forts – Cahergall (National Monument), 105 ft in diameter, with two stone structures within the walls; and, commandingly situated on a hill, Leacanabuaile (9th c; National Monument), with staircases and chambers set in the thickness of the walls, and others underground.

The N70 continues north-east up the wide valley of Kells. On the left rises Knockadober (2230 ft), on the right a range of peaks of much the same height. Between them are fine views of the sea and the hills. The road then keeps close to the foot of Drung Hill, at some points high above the sea, passing an old coaching inn with magnificent views of Dingle Bay and the hills of the Dingle Peninsula before descending to Glenbeigh.

Glenbeigh

The delightfully situated little resort of Glenbeigh has good fishing. A mile west is a beautiful sandy beach, Rossbeigh Strand.

Killorglin

From Glenbeigh it is 9 miles through an undulating moraine landscape to the little town of Killorglin, where the famous Puck Fair is held every year on August 10th–12th.

After crossing the River Laune (salmon fishing) the road forks, the N70 going straight on to Milltown, west of which are the ruins of Kilcoman Abbey (13th c.; National Monument), and then Tralee (➤ entry). The R562 meanwhile turns east and, following the river, continues the circuit of the Ring of Kerry.

Ballymalis Castle

4 miles beyond the fork the road passes Ballymalis Castle (16th c.; National Monument), the picturesque ruin of a four-storey tower house on the banks of the river ½ mile off to the right. Extensive views of Macgillicuddy's Reeks.

The route now traverses the Killarney lake district (➤ entry) then climbs, with fine views to the rear, to Moll's Gap before descending through lovely scenery, with many bends, back to its starting point at Kenmare (21 miles from Killarney).

Roscommon · Ros Comain   C 3

Republic of Ireland
Province: Connacht
County: Roscommon
Population: 1700

Roscommon (Ros Comain, Coman's wood), county town of Co.

Roscommon, is situated in gently undulating hill country in western central Ireland, at the junction of three main roads (the N60, N61 and N63). It takes its name from St Coman, who founded a monastery here in the 6th c.

Sights

In 1253 Felim O'Conor, king of Connacht, founded a Dominican fiary here, which is believed to have occupied the site of a 6th c. monastery. The friary church (National Monument), altered in the 15th c., still survives; a niche in the north wall contains the founder's tomb (ca 1290) with the figures of eight armed retainers.

Roscommon Friary

Roscommon Castle (National Monument) dates from the same period as the church but subsequently suffered much alteration. An imposing square structure with round towers at the corners and a twin-towered gatehouse, it occupies a commanding position on the hillside.

Roscommon Castle

Surroundings

11 miles north of Roscommon, at Tulsk, where the N5 crosses the N61, are the remains of a castle and a Dominican friary. 3 miles north-west of this, at Rathcroghan, is an area of high ground some 2 sq miles in extent, with a number of earthworks. The site (National Monument) is believed to have been the place of coronation of the kings of Connacht. The earliest feature is a low mound, probably a passage grave. There are also various square, round, oval or irregularly shaped enclosures bounded by earth walls. A standing stone within a stone ring-fort is said to mark the grave of Dathi, the last pagan king of Ireland. In the immediate vicinity are other ring-forts and megalithic tombs.

Rathcroghan

About 12 miles north-west of Roscommon the R367 branches right from the N60 to Ballintober, with the ruins of a castle built in about 1300 – a square structure with polygonal towers at the corners of its massive walls, two projecting gateway towers on the east side and a moat.

Ballintober

5 miles further north-west on the N60 lies Castlerea, a little town offering a variety of leisure activities (golf, tennis, fishing). Near the town stands Clonalis House, surrounded by its park. The present house dates only from the 19th c. The O'Conors, whose family seat this was, produced in earlier times a number of high kings and kings of Connacht, a period recalled by various documents and other items displayed in the Victorian house. Open Jun. to mid-Sep. Tue.–Sun. noon–5pm.

Castlerea

Roscrea · Ros Cre   D 4

Republic of Ireland
Province: Munster
County: Tipperary
Population: 4200

Roscrea (Ros Cre, Crea's wood), a small country town with some industry, lies in southern central Ireland at the junction of the N7, N62 and R421. It is a good base for walking and climbing in the Slieve Bloom Mountains.

Sights

★St Cronan's
Church

The town grew up around a monastery founded by St Cronan in the 7th c. Of the Romanesque St Cronan's Church (12th c.; National Monument), built on the old monastic site, there survives only the west front, with the doorway and blind arcading either side; above the doorway is the figure of a priest. The remainder was pulled down in 1812 to make way for the new parish church. To the north of the church is a high cross (12th c.) with representations of Christ, a bishop and two other figures (possibly the Virgin and St John). The round tower (10th c.; National Monument) is cut off from the church by the modern road which bisects the monastic site. Originally 80 ft high, the tower survives to a height of 60 ft.

Roscrea Castle

Nearby, in Castle Street, are the ruins of Roscrea Castle (13th c. National Monument), with massive curtain walls, several towers and an elaborate system of staircases and passages leading to various defensive stations. The holes in the walls for the chains of the drawbridge can be seen from the street.

In the 18th c., **Damer House** was erected within the castle walls. After thorough restoration it is now used for periodic exhibitions. Note in particular the staircase with its elaborate carving. Adjoining Damer House is the 'Heritage Annexe', occupying a building erected in the 19th c. for military purposes, in which exhibits detailing the history of the region are presented. Open Mon.–Fri. 9.15am–1pm, 2–5pm, May–Sep. also Sat. 11am–5pm, Sun. 2–5pm.

Franciscan Friary

In Abbey Street are remains of a 15th c. Franciscan friary – a gateway, the walls of the choir and the bell tower, the buttresses of which form the entrance to the modern parish church.

Surroundings

Monaincha Abbey

2 miles east of the town, near the golf course, stands the ruined church (12th–13th c.; National Monument) of Monaincha Abbey, founded in the 7th c. on an island in what was then an area of bog. The church retains a finely decorated west doorway and chancel arch.

Nenagh

A good 20 miles south-west of Roscrea on the N7, in a fertile plain, lies the town of Nenagh. Its main feature of interest is the massive keep of Nenagh Castle (early 13th c.; National Monument), a five-storey round tower 100 ft high with walls up to 20 ft thick; the upper part is 19th c. Of the other towers of this pentagonal Anglo-Norman stronghold of the Butlers, there remains only one of the towers of the gatehouse. An unusual museum can be found in Nenagh – housed in a building formerly used as a prison. The cells and the execution chamber are shown as they were in the 19th c. when prisoners were kept here. Biographical material explains the fate of 17 men who were executed here. In the adjoining octagonal governor's house are reconstructions of a 19th c. schoolroom, shop, smithy and kitchen. Open mid-May to mid-Sep. Mon–Fri. 10am–5pm, Sun. 2.30–5pm.

Lorrha

17 miles north of Nenagh, at Lorrha, are three churches (all National Monuments): a ruined Dominican church with good details (13th c., with later alterations); the remains of an Augustinian church (15th c.); and, to the south, another church, part of which is still in use, with sculptural decoration on the doorway, including a pelican, symbol of self-sacrificing love.

Rosguill Peninsula   A 4

Republic of Ireland
Province: Ulster
County: Donegal

The Rosguill Peninsula is one of the small peninsulas on the indented
coastline of Co. Donegal in the extreme north of Ireland; it is bounded
on the east by Mulroy Bay and on the west by Sheep Haven. The beauty
of its scenery attracts many visitors.

   Like much of Donegal, this is still a predominantly Irish-speaking area
(Gaeltacht). Hand-woven tweed is made here.

Atlantic Drive

The Atlantic Drive, encircling the greater part of the peninsula, is one of   **Carrigart**
Ireland's finest scenic roads. The starting point of the roughly 12-mile
circuit is Carrigart, a pleasant holiday resort (golf, tennis, swimming,
riding, sea fishing) reached either from the south-east via the N56 from
Letterkenny (➤ entry), along a beautiful stretch of road around Mulroy
Bay, or alternatively from the south-west.

From Carrigart a narrow road goes north skirting the west side of Mulroy   **Tranarossan Bay**
Bay, after 4 miles bearing west across the peninsula to beautiful
Tranarossan Bay (dunes with interesting flora in spring).

The road now follows the Atlantic coast before winding its way south-   **Downings**
wards, with views of Sheep Haven Bay, to Downings, a holiday resort
with a good sandy beach. Visitors can look round a tweed factory and
buy the Donegal tweed made there.

The Rosses · Na Rosa   A/B 3

Republic of Ireland
Province: Ulster
County: Donegal

The indented coastal area in north-west Donegal known as the Rosses
(Na Rosa, the headlands) extends from Gweebarra Bay in the south to
Inishfree Bay in the north – a tract of generally flat countryside of grey
rocks, little loughs and tiny fields enclosed by drystone walls. It is a predominantly Irish speaking (Gaeltacht) area.

Sights

The only place of any size in this still largely unspoilt region is Dungloe   **Dungloe**
on the N56. From here the N56 and another very scenic road further
east, run north-east to Gweedore (➤ Bloody Foreland).

Lough Anure, lying to the right of the N56, is of geological interest for its   **Lough Anure**
evidence of glaciation.

South-west of Dungloe is Crohy Head, with fine cliffs and some caves.   **Crohy Head**

From Dungloe the R259 arcs north-west, following the Atlantic coast   **Burtonport**
with its constantly changing views. At the fork in the road just outside
Dungloe branch left. Keeping close to the coast, with views of the

Drystone walls dominate the landscape at the Rosses

numerous islands offshore, the road next traverses the narrow strip of land between Lough Meela and the sea. To the left can be seen Rutland Island, with the sand-covered remains of a harbour constructed in 1796.

After 5 miles Burtonport is reached, a busy fishing haven where more salmon and lobsters are landed than at any other port in Ireland or indeed the British Isles. Not surprisingly there are several restaurants serving freshly caught lobster and other seafood.

Aranmore Island To the west, beyond a number of smaller islands, lies Aranmore or Aran Island (not to be confused with the Aran Islands; ➤ entry), to which a boat runs from Burtonport (hourly in summer), a crossing of about 20 minutes. Some 800 or so people live on the island, only 8 miles long and 3 miles wide. Their main sources of income are fishing and tourism.

The island's wild, heather-clad plateau terminates on its western side in cliffs and caves, the nesting ground of countless seabirds. Lough Shure, a small lough in the centre of the island, has an abundance of rainbow trout. There are sheltered beaches on the east side of the island.

Royal Canal   C 4/5

Republic of Ireland
Length: 90 miles

Like the Grand Canal (➤ entry), the Royal Canal starts from Dublin and links Dublin Bay with the Shannon (➤ entry). It follows a course further north than the Grand Canal, joining the Shannon above Lough Ree. Differences in height are overcome by 47 locks.

Construction of the Royal Canal was begun in 1792, the culmination of more than 30 years' planning and preparation. Each section was brought into use as it was completed; once the link with the Shannon was established in 1817, freight and passenger traffic increased considerably. Branch canals were constructed to link up with towns near the main canal. But, as with the Grand Canal, increasing competition from the railways brought economic difficulties. Finally the canal was purchased by a railway company and a railway line running west was built alongside it (1845). During the second half of the 19th c. traffic on the canal continued to decline, and some of the branch canals and canal harbours were filled in. By the middle of the 20th c. freight transport had stopped completely and in 1961 the canal was officially closed to commercial traffic. The Royal Canal Amenity Group now works for the preservation of the canal as a historical monument and recreational facility. — History

The Royal Canal offers excellent facilities for pleasure craft, the maximum permitted size of vessel – determined by the dimensions of the smallest lock – being as follows: length 75 ft, beam 13 ft wide, draught 4½ ft. The lowest bridges over the canal have a clearance of 10 ft. — Pleasure craft

The canal is well stocked with bream, roach, rudd, tench, pike and the occasional trout.

Shannon (River Shannon)   B–D 3/4

Republic of Ireland
Length: 230 miles

The Shannon, Ireland's longest river, rises in Co. Cavan, flows through the limestone plains of central Ireland and reaches the Atlantic just

River Shannon: popular with holiday boating enthusiasts

Shannon
River Shannon

20 km
12,5 mi

········· Canal

✕ Lock

––––––– Ferry

✕ Railway bridge

✕ Road bridge

Source of the Shannon

Lough Erne

Lough Allen

Shannon Erne Waterway

Heapstown Cairn

Lough Arrow

Lough Key

Drumshanbo

Boyle

Carrick-on-Shannon

Jamestown

Lough Bofin

Rinn Loughs

Lough Gara

Lough Bodergh

Roosky

Grange Lough

Kilglass Lough

Lough Forbes

Loch O'Flynn

River

Longford

Lanesborough

Roscommon

Royal Canal

Suck

Rindown Castle

Lough Ree

Athlone

Twyfort Cross

Shannonbridge

Clonmacnoise

River Brosna

Grand Canal

Meelick

Shannon Harbour

Derryhivenny Castle

Banagher

Portumna

Lough Derg

Old Court Castle

Lough Graney

Tuamgraney Church

Ennis

Nenagh

Killone Abbey

Quin Abbey

Balboru Fort

Killaloe

Ballina

Shannon Airport

Bunratty Castle

Montpelier

Ardnacrusha

Limerick

Battle Island

Kilrush

Carrigogunnel Castle

Scattery Island

Killimer

Foynes Island

Tarbert

Carrigafoyle Castle

Atlantic Ocean
Mouth of the Shannon

Newcastle West

Tipperary

Blossom Gate

© Baedeker

beyond Limerick. With its loughs, tributary streams and canals it forms a widely ramified system of waterways traversing a fifth of the area of Ireland. The banks of the Shannon, apart from the few places of some size through which it flows, are thinly populated and for much of their length bordered by pastureland. Since there is no industry along the river, the light over the water is of unusual clarity. Apart from a short non-navigable stretch on its upper reaches, the gradient down to Killaloe is so gentle that only six locks are required over this considerable distance.

Tourist and recreational facilities are now very well developed on the Shannon all the way from Battlebridge (at its outflow from Lough Allan, a lough well stocked with fish) to Killaloe. Since 1994, when the canal from Leitrim near Carrick-on-Shannon (➤ entry) to Lough Erne in Northern Ireland, which had lain unused for more than a century, was re-opened after restoration, the river has been part of the largest cruising area of inland waterways in Europe – a total of 500 miles of intercon-nected lakes, rivers and canals to explore by boat!

Tourism

A leisurely cruise along these peaceful waters is one of the great hol-iday pleasures that Ireland can offer. Though for the most part shel-tered, sudden increases in wind can whip up heavy waves on the two largest lakes on the Shannon waterway, Lough Ree just north of Athlone and Lough Derg just north of Killaloe. There are marinas for boats of all types and sizes on the Shannon at Carrick-on-Shannon, Athlone and Killaloe (see entries). For further information on cabin-cruiser hire see Practical Information, Boating.

★Cruising on the Shannon

Boats starting from Carrick-on-Shannon (➤ entry) are likely to want first to explore the upper reaches of the river; also the River Boyle and its loughs, especially the beautiful Lough Key near the town of Boyle (➤ entry), with its wooded islands and Forest Park in the demesne of a former mansion (forest trails, bog garden, restaurant, shop).

Carrick-on-Shannon

Downstream from Carrick-on-Shannon, the Jamestown Canal and lock (with detours possible to Drumsna and Jamestown) lead into the delightful Lough Boderg from which there is access via a narrow pass-age through reed beds to the lonely Corranadoe loughs, a paradise for birdwatchers and anglers.

Jamestown Canal Lough Boderg

Dromod on Lough Bofin has a pretty little harbour (with correspondingly few mooring places). Roosky, further south, has a quay.

Lough Bofin

Beyond Roosky a narrow tree-lined stretch of the Shannon leads into Lough Forbes and then on past the junction with the Royal Canal (➤ entry) to Termonbarry with its large lock. From Termonbarry, or from Cloondara across the river, Strokestown and Longford (➤ entry) can be visited.

Lough Forbes

Further downstream is an extensive tract of bogland worked by Bord na Móna, the Irish peat development board. At the little town of Lanesborough (➤ Longford: Surroundings, Lough Ree), the Shannon is spanned by a nine-arched bridge.

Lanesborough

The river then opens out into the great expanse of Lough Ree (lake of kings). Several islands in the lough, including Inchbofin (National Monument), Inishturk and Inchmore, have remains of early monastic settlements. On Inchclearaun (also known as Quaker Island after a 19th c. inhabitant), Clothra, sister of Queen Maeve, is said to have been killed by a slingstone hurled from the shore of the lough.

Lough Ree

Clonmacnoise

South of Athlone (➤ entry) and its lock, the river pursues a quiet winding course through flat countryside until the towers of Clonmacnoise (➤ entry) appear on the horizon. This is without question the finest way of approaching the ruins of the monastic settlement (which has a landing stage).

Shannonbridge

At Shannonbridge an old 16-arched bridge spans the Shannon. The fortifications here were built during the Napoleonic era.

Shannon Harbour

From Shannon Harbour barges once sailed to Dublin on the Grand Canal (➤ entry). Nearby ruins dating from that period still convey some feeling of Regency elegance.

Lough Derg

Below Shannon Harbour the river becomes wider, passing the old towns of Banagher (➤ Birr) and Portumna (➤ Loughrea) before entering Lough Derg (➤ Killaloe), the largest of the many Shannon lakes, studded with islands.

The landscape now changes: the shores become more fertile, farms and villages appear more frequently and there is an air of greater prosperity. The south end of Lough Derg is encircled by hills; ranges of red sandstone mountains mark out the horizon on both sides.

Killaloe

The town of Killaloe (➤ entry) is noted not only for its heritage but also its large marina and water-skiing facilities.

For hire boats Killaloe marks the end of navigation. Privately owned craft, on the other hand, can proceed further, though the lower reaches of the Shannon are considered difficult and hazardous. Over the next 18 miles or so the river, hitherto fairly sluggish, flows rapidly.

Ardnacrusha

At Ardnacrusha (hill of the cross) there is a huge hydroelectric power station, built in 1925, with a dam at Parteen, a head-race 8½ miles long bringing the water to the power station, four turbines and two locks. This first and largest of Ireland's power stations produces some 350,000 megawatts of electricity annually. Visiting the power station, reached by road from Limerick or Killaloe along the north bank of the Shannon, is an impressive experience. In the huge locks vessels are raised and lowered more than 100 ft. There is also a fish lift to ensure that fish – mainly salmon – have access to the upper canal (the lift takes three hours). The waters streaming out of the turbines are fed into the river below Ardnacrusha at a point where it is already tidal.

Limerick

Most of the city of Limerick (➤ entry) lies on the south bank of the Shannon, with docks and moorings for sea going vessels of up to 10,000 tons.

Beyond Limerick, on the right bank of the river, is Shannon International Airport (➤ Ennis).

Between here and its outflow into the Atlantic, a distance of some 60 miles, the Shannon opens out into a funnel-shape estuary. Near Kilkee (➤ entry) a car ferry operates between Tarbert in Co. Kerry and Killimer in Co. Clare.

★★Skellig Islands · Skellig Rocks E 1

Republic of Ireland
Province: Munster
County: Kerry

The Skellig Islands or Skellig Rocks, a group of small rocky islets, lie off the south-west coast of Ireland some 9 miles west of the Iveragh Peninsula. To protect the islands' unique bird life, landing has been prohibited since 1987 (although some local fishermen will still ferry tourists across from Caherdaniel; ➤ Ring of Kerry).

The islands with their curious topography can, however, be viewed from a distance. Comfortably equipped excursion boats sail to and around the Skelligs from Valentia Island (➤ Ring of Kerry), where the Skellig Experience Visitor Centre at the landing place provides a wealth of information about these isolated outcrops.

Skellig Experience

The islands

The boat first passes Little Skellig, an island inhabited by tens of thousands of seabirds of many species, particularly gannets. The dense flocks taking off from their nesting places, soaring up, swooping down again and all the time uttering their harsh cries, form a sight – and a sound – not to be forgotten. Binoculars should be taken.

Little Skellig

On Skellig Michael, the largest of the islands, the remains of a monastic settlement, said to have been founded in the 6th c. by St Finan, are visible. A total of 670 steps are hewn in the rock leading up to the saddle between the island's two rocky peaks (highest summit 713 ft). Below the lower of the two rocky pyramids, the well-preserved monastic remains (National Monument) can be seen laid out on little artificial terraces – six circular beehive huts with rectangular interiors; two boat-shaped oratories built in stone (6th–9th c.); lower down, the remains of a church, probably 12th c.; small areas of garden, a well, gravestones and the remains of a sundial; finally, enclosure walls on the edge of a dizzy precipice.

Skellig Michael

Until the 13th c. there were always 13 monks on the island. Since Skellig Michael is without a spring, water had to be collected with considerable difficulty from two small reservoirs. Later many pilgrims came to the island, climbing to the highest point to kiss the ancient stone standing upright in the rock. From 1820 until 1987 a lighthouse keeper kept permanent watch on the island.

Skibbereen · Sciobairin   E 2

Republic of Ireland
Province: Munster
County: Cork
Population: 2000

Skibbereen (Sciobairin, little boat harbour), one of the chief towns in Co. Cork, lies near the southern tip of Ireland, charmingly situated on the River Ilen, which, a mile below the town, opens out into a winding estuary with numerous islands.

Skibbereen is a fishing port and market town, and a good centre from which to explore the surrounding area.

Surroundings

From Skibbereen the R596 leads south-east to Castletownshend. Here in the middle of the steep and picturesque main street grow a clump of trees. On the south-western outskirts stands Drishane House, home during the last century of Edith Somerville and Violet Martin who, under the pseudonym 'Somerville and Ross', wrote novels and short stories vividly describing life in the Anglo-Irish houses of the period. Not far north-west of the village rises the massive Knockdrum Fort (National Monument), a ring-fort 95 ft in diameter, with stone walls 10 ft thick, a narrow entrance protected by a guard cell, and chambers underground.

Castletownshend

Creagh Gardens near Skibbereen

Creagh Gardens	The R595, heading south-west from Skibbereen, reaches in about 3 miles Creagh Gardens, romantically situated by the sea. Open Apr.–Sep. daily 10am–6pm.
Baltimore	The R595 terminates at the pleasant holiday resort of Baltimore, a well-known fishing centre also with a sailing school. From here it is possible to visit Sherkin Island and Clear Island by boat or take the regular ferry to Schull (➤ below) via Heir Island.
Sherkin Island	Sherkin Island, close offshore, sheltering the town's harbour like a break-water, has the ruins of a castle and a 15th c. Franciscan friary (daily ferry service from Baltimore in summer).
Clear Island	Further out, also with a boat service from Baltimore and in summer also from Schull, is Clear Island, whose 150 inhabitants, living isolated, have preserved something of the older way of life and still speak Irish. There are two Irish language colleges on the island. The ruins of a church (12th c.; National Monument) and a stone pillar with a cross motif bear witness to an Early Christian settlement here. The Fastnet Rock, the most southerly point of Ireland away out in the Atlantic, has magnificent cliff scenery.
Lough Ine	On the way back to Skibbereen a detour can be made eastwards on a side road which passes Lough Ine, a clear sea lough whose rich fauna is kept under observation by scientists at a marine biology research station belonging to University College, Cork. A waymarked path leads up to Hill Top (a good 20 minutes from the picnic place), from where there are excellent views of the lough and the sea with the outlying islands.
Schull	At Ballydehob, 10 miles west of Skibbereen, the R592 branches off

south-west to Schull where a planetarium can be visited. In the vicinity are a number of old copper mines. From Mount Gabriel (1312 ft) there is a good panorama. Ferries run from Schull to Baltimore and Clear Island.

From Schull there is an attractive run to Crookhaven, which has a safe, sheltered harbour. A narrow road makes its way to Mizen Head, from the highest point of which (765 ft) there is a splendid view of the Atlantic coast.

Crookhaven

Sligo · Sligeach

B 3

Republic of Ireland
Province: Connacht
County: Sligo
Population: 17,200

Sligo (Sligeach, river with many shells) lies in the north-west of Ireland, on a well-wooded plain encircled by hills. Most of the town is on the south side of the broad River Garavogue, which flows from Lough Gill (close east of the town) into Sligo Bay.

Sligo is not only the county town of Co. Sligo but also the chief town in north-west Ireland, and an important road junction where the N4, N15 and N16 all meet. It is also the terminus of a railway line from Dublin, with the most northerly railway station in the Irish Republic. The harbour is of little importance today on account of its shallow water.

The poet William Butler Yeats (➤ Famous People) lived for some time in Sligo, and there are many reminders of this famous resident both in and around the town. The Yeats Summer School holds courses every August for Irish and foreign students.

Sligo appears in the records for the first time in 537. In 807 it was plundered by Vikings. In 1245 Maurice Fitzgerald, earl of Kildare, took up residence here. Later, rival clans vied for possession of the castle. The town was devastated by Cromwell's troops in 1641 and again in 1645.

History

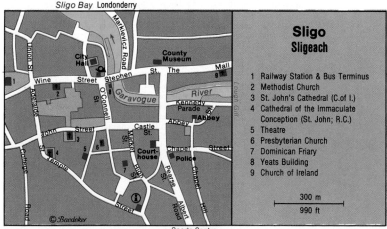

Sligo Bay Londonderry

Sligo
Sligeach

1 Railway Station & Bus Terminus
2 Methodist Church
3 St. John's Cathedral (C.of I.)
4 Cathedral of the Immaculate Conception (St. John; R.C.)
5 Theatre
6 Presbyterian Church
7 Dominican Friary
8 Yeats Building
9 Church of Ireland

300 m
990 ft

Sports Centre
Galway, Dublin

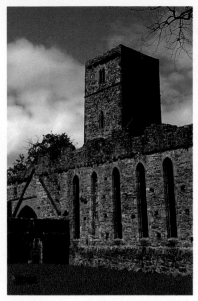 

Sligo Friary

Town

Sligo, a busy, lively town well supplied with shops and services, has few particularly outstanding sights.

Sights

County Museum
Art Gallery

In Stephen Street, on the north side of the River Garavogue, are the Sligo County Museum and adjoining Art Gallery. The County Museum (open Mon.–Fri. 10.30am–12.30pm, 2.30–4.30pm), occupying an old rectory, contains material on the history of the region and mementoes of W B Yeats, including first editions of his works, as well as letters and family photographs. The Art Gallery (open Apr.–May Tue., Thu., Sat. 10.30am–12.30pm; Jun.–Sep. Tue.–Sat. 10.30am–12.30pm, 2.30–4.30pm) has pictures by a variety of artists; of particular interest are the works by Jack Butler Yeats, the poet's brother.

★Sligo Friary

From the County Museum a bridge crosses to the south bank of the river. To the left are the oldest buildings in Sligo – the church, cloister and conventual buildings of Sligo Friary (National Monument), a Dominican friary founded by Maurice Fitzgerald in 1253 and rebuilt in 1416 after a fire. The church has a double nave and transepts; the choir dates from the original foundation, the transepts from the 16th c. Notable features are the canopied tomb of Cormack O'Crean (1506) on the north side of the nave, with a Crucifixion and other figures in bas relief, and the O'Conor Sligo Monument (1624) on the south side. Three sides of the beautiful 15th c. cloister have survived, with the sacristy and chapter house (13th c.).

St John's Church
St John's
Cathedral

About 550 yd further west are the town's two principal churches, St John's Church (Church of Ireland) in John Street, a neo-Gothic building of 1812, and the Roman Catholic St John's Cathedral (neo-Romanesque, 1869–74) in Temple Street.

The Art Gallery in the Yeats Memorial Building beside Hyde Bridge mounts temporary exhibitions; in summer there is an audio-visual presentation documenting Yeats' connection with Sligo.

Yeats Memorial Building

Lough Gill

To the east of the town lies the delightful Lough Gill, 5 miles long and well stocked with salmon, trout and pike. The 23-mile scenic circuit of the lough is an experience not to be missed. Also very enjoyable in summer are the boat trips on the lough (from Sligo or Parke's Castle).

Hazelwood House, a handsome little Palladian mansion (1731 by Richard Cassels) stands on a peninsula at the north-west end of the lough between the lough and the River Garavogue.

Hazelwood House

Almost immediately north is picturesque Lough Colgagh, above which are found a large ancient burial site, the Deerpark Monument (National Monument), and remains of other early structures.

Lough Colgagh

Proceeding round Lough Gill, Parke's Castle (National Monument), a fine rectangular three-storey building with a large 17th c. courtyard is seen on the east shore of the lough (see picture, below). The fortified mansion has been carefully restored and can be visited. Remnants of an earlier fortified building have been uncovered in the courtyard. Open Jun.–Sep. daily 9.30am–6.30pm; mid-Apr. to May Tue.–Sun. 10am–5pm; Oct. daily 10am–5pm.

★Parke's Castle

Parke's Castle on the shores of Lough Gill

285

★Dromahair	The circuit continues to Dromahair, an exceedingly attractive place of considerable historical importance. In the 12th c. Dervorgilla, wife of Tiernan O'Rourke, eloped from here with Dermot MacMurrough, king of Leinster. Subsequently outlawed by Ireland's high king, Dermot appealed to Henry II of England who sent his vassals to Dermot's aid. So occurred the first incursion of the Anglo-Normans into Ireland, landing near Wexford in 1169. The ruins of Breffni Castle, seat of the O'Rourkes, adjoin the Old Hall (1626) on the bank of the Bonet River.
Creevelea Friary	Across the river from Dromahair are the ruins of Creevelea Friary (National Monument), a Franciscan friary founded in 1508. The remains include a church with choir and tower, and monastic buildings set round a cloister. The pillars on the north side of the cloister have figural representations including of St Francis with the stigmata preaching to the birds.
Dooney Rock	The R287 now proceeds west, but after 4 miles turns north along a valley back to the south shore of Lough Gill. Soon Dooney Rock is reached. This popular viewpoint is celebrated in a song by Yeats, as also is Inishfree Island situated close to the southern shore. Also to be seen are Church Island with its ruined church (National Monument), and, further on, the smaller Cottage Island. To the north is Cairns Hill on which there are various prehistoric sites. Finally return to Sligo on the N4.

Lough Arrow

About 17 miles south-east of Sligo lies Lough Arrow. A road turning east off the N4 near Castle Baldwin skirts the lough, leading first to Heapstown Cairn (National Monument), possibly a passage grave, and then, further east, Lough Nasuil. In 1933 this remarkable little lough, roughly 330 yd in diameter and normally containing some 220 million gallons of water, suddenly emptied, remained dry for three weeks, and then just as suddenly filled up again. To the south, beautifully situated on the shores of Lough Arrow, is Ballindoon Friary (16th c.). After another 6 miles the N4 is regained at Ballinafad, which has a 16th c. castle (National Monument) with massive corner towers.

Carrowkeel	About 3 miles north of Ballinafad, on an isolated hill slope in the Bricklieve Mountains, is the Carrowkeel prehistoric site (National Monument), comprising 14 burial mounds, all circular except for one which is oval, and with various types of chamber tomb. They date from 2500–2000 BC. Below the burial site are the remains of 50 circular stone huts, perhaps occupied by those who constructed the graves. From the top of the hill there is a superb view of Lough Arrow.
Keshcorran Hill	Keshcorran Hill, a few miles further west (near Kesh, just off the R295), has a number of caves.
Ballymote	6 miles north is Ballymote, with the massive ivy-covered ruins of a castle with six round towers. Built in about 1300, the castle was subject to repeated attack until its fortifications were finally slighted about 1700.
Collooney	The R293 continues north to join up with the N17. 2½ miles north-east on the River Owenmore lies Collooney with, nearby, the pretty Makree Castle (18th c.).
Ballysodare	At Ballysodare, 1½ miles north, the River Owenmore descends a picturesque series of rapids, with a salmon-ladder 'bypass' for the benefit of the fish. On the left bank can be seen the ivy-clad ruins of a 7th c. monastery.

Strandhill, situated on a tongue of land jutting out into Sligo Bay 5 miles west of Sligo, is a family seaside resort with good sandy beaches which offer excellent surfing.

Strandhill

On the summit of the easily climbed Knocknarea (1096 ft), just to the south of Strandhill, stands a huge cairn (National Monument), 36 ft high and 197 ft in diameter, popularly supposed to be the grave of Queen Maeve. From the top of the hill there are magnificent views. On the south-west side is a deep chasm between sheer limestone cliffs.

Knocknarea

The Carrowmore burial site (National Monument) can be reached by driving south from Strandhill then turning north-east in the direction of Sligo. Here archaeologists have discovered some 60 graves, many destroyed and others severely damaged but comprising nevertheless the largest collection of megalithic graves in Ireland. Most are a mixture of passage graves and dolmens, the oldest dating from between 3000 and 2500 BC. Open Jun.–Sep. daily 9.30am–6.30pm.

Carrowmore

Rosses Point is another popular holiday resort situated north-west of Sligo. In addition to a championship golf course, it has good sheltered sandy beaches.

Rosses Point

Tara · Teamhair na Riogh   C 5

Republic of Ireland
Province: Leinster
County: Meath

25 miles north-west of Dublin, at the village of Tara (Teamhair na Riogh, Tara of the kings), a narrow side road leaves the N3 on the left and ascends the famous Hill of Tara, a low grassy hill from which there are extensive views to the north and west.

In prehistoric times Tara was already known as a ritual centre. From the 3rd c. onwards it became the seat of kings – at first minor priest-kings and later the high kings of Ireland. Every three years popular assemblies were held here at which laws were promulgated and disputes between the clans were settled. With the spread of Christianity Tara lost its importance as a cult site but remained the seat of the high kings of Ireland until its abandonment in 1022. Centuries later, in 1843, Tara was again the scene of a great assembly – a mass meeting at which Daniel O'Connell made a speech calling for the emancipation of Catholics in Ireland.

★Hill of Tara

The Hill of Tara (National Monument) boasts a whole series of grass-covered earthworks. Nothing remains of the timber or wattle-and-daub buildings of the Celtic period, the finest of which were said to have doors set with precious stones and furnishings of gold and bronze. For an appreciation of the importance of the site, visitors are referred to the audio-visual presentation in St Patrick's Church.

The central area of the complex, the Ráth of the Kings, is surrounded by a great rampart, the Royal Enclosure. In the centre of the enclosure are two mounds, Cormac's House and the Royal Seat. Near Cormac's House the coronation stone (the Lia Fail) is supposed to have stood; legend has it that the stone used to sound when the rightful king ascended it. Nearby is a memorial stone (erroneously referred to as the coronation stone), commemorating Irish rebels killed in the 1798 Rising.

Ráth of the Kings

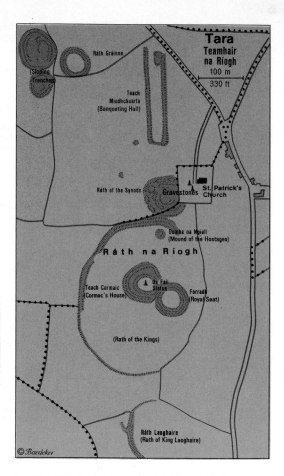

To the north, still within the enclosure, is the Mound of Hostages, a passage grave dating from 1800 BC in which were found the remains of 40 cremated corpses. On their accession the kings of Tara were accustomed to take hostages from the noble families of the kingdom as a way of ensuring their loyalty. After their death, which was certainly not always natural, they were buried in the Mound of Hostages.

Ráth of the Synods

Adjoining the Royal Enclosure to the north is the Ráth of the Synods (2–4th c.), a living area once surrounded by a ring wall. Part of it was destroyed at the beginning of the 20th c. because it was thought to conceal the Ark of the Covenant described in the Old Testament.

Banqueting Hall

Further north are two parallel earthworks 600 ft long and 100 ft apart. The depression between them is traditionally known as the Banqueting Hall – an old print depicts a banquet in progress, with the high king's guests seated in order of rank and precedence in a wooden structure.

Archaeologists, however, believe that it is more likely to have been the ceremonial approach to a cult site.

To the west of the Banqueting Hall lie other earthworks, firstly Gráinnes Fort, then adjacent the so-called Sloping Trenches, probably cult sites.

On a hill 875 yd south of the Hill of Tara is the fort known as Ráth Maeve (National Monument), 720 ft in diameter, surrounded by a rampart and a ditch.

Ráth Maeve

Thurles · Durlas Eile   D 4

Republic of Ireland
Province: Munster
County: Tipperary
Population: 7400

The little market town of Thurles (Durlus Eile, strong fort of Ely) lies in the fertile plain of the River Suir in the south of Ireland. It is an important road junction (N62, N75, R498) and is on the Dublin–Cork railway line. Thurles is the cathedral town of the archdiocese of Cashel and Emly.

Sights

Beside the bridge over the Suir stands the keep of Bridge Castle (12th c.), and near the Square the smaller Black Castle (?15th c.). The cathedral (1865–72), in Lombard Romanesque style, has a Baroque high altar by Andrea Pozzo (17th c.) which came from the Gesú Church in Rome. In a mortuary chapel is the tomb of Archbishop Croke (1824–1902), who took an active part in the struggle for Irish independence and was the first patron of the Gaelic Athletic Association (GAA), founded in 1884 and now one of Europe's largest amateur sports federations.

Surroundings

2 miles north of the town, Brittas Castle, an unfinished 19th c. building with an imposing battlemented tower, can be seen from the N62.

Brittas Castle

Definitely worth visiting is Holy Cross Abbey (13th–15th c.; National Monument), located 4 miles south of Thurles on the right bank of the Suir. The Cistercian monastery, founded in the 12th c., possessed a fragment of the True Cross, making it a place of great pilgrimage. The church, re-roofed and restored in 1975, has an aisled nave and two transepts with a massive tower over the crossing. The chancel, transepts and crossing are all vaulted. The choir (15th c.) with its east window and stone sedilia bearing coats of arms, is particularly fine. In the north transept, partly preserved, is a wall painting (a feature rare in Ireland) depicting a stag-hunting scene in shades of brown, red and green with three huntsmen, a stag and a dog. An arched structure situated between two chapel recesses in the south transept is probably the shrine in which the relic of the True Cross was displayed. From here a staircase leads to the upper floor with the monastic dormitory. On the east side of the attractive and well-preserved cloister lies the chapter house (not open to the public). The refectory on the south side has been destroyed. Open daily 10am–1pm, 2–6pm.

★Holy Cross Abbey

About 3 miles north-west of Holy Cross Abbey, Ballynahow Castle (16th c.; National Monument) has one of the few circular keeps in Ireland. Two of the five original vaulted roofs remain.

Ballynahow Castle

Tipperary · Tiobrad Arann   D 3

Republic of Ireland
Province: Munster
County: Tipperary
Population: 5000

Tipperary (Tiobrad Arann, well of Arann) is a market and industrial town (dairy products, linoleum) in the south of Ireland, situated in the fertile Golden Vale which extends west of Cashel into Co. Limerick. To the south of the town rises the long ridge of the Slievenamuck Hills.

Tipperary became a familiar name to many outside Ireland from the traditional song *It's a long way to Tipperary*. A favourite with British troops at the beginning of the 20th c., it became popularised before the start of the first world war – particularly the first verse:

It's a long way to Tipperary,
It's a long way to go,
It's a long way to Tipperary
To the sweetest girl I know.
Goodbye Piccadilly, farewell Leicester Square.
It's a long long way to Tipperary,
But my heart's right there.

Sights

Little is left of the old town. The most notable remains of the past are the chancel arch of a monastic church (13th c.) and the ruins of a 17th c. grammar school. The neo-Gothic parish church dates from the 19th c.

Surroundings

Thomastown
Castle

On the N74 about 6 miles east of Tipperary, in the Golden Vale, are the ruins of Thomastown Castle, built in the 17th c. and enlarged in neo-Gothic style about 1812. This was the birthplace in 1790 of Father Theobald Matthew, the 'Apostle of Temperance' (➤ Cork). The house fell into disrepair from the end of the 19th c.; the park, which once had a large French-style garden, now forms part of an afforestation scheme.

Golden

2 miles further east where the road crosses the Suir at the village of Golden, a ruined castle stands picturesquely on a rocky islet in the river.

★Athassel Priory

Beyond the bridge a road on the right leads to the ruins of Ireland's largest medieval monastery, Athassel Priory (13th–15th c.; National Monument), an Augustinian house founded by William de Burgh and dissolved in the mid-16th c. The remains cover an area of 4 acres. The church, 213 ft long, has an aisled nave, a choir and transepts, with an impressive tower over the crossing. In the choir is the tomb of a Norman knight (13th c.). Practically nothing survives of the cloister, around which are the extensive conventual buildings, surrounded by a high wall. In front of the gatehouse was a bridge giving access to the priory. Until the mid-14th c. there was a little town here, of which no trace remains.

Tralee · Tra Li   D 2

Republic of Ireland
Province: Munster
County: Kerry
Population: 17,500

Tralee (Tra Li, bay of the River Lee), the lively county town of Co. Kerry, lies in the south-west of Ireland, 2 miles above the outflow of the River Lee into Tralee Bay. Despite its relatively small population, Tralee fulfils an important role as the urban centre for Co. Kerry, a particularly large county. In addition to its administrative agencies, the town offers a good range of services and shopping facilities. Tralee is the home of the Kerry Group, a dairy cooperative established in 1974, which markets its products (such as butter) under the label Kerry Gold, exporting them to numerous countries.

For tourists Tralee is above all the gateway to the Dingle Peninsula (➤ entry), an area steeped in history, and the starting point for a drive around the famous Ring of Kerry (➤ entry).

Tralee was twice set on fire by its own garrison (in 1643 and again in 1691) before being given up to the enemy. As a result no older buildings have survived. There are, however, some fine Georgian houses in the centre of town.

Town

Sights

St John's Church, a 19th c. neo-Gothic building by the Dublin architect J J McCarthy, has fine stained glass by Michael Healy in the sacristy.

St John's Church

The early 19th c. Court House, to the north of the church, in Ashe Street, has an Ionic portico.

Court House

Housed in the Ashe Memorial Hall (open Mon.–Sat. 10am–6pm, Sun. 2–6pm, Aug. to 8pm) are three attractions collectively entitled 'Kerry the Kingdom'. The first, 'Kerry in Colour', is a slide show introducing visitors to the scenic beauties of the region. The second, 'Treasures of the Kingdom', is actually the local museum which brings to life the history of the county from the Stone Age to the present day by a series of imaginative displays; exhibits include various notable archaeological finds and objets d'art. The third, 'Geraldine Tralee', takes its name from the Desmond Geraldines, one of the Anglo-Norman families who ruled over Tralee and its surroundings. Eleven 'time vehicles' carry visitors through

Kerry the Kingdom

Siamsa Tire Theatre in Tralee

291

the medieval streets and squares of Tralee in 1450, reconstructed in impressive detail even down to the sounds and smells.

Siamsa Tire Theatre

Close to the Ashe Memorial Hall stands Tralee's Siamsa Tire Theatre, opened in 1991. The design of the theatre was inspired by Ireland's stone forts. Behind the name Siamsa Tire lies a national people's theatre dedicated to the promotion of Celtic culture. Programmes include music, dance and drama (performances May–Sep., 8.30pm).

Blennerville windmill and steam train

From 1891 until 1953 a narrow-gauge railway operated between Tralee and Dingle. In 1993 a section was reopened with trains running hourly between April and September from Tralee to the restored Blennerville windmill 2 miles away. The mill, which can also be reached by car via the R559 Dingle road, was erected at the end of the 18th c. and remained in operation until the end of the 19th c.; it was restored in the 1980s. Visitors can watch wheat being ground into flour between the huge millstones. A multi-media presentation recalls the history of the mill and tells the story of its restoration, while a further exhibition is devoted to the mass emigrations of the last century (in the 18th and 19th c. many ships carrying Irish emigrants sailed from Blennerville Quay). Open

May–Nov. Mon.–Sat. 10am–6pm, to 8pm in summer, Sun. 2–6pm.

Surroundings

Fenit

In 1994 Fenit Sea World opened on the harbour at Fenit just 6 miles west of Tralee. Visitors are brought face to face with every type of marine creature from tiny crustacea to rapacious-looking sharks. Open daily 10am–6pm.

Ardfert

5 miles north-west of Tralee on the R551 lies Ardfert, around which are some important medieval remains. St Brendan (483–578), born in neighbouring Fenit, founded a monastery here, to which a group of churches (National Monuments) in the churchyard belonged – the fortress-like 'cathedral', with a beautiful 12th c. west doorway and blind arcading and a 13th c. nave and choir (fine lancet windows); to the north-west the little Romanesque church of Temple na Hoe with columns at its outer corners; and the 15th c. church of Temple na Griffin.

A short distance east are the ruins of a Franciscan friary (13th–15th c.; National Monument). The church has arcade columns and a fine south window. Two sides of the 15th c. cloister have survived.

Ballyheige

Further north on the R551 lies the quiet seaside resort of Ballyheige. Nearby on lovely Kerry Head, jutting into the Atlantic west of the village, hexagonal quartz crystals from the Kerry Mountains can be found. Banna Beach, extending to the south, is the chief attraction for most holidaymakers. It was here that in 1916 Sir Roger Casement (➤ Famous People) landed from a German submarine to take part in the Easter Rising.

Crag Cave

Just off the N21, about 12 miles east of Tralee, is the impressive Crag Cave. Systematically explored for the first time in 1981, it was found to be one of the largest cave systems in Ireland, with passages almost 2½ miles long. With lighting and safe gangways installed, Crag Cave was opened to the public in 1989. Open daily 10am–6pm.

Trim · Baile Atha Truim   C 5

Republic of Ireland
Province: Leinster
County: Meath
Population: 2100

The little market town of Trim (Baile Atha Truim, town of the elder-tree
fort) lies on the River Boyne in a fertile plain north-west of Dublin. Here
within a small space are gathered remains of a rich past, both religious
and military.

In 1172 Hugh de Lacy, a vassal of Henry II, built a castle on a site close   History
to the spot where St Patrick had founded a monastery in the 5th c. The
castle subsequently changed hands several times, being successively
fought over, destroyed, rebuilt and enlarged. In the 14th c. the town that
had grown up around the castle was fortified with walls and gates. The
Irish parliament met here several times during the 15th c. In 1649 the
town fell into Cromwellian hands.

Sights

Trim's most prominent landmark is the Yellow Steeple (National   Yellow Steeple
Monument), the last relic of an Augustinian abbey built on a bare hill
above the river in the 14th c. The fine tower, still over 126 ft high, stood
on the north side of the church.

Nearby is the privately owned Talbot's Castle, which has been mod-   Talbot's Castle
ernised and converted into a school. Among its pupils was Arthur
Wellesley (1769–1852), the future duke of Wellington. He later lived in
Patrick Street, where there is a monument to him.

A little way south of the Yellow Steeple (near the river embankment) can   Sheep Gate
be seen the two-storey ruins of Sheep Gate, the only surviving town
gate.

Opposite, on the south side of the Boyne in the heart   ★Trim Castle
of town, rises a magnificent stronghold, Trim Castle
(National Monument), the largest Anglo-Norman
castle in Ireland, occupying an area of 3 acres. In the
very centre of the castle precinct, at its highest point,
stands the square keep, with turrets at the four corners and projecting towers (only three of the original
four survive) in the middle of each of the 11 ft-thick
walls, giving the massive structure a cruciform plan. The whole is surrounded by a curtain wall with semicircular towers (five of which
remain) and a moat. Entry was via a drawbridge operated from the
tower on the south side. The parapet walks originally linked with the
town walls.

On the edge of Trim lie the exceedingly pleasant Butterstream   Butterstream
Gardens, consisting of several adjoining gardens separated by box   Gardens
hedges, each with its own individual character. Open May–Sep.
Tue.–Sun. 2–5pm.

Surroundings

Almost a mile upstream to the east of the town, at an old bridge over the   **Newton Trim**
Boyne, lies Newton Trim, the ruins of the Abbey of St Peter and St Paul

(National Monument). Of the very large cathedral (13th c.; transitional Romanesque–Gothic), built for the see of Meath, there remain only the choir, the crossing and a small section of the nave. On the south side of the church are some remains of conventual buildings. To the east is a smaller church (13th c.) containing a fine late 16th c. double tomb.

Tuam · Tuaim C 3

Republic of Ireland
Province: Connacht
County: Galway
Population: 4500

Tuam (Tuaim, burial place) is situated in the west of Ireland on the N17 east of Lough Corrib. The little market town has some industry including a sugar factory; it is also a good centre for fishing.

Tuam was from quite early on a place of great ecclesiastical importance. The town's first two Protestant archbishops between them produced the first ever translation of the New Testament into Irish (1602). It is now the see of a Roman Catholic archbishop and a bishop of the Church of Ireland.

Sights

★St Mary's
Cathedral

The 19th c. St Mary's Cathedral (Church of Ireland) in Galway Road incorporates barrel-vaulted chancel (with beautifully carved chancel arch) and fine east window from the original 12th–14th c. church. In the south aisle is the ornamented shaft of a 12th c. high cross. The choir stalls are Italian baroque.

High cross

In the Market Square stands another high cross (12th c.; National Monument), assembled from various fragments, with a number of figures and interlace ornament.

Mill Museum

In nearby Shop Street is Mill Museum, with a working corn mill and milling equipment.

Surroundings

Dunmore

On the N83 some 8 miles north-east of Tuam lies Dunmore, a place of some age with the ruins of a castle and friary (both National Monuments). The castle (14th c.) consists of a four-storey rectangular tower with gables. The Augustinian friary was founded in 1425 by a member of the Bermingham family; all that survives is the church, with a massive central tower borne on arches.

Bermingham
House

2 miles north of Tuam stands Bermingham House (1730), with good stucco work and fine furniture. Open weekday afternoons.

Knockmoy

Picturesquely situated on a small lough 7 miles from Tuam, reached via the R347 and N63 (the Roscommon road), are the ruins of Knockmoy Abbey (National Monument), a Cistercian monastery founded in 1190. The nave is plain but the choir has some fine stonework. On the north wall is one of Ireland's few examples of medieval wall painting, dating from about 1400. Only the outlines, drawn in black, have survived. The scenes depicted are Christ in the attitude of blessing, the martyrdom of St Sebastian and the legend of the three dead and three living kings. Under the three dead kings is the inscription: 'That which you are, we were; that which we are, you will be'. The east wing of the conventual buildings is well preserved but nothing is left of the cloister.

On the site of an old Franciscan friary at Kilbennan, 2½ miles north-west of Tuam, are a partly collapsed round tower and the ruins of a small church (both National Monuments). **Kilbennan**

Tullamore · Tulach Mhor C 4

Republic of Ireland
Province: Leinster
County: Offaly
Population: 8000

Tullamore (Tulach Mhor, great hill of assembly), county town of Co. Offaly, lies almost exactly in the centre of Ireland at the junction of the N52 and N80 and on the Dublin–Galway railway line. Until 1804 the town was the terminus of the Grand Canal (➤ entry) from Dublin.
It is now an important agricultural centre and whiskey distilling town (Tullamore Dew Irish Whiskey) and the site of the Irish Republic's main radio transmitter.

Having been almost totally destroyed in 1790 – when it was a much smaller place than today – by the explosion of a large balloon that crashed, Tullamore has no really old buildings. Noteworthy among those of later date are St Catherine's Church (1818), the Market House and Court House (both likewise early 19th c.), and various buildings erected in the early years of the Grand Canal. Charleville Castle, off the N52 south-west of the town centre, was built at the end of the 18th c.; the interior has been sympathetically restored by the present owners. **Town**

Surroundings

4½ miles north of Tullamore is Durrow where in the 6th c. St Columcille founded a monastery. It was here in the 7th c. that the famous Book of Durrow (now in the library of Trinity College; ➤ Dublin), was written and illuminated. **Durrow**
Also preserved is a 10th c. high cross (National Monument) with figural reliefs of considerable art-historical importance: on the east side are the Sacrifice of Isaac and Christ in Glory, flanked by David with his harp on the left and David killing the lion on the right; on the west side the Vigil at the Tomb, the Scourging, the Arrest of Christ and the Crucifixion; on the south side Adam and Eve, Cain and Abel, a warrior and a horseman; and on the north side two groups of figures. The cross is in the grounds of the privately owned Durrow Abbey; visitors are asked to behave with due respect.

22 miles north-east of Tullamore, on the eastern edge of Co. Offaly, lies the pretty little market town of Edenderry, overlooked by Blundell's Castle. **Edenderry**

On the Grand Canal 6 miles west of the town is Rahan, where from the 8th to the 18th c. there was a monastery. Two churches belonging to the monastery (both National Monuments) can still be seen. The larger of the two (Romanesque) has a splendid doorway and good carving on the chancel arch and two windows; the nave is 18th c. on earlier foundations. The smaller church dates from the Early Christian period but has been much altered. **Rahan**

Boher Church   A good 12½ miles north-west of Tullamore, off the R436, the Roman Catholic parish church at Boher preserves the 12th c. Shrine of St Manchan. The yew casket containing the saint's relics is housed within a portable metal reliquary decorated with animal symbols and bronze figures, the latter being later additions.

Waterford · Port Lairge   D 4

Republic of Ireland
Province: Munster
County: Waterford
Population: 40,000

Waterford (Port Lairge, Lairge's landing place), county town of Co. Waterford, lies near the south-eastern tip of Ireland on the south bank of the River Suir, some 20 miles above its mouth. The river at this point is broad and deep, enabling the town to develop into a seaport of considerable importance.

The town has a variety of industries but is chiefly known for its glass (Waterford Crystal Factory). Waterford glass was already famous in the 18th c. and since its revival in 1947 is world renowned.

History   In 853 the Danes established a settlement here which they called Vadrefjord. In 1170 Richard Strongbow took the town, and it became second in importance only to Dublin among Anglo-Norman strongholds. Waterford remained loyal to Britain well into the 19th c., a loyalty recognised by Henry VII who, in 1487, granted the town its motto '*Urbs intacta manet Waterfordia*' ('The town of Waterford remains intact'), a reference to its refusal on two occasions to bow to rival claimants to the English throne. In 1649 Cromwell too was forced to abandon his siege of Waterford, though the town fell to his troops the following year. Thirty years later, having supported James II, it surrendered to William of Orange.

Town   The town centre has many houses dating from around 1800 when Waterford's glass industry was in its heyday. The Mall in particular is graced by quite a number of Georgian houses. There are also numerous hotels, restaurants and pubs.

Waterford
Port Láirge

1 Blackfriars Priory
2 Arts Centre
3 Chamber of Commerce
4 St. Patrick's Church
5 Holy Trinity Cathedral
6 St. Olaf's Church
7 French Church, Heritage Centre
8 Reginald's Tower
9 Christ Church Cathedral

450 m
1485 ft

Sights

Downstream of the bridge over the Suir a street known simply as the Quay – but in fact comprising Merchants Quay, Meaghers Quay and Parade Quay – runs along the south bank of the river for ¾ mile. Most of the principal sights of Waterford can be viewed by venturing down the various streets and lanes opening southwards off the Quay.

The Quay

The church tower seen on the corner of O'Connell Street and Bridge Street is all that now remains of an old Dominican friary, Blackfriars Priory (1226–1541).

Blackfriars Priory

The Garter Lane Arts Centre, further along O'Connell Street, exhibits modern Irish art.

Art Centre

O'Connell Street continues into Great George Street, on the right-hand side of which is the Chamber of Commerce, a handsome neoclassical building (1795) by John Roberts.

Chamber of Commerce

Nearby, off Broad Street, stands St Patrick's Church (mid-18th c.), with a charming gallery.

St Patrick's Church

Diagonally across from St Patrick's, between Parade Quay and High Street, lies Holy Trinity Cathedral, also by Roberts (1793), with a late 19th c. façade.

Holy Trinity Cathedral

Proceeding along Parade Quay, the ruined French Church (National Monument; in Greyfriars Street) stands on the right, its 15th c. nave, chancel and tower being all that remains of a monastery founded here in 1240. Between the 17th and the 19th c. the nave was used as a hospice for the poor; the choir served as a church for Waterford's Huguenot refugees, and the Lady Chapel became a place of burial for the leading families of the town.

French Church

On display in a building near the church are finds from excavations carried out in Waterford and the surrounding area since 1984 (open as for Reginald's Tower below).

Heritage Centre

At the far end of the Quay the attractive Mall branches off at a sharp angle to the right. On the corner stands the imposing circular Reginald's Tower, the walls of which are 10 ft thick. It is reputed to have been part of the old Viking fortifications – the date generally given is 1003 – but in its present aspect appears to be Anglo-Norman (13th c.). Today it houses the City Museum. Open Apr.–Sep. Mon.–Fri. 11am–1pm, 2–4pm, Sat. 11am–1pm.

★Reginald's Tower

South of the tower, in the Mall, is the City Hall (1788 by Roberts), preserved in very much its original state. Part of the building accommodates the Victorian Theatre Royal.

City Hall

Beyond City Hall can be seen Christ Church Cathedral (1779 by Roberts), Waterford's principal Protestant church, with a spacious interior and two fine tombs, the Rice Monument (1469) and the Fitzgerald Monument, the latter of Carrara marble.

Christ Church Cathedral

On the south side of Cathedral Square is the Bishop's Palace (18th c.; restored 1975).

Bishop's Palace

A short distance away, to the left off the Mall, is the dignified Court House (1849), from the grounds of which there is access to the wooded People's Park, to the south, over a little bridge spanning the Johns River.

Court House

Cromwell's Rock

In the Ferrybank district, across on the north side of the Suir from the People's Park, can be seen Cromwell's Rock, from which Cromwell is said to have watched the siege of the town (fine view).

Waterford Crystal factory

The Waterford Crystal Factory is located 1½ miles south of the city centre, on the Cork road (N25), the continuation of the Mall. Visitors to the works see glass being blown and cut by hand (guided tours Mon.–Fri. 10.15am, 11am, 11.45am, 1.45pm, 2.30pm and 3.15pm). Waterford glass can be bought in the Crystal Gallery adjoining the factory. Open Mon.–Fri. 9am–5pm; May–Sep. also Sat. 10am–1pm.

Surroundings

Passage East

Passage East lies 6 miles east of Waterford on the R683, at the point where the River Suir flows into the wide inlet known as Waterford Harbour. It was once a fortified town, where in 1170 Richard Strongbow landed with 1200 men before going on to take Waterford. There is a pedestrian and car ferry to Ballyhack, on the other side of Waterford Harbour.

Dunmore East

From Passage East, minor roads lead to the southern end of Waterford Harbour where Dunmore East, a pretty little seaside resort, clings to the hillside sloping up from the sea. It has a small harbour and a good beach (diving).

Knockeen Dolmen

A detour on minor roads to the west of the R675 (the road from Waterford south to Tramore Bay) leads, after 2½ miles, to the very fine Knockeen Dolmen (National Monument). Thought to be 4000 years old, it has a rectangular chamber roofed over with two partly overlapping capstones.

Making Waterford crystal ...

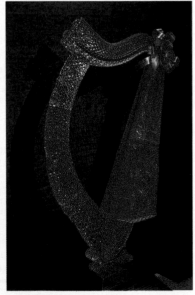

... and an Irish harp in glass

The R675 itself continues to Tramore, 8 miles south of Waterford, a popular family resort with a lovely 3-mile-long sandy beach and a range of recreational facilities including fishing, horse racing and golf.

'Celtworld', Tramore's latest attraction (opened in 1992), utilises all the resources of modern technology (holograms, lasers, computer graphics) in the course of an entertaining presentation, lasting just under an hour, that brings to life the myths and legends of the Celtic peoples. Open Mar.–May, Oct. daily 10am–5pm; Jun.–Sep. daily 10am–11pm.

Portlaw, an old Quaker settlement, is reached by following the Suir upstream from Waterford, first heading west on the N25 and then north-west on the R680 (9 miles). The town's tanneries produce a substantial proportion of Ireland's leather.

North-west and just outside Portlaw lies the Curraghmore demesne (open Thu. afternoons and bank holidays only). Here, situated 1¼ miles from the park entrance, in splendid gardens – among the many attractive features of which is a shell house – is the architecturally notable mansion (1745 by John Roberts) of the marquesses of Waterford. The house, with fine interior decorations and some famous pictures, is not open to public.

A few miles north-west of Waterford, over the county boundary in Co. Kilkenny (N9 then N24), the imposing ruins of Granagh Castle (National Monument) stand high above the north bank of the Suir; they comprise a 13th c. keep, curtain walls reinforced by towers, and a 16th c. great hall.

Westport · Cathair na Mart   C 2

Republic of Ireland
Province: Connacht
County: Mayo
Population: 3500

Westport (Cathair na Mart, stone fort of the cattle) is situated in the north-west of Ireland on Clew Bay, in the south-east corner of which the River Carrowbeg flows into Westport Bay.

Before the advent of the railways, Westport – a planned settlement established by the earl of Altamont in 1780, probably to the design of a French architect – was a considerable port. Today it has developed into an angling centre with good fishing in Clew Bay.

Many people consider Westport one of the prettiest small towns in Ireland. Lime trees line both banks of the little River Carrowbeg which, spanned by attractive old bridges, runs along the middle of the Mall, the town's main street.

The Protestant church (1880) has art-nouveau carvings. At the south end of the Mall is a pleasant square, the Octagon, with an unusual clock-tower erected on the site of a monument destroyed in 1922.

★Westport House

The entrance to Westport House, seat of the marquesses of Sligo, is reached by following the main road south from the Octagon and turning right towards Westport Quay. The house, built by Richard Cassels in 1730–4 and enlarged by James Wyatt, is one of the finest mansions in Ireland.

Westport House

Though few of the original furnishings survive, the Long Gallery is hung with portraits of the family, the Dining Room is decorated with good stucco work and on the first floor are a series of paintings of local views.

Installed in the basement are a not very attractive 'shopping arcade' and various forms of family amusement.

An unusual feature of the lovely English-style gardens are the fountains that operate by tidal power. Children will enjoy the small zoo.

Clew Bay Heritage Centre

Near Westport House, likewise on Westport Quay, is the Clew Bay Heritage Centre with information about the region's history. Open Mon.–Fri. 10am–1pm, Sat., Sun. 2–5pm.

Surroundings

Newport

Newport, 7 miles north of Westport, on the N59 leading into northern Mayo, is a fishing centre (sea fishing in Clew Bay, trout in the neighbouring loughs) dominated by an old railway viaduct. The church (1914) boasts a lovely stained-glass window ('The Last Judgement', 1930) by Harry Clarke. Drumlins – mounds of glacial deposits – abound in the countryside round Newport; many of the islets in Clew Bay are drumlins which have been engulfed by the sea.

Burrishoole Friary

North of Newport, on a quiet bay, are the ruins of a Dominican friary, Burrishoole Friary (15th c.; National Monument). Of the church there remain the nave, choir and south transept (windows), and the squat central tower. There is also a fragment of the cloister.

A few miles further west, on another inlet to the left of the road, stands Carrigahooley Castle (15th c.; National Monument). Formerly called Rockfleet Castle, the turreted four-storey tower once belonged to the notorious Grace O'Malley (➤ Famous People).

Carrigahooley Castle

Mulrany, 7½ miles further on, is a little place with a mild climate in which fuchsias, rhododendrons and Mediterranean heaths flourish. The village has facilities for golf and tennis.

Mulrany

From Mulrany the R319 crosses the sizeable Curraun Peninsula to Achill Island (➤ entry). It is well worth driving round the peninsula: a particularly delightful little road runs along the south side, with constantly changing coastal scenery and fine views over Clew Bay and across to Clare Island. The centre of the peninsula is dominated by the 1815 ft Curraun.

Curraun Peninsula

At the village of Aghagower, on a side road off the R330 4 miles southeast of Westport, are the ruins of a round tower and a church (National Monument), relics of a monastery founded by St Senach who St Patrick himself consecrated bishop. The round tower, the top of which is missing, stands 60 ft high; the entrance is modern. The church is 15th c.

Aghagower

Wexford · Loch Garman   D 5

Republic of Ireland
Province: Leinster
County: Wexford
Population: 15,000

In the Irish National Heritage Park

Wexford (Loch Garman, Garman's lough), county town of Co.
Wexford, lies at the south-eastern tip of Ireland on Wexford Harbour,
a sheltered inlet opening off the St George's Channel. Until 1970 the
town's economy was largely agricultural; today it is mainly industrial
(agricultural machinery, electronic metering equipment, submersible
pumps).

Town

Wexford's picturesque historic nucleus with its narrow winding streets is
a typical example of an Anglo-Norman settlement.

The principal thoroughfare, Main Street, extends roughly parallel with
the town's long harbour quay; almost all the places of interest can be
reached with ease via the side streets to right and left.

Sights

**Westgate Heritage
Centre**

The restored 13th c. Westgate, in the north-west of the town centre, is
the only one of the five original gates to survive. Today it houses the
Westgate Heritage Centre, where an audio-visual presentation lasting
about half an hour provides a wealth of information about the town
and the surrounding area. Open Mon.–Sat. 9.30am–12.30pm, 2–5pm,
Sun. 2–5pm.

Selskar Abbey

Nearby can be seen the ruins of Selskar Abbey, founded in the 12th c.
Still in evidence are a battlemented tower and the remains of St
Selskar's Church (15th c.; National Monument). The abbey was
destroyed by Cromwell's troops in 1649.

Bullring

At the intersection of Main Street and Quay Street is a little square called
the Bullring, recalling the medieval pastime of bull baiting; in it stands a
bronze memorial to the 1798 Rising.

Crescent Quay

Further along Main Street, Henrietta Street leads left into Crescent Quay,
a semicircular square in which stands a statue of Commodore John
Barry (1745–1803), erected by the US government to commemorate the
father of the American Navy.

Surroundings

**★★ Irish National
Heritage Park**
Dublin

The Irish National Heritage Park, near Ferrycarrig, about 3 miles north-
west of Wexford (reached via the N11, the Dublin road), is an open-air

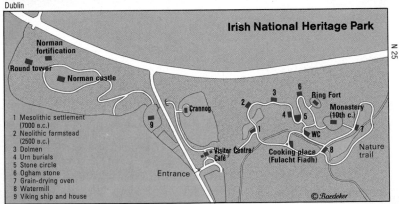

Irish National Heritage Park

N 25

Norman
fortification

Round tower

Norman castle

Crannog

1 Mesolithic settlement
  (7000 B.C.)
2 Neolithic farmstead
  (2500 B.C.)
3 Dolmen
4 Urn burials
5 Stone circle
6 Ogham stone
7 Grain-drying oven
8 Watermill
9 Viking ship and house

2
3
6 Ring Fort
4 5
Monastery
(10th c.)
1
WC
7
9
Visitor Centre/
Café
Cooking place
(Fulacht Fiadh)
8
Nature
trail

Entrance

© Baedeker

Johnstown Castle

museum with replicas of dwellings and other man-made structures (dolmens, a stone circle, ring-fort, Early Christian monastery, crannog, round tower, and so on) illustrating some 9000 years of Irish history. A nature trail has been laid out inside the park. Open Mar.–Oct. daily 10am–7pm; last admission 5pm.

On the northern edge of the wide bay of Wexford Harbour is a wildfowl reserve (open daily 9am–sunset), notable in particular for the great number of lesser white-fronted geese that winter here every year; there are also many swans and no fewer than 28 different types of duck. Entrance to the reserve is from the R741. Facilities include a car park, screened observation hides, an observation tower and a small Visitor Centre displaying the various species of bird that frequent the marsh.

Wildfowl reserve

Leaving Wexford by the Rosslare road (N25), a signposted turning on the right not far from the southern exit of the bypass, leads to Johnstown Castle, a neo-Gothic mansion built in the second half of the 19th c. incorporating the remains of a medieval fortress. Apart from the entrance hall the castle itself is closed to the public, but the landscaped park with its lakes and over 200 varieties of trees and shrubs is delightful. Farm buildings belonging to the castle have been turned into an agricultural museum, with displays of old implements and machinery and replicas of various workshops, and a farmhouse kitchen and bedroom ca 1900; also an interesting collection of Irish vernacular furniture. Park open daily 9am–5.30pm; museum Mon.–Fri. 9am–5pm, Sat., Sun. 2–5pm; low season closed noon, Nov.–Mar. closed Sat. and Sun.

★Johnstown Castle and Agricultural Museum

Proceeding south on the N25, turn left onto the R739 to reach Rathmacknee Castle (15th c.; National Monument). Excellently preserved, it is a good example of a typical 15th c. or 16th c. Irish castle. The five-storey tower, battlemented in the manner of the period, stands

Rathmacknee Castle

within an enclosure, the walls of which, more than 23 ft high and 4 ft thick, are punctuated by a massive round tower at the north-east corner and a smaller square tower at the north-west corner.

Rosslare

From the castle take the minor road leading back to the N25 at Killinick Station. Just beyond the village a road branches off on the left to the little town of Rosslare, which claims to be one of the driest and sunniest places in Ireland. The wide bay boasts several miles of safe shingle and sand beach.

Rosslare Harbour

About 3 miles away at the southern end of the bay lies Rosslare Harbour from where there are ferry services to Fishguard (Wales) and Le Havre (France). It has an extensive pier and a car ferry terminal (opened in 1989). Almost all passenger traffic from the European mainland passes through Rosslare; the harbour is also important for freight, handling about 10 per cent of Ireland's exports.

Lady's Island Lake

South of Rosslare Harbour, separated from the sea only by a thin strip of land, lies Lady's Island Lake. On an island in the lake, today linked to the shore by a causeway, are the ruins of an Augustinian monastery and a 12th c. Anglo-Norman castle with a leaning tower.

**Kilmore Quay
Saltee Islands**

South of Wexford the R739 leads south-west to Kilmore and Kilmore Quay, a remote and picturesque fishing centre on Forlorn Point. From here a boat can be taken to the rocky Saltee Islands (Little Saltee and Great Saltee). These uninhabited isles are Ireland's largest bird sanctuary, the nesting place of some 30 species, including cormorants, puffins, razorbills and fulmars.

Wicklow · Cill Mhantain

Republic of Ireland
Province: Leinster
County: Wicklow
Population: 5000

Wicklow (Cill Mhantain, St Mantan's church), county town of Co. Wicklow, lies not far south of Dublin at the southern end of a wide crescent bay on the Irish Sea coast.

The River Vartry reaches the sea here, first opening out into a 2-mile-long lagoon separated from the sea by a grassy spit (which today is a promenade and recreational area). Vikings, quick to appreciate the sheltered harbour, established themselves in what was an ancient monastic settlement founded in the 5th c. by St Mantan, which they renamed Wykingio.

Sights

The old town with its narrow streets grew up in the shelter of Black Castle (12th c.), an Anglo-Norman stronghold on a rocky promontory east of the town. Up until the 17th c. it was subject to repeated attacks . In the garden of the parish priest's house can be seen remains of a 13th c. Franciscan friary. The 18th c. parish church incorporates a good Romanesque doorway.

Surroundings

Wicklow Head

Wicklow Head, 2 miles south-east of the town, not only provides fine views but is unusual in having no fewer than three lighthouses on the point. Further south, the sandy beaches of the 'Silver Strand', today disfigured by excessive numbers of caravans, extend down the coast to Brittas Bay and Mizen Head.

Leaving Wicklow on the R750, follow the N11 north-westwards through Rathnew to Ashford, attractively situated on the River Vartry. Along the banks of the river close to the village are the superb Mount Usher Gardens, with many varieties of rare trees and shrubs, some of them subtropical. The gardens, a modest 1¼ acres at the time, were first laid out by Edmond Walpole in 1868; today, still privately owned, they cover some 20 acres. About 5000 different species of plant flourish in this quite enchanting demesne. The colours are particularly splendid in May and early June when the azaleas and rhododendrons are in bloom. Open mid-Mar. to Oct. Mon.–Sat. 10.30am–6pm, Sun. 11am–6pm.

★**Mount Usher Gardens**

The Devil's Glen, a noted beauty spot higher up the Vartry valley, is a deep chasm with craggy sides overgrown with trees and shrubs. On entering the glen the river plunges nearly 100 ft into the Devil's Punchbowl. There are fine views of the waterfall from well-sited paths in the glen.

★**Devil's Glen**

★Wicklow Mountains   C/D 5

Republic of Ireland
Province: Leinster
County: Wicklow

The Wicklow Mountains, a range of granite hills, extend for some 40 miles from just south of Dublin southwards through Co. Wicklow. Their

At the Sally Gap

eastern slopes descend towards the Irish Sea, while their western slopes border the plain of the River Barrow.

Only two passes, the Sally Gap and the Wicklow Gap, offer a route through the mountains from east to west. Until the 18th c. the inaccessible high valleys provided a relatively safe retreat for refugees, outlaws and criminals. Following the 1798 Rising, a strategic highway known as the Military Road was constructed, giving greater control of the area.

Topography

The Wicklow Mountains are a lonely region of purple-and-brown-flecked hills, dark lakes and conical peaks, often shrouded in mist. Moorland alternates with heath, deciduous with coniferous woodland.

Those intending to walk in the hills can obtain information from the Visitor Centre at Upper Lake, Glendalough (➤ entry). Open end Apr.–Aug. daily 10am–6.30pm; Sep. Sat. and Sun. only.

Touring the Wicklow Mountains

Rathfarnham to Laragh

From Rathfarnham (➤ Dublin) the R115 leads south, climbing steadily. Ahead, half right, can be seen Kippure (2517 ft) with its television tower; to the rear there is a fine view of Dublin. At Glencree, shortly before the Enniskerry road branches off to the left, there is a German military cemetery. From here the route continues south, passing two small loughs and traversing a boggy plateau.

On gaining the watershed at the Sally Gap (1657 ft), the R115 crosses the R759, afterwards winding its way south over bare moorland, negotiating several streams flowing down from the hills on the right – Gravate (2396 ft), Duff Hill (2406 ft) and Mullaghcleevaun (2839 ft) – before descending the rugged Glenmacnass valley with its splendid waterfall (best seen from the valley side) to Laragh. Here a choice of onward routes presents itself.

Laragh to Hollywood and Dublin

From Laragh the R756 climbs steadily west, past the famous monastic site of Glendalough (➤ entry) in a side valley to the left, and on up to the Wicklow Gap (1595 ft) between Tonelagee (2734 ft) to the north and Camaderry (2337 ft) to the south. Camaderry lies within the Glendalough Forest Park (nature reserve), the boundary of which the road skirts. About 2½ miles beyond the pass a narrow road branches off right to the Glenbridge Youth Hostel, situated in a lonely valley bottom. 4 miles further on another road goes off on the right, this time leading north to the 1938 Lacken Reservoir (or Poulaphuca Lake) which, with a surface area of 8 sq miles, both contributes to Dublin's water supply and is also harnessed to produce electricity.

The R756 meanwhile continues down to Hollywood. Somewhat over a mile south of the village, at **Athgreany**, there is a large stone circle of uncertain age (National Monument) known as the 'Piper's Stones' – the 'Piper' being another monolith standing alone outside the circle.

4 miles north of Hollywood, on the left of the N81 beyond the reservoir, lies ★**Russborough House**, a Palladian mansion (1740–50) by Richard Cassels and Francis Bindon, now the home of the Beit family. The main house, with a great flight of steps leading up to the entrance, is linked by colonnades to substantial wings. The interior has fine stucco work by Francini and contains the Beit Art Collection – including works by Goya, Rubens, Velázquez and Vermeer – and a display of Irish silver. From Russborough House it is 19 miles or so back to Dublin on the N81. Open Easter–Oct. daily 2.30–5.30pm.

Detour to the Glenmalure valley and Lugnaquilla Mountain

This route ventures into an isolated part of the Wicklow Mountains, where the landscape can appear dark and eerie – though with much impressive scenery. Proceed south from Laragh, turning off right after 1¼ miles to follow the old Military Road into the mountains where it climbs steadily to 1267 ft before dropping down again into the

Glenmalure valley. At the crossroads in the hamlet of Drumgoff, take a narrow road to the right, soon reaching a car park. From here Lugnaquilla (3095 ft) can be climbed (unmarked path; 10½ miles there and back; about 2625 ft of ascent).

From Laragh the R755 makes its way through the charming scenery of the Vale of Clara, running south-east along the Avonmore River to Rathdrum. To the south extends the Avondale Forest Park (➤ Arklow).

Laragh to Wicklow and Dublin

Take the R752 in the direction of Wicklow, but before reaching the town turn onto the N11 and drive north to Ashford, with the truly delightful Mount Usher Gardens (➤ Wicklow). Here the R764 heads inland, passing the large Vartry Reservoir. At the junction near the pretty little village of Roundwood, take the R755 northwards.

Further along, to the right of the road, rises the **Great Sugar Loaf** (1644 ft); it can be climbed in about 45 minutes from the large car park on its south side (689ft of ascent).

Another recommended stop on this stretch of the route is at **Enniskerry** (➤ entry) for a visit to the magnificent Powerscourt Gardens nearby. From Enniskerry the R117 leads back to Dublin (9 miles).

Opened in 1983, the long-distance trail known as the Wicklow Way runs for 80 miles from Marlay Park, Co. Dublin (car park; bus service from Dublin), to Clonegal in Co. Carlow. A series of parking places conveniently sited within easy reach of the well-signposted Way, make it possible to walk individual sections of the route.

Wicklow Way

The first section follows the eastern slopes of the hills, ending at Luggala near Lough Tay, on the R759 between Sally Gap and Roundwood. The second section makes towards Laragh, passing the end of Glenmacnass before turning west and south-west via Drumgoff and Aghavannagh to Moyne. The final section runs south through the Ballycumber and other ranges of hills, by way of Tinahely and Shillelagh, to Clonegal. From there it is possible to continue even further – though of course no longer in the Wicklow Mountains – on the South Leinster Way to Graiguenamanagh in Co. Kilkenny (25 miles). For those who would like more information, a leaflet, *The Wicklow and South Leinster Way*, is available from the Irish Tourist Board.

Youghal · Eochail   E 4

Republic of Ireland
Province: Munster
County: Cork
Population: 6000

Pronounced 'Yaul', Youghal (Eochail, yew wood) is situated on the south coast of Ireland on Youghal Bay. Here the Blackwater River opens out into a sea lough, forming a fine sheltered harbour. Youghal is a popular seaside resort, with good sandy beaches.

Youghal point lace, distinguished by its vivid patterns, is justly renowned.

From the 13th c. until its destruction by the rebel earl of Desmond in 1579, Youghal was a flourishing place. At the end of the 16th c. it was governed by Sir Walter Raleigh, and later by Richard Boyle. In 1649 the town surrendered to Cromwell, who made it the base for his Irish campaigns.

History

Youghal is an ancient little market town and fishing port with a main street running parallel to the Blackwater embankment. A considerable number of 18th and 19th c. houses still grace the centre of town. There

Town

are also remains of old fortifications: on the west side, a section of the 15th–16th c. town walls, with towers, extends south-east for a distance of about 650 yd.

Sights

North Abbey

Approaching the town from the north, the road passes, in a churchyard on the right, the ruins of North Abbey (National Monument), a Dominican friary founded in 1268.

St Mary's Church

William Street, branching right off North Main Street, leads to St Mary's Church, a collegiate church founded in the early 13th c. and subsequently much rebuilt (most recently the choir, in 1854). The church has an aisled nave and a detached tower. Notable features of the interior include the oak carving in the nave, the font, and a number of tombs, in particular the elaborately sculpted monument (1619) of Richard Boyle in the south transept, where he lies buried with his two wives and nine of his 16 children.

Myrtle Grove

North-east of the parish church stands Myrtle Grove, a stately Elizabethan mansion which belonged to Sir Walter Raleigh.

Clockgate Tower

At the south end of Main Street rises the five-storey Clockgate Tower, erected in place of an old town gate in 1771; until 1837 it was the town prison. Today it houses a small museum.

Surroundings

Molana Abbey

North of Youghal a side road branching off the N25 skirts the west bank of the Blackwater. Passing by the ruins of Rinncru Abbey and Templemichael Castle, it comes to the remains of Molana Abbey, beautifully situated on the river, with church and conventual buildings (chapter house, refectory, kitchen) laid out round a cloister.

Ballycotton

The fishing village of Ballycotton, about 15 miles south-east of Youghal, has good beaches and splendid cliff scenery.

Cloyne

5 miles north-west of Ballycotton is Cloyne, which in the 12th c. was the see of a bishop. Though dating from 1250, the cathedral has undergone much alteration and modernisation; it contains a number of fine monuments and, by the north door, crude carvings representing pagan symbols. On the opposite side of the street stands a 100-ft round tower, its original roof replaced by a battlemented top.

Killeagh

Killeagh is situated on the N25 7½ miles west of Youghal. North of the village, extending for some miles up the valley of the River Dissour, lies the Glenbower State Forest, which retains something of the character of Ireland's ancient woodland. South-east of Killeagh stands the round keep of Inchiquin Castle (13th c.).

Castlemartyr

Further west, also on the N25, is Castlemartyr, where, in the grounds of a Carmelite priory, are the remains of Seneshal's Castle – a 15th c. enclosure with corner towers, a keep of the same period, and 17th c. domestic quarters.

Midleton

About 6 miles west again is Midleton, a thriving little market and industrial town with a handsome 18th c. Market House and a church designed by the Pain brothers (19th c.).

The principal feature, however, is the Jameson Heritage Centre (► picture, p. 323), housed in old mill buildings dating from the end of the

18th c. From 1825 to 1975 the premises were in use as a whiskey distillery. Models, lectures and displays explain the process of whiskey production. Open May–Sep. daily 10am–4pm.

Practical Information

Air Travel

In the Republic of Ireland there are four international airports (Dublin, Cork, Shannon and Knock). In Northern Ireland the only one is near Belfast (Aldergrove). Regional airports, including Carrickfinn, Kerry and Waterford in the Irish Republic, as well as Belfast City and Londonderry/Derry in Northern Ireland, have connections with UK airports as well as operating inland flights. Galway and Sligo in the Republic are used by small aircraft in inland flights. Airports

Aer Lingus flies several times daily from Dublin to Cork and Shannon. There are two services a day to Galway and Kerry (except one on Saturday and three on Sunday). There is also one service daily to Sligo. Ryanair offer a range of budget flights to the UK. Airlines
  In addition there are services by smaller domestic airlines, including Aer Arann, which flies from airports at Caislean, Inverin, Connemara, near Galway to the Aran Islands.

Aer Lingus:
40–41 Upper O'Connell Street, Dublin 1
Tel. (01) 8862222

12 Upper George's Street, Dun Laoghaire
Tel. (01) 8868888

2 Academy Street, Cork
Tel. (021) 4327155

136 O'Connell Street, Limerick
Tel. (061) 474239

46–48 Castle Street, Belfast 1
Tel. (0845) 9737747
Email bookings@aerlingus.ie, web site www.aerlingus.ie

Ryanair:
Tel. (01) 6097800, email info@ryanair.ie, web site www.ryanair.ie

Aer Arann:
Tel. (01) 8141058, email info@aerarann.ie, web site www.aerarann.ie

Arriving

Getting to Ireland

The Republic of Ireland has four international airports: Dublin, Cork, Shannon and Knock; Northern Ireland has one, Belfast Aldergrove. The Republic's national airline is Aer Lingus, which flies both international and domestic services. By air

◀ *Powerscourt Town House Centre in Dublin*

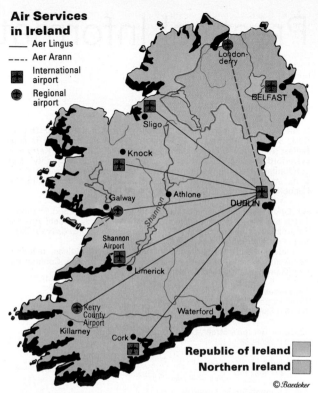

Air Services in Ireland

—— Aer Lingus

---- Aer Arann

▣ International airport

◉ Regional airport

London-derry

BELFAST

Sligo

Knock

Galway

Athlone

DUBLIN

Shannon

Shannon Airport

Limerick

Kerry County Airport

Killarney

Waterford

Cork

Republic of Ireland ▢

Northern Ireland ▢

© *Baedeker*

There are regular services from many airports in Britain to the Irish international airports and (less frequently) to certain regional airports (➤ Air Travel); from the United States and Canada to Belfast direct but usually via London Heathrow, Gatwick or Glasgow (Scotland), and to Dublin, Shannon and Knock in the Irish Republic; and from many European cities to Dublin and Belfast. Many visitors from Europe, America and other parts of the world will usually fly to a British airport and get a connecting service from there.

The flight from British airports takes about an hour.

By sea

There are several passenger and car ferry services between British and Irish ports:

From Welsh ports to the Irish Republic: Fishguard–Rosslare and Holyhead–Dun Laoghaire (Stena Line); Holyhead–Dublin and Pembroke–Rosslare (Irish Ferries); Swansea–Cork (Swansea–Cork Ferries) – summer only. Crossing times vary from 1 hour 40 minutes to 10 hours depending on the type of vessel and the route.

From Liverpool to Belfast (Norse Irish Ferries). Crossing time 11 hours.

Liverpool and Holyhead can be reached by direct rail services from London Euston Station; Fishguard and Pembroke from London Paddington Station.

From the Isle of Man to Dublin and Belfast (Isle of Man Steam Packet Company) – summer only. The crossing to Dublin takes 2¾ hours and to Belfast 4½ hours.

From Scottish ports to Northern Ireland: Stranraer–Belfast (Stena Line) and Cairnryan–Larne (P&O). Crossing times vary from 1½ to 3 hours depending on the type of vessel and the route.

There are also a number of services from French ports: Le Havre–Rosslare (Irish Ferries) 2–4 sailings weekly; Le Havre–Cork (Irish Ferries) weekly; Cherbourg–Rosslare (Irish Ferries) 1–3 sailings weekly; Roscoff–Cork (Brittany Ferries) spring to autumn 2 sailings weekly; St Malo–Cork (Brittany Ferries) in summer weekly.

Accommodation

For visitors who would prefer to be free in their choice of route and overnight accommodation, the solution is bed and breakfast – comfortable rooms in private houses or farmhouses at reasonable prices with a substantial Irish breakfast. Some package tours also include vouchers for bed and breakfast accommodation. Information may be obtained from the Irish Tourist Board (*Bed & Breakfast*) and Northern Irish Tourist Board (*Where to Stay*; ➤ Information).

Bed and breakfast

In the Republic of Ireland there are some 120 camping and caravanning sites which are officially recognised by the Irish Tourist Board and classified according to their facilities with from one to four stars. Details can be found in the brochure *Caravan & Camping Parks* published by the Board. Overnight stays other than on camping sites is generally not permitted. Permission should be sought from the landowner or proprietor before camping on private property. For further information contact:

Camping and caravanning

Irish Caravan and Camping Council
PO Box 4443, Dublin 2
email info@camping-ireland.ie, web site www.camping-ireland.ie

Camping and caravanning is also widespread in Northern Ireland. A list of sites can be found in the brochure *Where to Stay* (see above).

Many country houses and mansions in the Irish Republic have been converted into hotels and restaurants. Establishments of this kind belong to the Irish Country Houses and Restaurants Association, which issues a brochure entitled *Ireland's Blue Book* that lists them. They are also included in the list of hotels, restaurants and guest houses published by the Irish Tourist Board.

Country houses

Some of these houses serve meals only to residents; others cater also for non-residents; and others again are restaurants but have no accommodation for residents.

Hidden Ireland is an association of exclusive, privately owned country houses with a limited number of rooms. The choice ranges from castles by the sea to luxurious farmhouses. The accommodation list is available from the Irish Tourist Board or direct from:

The Hidden Ireland
37 Lower Baggot Street, Dublin 2
Tel. (01) 6627166, fax (01) 6627144

Self-catering accommodation is available throughout Ireland in cottages, bungalows, chalets, apartments, country houses, even castles. The Irish Tourist Board and the Northern Ireland Tourist Board can provide lists of such holiday homes.

Holiday homes

Boating

Ireland has a great many inland waterways where the water is generally clean, and these rivers and lakes are ideal for boating. The best areas are the Shannon, the Shannon–Erne Waterway, Lough Erne in Northern Ireland the Grand Canal, which was once an important route between the east and the west of the Irish Republic.

More than 500 cabin cruisers are available for hire at the numerous marinas; a visitor wishing to hire a boat must be at least 21 years old, but a permit to navigate a boat is not necessary, the only proviso being that at least two persons must be on board. Equipment provided depends on the size of the boat. No provisions are supplied and these must either be ordered in advance from the hirer to bought beforehand.

Handling a boat demands considerable common sense. Average speed is 6 mph and most Shannon cruisers manage 30 miles per day. On each cruiser will be found a copy of the *Shannon Guide*; this contains detailed information about the various stretches of water as well as information concerning facilities for obtaining fuel, water and provisions. Lifebelts, one lifejacket per bed, a first-aid kit and signal rockets in case of emergency must be taken and weather reports heeded.

Basic rules are: always travel on the right, especially when negotiating narrow river passages, always keep black markers (buoys, markers or posts) on the port side – that is, on the left. For general information and technical queries contact:

Dúchas The Heritage Service – Waterways
Department of Arts, Heritage, Gaeltacht & the Islands, 17–19 Lower Hatch Street, Dublin 2
Tel. (01) 6613111, fax (01) 6761714, email info@heritageireland.ie, web site www.heritageireland.ie.

Shannon

The Shannon has six locks; in general these are operational April to September weekdays 9am–6 or 8pm, on Sundays 9am–6pm. At other times delays may be expected. No boat may move after dusk. The cruising season is generally from St Patrick's Day (March 17th) until the end of October because of high water levels in winter.

Shannon–Erne Waterway

The 39-mile Shannon–Erne Waterway connects Ireland's two main rivers. This canal was completely restored in 1994 and has six new mooring zones. There are 16 fully automatic locks to negotiate between Leitrim in the Republic of Ireland and Belturbet in Northern Ireland. There are no passport controls at the border.

Grand Canal

The Grand Canal is an idyllic stretch of water that is considerably less used than the Shannon. Since this artificial waterway is never wider than 39 ft, the large Shannon cabin cruisers cannot use it. Instead of these, special narrowboats between 32 ft and 46 ft long are in service; the internal space is considerably restricted.

Package holidays

Numerous tour operators offer organised holidays in cabin cruisers. Details can be found in *Ireland: A Romantic Blend*, published by the Irish Tourist Board.

Car Rental

Rental conditions

Irish and international car rental firms are represented in the whole country, especially in the international air and sea ports and in the larger towns. The minimum age for renting a car depends on the firm and type of vehicle but is usually between 21 and 25; the maximum age is 70.

Most firms require a driving licence to have been held for at least one year.

Crossing the frontier between the Irish Republic and Northern Ireland must be agreed with the rental firm beforehand; usually there is no objection.

Republic of Ireland

Dublin
1 Hanover Street East; tel. (01) 774010
Dublin Airport; tel. (01) 6057555

Cork (head office)
Emmet Place; tel. (021) 4281111, fax (021) 4281122, email dcarberry@jandp.iol.ie, web site www.avis.com
Cork Airport; tel. (021) 4281169

Galway
Higgins Garage, Headford Road; tel. (091) 568886
Galway Airport; tel. (091) 568901

Offices also at Farranfore, Kerry; Donegal, Shannon and Sligo airports.

Dublin
151 Drumcondra Road, Ferry Port; tel. (01) 8379611
Dublin Airport; tel. (01) 8445150

Cork
c/o Tourist Information Center, Grand Parade, Ferry Port
Tel. (021) 4274755
Cork Airport; tel. (021) 4314000

Galway
3 Foster Street, Eyre Square; tel. (091) 556376

Killarney
International Best Western Hotel, Kenmare Place; tel. (064) 34341

Roscommon (head office)
Athlone Road; tel. (0903) 27711, fax (0903) 27744, email reservations@budgetcarrental.ie, web site www.budgetcarrental.ie

Waterford
41 The Quay; tel. (051) 21550

Offices also at Kerry, Knock, Shannon and Sligo airports.

Dublin (head office)
Baggot Street Bridge; tel. (01) 6142888, 6142800 (reservations), fax (01) 6142899, email reserve@europcar.ie, sales@europcar.ie, web site www.europcar.ie
Dublin Airport; tel. (01) 8120410

Galway
Headford Road; tel. (091) 562222

Killarney
Muckross Road; tel. (064) 31237

Strokestown
Westward Garage; tel. (078) 33029

Waterford
Sheridan Garage, Cork Road; tel. (051) 373144

Wexford
Redmond Place; tel. (053) 22122

Offices also in Rosslare Harbour; Shannon and Sligo airports.

Hertz

Dublin
Leeson Street; tel. (01) 6602255
Dublin Airport; tel. (01) 8445466

Galway
Galway Airport; tel. (091) 770005

Killarney
28 Plunket Street; tel. (064) 34126

Sligo
Sligo Airport; tel. (071) 44068

Waterford
Auto Boland, Newrath; tel. (051) 878737
Waterford Airport; tel. (051) 878737

Wexford
Ferrybank; tel. (053) 235111, fax (053) 232405, email sboland@hertz.ie,
web site www.hertz.com

Offices also at Cork, Kerry, Knock and Shannon airports; Rosslare
Harbour.

Northern Ireland

Avis

Belfast
69 Great Victoria Street; tel. (028) 90240404
Aldergrove Airport; tel. (028) 9422333

Coleraine
1 New Mills Road; tel. (028) 70343654

Larne
96–98 Glenarm Road; tel. (028) 28260799

Budget

Belfast
96 Great Victoria Street; tel. (028) 90230700
Belfast City Airport; tel. (028) 98451111

Londonderry
173 Strand Road; tel. (028) 71360420

Europcar

Belfast
58 Antrim Road; tel. (028) 90757401
Aldergrove Airport; tel. (028) 9423444

Hertz

Aldergrove Airport; tel. (028) 9422533
Belfast Harbour Airport; tel. (028) 71732451

Climbing and Hill Walking

For the Irish climbing and hill walking is a relatively new pastime. Much
has been undertaken recently to build up an extensive, waymarked network of trails. The *Walking Ireland* brochure published by the Irish
Tourist Board provides information about the long-distance footpaths
covering most of Ireland. All of these paths are well marked and some
are circular (e.g. the 133-mile Kerry Way of the 41-mile Slieve Bloom
Way). For further information contact:

Sports Unit, Department of Tourism, Sport and Recreation
Frederick Buildings, South Frederick Street, Dublin 2
Tel. (01) 6621444, fax (01) 6799291

Northern Ireland is traversed by the Ulster Way, 435 miles in length.
Information from:

Field Officer, Sports Council for Northern Ireland
House of Sport, Upper Malone Road, Belfast BT9 5LA
Tel. (028) 90381222

Good places for shorter rambles are the National Parks (Killarney,
Connemara, Glenveagh, the Burren, Wicklow Mountains) and the 12
Forest Parks.

Shorter rambles

Apart from these (and the long-distance footpaths) there are hardly
any waymarked footpaths. What paths there are have arisen in connection with farming. Most paths over fields are asphalted and often there
is nothing else but to go cross-country, so good maps are essential and
guide books will come in very useful.

You should never walk alone. As most paths cross thinly populated terrain and there are few other ramblers about, you will have to be self-
reliant in case of accidents and emergencies. It is not advisable to take a
dog because of the many sheep. Generally farmers do not mind you
crossing their land, but you should make sure to close gates again
behind you.

Tips

The Irish Tourist Board can provide a list of companies that organise
walking holidays.

Walking holidays

Conversions

To convert metric to imperial multiply by the imperial factor; e.g. 100 km
equals 62 miles (100 × **0.62**).

Linear measure

1 metre	**3.28** feet, 1.09 yards
1 kilometre (1000 m)	**0.62** mile

Square measure

1 square metre	**1.2** square yards, 10.76 square feet
1 hectare	**2.47** acres
1 square kilometre (100 ha)	**0.39** square mile

Capacity

1 litre (1000 ml)	**1.76** pints (**2.11** US pints)
1 kilogram (1000 grams)	**2.21** pounds
1 metric ton (1000 kg)	**0.98** ton

Temperature

°C	°F	°C	°F
−5	23	20	68
0	32	25	77
5	41	30	86
10	50	35	95
15	59	40	104

Crafts

In many parts of Ireland the old, traditional crafts are still practised; these include pottery, weaving, basket-making and glass-blowing. Residential courses are often available. Information from:

Crafts Council of Ireland
The Castle Yard, Kilkenny, Co. Kilkenny
Tel. (05) 661804, fax (05) 663754

Currency

Republic of Ireland

Currency

The unit of currency is the Irish pound or punt (IR£) of 100 pence (p).

There are banknotes for £5, £10, £20, £50, and £100, and coins in denominations of 1p, 2p, 5p, 10p, 20p, 50p and £1.

Euro

On January 1st 1999 the euro became the official currency of the Republic of Ireland, and the Irish pound became a denomination of the euro. Irish pound notes and coins continue to be legal tender during a transitional period. Euro bank notes and coins are likely to be introduced by January 1st 2002.

Currency
regulations

There are no restrictions on either the import or export of currency.

Northern Ireland

Currency

The unit of currency is the pound sterling (£) of 100 pence (p). There are banknotes for £5, £10, £20 and £50, and coins in denominations of 1p, 2p, 5p, 10p, 20p, 50p, £1 and £2.

Currency
regulations

There are no restrictions on either the import of export of currency.

Eurocheques

In the Irish Republic Eurocheques can be cashed up to a limit of IR£140, in Northern Ireland up to £100 sterling; the same limits apply to cash obtained from ATMs, which often accept valid credit cards.

Credit cards

Banks, larger hotels, established restaurants, car rental firms, petrol stations and a number of shops accept most international credit cards.

Customs Regulations

Allowances
between EU
countries

In theory there is now no limit to the amount of goods that can be taken from one EU country to another provided they have been purchased tax paid in an EU country, are for personal use and not intended for resale.

However, customs authorities have issued guidelines to the maximum amounts considered reasonable for persons over 16 years of age. These are: 800 cigarettes; 400 cigarillos; 200 cigars; 1 kg tobacco; 10 litres of spirits; 20 litres of aperitifs; 90 litres of wine, of which 60 litres of sparkling wine; 110 litres of beer. A passport is still required for crossing the border.

For those coming from a country outside the EU, the allowances for goods obtained anywhere outside the EU for persons over the age of 16 are: 200 cigarettes or 100 cigarillos or 50 cigars or 250 grams of tobacco; 1 litre of spirits or 2 litres of fortified or sparkling wine; 2 litres of wine. Also (all ages) 60 millilitres of perfume and 250 millilitres of toilet water.
This applies to Northern Ireland and the Republic of Ireland.

Entry from non-EU countries

Cycling

With its delightfully varied countryside, the relatively short distances and comparatively little traffic, Ireland is an ideal country to explore by bicycle.

Many airlines transport bicycles free as they are included in the weight limit of 20 kg. There is a surcharge of 25 per cent of the normal fare for taking your bicycle on the train, up to a maximum of IR£6 (single). A charge is also made on the cross-country buses.

Transport of cycles

There are various cycle-hire firms in most cities. As the bicycles are bought new at the beginning of each season, they are usually in good condition. Cycles with three or five gears and also sports cycles with 12 or 18 gears and mountain bikes are all available for hire. In July and August it is advisable to book in advance.
The weekly hire charge (including insurance) depending on the type and the firm is usually between £25 and £50. A deposit is usually required. For an additional charge the cycles can be returned to any hire depot. The Irish Tourist Board has information on bicycle hire. For further details contact:

Cycle hire

Walking/Cycling Ireland
PO Box 5520, Ballsbridge, Dublin 4
Tel. (01) 6688278, fax (01) 6605566, email wci@kerna.ie

A list of tour operators who organise cycling holidays can be found in *Europe's Green Holidays*, published by the Irish Tourist Board.

Cycling holidays

The brochure *Cycling Ireland* (obtainable for the Irish Tourist Board) gives information on 23 cycle tours (most between 120 and 190 miles). For additional information on cycle tours tel. (016) 7908899.

Tours

City Cycle Tours (1A Temple Lane, Dublin 2; tel. (01) 6715610) organises sightseeing tours of Dublin by bicycle.

Sightseeing Dublin by bike

Electricity

In the Irish Republic 220 volts (50 cycles); in Northern Ireland 240 volts (50 cycles). Power sockets are of the British type, although two-pin round sockets may still be found in some parts of the Republic; visitors from countries with a different type should take an adaptor.

Embassies and Consulates

In the Republic of Ireland

United Kingdom Embassy:
29 Merrion Road, Dublin 4
Tel. (01) 2053700, fax (01) 2053885

United States Embassy:
42 Elgin Road, Ballsbridge, Dublin 4
Tel. (01) 6687122

Canada Embassy:
65–68 St Stephen's Green, Dublin 2
Tel. (01) 4781988

Australia Embassy:
2nd Floor, Fitzwilton House, Wilton Terrace, Dublin 2
Tel. (01) 6761517

In Northern Ireland

United States Consulate General:
Queen's House, 14 Queen Street, Belfast BT1 6EQ
Tel. (028) 90328239

Canada Jeanne Rankin, c/o Roscoff
Lesley House, Shaftesbury Square, Belfast 2
Tel. (028) 32331532

Emergencies

Police, fire, ambulance (throughout Ireland): tel. 999

Breakdown
assistance Republic of Ireland (freephone): (1800) 667788 (AA)

Northern Ireland (freephone): (0800) 887766 (AA); (0800) 828282 (RAC)

Events

Events which take place in particular locations will be found in the Sights
from A–Z section of this guide. In addition, the following events are held
at various places in the Irish Republic and Northern Ireland:

Febuary 1st **Kildare** St Brigid's Festival (d February 1st 523 in Kildare)

March 17th St Patrick's Day, with processions in the major towns (both parts of
Ireland)

April **Cork** International Choral and Folk Dance Festival
Dublin Grand Opera Season (spring)

May **Belfast** Lord Mayor's Show (parade with decorated floats and bands)
Dublin Spring Show and Industrial Fair; Feis Ceoil (folk music)
Dundalk International Maytime Festival
Ennis Fleadh Nua (festival of music and dance)

Killarney Pan Celtic Week

Boyle Angling Festival	June
Letterkenny Donegal International Car Rally	
Listowel Writers' Week	
Westport Westport Horse Show	
Many places: Music Festival in Great Irish Houses	

Athlone Athlone International Freshwater Angling Festival; Shannon July
Boat Rally
Cobh Cobh International Folk Dance Festival
Dublin Dublin International Folk Festival; International Horse Show
Enniscorthy Strawberry Fair
Galway Race Week (last week in July)
Glenariff Glens of Antrim Feis (Irish dancing and music)
Killarney Bach Festival

Ballycastle Oul' Lammas Fair (popular festival in Northern Ireland) August
Birr Birr Vintage Week
Carlingford Carlingford Oyster Festival
Clifden Connemara Pony Show
Dublin Antiques Fair
Killorglin Puck Fair
Killybegs Killybegs Sea Angling Festival
Kilkenny International Arts Week Festival (including concerts and exhi-
bitions)
Letterkenny Letterkenny International Folk Festival
Stradbally (Co. Laois) Stradbally Steam Rally (for rail enthusiasts)
Tralee Rose of Tralee International Festival
Wexford Mussel Festival
In various places: All Ireland Fleadh (pronounced 'flah' – music festival)
takes place in a different town each year on the last weekend in
August; during this festival not only the official events are worth
seeing but also the musicians improvising in crowded pubs and hotels
and in the streets.

Clifden Community Festival (street festival) September
Dublin All Ireland Hurling Finals
Galway Galway Oyster Festival
Waterford Waterford International Festival of Light Opera (in the Royal
Theatre)

Ballinasloe Horse Fair October
Cork Guinness Cork Jazz Festival; Film Festival
Dublin Dublin City Marathon
Kinsale Gourmet Festival (cooking demonstrations, wine and food tast-
ing and various events)
Wexford Wexford Festival of Opera

Belfast Belfast Festival of Queen's (theatre and musical events at November
Queen's University)

Dublin Dublin Grand Opera Society Winter Season December

Fishing

Owing to its numerous loughs (lakes) and rivers and its extensive
coastal waters, Ireland is one of the great fishing countries, offering an
enormous variety of angling opportunities – coarse fishing, game fishing (salmon and trout), and deep-sea fishing.

© Baedeker

**Common Irish
freshwater fishes**

Rudd
*Scardinius
erythrophthalmus*

Perch
Perca fluviatilis

Brown trout
Salmo trutta

Bream
Abramis brama

Pike
Esox lucius

Salmon
Salmo salar

Since Irish fishermen are mainly interested in trout and salmon, no licence is required for coarse fishing, either in the Irish Republic or Northern Ireland (only in the area of the north Shannon is a 'Share Certificate' required). There is no closed season. Fishing with live bait is not permitted. Fishing with more than two rods at the same time is not allowed. The best fishing is in the Irish 'Lake District', which encompasses parts of counties Westmeath, Longford, Cavan and Monaghan; the lake district of County Clare is also beautiful.

The principal species of coarse fish are pike (Nov.–Mar. in large loughs), bream (best Apr.–Aug.), tench (best May–Sep.), rudd (best Apr.–Sep.), roach (best Apr.–Sep.), perch, carp and eels.

For game fishing a licence is required: it can be obtained from the office of the fishery board or district concerned and from certain tackle dealers, shops and hotels. Most game-fishing waters are privately owned (enquire locally). The commonest species of trout are the brown trout and rainbow trout. The best-stocked waters are found in the west of Ireland (such as Lough Corrib). Note that the closed season is from the end of August to the beginning of January. Salmon can be found in almost all rivers which enter the sea.

There are excellent deep-sea fishing grounds off the west and south coasts of Ireland, in the warmer water brought by the Gulf Stream. The fish that can be caught in these waters include shark, ray, cod, pollack, hake, bass, grey mullet and sea bream. Tackle can be hired locally. The season is from spring to autumn. The main centres are Youghal, Kinsale, Courtmacsherry, Cahirciveen, Galway, Westport, Killala, Killybegs, Dungarvan, Baltimore, Schull, Valentia, Cleggan, Rosses Point, Mullaghmore and Bunbeg.

There are numerous organisers of fishing holidays and information on these can be obtained from the Irish Tourist Board.

Information

Irish Tourist Board
Loveitts Farm, Brinklow, Rugby, Warwickshire CV23 0LG

Department of the Marine Fisheries Administration
Leeson Lane, IRL – Dublin 2
Tel. (01) 785444

Central Fisheries Board
Mobhi Boreen, Glasnevin, Dublin 9
Tel. (01) 8379206, fax (01) 8360060, email info@cfb.ie

Food and Drink

The principal meals of the day in Ireland are breakfast, lunch, tea and dinner. Formerly the traditional Irish evening meal was 'high tea', between tea and dinner, but this is now rarely served.

The Irish breakfast is a substantial meal, consisting of cereal or porridge, bacon and eggs and sausages, toast, brown bread, butter and jam or marmalade, accompanied by coffee, tea, milk or fruit juice.

Lunch is usually a modest meal, often consisting only of sandwiches and tea. Hotels and restaurants, however, offer a full menu; many have a reasonably priced tourist menu.

Food and Drink

Afternoon tea

Afternoon tea may be accompanied by cakes, buns, scones or biscuits.

Dinner

Dinner in a restaurant always consists of several courses, with a choice of dishes for each course. Sherry, whiskey or gin may be taken as an aperitif and wine with the meal (few restaurants are licensed to sell beer).

Courses

A traditional first course may consist of smoked Irish salmon, seafood cocktail or egg mayonnaise. This may be followed by leg of lamb with mint sauce, roast rib of beef, gammon steak, grilled sirloin steak, fried fillet of plaice with tartare sauce, or poached or grilled salmon, accompanied perhaps by Brussels sprouts, creamed mushrooms, celery au gratin, carrots Vichy, creamed potatoes or baked potatoes. Among popular desserts of a traditional variety are lemon meringue pie, hot apple pie with ice cream and fruit salad with fresh cream.

Irish stew

One celebrated Irish specialty is Irish stew, consisting of mutton, potatoes, onions and seasoning, cooked slowly in a pot for several hours.

Drinks

Favourite Irish drinks are beer and whiskey. There is a wide range of beers, from light English ales to the dark Guinness stout with its foaming head, brewed in the celebrated Guinness Brewery in Dublin (➤ Baedeker Special, p. 326). A light lager is now also popular.

Irish whiskey

With its smoother taste (and different form of spelling), Irish whiskey is quite different from its Scottish or American counterparts. It is drunk neat or with water.

Irish coffee

Whiskey is also drunk in the form of 'Irish' or 'Gaelic' coffee. To make this warm and comforting drink, first warm a glass by washing it out

Jameson Heritage Visitor Centre in Midleton: a former whiskey distillery

with hot water, then pour in a measure of Irish whiskey with a little sugar, full up with hot black coffee, stir well and, after the mixture has settled, top it up over a spoon with pouring cream.

Irish whiskey is also the basis of a liqueur, 'Irish Mist', which is said to have originated in the town of Tullamore, in a process involving the addition of heather honey.

Irish Mist

Medieval banquets

Among tourist attractions which have become popular in Ireland are the 'medieval banquets' held in old castles such as Bunratty, Knappogue (near Quin, Co. Clare) and Dunguaire (Kinvara, Co. Galway). At these events substantial medieval-style meals, with wine are served by young men and women in appropriate costume to the accompaniment of old ballads and music.

Generally there are two banquets per evening at about 5.30 and 8.45pm. The inclusive price is approximately IR£30 per person.

Bookings can be made at any tourist office (➤ Information) or at:

Information and booking:

Shannon Mediaeval Castle Banquets
Tel. (061) 360788

Dunguaire Castle
Tel. (091) 37108

Bunratty Castle
Bunratty, Co. Clare
Banquets throughout the year

Castles

Knappogue Castle
Near Quin, Co. Clare
Banquets only from May to September

Dunguaire Castle
Kinvara, Co. Galway
Banquets only from May to September

In Bunratty Folk Park (Co. Clare) traditional Irish nights (*céilís*) are organised with Irish food, wine, music, singing and dancing (from May to October): daily 5.30 and 8.45pm.

Irish nights

Golf

Golf is a popular sport in Ireland, and on summer evenings and at weekends large numbers of people play the game, often without any elaborate equipment. There are over 200 golf clubs, and numerous courses, about half of them 18 holes. Equipment can often be hired by visitors. There are golf courses near most holiday hotels.

Considered by experts to be the best golf courses are Portmarnock (Republic of Ireland, no. 1), Royal Portrush (Northern Ireland, no. 13), Royal County Down (Northern Ireland, no. 36), Ballybunion (Republic of Ireland, no. 76), Waterville (Republic of Ireland, no. 81) and Killarney (Republic of Ireland, no. 79).

Ranking

Guinness is Good for You

The heart of Ireland beats in St James's Gate in Dublin. Guinness is brewed here – the 'wine of the country', as James Joyce (in *Ulysses*) calls the almost black beer which everybody in Ireland drinks as medicine, basic food and to raise the spirits. And in *Finnigans Wake* Joyce asks, 'Is Ireland sober, is Ireland stiff.'

Soberly considered, Guinness is a dark, top-fermented beer, but which is brewed in a special way. The brewers by the River Liffey make their wort not only from dried malt but also add a little grain, roasted over beech wood but not malted, in order to obtain the dark colour, skilfully mixing several worts and hops to create the unique dry taste. The result is an 'Extra Stout', which in spite of its name has an alcohol content of only 4.3 per cent, for nowadays the word 'stout' describes the colour and not the strength of the beer. In Ireland draught Guinness tastes strongest and freshest, for here, thanks to the amount consumed, the beer is not pasteurised. Visitors who drink Guinness in their own country will not only be surprised at the taste but also at the colour of the beer in Dublin – much darker and with an almost white head. For every country in which it is sold, Guinness is brewed with a different recipe; the strongest is found in the tropics as 'Foreign Extra Stout', the second strongest in Germany.

However, Guinness is not just a type of beer and the national drink, it also represents the successful history of a family and a product that has become a world-wide legend.

With an inherited £100 in his pocket, Arthur Guinness from Celbridge in County Kildare came to Dublin in 1759. Here he bought a small brewery and produced the 'entire beer', a mixture of several worts which at that time was to the taste of customers. Since this strong ale was popular especially with porters, it had acquired the nickname of 'porter'. When Arthur Guinness I bequeathed the brewery to his son, who, as was customary at the time, was also called Arthur, he already dominated the Irish beer scene and also the cereal market – there were indeed times when almost the entire Irish cereal production found its way into the Guinness brewery. Arthur Guinness II set about capturing English beer drinkers, and straight away even the British upper classes took to the popular brew. The continuing thirst for Guinness increased the fame and fortune of the family. Benjamin Lee, the third member of the dynasty, became mayor of Dublin, distinguished himself as a patron and introduced – what was probably his most important achievement in an international context – bottled beer. His successor, Edward Cecil, who turned the brewery, now the largest in the world, into a limited company, was ennobled and henceforth the head of the Guinness dynasty bore the title of earl of Iveagh. As if this was not enough, James Joyce brought him literary immortality: in *Ulysses* 'Noble Buniveagh' is none other than Edward Cecil. He it was, too, who gave the Australian South Pole explorer Douglas Mawson a few bottles of Guinness; they were buried in permanent ice and when they were found 18 years later they were, of course, perfectly drinkable. Finally Edward Cecil had a tower built near his mansion on his Eleveden estate in Phoenix Park, and each morning he would climb the tower after drinking his early morning tea, in order to see whether the chimneys of his brewery at the far end of the city were still smoking. Even today every member of the Guinness family can climb the tower. After Edward Cecil, his successor, Rupert, was understandably less charismatic. Although a member of the House of Lords, he attended only once, on a matter which concerned him personally. When in a debate a complaint was made that his advertisement hoardings with the slogan 'Guinness is Good for You' desecrated the countryside, Lord Rupert rose and could only reply truthfully, 'But Guinness *is* good for you!'

This slogan, invented by the writer Dorothy Sayers, is indicative of the great advertising success of Guinness from the 1920s to the 1940s. As well as well-known authors, equally celebrated artists, such as Rex Whistler, HM Bateman and the caricaturist 'Vicky', worked for Guinness and illustrated the advertising slogans. The most popular was a series featuring a zookeeper who was constantly being surprised by the antics of the animals in his charge but who recovered with the aid of a porter – 'My Goodness, My Guinness'. The campaign was so successful that in 1953, at the coronation of Queen Elizabeth II, Guinness had advertising posters printed without any text or any reference to beer, only a sealion, a toucan and a kangaroo, for everybody knew to what the posters referred.

If he can say as you can
Guinness is good for you
How grand to be a Toucan
Just think what Toucan do

*My Goodness —
My GUINNESS*

In the course of time porter lost its popularity and since 1973 it has only been produced by a few breweries in England. The last barrel of Irish porter was consumed in a Belfast pub in May 1973 with due obsequies. Guinness, however, had already replaced the stronger stout and was successfully filling the gap which porter had relinquished. Today, behind the name of Guinness lies not only the largest brewery in Europe but also a group of companies which is active in the automobile and food industries, which owns a fleet of pleasure boats on Ireland's rivers and lakes, and which, of course, publishes *The Guinness Book of Records*. Members of the family have married into European aristocracy. For the ordinary Irish people, however, and especially for the men, the dream is to be appointed by Guinness to the post of 'test drinker' – and there is, indeed, such a person.

Golf-courses in the Republic of Ireland

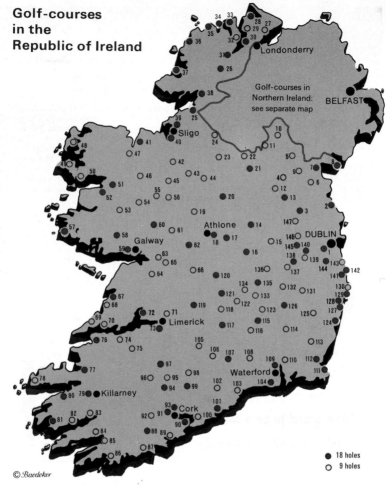

© Baedeker

● 18 holes
○ 9 holes

Golf courses in the Republic of Ireland (see map)

1 Dublin and surroundings:

Balbriggan Golf Club (18)
Ballinascorney Golf Club (18)
Beaverstown Golf Club (18)
Beechpark Golf Club (18)
Black Bush Golf Club (18)
Carrickmines Golf Club (9)
Castle Golf Club (18)
Clontarf Golf Club (18)
Deerpark Hotel Golf Club (18)
Donabate Golf Club (18)
Dublin and County Golf Club (18)

Dun Laoghaire Golf Club (18)
Edmondstown Golf Club (18)
Elm Park Golf Club (18)
Forrest Little Golf Club (18)
Foxrock Golf Club (9)
Gormanston Gold Club (9)
Grange Golf Club (18)
Hazel Grove Gold Club (9)
Hermitage Golf Club (18)
Howth Golf Club (18)
Killiney Golf Club (9)
Lucan Golf Club (18)

Beautiful view from Howth Golf Club near Dublin

Malahide Golf Club (9)
Milltown Golf Club (18)
Newlands Golf Club (18)
Portmarnock Golf Club (18 and 9)
Rathfarnham Golf Club (9)
Royal Dublin Golf Club (18)
Rush Golf Club (9)
Skerries Golf Club (18)
Slade Valley Golf Club (18)
Stackstown Golf Club (18)
St Anne's Golf Club (9)
Stepaside Golf Club (9)
Sutton Golf Club (9)
The Island Golf Club (18)
Woodbrook Golf Club (18)

2 Laytown and Bettystown Gold Club (18)
County Louth Golf Club (18)
3 Royal Tara Golf Club (18)
4 Cabra Castle Golf Club (9)
5 Castleblayney Golf Club (9)
6 Ardee Golf Club (18)
7 Dundalk Golf Club (18)
8 Greenore Golf Club (18)
9 Nuremore Golf Club (9)
10 Rossmore Golf Club (9)
11 Clones Golf Club (9)
12 Virginia Golf Club (9)
13 Headfort Golf Club (18)
14 Mullingar Golf Club (18)

15 Edenderry Golf Club (9)
16 Tullamore Golf Club (18)
17 Moate Golf Club (18)
18 Athlone Golf Club (18)
19 Roscommon Golf Club (9)
20 County Longford Golf Club (18)
21 County Cavan Golf Club (18)
22 Belturbet Golf Club (9)
23 Ballinamore Golf Club (9)
24 Blacklion Golf Club (9)
25 Bundoran Golf Club (18)
26 Ballybofey and Stranorlar Golf Club (18)
27 Greencastle Golf Club (9)
Redcastle Golf Club (9)
28 Ballyliffen Golf Club (18)
29 Buncrana Municipal Golf Club (9)
30 North West Golf Club (18)
31 Letterkenny Golf Club (18)
32 Otway Golf Club (9)
33 Portsalon Golf Club (18)
34 Rosapenna Golf Club (18)
35 Dunfanaghy Golf Club (18)
36 Gweedore Golf Club (18)
Cruit Island Golf Club (9)
37 Narin and Portnoo Golf Club (18)
38 Donegal Town Golf Club (18)
39 County Sligo Golf Club (18)
40 Strandhill Golf Club (18)
41 Enniscrone Golf Club (18)

42 Ballymote Golf Club (9)
43 Boyle Golf Club (9)
44 Carrick-on-Shannon Golf Club(9)
45 Ballaghaderreen Golf Club (9)
46 Swinford Golf Club (9)
47 Ballina Golf Club (9)
48 Belmullet Golf Club (9)
49 Achill Golf Club (9)
50 Mulrany Golf Club (9)
51 Castlebar Golf Club (18)
52 Westport Golf Club (18)
53 Ballinrobe Golf Club (9)
54 Claremorris Golf Club (9)
55 Ballyhaunis Golf Club (9)
56 Castlerea Golf Club (9)
57 Connemara Golf Club (18)
58 Oughterard Golf Club (18)
   Ashford Castle Golf Club (9)
59 Galway Golf Club (18)
60 Tuam Golf Club (18)
61 Mountbellew Golf Club (9)
62 Ballinasloe Golf Club (18)
63 Athenry Golf Club (9)
64 Gort Golf Club (9)
65 Loughrea Golf Club (9)
66 Portumna Golf Club (9)
67 Lahinch Golf Club (18 and 18)
68 Spanish Point Golf Club (9)
69 Kilkee Golf Club (9)
70 Kilrush Golf Club (9)
71 Clonlara Golf Club (9)
72 Shannon Golf Club (18)
   Ennis Golf Club (18)
   Dromoland Castle Golf Course
   (18)
73 Limerick Golf Club (18)
   Castleroy Golf Club (18)
   Adare Manor Golf Club (18)
74 Foynes Golf Club (9)
75 Newcastle West Golf Club (9)
76 Ballybunion Golf Club (18 and 18)
77 Tralee Golf Club (18)
78 Ceann Sibeal Golf Club (9)
79 Killarney Golf Club (18)
   Mahony's Point Course (18)
80 Dooks Golf Club (18)
81 Waterville Golf Club (18)
82 Parknasilla Golf Club (9)
83 Kenmare Golf Club (9)
84 Glengarriff Golf Club (9)
85 Bantry Golf Club (9)
86 Skibbereen Golf Club (9)
87 Dunmore Golf Club (9)
88 Bandon Golf Club (18)
89 Kinsale Golf Club (9)
90 Monkstown Golf Club (18)
91 Muskerry Golf Club (18)
92 Macroom Golf Club (9)
93 Mahon Municipal Golf Course
   (18)
   Douglas Golf Club (18)
   Cork Golf Club (18)

   Frankfield Golf Club (9)
94 Mallow Golf Club (18)
95 Doneraile Golf Club (9)
96 Kanturk Golf Club (9)
97 Charleville Golf Club (18)
98 Mitchelstown Golf Club (9)
99 Fermoy Golf Club (18)
100 East Cork Golf Club (18)
    Raffeen Creek Golf Club (9)
    Cobh Golf Club (9)
101 Youghal Golf Club (18)
102 Lismore Golf Club (9)
103 Dungarvan Golf Club (9)
104 Tramore Golf Club (18)
105 Tipperary Golf Club (9)
106 Cahir Park Golf Club (9)
    Rockwell Golf Club (9)
107 Clonmel Golf Club (18)
108 Carrick-on-Suir Golf Club (9)
109 Waterford Golf Club (18)
110 New Ross Golf Club (9)
111 Rosslare Golf Club (18)
112 Wexford Golf Club (18)
113 Enniscorthy Golf Club (9)
114 Borris Golf Club (9)
115 Kilkenny Golf Club (18)
116 Callan Golf Club (9)
117 Thurles Golf Club (18)
118 Templemore Golf Club (9)
119 Nenagh Golf Club (18)
120 Birr Golf Club (18)
121 Roscrea Golf Club (18)
122 Rathdowney Golf Club (9)
123 Castlecomer Golf Club (9)
124 Courtown Golf Club (18)
125 Coolattin Golf Club (9)
126 Carlow Golf Club (18)
127 Arklow Golf Club (18)
128 Woodenbridge Golf Club (9)
    The European Golf Club (18)
129 Blainroe Golf Club (18)
130 Wicklow Golf Club (9)
131 Baltinglass Golf Club (9)
132 Athy Golf Course (9)
133 Abbeyleix Golf Club (9)
134 Mountrath Golf Club (9)
135 Heath Golf Club (18)
136 Portarlington Golf Club (9)
137 Cill Dara Golf Club (9)
138 Curragh Golf Club (18)
139 Naas Golf Club (9)
140 Bodenstown Golf Club (18)
    Four Lakes Golf Club (18)
141 Delgany Golf Club (18)
142 Greystones Golf Club (18)
143 Bray Golf Club (9)
144 Kilternan Golf Club (18)
    Old Conna Golf Club (18)
145 Knockanally Golf Club (18)
    Clongowes Golf Club (9)
146 Kilcock Golf Club (9)
147 Trim Golf Club (9)

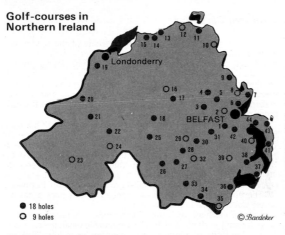

Golf-courses in Northern Ireland

● 18 holes
○ 9 holes

© *Baedeker*

Golf courses in Northern Ireland (see map)

1 Belfast and surroundings
Aberdelghy Golf Club (9)
Ballyearl Golf Club (9)
Balmoral Golf Club (18)
Belfast Parks Golf Course (9)
Belvoir Park Golf Club (18)
Cliftonville Golf Club (9)
Dunmurry Golf Club (18)
Fortwilliam Golf Club (18)
Gilnahirk Golf Club (9)
Knock Golf Club (18)
Knockbracken Golf Club (18)
Malone Golf Club (18 and 9)
Ormeau Golf Club (9)
Shandon Park Golf Club (18)
Holywood Golf Club (18)
Royal Belfast Golf Club (18)
2 Greenisland Golf Club (9)
3 Massereene Golf Club (18)
4 Ballymena Golf Club (18)
5 Ballyclare Golf Club (18)
6 Carrickfergus Golf Club (18)
7 Whitehead Golf Club (18)
Bentra Golf Club (9)
8 Larne Golf Club (9)
9 Cairndhu Golf Club (18)
10 Cushendall Golf Club (9)
11 Ballycastle Golf Club (18)
12 Bushfoot Golf Club (9)
13 Royal Portrush Golf Club (18, 18 and 9)
14 Portstewart Golf Club (18, 18 and 9)
Ballyreagh Golf Course (9)
Benone Golf Course (9)
15 Castlerock Golf Club (18 and 9)
16 Kilrea Golf Club (9)
Brown Trout Golf Club (9)

Manor Golf Club (9)
17 Moyola Park Golf Club (18)
18 Killymoon Golf Club (18)
19 City of Derry Golf Club (18 and 9)
20 Strabane Golf Club (18)
21 Newtownstewart Golf Club (18)
22 Omagh Golf Club (18)
23 Enniskillen Golf Club (18)
Ashwoods Golf Centre (9)
Castle Hume Golf Course (9)
24 Fintona Golf Club (9)
25 Dungannon Golf Club (18)
26 County Armagh Golf Club (18)
27 Tandagree Golf Club (18)
28 Portadown Golf Club (18)
29 Craigavon Golf Centre (18)
30 Lurgan Golf Club (18)
31 Lisburn Golf Club (18)
32 Banbridge Golf Club (18)
33 Newry Golf Club (18)
34 Warrenpoint Golf Club (18)
35 Kilkeel Golf Club (9)
36 Royal County Down Golf Club (18 and 18)
37 Ardglass Golf Club (18)
38 Downpatrick Golf Club (18)
Bright Castle Golf Club (18)
39 Spa Golf Club (18)
40 Mahee Island Golf Club (9)
41 Kirkistown Castle Golf Club (18)
42 Scrabo Golf Club (18)
43 Donaghadee Golf Club (18)
44 Bangor Golf Club (18)
Carnalea Golf Club (18)
Clandeboye Golf Club (18 and 18)
Helen's Bay Golf Club (9)
45 Ashfield Golf Club (18

Horse-drawn Caravans

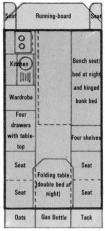

The brightly painted round-topped caravans of the tinkers who used to travel the roads of Ireland – and who are thought to be descended from Irish people driven into the west of the country by Cromwell's forces and unrelated to the gypsies of the Continent – are now rarely seen. However, in recent years modern replicas of these picturesque vehicles have become popular with holiday-makers as a means of enjoying a leisurely holiday on the quiet roads of the Irish Republic.

These caravans, drawn by sturdy horses, are some 13 ft long by 8 ft wide and usually have room for not more than four people. They have seats and a table, which can be converted into beds, and a two-burner cooker working on bottled gas. Bedding and bed linen is provided. The caravan operators have fixed itineraries – there is a choice of routes – with suitable overnight stopping-places. The day's journey is unlikely to be more than 10 miles or so. The horse must be given its nosebag of oats once a day and turned out to graze in the evening.

To rent a caravan, with most companies, it is necessary to put down a damage deposit of IR£200, refundable when the caravan is returned in good condition. Rental charges range from IR£300 to IR£550 a week, varying according to season.

Hotels

Hotels in the Republic of Ireland

In the Republic of Ireland there is a wide range of hotels, from the castle hotel, through modern luxury and medium-class hotels, to simple accommodation. Popular with foreign guests are the many beautifully situated country-house hotels (➤ Arriving, Accommodation). In addition to the hotels, guest services are also available and price themselves on personal service. Also numerous private houses (➤ Arriving, Accommodation) can generally be recommended, but are not listed in this guide.

Categories

Hotels are officially classified in five categories: luxury hotels have five stars, medium-class have two or three, and basic hotels have one star.

Reservations

Visitors are recommended, especially in the main season, to reserve accommodation in advance through a travel agent or direct at a hotel. Bookings in advance can also be made by calling personally at tourist offices (➤ Information) or by phoning the credit-card reservation service (with access to more than 11,000 properties approved by the Irish Tourist Board and Northern Ireland Tourist Board; tel. (00800) 66866866, email reservations@gulliver.ie).

Price

Price for hotels in Dublin and popular holiday centres are considerably higher than in the more remote parts of the country. There can also be marked differences in costs depending on the season, and therefore only a general indication can be given of prices. In the table below the prices are per room per night.

Category	Double room
*****	IR£200–300
****	IR£90–200
***	IR£70–120
**	IR£60–90
*	IR£40–60

In the following list of hotels, the official category and number of rooms is given together with the address, telephone and fax numbers, and any email addresses and web sites.

***Dunraven Arms

75 rooms; tel. (061) 396633, fax (061) 396541, email dunraven@iol.ie, web site www.dunravenhotel.com
The rooms of this hotel, which dates from 1792, contain antique furniture; there is an attractive garden and stables, and a leisure centre with a swimming pool.

***Nesbitt Arms

19 rooms; tel. (075) 41103, fax (075) 41895, email nesbitta@indigo.ie
The hotel, dating from 1834, is located in the centre of the town. Bar, bistro, restaurant.

**Cullenmore Hotel

12 rooms; tel. (0404) 40187, fax (0404) 40471, email cullenmore@eircom.net
Bar, restaurant.

***Hodson Bay

133 rooms; tel. (0902) 92444, fax (0902) 80520, email info@hodsonbay hotel.com, web site www.hodsonbayhotel.com
This well-appointed hotel on the shore of Lough Ree has many sports facilities (golf course, tennis, marina) and is suitable as a conference centre.

***Haydens Gateway Hotel

48 rooms; tel. (065) 6823000, fax (065) 6823759, email cro@lynchotels.com, web site www.lynchotels.com
Guests can enjoy the stylish atmosphere in this hotel, which has an award-winning restaurant and coffee shop.

***Kee's

Stranorlar, 53 rooms; tel. (074) 31018, fax (074) 31917
The former coaching inn is now a comfortable hotel. Bistro, conservatory lounge, restaurant.

****Slieve Russell

151 rooms; tel. (049) 9526444, fax (049) 4526474, email slieverussell@quinn-hotels.com, web site www.quinn-group.com
Luxury hotel with a wide range of leisure facilities. A popular place for golfers to stay (18- and 9-hole courses)

***Bay View

35 rooms; tel. (021) 646746, fax (021) 646075, email bayhotel@iol.ie
A magnificent location with views over Ballycotton Bay.

***Sea View

17 rooms; tel. (027) 50073, fax (027) 51555
Surrounded by an extensive park, this comfortable hotel has a good restaurant specialising in seafood.

****Ballynahinch Castle

Recess, 40 rooms; tel. (095) 31006, fax (095) 31085, email bhinch@iol.ie, web site www.commerce.ie/ballynahinch
This 18th c. castle stands on the Owenmore River.

***Westlodge

90 rooms; tel. (027) 50360, fax (027) 50438, email info@westlodge hotel.ie, web site www.westlodgehotel.ie
Popular with families; new health and leisure centre.

Hotels

Birr
***County Arms
Railway Road, 24 rooms; tel. (0509) 20791, fax (0509) 21234, email countyarmshotel@tinet.ie
Fresh fruit and vegetables served in the restaurant are grown in the hotel's own garden.

Blarney
***Christy's Hotel
49 rooms; tel. (021) 385011, fax (021) 385350, email christys@blarney.ie
Former mill buildings are now a comfortable hotel.

Bray
***Royal
Main Street, 91 rooms; tel. (01) 2862935, fax (01) 2867373, email royal@regencyhotels.com, web site www.regencyhotels.com
Swimming pool, whirlpool, sauna and solarium.

Bunratty
***Fitzpatrick Bunratty
115 rooms; tel. (061) 361177, fax (061) 471252, email info@fitzpatrick.com, web site www.fitzpatrickhotels.com
Situated in wooded grounds with a fitness centre, one of the advantages of this hotel is its accessible location: only 5 miles from Shannon Airport and 9 miles from Limerick.

Caherdaniel
***Derrynane
74 rooms; tel. (066) 9475136, fax (066) 9475160, email info@derrynane.com
A modern hotel on the Ring of Kerry overlooking the sea. Quiet beaches nearby.

Carlow
***Seven Oaks
Athy Road, 32 rooms; tel. (0503) 31308, fax (0503) 32155, email sevenoak@tinet.ie, web site www.beourguest.ie
Individually styled rooms, excellent Irish cooking and a comfortable bar.

Cashel (Co. Galway)
***Cashel House
32 rooms; tel. (095) 31001, fax (095) 31077, email info@cashel-house-hotel.com, web site www.cashel-house-hotel.com
The gardens surrounding Cashel House have won several awards. The hotel also has tennis courts, its own riding stables and a small private beach.

Cashel (Co. Tipperary)
***Cashel Palace
Main Street, 23 rooms; tel. (062) 62707, fax (062) 61521, email reception@cashel-palace.ie, web site www.cashel-palace.ie
In the 18th c. Cashel Palace was the archbishop's residence. In the park are trees that were planted on the coronation of Queen Anne; private walk to the famous Rock of Cashel.

Castlebar
***Breaffy House
59 rooms; tel. (094) 22033, fax (094) 22276, email breaffyhotel@anu.ie, web site www.breaffyhouse.ie
This country house, set in a large park, belongs to the Best Western group of hotels.

Cavan
***Kilmore
Dublin Road, 39 rooms; tel. (049) 4332288, fax (049) 4332458, email kilmore@quinn-hotels.com
A comfortable hotel with a good restaurant.

Clifden
***Abbeyglen Castle
36 rooms; tel. (095) 21201, fax (095) 21797, email info@abbeyglen.ie, web site www.abbeyglen.ie
This imposing castle stands in the centre of a romantic park with waterfalls and a panoramic view of Clifden.

***Ardagh Hotel
Ballyconneely Rd., 21 rooms; tel. (095) 21384, fax (095) 21314, email ardaghhotel@eircom.net, web site www.commerce.ie/ardaghhotel
A quiet family-run hotel 1 mile outside Clifden with a good restaurant (lobster and seafood specialities).

****The Lodge & Spa at Inchydoney Island
Clonakilty

67 rooms; tel. (023) 33143, fax (023) 35229, email reservations@ incheydoneyisland.com
A luxury hotel on a scenic coastline, close to the sandy beach. Bar, restaurant.

***Minella
Clonmel

Coleville Road, 70 rooms; tel. (052) 22388, fax (052) 24381, email hotel-minella@tinet.ie, web site www.tipp.ie/hotel-minella.htm
An elegantly appointed country house on the banks of the River Suir.

****Jurys
Cork

Western Road, 185 rooms; tel. (021) 276622, fax (021) 274477, email enquires@jurys.com, web site www.jurys.com
Situated on the banks of the River Lee, it is only a 5-minute walk to the centre of Cork. There are two restaurants to choose from.

***Jurys Inn
Anderson's Quay, 133 rooms; tel. (021) 276444, fax (021) 276144, email enquiry@jurys.com, web site www.jurys.com
A new concept for Ireland: modern, purpose-built rooms let to up to three adults or two adults and two children.

**Courtmacsherry
Courtmacsherry

12 rooms; tel. (023) 46198, fax (023) 46137, email cmv@indigo.ie
This former residence of the earls of Shannon overlooks Court-macsherry Bay. Self-catering cottages to let.

***Dingle Skellig
Dingle

116 rooms; tel. (066) 9150200, fax (066) 9151501, email dsk@iol.ie, web site www.dingleskellig.com
Attractively situated near Dingle harbour, this hotel has a swimming pool, playground, tennis courts, sauna and gym; new conference and banqueting centre.

***Harvey's Point
Donegal

Lough Eske, 32 rooms; tel. (073) 22208, fax (073) 22352, email harveyspoint@eircom.net
About 3 miles outside Donegal, this hotel is set in beautiful scenery on the Lough Eske. Excellent French and Swiss gourmet cuisine.

***Aran View House
Doolin

Coast Road, 19 rooms; tel. (065) 7074061, fax (065) 7074540, email aranview@gofree.indigo.ie
This Georgian house is magnificently located within view of the Aran Islands, the Burren and the Cliffs of Moher.

***Boyne Valley
Drogheda

35 rooms; tel. (041) 9837737, fax (041) 9839188, email reservations@boyne-valley-hotel.ie, web site www.boyne-valley-hotel.ie
Country house with lovely gardens.

****Conrad
Dublin

Earlsfort Terrace, 191 rooms; tel. (01) 6765555, fax (01) 6765424, email info@conrad-international.ie, web site www.conradinternational.ie

This luxury hotel offers the standard of comfort and facilities appropriate to this price category.

****Shelbourne
St Stephen's Green, 164 rooms; tel. (01) 6634500, fax (01) 661006, email shelbourneinfo@forte-hotels.com, web site www.shelbourne.ie
One of the most distinguished addresses in Ireland. Rooms are furnished with antiques.

****Burlington
Upper Leeson Street, 526 rooms, tel. (01) 6605222, fax (01) 6603172, email burlington@doylehotels.com, web site www.doylehotels.com
Ireland's largest hotel, with a cosmopolitan atmosphere.

****Clarence Hotel
6–8 Wellington Quay, 50 rooms; tel. (01) 4070800, fax (01) 4070820, email reservations@theclarence.ie, web site www.theclarence.ie
Reopened in 1995 after extensive refurbishment, all the rooms have been individually designed in contemporary, elegant style.

***Temple bar
Temple Bar, 129 rooms; tel. (01) 6773333, fax (01) 6773088, email templeb@iol.ie, web site www.towerhotelgroup,ie
Centrally situated in the vibrant Temple Bar district.

***Jurys Tara
Merrion Road, 113 rooms; tel. (01) 2694666, fax (01) 2691027, email michelle-bernie@jurys.com
2 miles from city centre with good view of Dublin Bay.

***Jurys Christchurch Inn
Christchurch Place, 182 rooms; tel. (01) 454000, fax (01) 4540012, email info@jurys.com, web site www.jurys.com
Centrally located with attractive modern rooms.

Dundalk

**Imperial
Park Street, 47 rooms; tel. (042) 9332241, fax (042) 9337909
A comfortable hotel in the town centre. Bar, coffee shop, restaurant.

Dungarvan

***Lawlors
89 rooms; tel. (058) 41122, fax (058) 41000
Welcoming family-run hotel.

Dun Laoghaire

***Royal Marine
Marine Road, 103 rooms; tel. (01) 2801911, fax (01) 2801089, email ryan@indigo.ie, web site www.ryanhotels.com
This comfortably furnished house stands in the middle of magnificent parkland with panoramic views of Dublin Bay.

Ennis

**Magowna House
Inch, 10 rooms; tel. (065) 6839009, fax (065) 6839258, email magowna@iol.ie
Country house (4 miles outside Ennis) with views of the Shannon.

Enniscorthy

*Murphy-Flood's
Market Square, 21 rooms; tel./fax (054) 33413, email mfhotel@indigo.ie, web site indigo.ie/~mfhotel
Georgian-style hotel with restaurant overlooking Market Square.

Galway

****Glenlo Abbey
Bushy Park, 45 rooms; tel. (091) 526666, fax (091) 527800, email glenlo@iol.ie, web site www.glenlo.com

This classy hotel, with marble baths and many other luxurious facilities, stands in the middle of beautiful private gardens.

****Ardilaun
Taylor's Hill, 89 rooms; tel. (091) 521433, fax (091) 521546, email ardilaun@iol.ie, web site www.ardilaunhousehotel.ie
This beautiful house stands in lovely grounds halfway between Galway and Salthill.

***Lochlurgain
22 Monksfield, Upper Salthill, 13 rooms; tel. (091) 529595, fax (091) 522399, lochlurgain@eircom.net
Good service is provided in this family-run hotel in the city centre.

***Glendalough
Glendalough

44 rooms; tel. (0404) 45135, fax (0404) 45142, email info@glendalough hotel.ie
Built at the beginning of the 19th c, this hotel has been completely modernised. It lies in Glendalough National Park in the heart of Wicklow's most scenic valley.

***Marlfield House
Gorey

19 rooms; tel. (055) 21124, fax (055) 21572, email marlf@iol.ie, web site www.marfieldhouse.com
Mansion house surrounded by gardens and woodland.

****Park
Kenmare

49 rooms; tel. (064) 41200, fax (064) 41402, email phkenmare@iol.ie, web site www.parkkenmore.com
Top hotel surrounded by superb parkland; 18-hole golf course, tennis and croquet.

***Riversdale House
64 rooms; tel. (064) 41299, fax (064) 41075
Located on Kenmare Bay close to the town centre.

**Halpin's
Kilkee

2 Erin Street, 12 rooms; tel. (065) 56032, fax (065) 56317, email halpins@iol.ie, web site www.gueenbook.ie/halpins
Centrally situated, privately run hotel.

***Langton House
Kilkenny

69 John Street, 26 rooms; tel. (056) 65133, fax (056) 63693
Period town house with very comfortable rooms. Popular bar and restaurant.

***Newpark
Castlecomer Road, 111 rooms; tel. (056) 22122, fax (056) 61111, email info@newparkhotel.com, website www.newparkhotel.com
This hotel has a swimming pool, sauna, steam bath and fitness room.

****Aghadoe Heights
Killarney

75 rooms; tel. (064) 31766, fax (064) 31345, email aghadoeheights@eircom.net, web site www.aghadoeheights.com
Luxury hotel with corresponding level of comfort and panoramic views.

***Gleneagle
213 rooms; tel. (064) 31870, fax (064) 32646, email gleneagle@iol.ie, web site www.gleneagle-hotel.com
Not a particularly attractive building from the exterior but has many entertainment and sports facilities, plus two restaurants.

Hotels

Killiney

***Fitzpatrick Castle
113 rooms; tel. (01) 2840700, fax (01) 2850207
Castle hotel, 9 miles from Dublin, with views of Dublin Bay; fitness centre and swimming pool.

***Court
86 rooms; tel. (01) 2851622, fax (02) 2852085, email book@killiney court.ie, web site www.killineycourt.ie
Victorian mansion with a breathtaking view of Killiney Bay; conference centre.

Kinsale

***Actons
Pier Road, 76 rooms; tel. (021) 4772135, fax (021) 4772231, email actonsh@indigo.ie
Situated above the harbour; noted for its special atmosphere and fine cooking.

Limerick

****Castletroy Park
Dublin Road, 107 rooms; tel. (061) 335566, fax (061) 331117, email sales@castletroy-park.ie, web site www.castletroy-park.ie
New hotel furnished in traditional style and standing in 14 acres of gardens; health and fitness club.

***Jurys
Ennis Road, 95 rooms; tel. (061) 327777, fax (061) 326400, email info@jurys.com, web site www.jurys.com
Centrally located in 5-acre garden on the banks of the Shannon.

***Greenhills
Caherdavin, 58 rooms; tel. (061) 453033, fax (061) 453307
Modern hotel with many comforts, plus leisure centre and swimming pool. Speciality of the restaurant are lamb dishes (the lamb comes from the hotel's own farm).

**Woodfield House
Ennis Road, 26 rooms; tel. (061) 453022, fax (061) 326755, email woodfieldhotel@eircom.net
A pleasant hotel both inside and out.

Lisdoonvarna

**Sheedy's Restaurant & Hotel
11 rooms; tel. (065) 7074026, fax (065) 7074555, email cmv@indigo.ie
Set in mature gardens with a good restaurant.

Lismore

**Ballyrafter House
10 rooms; tel. (058) 54002, fax (058) 53050, email ballyrafter@esatclear.ie, web site www.ballyrather.ie
Georgian manor house of special charm.

Lucan

***Finnstown Country House
Newcastle Road, 51 rooms; tel. (01) 6280644, fax (01) 6281088, email manager@finnstown-hotel.ie, web site www.finnstown-hotel.ie/finnstown
Comfortable house about 8 miles west of Dublin with a sauna, Turkish baths and various sports facilities.

Macroom

**Castle
Main Street, 42 rooms; tel. (026) 41074, fax (026) 41505, email castle hotel@tinet.ie, web site www.castlehotel.ie
Centrally located hotel with a good restaurant and a new health and leisure club.

Midleton

***Midleton Park
Old Cork Road, 40 rooms; tel. (021) 631767, fax (021) 631605
Relatively new hotel with a popular restaurant, bar and conference facilities.

****Hillgrove
44 rooms; tel. (047) 81288, fax (047) 84941
Opened in 1994, this hotel has live music at the weekends.

Monaghan

***Ardboyne
Dublin Road, 29 rooms; tel. (046) 23119, fax (046) 22355, email
ardboyne@quinn-hotels.com
Recently refurbished with a fine restaurant, the hotel is part of the Quinn
Hotel Group.

Navan

***Abbey Court Hotel
Dublin Road, 46 rooms; tel. (067) 41111, fax (067) 41022, email
abycourt@indigo.ie
Located on the Dublin side of the town.

Nenagh

*****Dromoland Castle
75 rooms; tel. (061) 368144, fax (061) 363355, email sales@dromoland.ie,
web site www.dromoland.ie
A comfortable castle hotel with an 18-hole golf course.

Newmarket-on-
Fergus

***Clare Inn
Dromoland, 182 rooms; tel. (061) 6823000, fax (061) 6823759
Reasonably priced alternative to Dromoland Castle, set by Dromoland's
18-hole golf course with views of Shannon estuary.

***Clarion Brandon House
61 rooms; tel. (051) 421703, fax (051) 421567, email
brandonhouse@eircom.net, web site www.brandonhousehotel.ie
19th c. mansion with a modern extension; new leisure centre.

New Ross

**Old Rectory
Rosbercon, 12 rooms; tel. (051) 421719, fax (051) 422974, email new
rossoldrectoryhot@eircom.net, web site www.amireland.com/oldrectory
Both hotel and restaurant are extremely tastefully furnished.

***Ross Lake House
Rosscahill, 13 rooms; tel. (091) 550109, fax (091) 550184, email
rosslake@iol.ie
Georgian house set in woodland; the hotel provides good food.

Oughterard

*Pier
Near harbour, 10 rooms; tel. (074) 58178, fax (074) 58115
The hotel stands near the sandy shore of Lough Swilly. Bar, dining room

Rathmullan

***Tinakilly Country House
52 rooms; tel. (0404) 69274, fax (0404) 67806, email
jandrpower@tinakilly.ie, web site www.tinakilly.ie
Good cuisine in this 19th c. house set in 7 acres of gardens.

Rathnew

***Renvyle House
Connemara, 65 rooms; tel. (095) 43511, fax (095) 43515, email
renvyle@iol.ie, web site www.renvyle.com
Historic coastal hotel set among sea, lake and mountains, with turf fires
and cosy lounges.

Renvyle

***Abbey
Galway Road, 25 rooms; tel. (0903) 26240, fax (0903) 26021, email
cmv@indigo.ie
Stylish 19th c. manor with attractively furnished rooms, set in 4 acres of
grounds.

Roscommon

Hotels

Rosslare   ******Kelly's Resort**
99 rooms; tel. (053) 32114, fax (053) 32222, email kellyhot@iol.ie
Popular seafront hotel with extensive facilities. Bistro, renowned restaurant.

Rossnowlaugh   *****Sand House**
46 rooms; tel. (072) 51777, fax (072) 52100, email info@sandhouse-hotel.ie, web site www.sandhouse-hotel.ie
Comfortable accommodation in a beautiful seaside location.

Shannon   *****Quality Shannon Hotel**
Ballycasey, 54 rooms; tel. (061) 364588, fax (061) 364045, email sales@qualityshannon.com
Friendly hotel near Shannon Airport. Bar, carvery, restaurant.

Skibbereen   ****Eldon**
Bridge Street, 19 rooms; tel. (028) 22000, fax (027) 22191, email welcome@eldon-hotel.ie, web site www.eldon-hotel.com
Central family-run hotel.

Sligo   ****Silver Swan**
29 rooms; tel. (071) 43231, fax (071) 42232
Family-owned hotel in the centre of town beside the Garavogue River. Bar.

Straffan   *******Kildare**
45 rooms; tel. (01) 6017200, fax (01) 6017299, email hotel@kclub.ie, web site www.kclub.ie
One of the most exclusive and expensive hotels in Ireland. It has an 18-hole golf course, tennis courts, swimming pool, sauna and other facilities.

Thomastown   ******Mount Juliet**
59 rooms; tel. (056) 73000, fax (056) 73019, email info@mountjuliet.ie, web site www.mountjuliet.ie
Guests can choose between the grand 18th c. Mount Juliet House, the sportier atmosphere of Hunters Yard of the Rose Garden Lodges – all of which are expensive!

Tralee   *****Brandon**
Princes Street, 185 rooms; tel. (066) 7123333, fax (066) 7125019, email info@brandon.ie
Elegantly furnished house with swimming pool, sauna and restaurant.

Tramore   *****Majestic**
57 rooms; tel. (051) 381761, fax (051) 381766
The hotel overlooks Tramore Bay. Restaurant (local seafood).

Waterford   ******Waterford Castle**
The Island, Ballinakill, 19 rooms; tel. (051) 878203, fax (051) 879316, email info@waterfordcastle.com, web site www.waterfordcastle.com
This magnificent castle stands on a small island in the River Suir, not far from Waterford. It has an 18-hole golf course, tennis courts and a pool.

***Tower
The Mall, 142 rooms; tel. (051) 875801, fax (051) 870129, email towerw@iol.ie, web site www.towerhotelgroup.ie
Modern, well-equipped hotel in the heart of the city; leisure and fitness centre.

Waterville   *****Butler Arms**
30 rooms; tel. (066) 9474144, fax (066) 9474520, email butarms@iol.ie, web site www.kerry-insight.com/butler-arms/

Charlie Chaplin spent many holidays in this stylish hotel that overlooks the Atlantic.

***Hotel Westport
Westport
The Demense, Newport Road, 129 rooms; tel. (098) 25122, fax (098) 26739, email sales@hotelwestport.co.uk, web site www.hotelwestport.ie
Not far from the town centre in the middle of a park. Entertainment in the bar in summer; conference centre and modern swimming pool/leisure centre.

***River Bank House
Wexford
The Bridge, 24 rooms; tel. (053) 23611, fax (0530 23342, email river@indigo.ie
Quiet location close to the centre; magnificent views of town, river and beach.

***White's
George Street, 82 rooms; tel. (053) 22311, fax (053) 45000, email info@whiteshotel.iol.ie, web site www.wexfordirl.com
Established in 1779, this charming, centrally located hotel in the centre is part of the Best Western group.

**Devonshire Arms
Youghal
Pearse Square, 10 rooms; tel. (024) 92827, fax (024) 92900
Pleasant 19th c. hotel with individually decorated rooms.

Hotels in Northern Ireland

In Northern Ireland the hotels are officially classified according to their facilities, ranging from high-standard hotels (five stars) to modest hotels (one star) while some hotels are unclassified.
Categories

Bookings can be made in advance by calling in person at tourist offices (➤ Information). Credit card bookings can be made by telephone (freephone): (0800) 404050 (from the UK), (1850) 230230 (from the Irish Republic), or for accommodation in the whole of Ireland: tel. (00800) 66866866, email reservations@gulliver.ie.
Bookings and reservations

In Belfast, hotel prices are markedly higher than elsewhere in Northern Ireland. Here they tend to be at the top end of the average prices. Price-ranges for hotels and guest houses are similar to those for the Republic of Ireland.
Prices

***Clandeboye Lodge
Bangor
10 Estate Road, Clandeboye, 43 rooms; tel. (028) 91852500, fax (028) 91852772, email info@clandeboyelodge.com
The hotel is set in wooded grounds and offers good service. Bar, lounge, restaurant.

***The Crescent Townhouse
Belfast
13 Lower Crescent, 11 rooms; tel. (028) 90323349, fax (028) 90320646, email info@crescenttownhouse.com
Regency hotel near Botanic Station. Bar, brasserie.

**Balmoral
Blacks Road, Dunmurry, 44 rooms; tel. (028) 90301234, fax (028) 90601455
Purpose-built hotel with smart, spacious public rooms.

***Killyhevlin
Enniskillen
Dublin Road, 43 rooms; tel.(028) 66323481, fax (028) 66324726, email info@killyhevlin.com

This hotel, picturesquely situated on Lough Erne, is suitable for a longer stay.

Londonderry
Derry

***Beech Hill
32 Ardmore Road, 27 rooms; tel. (028) 1349279, fax (028) 71345366, email info@beech-hill.com
Privately owned country manor 2½ miles from the city centre.

Newcastle

**Enniskeen House
98 Bryansford Road, 12 rooms; tel. (028) 43722392, fax (028) 43724084, email enniskeen-hotel@demon.co.uk
Welcoming family hotel near the Mourne Mountains. Two dining rooms.

Portaferry

***Portaferry
10 The Strand, 14 rooms; tel. (028) 42728231, fax (028) 42728999, email portaferry@iol.ie
Lovely setting by the sea.

Bushmills

**Beach House
61 Beach Road, Portballintrae, 32 rooms; tel. (028) 20731214, fax (028) 20731664, email info@beachhousehotel.com
Owned by the same family for three generations.

Portrush

***The Royal Court
233 Ballybogey Road, 18 rooms; tel. (028) 70822236, fax (028) 70823176, email royalcourthotel@aol.com
The modern hotel overlooks the beach and has extensive sea views. Dining room.

Hunting and Shooting

Shooting

Game shooting in Ireland is for pheasant grouse, partridge, snipe and various species of wild duck. A gun licence is required, which is issued only against proof that a shooting holiday has been booked. Relaxed quarantine regulations mean that visitors are now allowed to take more than one dog. Deer stalking is rarely available for visitors.

The shooting season is fixed each year by the Department of Agriculture; it is usually from the beginning of September to the end of January.

For the addresses of shooting clubs and organisers of shoots, apply to the Irish Tourist Board.

Hunting

Fox hunting is a popular Irish sport, not only for the 'gentry', but for any small farmer who possesses a horse. The hunt can also be followed on foot. There are still some 40 hunts in Ireland with the season lasting from the beginning of November to the end of March. Participants must be experienced riders.

Information

Internet

www.ireland.travel.ie

Ireland

All Ireland Information
Britain Visitor Centre
1 Regent Street, London SW1Y 4XT

Tourist information: tel. (020) 74933201, fax (020) 74939065, email
info@irishtouristboard.co.uk.

Bord Fáilte/Irish Tourist Board

Baggot Street Bridge, Dublin 2   Head office
Tel. (01) 6024000, fax (01) 6024100, email user@irishtouristboard.le

53 Castle Street, Belfast BT1 1GH   Northern Ireland
Tel. (028) 90327888, fax (028) 90240201, email info@irishtourist
boardni.ie

44 Foyle Street, Londonderry BT48 6AT
Tel./fax (028) 71369501

Ireland House, 150 New Bond Street, London W1Y 0AQ   United Kingdom
Tel. (020) 74933201, fax (020) 74939065, email
info@irishtouristboard.co.uk

5–8 Temple Row, Birmingham B2 5HG
Tel. (0121) 2369724

19 Dixon Street, Glasgow G1 4AJ
Tel. (0141) 2212311

28 Cross Street, Manchester M2 3NH
Tel. (0161) 8325981

345 Park Avenue, New York NY 10154   Canada and
Tel. (212) 4180800 or (1800) 2236470, fax (212) 3719052, email   United States
info@irishtouristboard.com, web site www.ireland.travel.ie

Information in the Republic of Ireland

In the Irish Republic information can be obtained locally from tourist
offices or, in a few cases, from community tourist offices. Offices are
generally open Mon.–Fri. 9am–6pm, Sat. 9am–1pm.

➤ Keel (below)   Achill Island

Church View; tel. (061) 396255   Adare
Open Apr.–Oct.

➤ Kilronan (below)   Aran Islands

Tel. (024) 94444   Ardmore
Open Jun.–Sep.

Grand Parade; tel. (0402) 32484   Arklow
Open mid-Jun. to Aug.

Athlone Castle; tel. (0902) 94630   Athlone
Open: mid-April to October

Tel. (0905) 73939   Aughrim
Open mid-Jun. to Sep.

Cathedral Street; tel. (096) 70848   Ballina
Open Jun.–Aug.

Information

Ballinasloe	Tel. (0905) 42131 Open Jul.–Aug.
Bantry	Tel. (027) 50229 Open Jun.–Sep.
Birr	Emmet Square; tel. (0509) 20110 Open mid-May to mid-Sep.
Boyle	Courthouse; tel. (079) 62145 Open Jun.–Aug.
Bray	Tel. (01) 2867128 Open mid-Jun. to Aug.
Bundoran	Tel. (072) 41350 Open Jun.–Aug.
Bunratty	Bunratty Folk Park; tel. (061) 360788 Open May–Sep.
Cahir	Castle Street; tel. (052) 41453 Open May–Sep.
Carlow	Tel. (0503) 31554 Open all year
Carrick-on-Shannon	The Quays; tel. (078) 20170 Open May–Sep.
Carrick-on-Suir	West Gate; tel. (051) 40726 Open Jun.–Aug.
Cashel	Town Hall, Main Street; tel. (062) 61333 Open Apr.–Sep.
Castlebar	Tel. (094) 21207 Open Jul.–Aug.
Cavan	1 Farnham Street; tel. (049) 4331942 Open all year
Clifden	Tel. (095) 21163 Open mid-Apr. to mid-Oct.
Cliffs of Moher	Liscannor; tel. (065) 81171 Open mid-May to Oct.
Clonakilty	Tel. (023) 33226 Open Jul.–Aug.
Clonmacnoise	Tel. (0905) 74134 Open mid-Apr.–Oct.
Clonmel	Tel. (052) 22960 Open mid-Jun.–Aug.
Cork	Tourist House, Grand Parade, tel. (021) 4273251, fax (021) 4273504, email user@cktourism.ie Open all year

Tel. (066) 51188   Dingle
Open May–Oct.

Tel. (073) 21148   Donegal
Open May–Sep.

Bus Éireann Depot, tel. (041) 9837070, fax (041) 9845340   Drogheda
Open Jun.–Aug.

11 Suffolk Street; tel. (01) 2844768, email information@dublintourism.ie,   Dublin
web site www.visitdublin.com
Open all year

Baggot Street Bridge; tel. (01) 2844768
Open all year

Dublin Airport; tel. (01) 8445387
Open all year

Market Square; tel. (042) 35484
Open all year

Jocelyn Street; tel. (042) 9335484, fax (042) 9338070, email dundalk   Dundalk
touristoffice@tinet.ie
Open all year

St Mary Street; tel. (058) 41741   Dungarvan
Open mid-Jun.–Aug.

Tel. (075) 21297   Dungloe
Open Jun.–Aug.

St Michael's Wharf; tel. (01) 2806984   Dun Laoghaire
Open all year

Arthur's Row; tel. (065) 628366   Ennis
Open all year

Castle Hill; tel. (054) 34699   Enniscorthy
Open mid-Jun.–Aug.

Victoria Place, Eyre Square; tel. (091) 563081, fax (091) 565201   Galway
Open all year

Galway Airport; tel. (091) 55252
Open Jun. to mid-Sep.

Tel. (027) 63084   Glengarriff
Open Jul.–Aug.

Main Street; tel. (055) 21248   Gorey
Open Jul.–Aug.

Courthouse; tel. (098) 45384   Keel
Open Jul.–Aug.

The Square; tel. (064) 41688   Kenmare
Open Jun.–Sep.

O'Connell Street; tel. (065) 56112   Kilkee
Open Jun.–Aug.

Information

Kilkenny
Rose Inn Street; tel. (056) 51500, fax (056) 63955
Open all year

Killaloe
Visitor Centre, The Bridge; tel. (061) 376866
Open Jun. to mid-Sep.

Killarney
Beech Road; tel. (064) 31633, fax (064) 34506
Open all year

Kilronan
Tel. (099) 61263
Open Jun. to mid-Sep.

Kilrush
Town Hall; tel. (065) 51577
Open Jun.–Aug.

Kinsale
Pier Road; tel. (021) 772234
Open Mar.–Nov.

Knock
Knock Airport; tel. (094) 67247
Open all year

Village; tel. (094) 88193
Open May to mid-Sep.

Letterkenny
Derry Road; tel. (074) 21160, fax (074) 25180, email irelandnorthwest@itnet.ie, web site www.ireland-northwest.travel.ie

Limerick
Arthur's Quay; tel. (061) 317522, fax (061) 317939
Open all year

Lismore
Community Office; tel. (058) 54588
Open May–Sep.

Listowel
St John's Square; tel. (068) 22590
Open mid-may to mid-Sep.

Longford
Main Street; tel. (043) 46566
Open Jun.–Aug.

Monaghan
Market House; tel. (047) 81122
Open all year

Mullingar
Market House; tel. (044) 48650, fax (044) 40413, email midlandseast tourism@tinet.ie
Open all year

Nenagh
Connolly Street; tel. (067) 31610
Open mid-May to mid-Sep.

Newbridge
Tel. (045) 33835
Open mid-Jun. to Aug.

Newgrange
Tel. (041) 24274
Open mid-Apr. to Oct.

New Ross
The Quay; tel. (051) 21857
Open mid-Jun. to Aug.

Portlaoise
James Fintan Lalor Avenue; tel. (0502) 21178
Open Jun.–Aug.

Tel. (0903) 26342 Open mid-Jun. to Aug.	Roscommon
Tel. (053) 33232/33622, fax (053) 33421 Open May to mid-Sep.	Rosslare Harbour
Rosslare Terminal; tel. (053) 33622 Open all year	
Tel. (091) 63081 Open Jun.–Aug.	Salthill
Tel. (061) 471664, fax (061) 471661 Open all year	Shannon Airport
Town Hall; tel. (028) 21766, fax (028) 21353 Open all year	Skibbereen
Temple Street; tel. (071) 61201, fax (071) 60360 Open all year	Sligo
Community Office; tel. (062) 51457 Open all year	Tipperary
Ashe Memorial Hall, Denny Street; tel. (066) 7121288, fax (066) 7121700 Open all year	Tralee
The Square; tel. (051) 381572 Open mid-Jun. to Aug.	Tramore
Mill Museum; tel. (093) 24463 Open Jul.–Aug.	Tuam
41 The Quay; tel. (051) 75788, fax (051) 877388 Open all year	Waterford
James Street; tel. (098) 25711, fax (098) 26709 Open all year	Westport
Crescent Quay; tel. (053) 23111, fax (053) 41743 Open all year	Wexford
Fitzwilliam Square; tel. (0404) 69117, fax (0404) 69118, email wicklow-touristoffice@tinet.ie Open all year	Wicklow
Tel. (024) 92390 Open Jun.–Sep.	Youghal

Northern Ireland Tourist Board

www.ni-tourism.com

59 North Street, Belfast BT1 1NB Tel. (028) 90246609, fax (028) 90240960	Head office
16 Nassau Street, Dublin 2 Tel. (01) 6791977, fax (01) 6798163	Republic of Ireland

Insurance

Information in Northern Ireland

In Northern Ireland information can be obtained from tourist offices and
visitor centres as well as district councils and local councils.

Insurance

Visitors are strongly advised to ensure that they have adequate holiday
insurance, including cover for loss or damage to luggage, loss of currency and jewellery.

Health   Nationals of other European Union countries are entitled to obtain medi-
cal care when on holiday in Ireland. Treatment can be obtained free of
charge, but medicines must be paid for. Form E111 should be obtained
(by British nationals from post offices in the UK, contained inside the
booklet *Health Advice for Travellers*) before departure.
   Visitors from non-EU countries are recommended, and nationals of EU
countries are advised, to take out some form of short-term health insurance providing complete cover and thereby possibly avoiding delays.

Vehicles   Visitors travelling by car should ensure that their insurance is comprehensive and covers use of the vehicle in Ireland (➤ Travel Documents).

Language

English is spoken throughout Ireland. The old Celtic language of Ireland,
known as Irish, Erse or Gaelic (➤ Facts and Figures, Language), is an
official language of the Republic of Ireland jointly with English. However,
it is the everyday language only in certain of the more remote parts of
the country.

The Irish alphabet has fewer letters than the Latin alphabet – no j, k, v, w, x, y or z. An acute accent over a vowel means that it is long. The traditional Irish uncial script will frequently be seen on road signs.

The following list of Anglicised forms of Irish words may help in interpreting place names and other names.

abha	river
ard	hill, high ground
áth	ford
ball	town, settlement
béal	estuary
ben	hill, mountain
bord	office, board
bun	end
burren	stone
cahir	stone fort
cashel	stone fort
cavan	cave
cill	church
clochán	beehive-shape stone hut
cnoc	hill
croagh	conical hill
derry	oak
drum	chain of hills
dún	hill fort
éireann	Irish
ennis (innis)	island, meadow
gal	river
grianán	palace
lis	stone fort
lough	lake, arm of the sea
mac	son
monaster	monastery
ráth	ring-fort
skerry	small rocky islet
slieve	hill, mountain
tholsel	town hall

Motoring

In the Irish Republic, apart from a short stretch around Dublin, there are no motorways. Trunk roads are designated as National roads (N), divided into National Primary (N1–25) and National Secondary (N over 50), and Regional roads (R). Many roads are extremely narrow but traffic is generally light. Drivers must be careful to avoid cattle and sheep and beware of agricultural vehicles crossing the roads.

Roads

Since many roads are not in very good condition, average speeds must be reduced (for example, for the 185 mile stretch between Dublin and Killarney, a good 5 hours should be allowed).

The classification of roads in Northern Ireland is the same as in the rest of the United Kingdom, with A (trunk) roads, B (secondary) roads and M for motorways.

Motorists travelling between the Republic of Ireland and Northern Ireland can cross the border at a large number of official border points, but the following are commended (see below). At each entry or exit you may be required to produce identification and your luggage and vehicle may be checked.

Cross-border routes

The customs regulations for entry to Northern Ireland are the same as those for the United Kingdom (➤ Customs Regulations).

Motoring

Recommended route	Republic of Ireland	Northern Ireland
R238–A2	Moville	Londonderry
R238–A2	Buncrana	Londonderry
N13–A2	Letterkenny	Londonderry
R236–A40	Raphoe	Londonderry
N14–A38	Letterkenny	Strabane
R235–C675a	Castelfin	Castlederg
R232–A35	Donegal	Enniskillen (via Pettigoe)
R230–A46	Ballyshannon	Enniskillen (via Belleek)
N16–A4	Manorhamilton	Enniskillen (via Belcoo)
R202–A32	Swanlibar	Enniskillen
F183–A34	Clones	Newtownbutler
R187–B36	Monaghan	Rosslea
N2–A5	Monaghan	Aughnacloy
N12–A3	Monaghan	Armagh
R181–B32	Castleblaney	Keady
R177–A29	Dundalk	Newtownhamilton
R179–B30	Carrockmacross	Newry (via Crossmaglen)
N1–A1	Dundalk	Newry
R173–B79	Carlingford	Newry

Maps

Visitors who propose to drive off the main roads in Ireland should supplement the general map in this guide with more detailed maps of the areas they want to explore. The 1:250,000 holiday maps of Ireland, published by the Ordnance Survey, Dublin (four sheets, North, East, South and West), show every motorable road, with places of interest marked; additional holiday information on the reverse side.

Regulations

Throughout Ireland traffic travels on the left, with overtaking on the right. At a junction of two roads of equal importance, unless otherwise indicated, traffic coming from the right has priority. Other driving regulations and road signs are in line with European standards.

Seat belts

Seat belts must be worn by drivers and front-seat passengers and, where fitted, by rear-seat passengers. Children under 12 years of age may travel only in the rear.
  Motorcyclists and moped riders must wear helmets.

Drink-driving

Drink-driving laws are strict. The blood alcohol limit in the Republic of Ireland and Northern Ireland is 0.8 per mille.

Car parking

On roads with a 'no waiting' sign parking is prohibited. A continuous double yellow line means no parking, a single yellow line indicates that parking is permitted only at certain times.

Fines

Exceeding the speed limits by up to 19 miles per hour is punished in Ireland by fines between £15 and £150; failing to give priority or failing to obey a 'no overtaking' sign incurs a fine of up to £125. Parking tickets for illegal parking incur a penalty of up to £20 and drink-driving offences may cost over £1,000.

Motor fuel

At almost all filling stations throughout Ireland Diesel, Super Plus Unleaded (98 octane) and Unleaded (95 octane) can be obtained.

Speed limits

In the Republic of Ireland the maximum permitted speed in built-up areas is 30 mph, on most country roads 55 mph; on some stretches of road there may be a 40 mph limit, indicated by signs. In Northern Ireland

Distances in kilometres and miles	Athlone	Belfast	Cork	Donegal	Dublin	Dundalk	Galway	Kilkenny	Killarney	Limerick	Londonderry	Portlaoise	Roscommon	Sligo	Waterford	Wexford
Athlone	●	227	219	183	126	145	93	126	232	121	209	74	32	117	174	188
Belfast	141	●	424	180	167	84	306	284	436	323	117	253	224	206	333	309
Cork	136	264	●	402	257	325	209	148	87	105	428	174	251	336	126	187
Donegal	114	112	250	●	222	158	204	309	407	296	69	257	151	66	357	372
Dublin	78	104	160	138	●	85	219	117	309	198	237	84	146	217	158	142
Dundalk	90	52	202	98	53	●	238	198	352	241	156	151	151	167	243	227
Galway	58	190	130	127	136	148	●	172	193	105	272	150	82	138	220	253
Kilkenny	78	177	92	192	73	123	107	●	198	113	335	51	158	245	48	80
Killarney	144	271	54	253	192	219	120	123	●	111	441	225	264	343	193	254
Limerick	75	201	65	184	123	150	65	70	69	●	328	114	151	232	129	190
Londonderry	130	73	266	43	147	97	169	208	274	204	●	282	211	135	383	378
Portlaoise	46	157	108	160	52	94	93	32	140	71	175	●	106	191	100	114
Roscommon	20	139	156	94	91	94	51	98	164	94	131	66	●	85	208	222
Sligo	73	128	209	41	135	104	86.	152	213	144	84	119	53	●	293	307
Waterford	108	207	78	222	98	151	137	30	120	80	238	62	129	182	●	63
Wexford	117	192	116	231	88	141	157	50	158	118	235	71	138	191	39	●

the speed limit in built-up areas is 30 mph, unless a higher limit (40 or 50 mph) is indicated, on ordinary country roads 60 mph and on motorways 70 mph.

AA Breakdown Freephone Service
Tel. (1800) 667788 (Irish Republic); (0800) 887766 (Northern Ireland)

Breakdown

Opening Hours

➤ Pubs

Pubs

Mon.–Sat. 9 or 9.30am–5.30 or 6pm, Sun. 11am–1pm. Details of chemists open outside these hours are displayed in the windows of chemists' shops.

Chemists/ Pharmacies

Opening times vary in the Republic of Ireland, but are usually from 9 or 9.30am–5.30 or 6pm. There is an early closing day Wed. or Thu. (Outside Dublin). Shopping centres and supermarkets stay open until 8 or 9pm on Thu. and/or Fri. In some places shops remain open until 8 or 9pm on Sat. and even on Sun. in most places there is one food shop open.
    Shops in Belfast are open Mon.–Sat. 9am–5.30pm; many large shop-

Shops

ping centres stay open until 9pm. Smaller places in Northern Ireland have an early closing day during the week (variable) and generally every day at lunchtime.

Banks

Banks in the Republic of Ireland open Mon.–Fri. 10am–12.30pm, 1.30–3pm, in Dublin to 5pm on Thu. (Dublin Airport daily 8am–10pm; Shannon Airport daily 6.30am–5.30pm, in winter from 7.30am). Money can also be changed at the General Post Office in Dublin Mon.–Sat. 9.30am–6pm, Sun. 10.30am–5.30pm.

In Northern Ireland the banks are open Mon.–Fri. 10am–12.30pm, 1.30–3.30pm. In smaller places banks are often open only three days a week.

Petrol (gas) stations

These are usually open 9am–6pm. On Sun. they have restricted opening times. In Dublin and Cork some fuel (gas) stations are open 24 hours a day.

Post

Post offices

Post offices are usually open 9am–6pm in the Irish Republic (to 5.30pm and Sat. until 12.30pm in Northern Ireland).

Small country post offices close at lunchtime.

Postage rates

Letters from the Republic of Ireland to Britain and other EU countries cost 32p (44p to non-EU countries in Europe), postcards 28p (37p).

Letters to the United States and Canada cost 52p.

Letters and postcards from Northern Ireland cost 19p (second class) or 27p (first class) to Britain, 27p to EU countries (36p to non-EU countries in Europe) and 45p (for 10 g air mail) to the United States and Canada.

Postboxes in the Republic of Ireland are green.

Public Holidays

Republic of Ireland

January 1st (New Year's Day)
March 17th (St Patrick's Day)
Good Friday
Easter Monday
First Money in May (Labour Day)
First Monday in June (June Bank Holiday)
First Monday in August (August Bank Holiday)
Last Monday in October (Autumn Bank Holiday)
December 25th and 25th (Christmas and St Stephen's Day)

Northern Ireland

January 1st (New Year's Day)
March 17th (St Patrick's Day)
Good Friday
Easter Monday
First Monday in May (May Day Bank Holiday)
Last Monday or May or first Monday in June (Spring Bank Holiday)
July 12th (Orangemen's Day; commemorating the Battle of the Boyne, 1690)
Last Monday in August (August Bank Holiday)
December 25th and 26th (Christmas and Boxing Day)

Irish postbox

Irish telephone box

Movable holidays in Ireland (known as Bank Holidays) generally fall on a Monday.

Public Transport

In the Republic of Ireland the public transport authority responsible for running rail and bus services is the Córas Iompair Éireann (CIE). Modern trains run between Dublin and the larger towns, and there are bus services linking the smaller as well as the larger places. The principal routes are shown opposite.

Visitors can buy an 'Irish Explorer' ticket covering rail and bus travel (but not in the central areas of Dublin, Cork, Limerick and Galway). Information about this ticket can be obtained from all CIE offices and larger railway stations. Information on timetables: tel. (01) 8366222, web site www.irishrail.ie.

Northern Ireland also has an extensive network of rail and bus services, with particular good bus links between towns not served by the railway system.

Special tickets offer substantial savings, such as the 'Emerald Card' which allows unlimited travel by bus and train for 8 or 15 days in Ireland and Northern Ireland. Further information is available from main railway stations (and bus stations in the case of the 'Emerald Card') in the Republic and Northern Ireland.

Republic of
Ireland

Northern Ireland

Rail, bus and ferry services in Ireland

—— Rail services

—— Buses (all year)

- - - Buses (summer only)

- - - Ferries

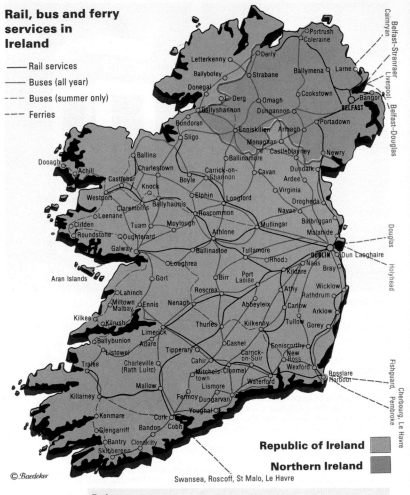

Republic of Ireland

Northern Ireland

© Baedeker

Swansea, Roscoff, St Malo, Le Havre

Pubs

Pubs serve alcoholic drinks of all kinds, which are normally ordered at the bar and paid for immediately. It is an easy matter to get into a conversation with local customers; if a drink is offered it is usual for this to be reciprocated.

Most pubs in the Republic of Ireland are open weekdays 10.30am–11.30pm in summer and until 11pm in winter. On Sundays the hours are 12.30–2pm, 5–11pm. Since August 2000 pubs may stay open all day until late in the evening. However, 'closing time' is strictly enforced.

In Northern Ireland pubs are open weekdays 11.30am–11pm, Sundays 12.30–2pm, 7–10pm.

In the so-called 'Singing Pubs' singers and instrumentalists perform without pay and customers can join in the songs.

The following is a selection of typical pubs in the Republic of Ireland and Northern Ireland. In many of the oldest pubs traditional ballads are often heard.

The **Crosskeys Inn** Toome, Crosskeys; tel. (028) 79650694 (music pub with Saturday sessions; often Sundays and Wednesdays as well)

The **Crown Liquor Saloon** 44 Great Victoria Street; tel. (028) 90325368 (Victorian furnishing with wood-panelled partitions, tinted glass and tiles)

Duke of York Commercial Court; tel. (028) 90241062 (one of the oldest bars in Belfast, beautifully restored, live music in the evenings)

The Liverpool Lounge 11 Donegal Quay; tel. (028) 90321796 (traditional music sessions on Saturdays and Mondays)

Madden's 1 Berry Street; tel. (028) 90244114 (pub with authentic ambiance, restored and decorated with gas lamps, music nearly every evening)

Whites Tavern High Street; tel. (028) 90243080 (traditional pub; Printer's Lounge recalls that the oldest newspaper in the town was founded here)

The Bailey 2 Duke Street, Dublin 2 (a meeting place for Joyce enthusiasts and for yuppies)

The Brazen Head 20 Lower Bridge Street, Dublin 8; tel. (01) 6795186 (Dublin's oldest pub, dating from the 17th c.; evening music sessions)

Davy Byrne's 2 Duke Street, Dublin 2; tel. (01) 6775217 (another pub mentioned in Joyce's *Ulysses*)

Doheny and Nesbitt 5 Lower Baggot Street, Dublin 2; tel. (01) 6762945 (interior unchanged from the last century, small and smoky)

The Duke 9 Duke Street, Dublin 2; tel. (01) 6799553 (meeting point for those interested in literature)

Hughe's Bar Dublin 7, 19 Chancery Street; tel. (01) 8726540 (traditional dances performed every Monday, Wednesday and Thursday)

The International Bar 23 Wicklow Street, corner of St Andrew Street, Dublin 2; tel. (01) 6779250 (blues music)

The Irish Whiskey Corner 77 Bow Street, Dublin 7; tel. (01) 8725566 (museum of whiskey with tasting room)

Mooney's 1 Lower Abbey Street, Dublin 1 (one of the well-known pubs frequented by James Joyce's character Leopold Bloom)

Kitty O'Shea's 23–25 Upper Grand Canal Street, Ballsbridge, Dublin 4 (live music daily; also well known for brunch at the weekends)

The Long Hall 51 South Great George's Street, Dublin 2 (furnished in Victorian style)

Mulligan's 8 Poolbeg Street, Dublin 2 (antique furnishing; another pub mentioned by Joyce)

O'Donoghue's 15 Merrion Row, Dublin 2; tel. (6) 607194 (birthplace of the Dubliners, therefore much visited)

The Old Stand Wicklow Street, Dublin 2; tel. (01) 6777220 (traditional pub, cosy atmosphere with quality wood panelling; popular with business people)

Slattery's 129 Chapel Street, Dublin 2 (well known for traditional Irish music)

Stag's Head Dame Court, Dublin 2 (interior in late 19th/early 20th c. style)

Abbey Tavern Howth

Jack O'Rourke's 15 Main Street, Blackrock

The Purty Kitchen Old Dunleary Road, Dun Laoghaire (dating from 1728)

Derragarra Inn Butlersbridge

Durty Nelly's Bunratty

Restaurants

Gus O'Connor's Doolin Tel. (065) 74168 (family owned since 1832; sessions on Fridays, Saturdays and Sundays)

Co. Cork **The Lobby** Cork City 1 Union Quay; tel. (021) 319307 (blues sessions on Monday evenings; Tuesdays and Fridays traditional Irish music)
Dan O'Connell's Slieve Luchra, Knocknagree; tel. (064) 56238 (live music on Friday and Sunday evenings, particularly the region's special fiddle style)

Co. Donegal **Huidi Beag's** Bunbeg; tel. (074) 32316 (traditional sessions every Monday)

Co. Galway **The Crane** Galway City, 2 Sea Road; tel. (091) 587419 (Irish music)
Roísín Dubh Galway City, Dominic Street; tel. (091) 586540 (live music)
Taylor's Galway City, Dominic Street; tel. (091) 587239 (traditional music)
Day's Pub Inishbofin; tel. (095) 45829 (sessions at weekends in summer and at Easter; can be reached by the Kings of Cleggan ferry)

Co. Kerry **An Droiched Beag** Dingle, Lower Main Street; tel. (066) 51723 (live music in the evenings)

Co. Limerick **Collin's Bar** Main Street, Adare
Bell Tavern 11 Broad Street, Limerick

Co. Louth **Monasterboice Inn** Monasterboice (near Drogheda)

Co. Mayo **Matt Molloy's** Westport, Bridge Street; tel. (098) 26655 (music pub)

Co. Offaly **Hough's Bar** Main Street, Banagher

Co. Sligo **Hargadon's** O'Connell Street, Sligo
Mac Lynn's Old Market Street, Sligo

Co. Tipperary **Ivy Bridge Bar** Main Street, Newport
The Monk's Bar Mitchel Street, Thurles

Co. Waterford **Katie Reilly's Kitchen** Tramore Road, Waterford
Seanachie Dungarvan

Co. Wicklow **Laragh Inn** Laragh

Restaurants

Menus
The restaurants listed are in three categories according to their charges.

The lowest category (Cat. 3) indicates restaurants where a three-course meal can be obtained for about the equivalent of £10 sterling; in restaurants of the middle category (Cat. 2) a similar meal costs up to £20 and in the first category (Cat. 1) prices are somewhat higher.

Medieval banquets
In a few old castles so-called medieval banquets (➤ Food and Drink) take place on some evenings.

Pub grub
Modest meals and snacks are served in pubs and are designated as 'pub grub'.

Alcohol licence
It is sensible to note the type of licence held by a restaurant before going in for a meal. 'Full licence' means that during the licensing hours a full selection of drinks is on sale. 'Wine licence' means that only wine can be served.

Restaurants in the Republic of Ireland

The Chalet　　　　　　　　　　　　　　　　　　　Achill Island
Keel; tel. (098) 43157; Cat. 2.
Known for its fresh fish; speciality brill.

The Mustard Seed　　　　　　　　　　　　　　　　Adare
Tel. (061) 396451; Cat. 1.
Very good Irish and international cooking; a picture-book cottage.

Shiro　　　　　　　　　　　　　　　　　　　　　Ahakista
Ahakista; tel. (027) 67030; Cat. 1.
Japanese eating house with family atmosphere; view of Dunmanus Bay.

Ard Einne　　　　　　　　　　　　　　　　　　　Aran Islands
Inishmore; tel. (099) 61126; Cat. 3.
Beautifully situated guest house with wonderful views.

Aran Fisherman
Kilroan, Inishmore; tel. (099) 61104, fax (099) 61225; Cat. 2.
Restaurant near harbour with large selection of fish, meat, pasta and
vegetarian dishes.

Swiss Barn Speciality Restaurant　　　　　　　　Ballina
Foxford Road, tel. (096) 21117; Cat. 2.
Specialities: fondues, lobster and steak tartare.

The Mustard Seed at Echo Lodge　　　　　　　　Ballingarry
Ballingarry; tel. (069) 68508, fax (069) 68511; Cat. 1.
Interesting surroundings in a converted monastery with mementoes
from many countries; exquisite cooking and a large range of Irish
whiskey and Scotch.

Mac Closkey's　　　　　　　　　　　　　　　　　Bunratty
Bunratty House Mews; tel. (061) 36408; Cat. 1.
Exclusive restaurant in the vaults of a Georgian house; excellent Irish
cooking.

Rusheen Lodge Guesthouse　　　　　　　　　　　Burren
Knocknagrough, Ballyvaughan; tel. (065) 77092l; Cat. 2.
Pretty country guest house about 2 miles outside Burren; Irish cooking.

Scarriff Inn Guest House　　　　　　　　　　　　Caherdaniel
Caherdaniel; tel. (066) 75132; Cat. 2.
Direct on the Ring of Kerry, restaurant with marvellous view of the sea.

The Old School House　　　　　　　　　　　　　　Cahirsiveen
Cahersiveen; tel. (066) 72426; Cat. 2.

Chez Hans　　　　　　　　　　　　　　　　　　　Cashel
Rockside Cashel; tel. (062) 61177; Cat. 1.
In a restored 19th c. church; well known for its excellent seafood cre-
ations.

O'Grady's Seafood Restaurant　　　　　　　　　Clifden
Clifden; tel. (095) 21450, fax (095) 21994; Cat. 2.
Speciality restaurant for seafood and salmon.

Blackrock Castle　　　　　　　　　　　　　　　　Cork
Blackrock; tel. (021) 357414; Cat. 2.
A restored castle on the north bank of the river outside town; stylish
decor and view over the River Lee.

Cliffords Restaurant
18 Dyke Parade; tel. (021) 275333; Cat. 1.
Popular restaurant, modern cuisine.

Eastern Tandoori
1 Emmet Place; tel. (021) 272020; Cat. 2.
Indian cuisine with several awards; peaceful ambiance.

Jacques Restaurant
Phoenix Street; tel. (021) 277387; Cat. 1.
Small French restaurant in the centre of Cork, delicious hors d'oeuvres
and traditional desserts.

The Minstrel
Maylor Street (Patrick St); tel. (021) 357414; Cat. 3.
Breakfast and simple snacks; the soups and salads are high rec-
ommended.

The Tea House
Fitzgerald's Park, in front of the museum; Cat. 3.
Light dishes such as soups, toasted snacks, pâté and cake; situated at
entrance to Fitzgerald's Park.

The Wine Vault
Western Road; Cat. 2.
Large bar with restaurant, stylish decor, opposite Jurys Hotel.

Dingle   **Doyle's Seafood Restaurant**
John Street; tel. (066) 51174; Cat. 2.
Excellent fish restaurant; speciality: lobster.

Donegal   **Diamond in the Highland Centre Hotel**
Tel. (073) 21027; Cat. 2.
Excellent restaurant with international cuisine; views of Donegal Castle
and the Bay.

Dublin   **Aisling**
Shelbourne Hotel, 27 St Stephen's Green, Dublin 2; tel. (01) 6766471, fax
(01) 6661600, email shelbourneinfo@forte-hotels.com, web site
www.shelbourne.ie; Cat. 1.
Traditional Irish cooking; elegant surroundings in Dublin's most beautiful hotel.

Ante Room
20 Lower Baggot Street, Dublin 2; tel. (01) 67621; Cat. 2.
Cosy cellar restaurant in Maguire's Pub; specialises in seafood.

Bewley's Oriental Café
78–79 Grafton Street, Dublin 2; tel. (01) 6355470, fax (01) 6799237; Cat. 3.
Popular coffee house with genuine Dublin atmosphere, right in the
shopping centre.

Café en Seine
40 Dawson Street, Dublin 2; tel. (01) 6774369; Cat. 2.
Coffee house with a relaxed atmosphere, jazz on Sundays.

Chapter One
18–19 Parnell Square North; tel. (01) 8732266, fax (01) 8732330; Cat. 2.
Pleasant restaurant in the historic surroundings of the Dublin Writers'
Centre on a Georgian town square.

Bewley's Café in Grafton Street, Dublin

The Chocolate Bar
Harcourt Street, Vaults, Dublin 2; tel. (01) 4780225; Cat. 3.
Blend of café, pub and disco in the Findlaters Wine Merchants building;
speciality giant sandwiches/rolls.

Clarence Hotel Restaurant
6–8 Wellington Quay, Dublin 2; tel. (01) 6709000, fax (01) 6707800; Cat. 2.
Old hotel-restaurant in the Temple Bar district, bought and renovated by
the Irish rock group U2.

The Commons
85–86 St Stephen's Green, Dublin 2; tel. (01) 4780530, fax (01) 4780551;
Cat. 1.
Elegant restaurant in Newman House; French cuisine with Irish influence, fine wines.

Cooke's Café
14 South William Street, Dublin 2; tel. (01) 6790536/7/8, fax (01) 6790546;
Cat. 2.
'New age' restaurant, Mediterranean-Californian cuisine; known for its
chocolate cake.

Davy Byrnes
21 Duke Street, Dublin 2; tel. (01) 6775217; Cat. 3.
Pub and restaurant, specialising in fish, prawns and oysters.

L'Ecrivain Restaurant
109 Lower Baggot Street, Dublin 2; tel. (01) 6611919, fax (01) 6610617;
Cat. 1.

Exclusive restaurant with French and Irish cooking, friendly atmosphere, small terrace.

Ernie's
Mulberry Gardens, Donnybrook, Dublin 4; tel. (01) 2693300, fax (01) 2693260; Cat. 1.
Luxury restaurant with inner courtyard and water features, specialising in Irish fish and game dishes with a French touch.

Fitzers National Gallery Restaurant
National Gallery, Merrion Square West, Dublin; Cat. 3.
Pleasant small restaurant reached through the National Gallery.

Kitty's Kaboodle
14 Merriot Row, Dublin 2; tel. (01) 6623350; Cat. 3.
Light Italian dishes such as pizza, pasta and garlic bread, low prices

Kitty O'Shea's
23 Upper Grand Canal Street, Dublin 4; tel. (01) 6609965; Cat. 2.
Typical Irish cooking, idyllic inner courtyard restaurant.

The Oliver St John Gogarty
Irish Bar & Restaurant, 57–58 Fleet Street, Temple Bar, Dublin 2; tel. (01) 6711822; Cat. 2.
Traditional Irish cooking; brunch and Irish breakfast on Sunday mornings.

Patrick Guilbaud Restaurant
46 James Place, Dublin 2; tel. (01) 764192; Cat. 1.
Delicious French gourmet dishes; the building was designed by the Irish architect Arthur Gibney.

Roly's Bistro
7 Ballsbridge Terrace, Dublin 4; tel. (01) 6682611; Cat. 2.
Lovely restaurant with relaxed atmosphere; Irish cooking, popular for its fish dishes.

La Stampa
36 Dawson Street, Dublin 2; tel. (01) 6772119; Cat. 2.
Good restaurant with clever dishes influenced by Irish, Italian and Japanese cuisine.

Thomas Read
4 Parliament Street, Dublin 2; tel. (01) 6771487; Cat. 3.
Mixture of bar, bistro and restaurant, light international dishes; named after the famous knife and scissors shop – the oldest shop in Dublin.

Thornton's
1 Portobello Road, Dublin 8; tel. (01) 4549067, fax (01) 4532947, email thornton.k.@isite.ie; Cat. 1.
Luxury restaurant with modern Irish cooking.

Turk's Head Chop House
Parliament Street, Dublin 2; tel. (01) 6792606; Cat. 2.
Light dishes and fish specialities in a restaurant styled after the Spanish art-nouveau architect Gaudí.

Dun Laoghaire | **Morels Bistro**
18 Glasthule Road; tel. (01) 2300210, fax (01) 2300466; Cat. 2.
Pleasant restaurant with Mediterranean cooking, near to sea.

Na Mara
1 Harbour Road; tel. (01) 2806767; Cat. 1.
Excellent fish restaurant in the old station building of Dun Laoghaire.

Blairs Cove   Durrus
Tel. (027) 61127, fax (027) 61487, email blairscove@tinet.ie; Cat. 1.
Elegant restaurant in a Georgian mansion.

GBC Bistro & Coffeeshop   Galway
Williamsgate Street; tel. (091) 563087, fax (091) 569263, email
gbc@tinet.ie; Cat. 2.
Originally specialising in baking, now the menu is very diverse.

The Hungry Grass
Cross Street; tel. (091) 65719; Cat. 3.
Popular café with organic cooking, vegetarian food and delicious sand-
wiches.

McDonagh's Seafood Bar
2 Quay Street; tel. (091) 565001; Cat. 2.
A very popular restaurant with the Irish, specialising in seafood.

The Oyster Room
In the Great Southern Hotel, Eyre Square; tel. (091) 564041; Cat. 1.
Top restaurant with a view of Eyre Square.

King Sitric Fish Restaurant   Howth
East Pier; tel. (01) 8325235; fax (01) 83923442, email info@kingsitric.ie;
Cat. 1.
Restaurant on two floors with a seafood and oyster bar, unusual wines;
situated at the tip of the Howth Peninsula outside Dublin.

Park Hotel Kenmare   Kenmare
Kenmare; tel. (064) 41200, fax (064) 41402, email phkenmare@iol.ie, web
site www.parkkenmare.com; Cat. 1.
Beautiful situation on Ring of Kerry with exquisite Irish food.

Kilkenny Shop   Kilkenny
Castle Yard; tel. (056) 22118; Cat. 3.
Coffee shop with delicious snacks, in historical surroundings.

Kyteler's Inn
Kieran Street; tel. (056) 21064; Cat. 2.
Medieval building with courtyard and vaulted cellar (➤ Sights from A to
Z, Kilkenny).

Lacken House
Dublin Road; tel. (056) 661085; Cat. 1.
One of the best restaurants in the area with home Irish cooking.

Parliament House
24–25 Parliament Street; tel. (056) 63666; Cat. 2.
Steaks and seafood dishes.

Crock o'Gold Restaurant   Killarney
19 High Street; tel. (064) 32432; Cat. 2.
Popular for its steak and seafood dishes.

Hotel Dunloe Castle
Beaufort; tel. (064) 44111, fax (064) 44583, email khl@iol.ie, web site
www.iol.ie/khl; Cat. 2.
Irish and international cuisine; views of the Gap of Dunloe.

Attractive restaurant façades in Kenmare

Dingle's Restaurant
40 New Street; tel. (064) 31079, email dingles@tinet.ie; Cat. 1.
Charming restaurant with varied cuisine.

Foley's Seafood & Steak Restaurant
23 High Street; tel. (064) 31217, fax (064) 364683; Cat. 2.
Pleasant restaurant with good service.

Limerick

Jasmine Palace
O'Connell Street; tel. (061) 412484, fax (061) 410201; Cat. 2.
Best Chinese restaurant in town; Cantonese cooking.

Papa Gino Pizza Parlour
Denmark Street; tel. (061) 418945; Cat. 2.
Simple decor, delicious Italian cooking, including takeaway pizzas.

Silver Plate
74 O'Connell Street; tel. (061) 316311; Cat. 1.
Fine French cooking in Georgian ambiance; speciality fish dishes.

Moycullen

Drimcong House Restaurant
Tel. (091) 85115; Cat. 1.
Luxury restaurant with creative dishes in a 17th c. mansion.

Nenagh

Gurthalougha House, Ballinderry
Tel. (067) 22080; Cat. 1.
Candlelight dinner in a country house; reservation necessary.

Shanagarry

Ballymaloe House
Shanagarry; tel. (021) 652531, fax (021) 652021, email bmaloe@iol.ie;
Cat. 1.

Elegant restaurant in a 14th c. castle; organic vegetables and fruit; specialities prawns, ham cooked in whiskey and 'black' sole. Cooking courses are organised.

Beezie's Dining Saloon Sligo
O'Connell Street; tel. (071) 45030; Cat. 2.
Lunch and supper in a typical pub atmosphere.

Bonne Chère
High Street; tel. (071) 42014; Cat. 2.
Very popular with families.

Reveries
Rosses Point, north-west of the town; Cat. 1.
Modern Irish cooking, speciality freshly caught salmon.

Truffles
11 The Mall; tel. (071) 44226; Cat. 3.
Specialises in delicious pizzas.

Dwyers Waterford
8 Mary Street; tel. (051) 77478; Cat. 2.
Sophisticated international cuisine; stylish decor in a former police station.

Angler's Rest Westport
Castlebar Street; tel. (098) 26412; Cat. 2.
Solid restaurant in a small hotel; the menu includes vegetarian dishes.

Quay Cottage
The Harbour (at the entrance to Westport House); tel. (098) 26412; Cat. 2.
Fish specialities, vegetarian dishes; ideal for guests interested in seafaring.

O'Mulleys
Bridge Street; tel. (098) 27308; Cat. 3.
Draws young people, organic food.

The Granary Wexford
Near Westgate; tel. (053) 22196; Cat. 2.
Specialises in fish and seafood.

Restaurants in Northern Ireland

Glassdrumman Lodge Annalong
85 Mill Road; tel. (028) 43768451; Cat. 1.
Situated in a large estate before the Mourne Mountains in silhouette; views of the coast. Specialities: salmon and shrimps.

Galgorm Manor Ballymena
1 mile outside Ballymena; tel. (028) 91852500; Cat. 2.
Modern Irish cooking with French influence.

Lodge Hotel Bangor
10 Estate Hotel, Clandeboye; tel. (028) 91852500; Cat. 2.
Good Irish cooking with local produce; situated near Blackwood Golf Course.

Deanes on the Square
7 Station Square, Helen's Bay; tel. (028) 91852841; Cat. 1.
Excellent international cuisine with Asian and Oriental influence; situated in a former station built in the style of a Scottish castle.

Shanks
The Blackwood, Crawfordsburn Road; tel. (028) 91853313; Cat. 1.
One of the best restaurants in Northern Ireland, attentive service; situated near Blackwood Golf Course.

Belfast

Culloden
Bangor Road, Belfast BT18 0EX; tel. (028) 90425223; Cat. 1.
Stylish decor in a former country mansion; Irish cooking with European influence.

Rayanne Country House
60 Desmesne Road, Belfast BT18 9EX; tel. (028) 90425859; Cat. 1.
Attentive service in a small Victorian country manor; fine Irish cooking.

Roscoff
7 Lesley House, Shaftesbury Square, Belfast BT2 7DB; tel. (028) 90331532; Cat. 1.
Luxury restaurant in the centre of town, fine Irish cooking.

The Strand Wine Bar & Restaurant
12 Stramillies Road; tel. (028) 90682266; Cat. 2.
Very good Irish cooking; pleasant service and relaxed atmosphere.

Thompson's
47 Arthur Street; tel. (028) 90323762; Cat. 2.
Highly recommended; fish, seafood and steaks.

Coleraine

The Buck's Head
77 Main Street; tel. (028) 70351858; Cat. 1.
18th c. pub with beer garden and its own greenhouse; traditional Irish cooking.

Dundrum

MacDuff's
Blackhill, 112 Killeague Road; tel. (028) 70868433; Cat. 1.
Traditional country-house cooking with modern influence; speciality game.

Londonderry

Brendan's Dinner
154 Spencer Road; tel. (028) 77744875; Cat. 2.
Good restaurant with Irish cooking.

Radisson Roe Park Hotel
Limavady; tel. (028) 77722212, fax (028) 77722313; Cat. 2.
Good Irish cooking with a French influence.

Newtownards

Eastern Tandoori
16 Castle Street; tel. (028) 91819541; Cat. 2.
Indian restaurant; delicious cooking, and some very good tandoori dishes.

Portaferry

Portaferry Hotel
10 The Strand; tel. (028) 42728231, fax (028) 42728999; Cat. 2.
Fine international cuisine.

Portrush

Ramore
The Harbour; tel. (028) 70824313; Cat. 1.
Popular restaurant on the coast, specialising in fish and seafood, fine wines.

Riding

Ireland is ideal for a riding holiday, whether as a beginner or an experienced rider. Package riding holidays are offered by some travel firms.

Riding schools organise courses for beginners, with experienced instructors. There are also courses in jumping and dressage – usually lasting a fortnight – for more experienced riders.

Another possibility is a pony-trekking holiday, usually lasting a week, with perhaps four hours spent in the saddle each day. In the Irish Republic the most interesting treks are in Connemara, on the Dingle Peninsula, Co. Sligo, and near Killarney.

Pony-trekking

Addresses and information about riding holidays in the Irish Republic can be obtained from:

Riding holidays

Equestrian Holidays Ireland
c/o Clonshire Equestrian Centre, Adare, Co. Limerick
Tel. (061) 396770, fax (061) 396726, email info@clonshire.iol.ie, web site www.ehi.ie.

The Northern Ireland Tourist Board issues a leaflet on pony trekking holidays.

Ireland is a great horse-breeding country, and horse racing is a very popular spectator sport. There are more than 250 race meetings every year on the country's 28 racecourses. The sport is promoted by the Racing Board and supervised by the Turf Club. Ireland's best-known racecourse is the Curragh in Co. Kildare.

Horse racing

The Dublin Horse Show, run by the Royal Dublin Society every year at the beginning of August, offers a full programme of events. It is also the largest market for Irish bloodstock and attracts numerous foreign buyers.

Dublin Horse Show

Souvenirs

Among the most popular souvenirs of a visit to Ireland are hand-woven tweed, fine lace, hand-knitted jerseys, pipes, china, pottery, silver and hand-cut crystal.

Fine antiques can be found in antique shops, at auctions and in flea markets at Dublin, Cork and Limerick.

Sport

The desire to establish Irish independence from Britain in sport led to the establishment in 1884 of the Gaelic Athletic Association. Gaelic football, which combines features of association football and rugby, was also actively promoted. Football finals are in Dublin on the third Sunday in September.

Irish sports

There is also a special Irish form of bowling, fought out with a heavy steel ball on quiet country roads in the south of Ireland between two towns or villages.

The great Irish game, however, and one mentioned in ancient legend and regarded by many as the fastest game played on grass, is hurling, played by teams of 15 men with hurling sticks, which are rather like hockey sticks but with broader blades. The All Ireland Hurling Final, at

Irish Derby: an annual social occasion

Croke Park in Dublin on the first Saturday in September, is watched by over 80,000 fanatical spectators.

Greyhound racing is also a popular spectator sport.

See Climbing and Hill Walking, Fishing, Golf, Hunting and Shooting, Riding, Water Sports.

Sport for the disabled

The Irish Tourist Board produces a guide for the disabled, with the addresses of organisations and clubs (including the Irish Wheelchair Association and the National League of the Blind) which will advise disabled people interested in sport.

Telephone

Local, long-distance and international calls can be made from public telephone boxes. A reduced tariff operates between 6pm and 8am and all day on Saturdays and Sundays. The more modern telephone boxes accept coins of 5, 10, 20, 50p and £1; from others a phonecard can be used in denominations of £2, £3.50, £8 and £16. These are obtainable from post offices and various shops.

International telephone codes

From the United Kingdom to the Republic of Ireland: 00 353
From the Republic of Ireland to the United Kingdom: 00 44
From the Republic of Ireland to Belfast: 00 4428

From the United States or Canada to the Republic of Ireland: 011 353
From the Republic to the United States or Canada: 00 1

Greyhound racing

From the United States or Canada to Northern Ireland: 011 44
From Northern Ireland to the United States or Canada: 00 1

The international code is followed by the local dialling code followed by the customer's number; if there is a zero at the beginning of the local dialling code this should be omitted.

The following are the local codes (with initial zero omitted for some of the major towns and cities in Ireland; others can be found in the international section of your telephone directory or web site www.golden pages.ie:

Athlone: 902, Belfast: 28, Cork: 21, Donegal: 73, Dublin: 1, Galway: 91, Killarney: 64, Killkenny: 56, Limerick: 61, Londonderry: 28, Sligo: 71, Wexford: 53.

Daytime public telephone calls to the United Kingdom are charged at the rate of IR£0.10 per minute, but cheaper calls are available 6pm–8am each day, at weekends and public holidays.

Direct dial

Daytime public telephone calls to the United States and Canada are charged at the rate of IR£0.12 per minute. All international calls are subject to a minimum call charge.

Time

The whole of Ireland observes Greenwich Mean Time, which is 5 hours ahead of New York time. Summer Time is one hour in advance of Greenwich Mean Time and is in force from late March to late October.

Tipping

In most hotels and restaurants a service charge of 10, 12 or 15 per cent is automatically added to the bill. Otherwise a tip of between 10 and 15 per cent can be given.

Travel Documents

British citizens do not, of course, require a passport to go to Northern Ireland and do not need one to enter the Irish Republic if they are travelling direct from Britain. Nationals of other countries require a passport or, in some cases, a national identity card.

Vehicle
documents

Visitors driving their own car should carry their national driving licence and car registration document, as well as a Green Card (international insurance certificate) obtainable from their normal insurers of the vehicle.

In Northern Ireland and in the Republic of Ireland foreign cars must display an International Distinguishing Sign of the approved type and design.

Visitors with Disabilities

Further
information

The Irish Tourist Board publishes a free booklet, *Discover Ireland*, which lists hotels and guest houses with facilities for the disabled and wheelchair users. The Northern Ireland Tourist Board's booklet *Accessible*

Yacht basin in Dingle

Accommodation in Northern Ireland lists places to stay and things to see.

National Rehabilitation Board
25 Clyde Road, Ballsbridge, Dublin 4
Tel. (01) 6684181

Disability Action
2 Annadale Avenue, Belfast BT7 3JH.
Tel. (028) 90491011, fax (028) 90491627

Water Sports

The Atlantic Ocean and the Irish Sea offer excellent sailing waters. In addition, sailing on the inland lakes, above all in south-west Ireland, is increasing in popularity. Around the Irish coast are numerous sailing centres and schools for both beginners and the more experienced.

Sailing

Sailing packages can be booked. Operators can be found in the 'Green Holiday Pages' of the Irish Tourist Board, or can be obtained from:

Irish Sailing Association
3 Park Road, Dun Laoghaire, Co. Dublin
Tel. (01) 2800239, fax (01) 2807558, email isa@iol.ie, web site www.sail
ing.org/isa

For Northern Ireland contact:

Sail Northern Ireland
The Marina, Rodger Quay, Carrickfergus BT38 8BE
Tel. (028) 93366666

Boats can be hired at the following sailing centres:

Hiring boats

Baltimore Sailing School
Baltimore, Co. Cork

Irish National Sailing School
115 Lower Georges Street, Dun Laoghaire, Co. Dublin

Fingall Sailing School
Upper Strand, Malahide, Co. Dublin

Galway Sailing Centre
Oranmore, Co. Galway

Glenans Irish Sailing Centre
28 Marrion Square, Dublin 2

International Sailing Centre
5 East Beach, Cobh, Co. Cork

Shannon Sailing
New Harbor, Dromineer, Co. Tipperary

Shannonside Sailing Centre
Killaloe, Co. Clare

When to Go

Water-skiing

There are opportunities for water-skiing on loughs (lakes) and rivers and especially off flat coastal areas. The necessary equipment and boats can be hired at many places (including Farran, Castleblayney, Macroom, Sligo).

Surfing

Surfing can be practised in Ireland anywhere there is water: the necessary breeze can usually be relied on. Surfboards can be hired at many places and courses for beginners and the more experienced are available (e.g. at Kinsale, Killaloe, Rosslare, Caherdaniel, Schull and Carlingford). Information:

Chris Sparrow
Irish Windsurfing Association
Naas, Co. Kildare
Tel. (045) 875168

For experts Ireland's west coast offers excellent conditions for surfing throughout the year. Waves of 3–13 ft high can be expected (especially at Doolin, Strandhill and Rossnowlagh).

Scuba diving

Irish coastal waters present ideal conditions for scuba diving. The warm Gulf Stream keeps up the temperature of the water so that it is relatively pleasant even at some depth. At certain points the coast falls steeply down, offering a variety of submarine fauna and flora. Some diving centres have equipment for hire (e.g. Bay View Hotel on Clare Island, Dolphin Diving in Ballyvaughan, Valentia Diving Centre on Valentia Island, Skellig Aquatic Dive Centre in Caherdaniel).

Rowing

Ireland's numerous rivers and loughs also provide ample scope for rowing. Information:

P Casey
Irish Amateur Rowing Union
House of Sport, Long Mile Road, Walkinstown, Dublin 12
Tel. (01) 4509831, fax (01) 4502805, email infor@iaru.ie

Canoeing

The Irish loughs and rivers offer opportunities both for canoe touring and white-water canoeing. The best rivers are the Liffey, Barrow, Nore, Boyne, Slaney, Lee, Shannon, Suir and Munster Blackwater. Canoes can be hired. Information:

Michael Scanlan
Irish Canoe Union
House of Sport, Long Mile Road, Walkinstown, Dublin 12
Tel. (01) 4509838/4501633, fax (01) 4601064, email office@irishcanoeunion.ie

When to Go

The best time to go to Ireland is between the end of March and the end of October. July and August, the warmest months, are best for seaside holidays but the popular places may be crowded. Autumn can also be very pleasant, since the weather in September and October tends to be mild and dry. Visitors who can be flexible in their choice of dates should visit Ireland in May or June when there is the greatest chance of sunny weather.

Although, due to the oceanic climate, it is never particularly cold in Ireland, there is a good deal of rain. As a rule, however, it takes the form of showers and does not last long.

➤ Facts and Figures, Climate

Youth Hostels

Youth hostels offer overnight accommodation primarily for young people at reasonable cost. In the Republic of Ireland the Irish Youth Hostel Association (An Óige) maintains 36 hostels. An international youth hostel card must be produced; advance booking is advisable. Charges for accommodation depend on the season, location of hostel and the age of the visitor, varying from IR£3–7 (Dublin up to IR£9).

For information and lists of hostels, apply to the relevant association:

Republic of Ireland:
Irish Youth Hostel Association (An Óige)
61 Mountjoy Square, Dublin 7
Tel. (01) 8304555, fax (01) 8305808, email anoige@iol.ie

Northern Ireland:
Hostelling International Northern Ireland (HINI)
22 Donegall Road, Belfast BT12 5JN
Tel. (028) 90324733, fax (028) 90439699

Index

Index

Index

Source of Illustrations

Front cover: AA Photo Library (S McBride)
Back cover: AA Photo Library (M Short)

Archiv für Kunst und Geschichte: 45 (middle)
Anthony Verlag (Löhr): 132
AP: 45 (right)
Baedeker Archiv: 327 (2x)
Bildagentur Schuster: 133
Bilderdienst Süddeutscher Verlag: 42 (left)
Birgit Borowski: 3 (top), 6 (bottom), 7 (top), 11, 27, 28, 51, 57 (bottom), 68, 74, 82, 90, 94, 106 (2x), 106, 130 (right), 142 (2x), 143, 145 (2x), 147, 155, 170, 175, 179, 183, 189, 202, 203 (2x), 207, 209 (2x), 216, 229, 230, 231, 233, 236, 257, 261 (left), 270, 271, 276, 282, 285, 291, 300, 301, 310, 329, 353 (2x), 362 (2x)
Ina Brödel: 8, 10, 13 (3x top and bottom left), 25, 29, 52, 53, 61, 62 (3x), 77, 87, 107, 116 (2x), 128, 146, 149, 160, 161 (2x), 167 (2x), 172, 174, 176, 178, 180 (2x), 184, 190, 192, 193 (2x), 200 (2x), 204, 215 (2x), 235 (2x), 258, 261 (right), 269, 284 (2x), 292, 359, 368
Fotoagentur Helga Lade: 1, 5 (left), 6 (top), 7 (bottom left), 50, 125
Green Studio: 59
Klaus Hartmann: 15, 76, 130 (left), 138, 164, 195, 238
Historia-Photo: 43 (2x middle and right), 46 (left)
Reinhard Hoene: 113, 115
Renata Holzbachová: 13 (bottom right), 16, 32, 71, 117, 122, 135, 137, 151, 166 (2x), 206 (2x), 218, 222, 298 (2x), 303, 305, 324, 366 (2x), 367
IFA Bilderteam: 3 (bottom), 5 (right), 6/7, 7 (bottom right), 100
Irish Tourist Board, Dublin: 239
Irish Tourist Board, Frankfurt: 277
Kai Ulrich Müller: 37, 72, 97, 187, 247 (2x), 248, 252
Klaus Thiele: 211
L Wüchner: 14

Imprint

168 photographs, 38 maps and plans, 1 large country map

German text: Birgit Borowski, Achim Bourmer, Rainer Eisenschmid, Peter Harbison, Wilhelm Jensen, Brian Reynolds, Margit Wagner, Beate Szerelmy

General direction: Rainer Eisenschmid, Baedeker Ostfildern

Cartography: Franz Kaiser, Sindelfingen: Franz Huber, Munich; Mairs Geographischer Verlag, Ostfildern (large fold-out map)

Editorial work English edition: g-and-w PUBLISHING, Wina Gunn

English translation: James Hogarth, David Cocking

English revision: Carol Porter

4th English edition 2001

© Baedeker Ostfildern
Original German edition 2000

© Automobile Association Developments Limited 2001
English language edition worldwide

Published by AA Publishing (a trading name of Automobile Association Developments Limited, whose registered office is Norfolk House, Priestley Road, Basingstoke, Hampshire RG24 9NY; registered number 1878835).

Distributed in the United States and Canada by:
Fodor's Travel Publications, Inc.
201 East 50th Street
New York, NY 10022

A CIP catalogue record of this book is available from the British Library.

Licensed user: Mairs Geographischer Verlag GmbH & Co, Ostfildern

Typeset by Fakenham Photosetting Ltd, Fakenham, Norfolk, UK

Printed in Italy by G Canale & C SpA, Turin

ISBN 0 7495 2962 8

Principal Sights

★
- National Gallery
- Merrion Square
- Powerscourt House
- Dublin Castle
- St. Patrick's Cathedral
- Custom House
- Four Courts
- Phoenix Park
- Howth
- Irish Museum of Modern Art
- St. Doulagh's Church
- Malahide Castle
- Dunsoghly Castle

DUNDALK
- Proleek Dolmen

ENNIS
- Quin Abbey
- Craggaunowen Project
- Dysert O'Dea

GALWAY
- Lynch's Castle
- St. Nicholas Church

GLENGARRIFF
- Ring of Beara

GORT
- Thoor Ballylee
- Kilmacduagh

INISHOWEN PENINSULA
- Grianán of Aileach

KELLS
- South Cross
- St. Columba's House

KILKENNY
- St. Canice's Cathedral
- Rothe House
- Kilkenny Castle
- Kilkenny Design Centre
- Dunmore Cave
- Kilcooly Abbey

KILLARNEY
- Muckross Friary
- Ladies' View
- Aghadoe (Aussicht)

KILLYBEGS
- Slieve League

KINSALE
- Ortsbild

LETTERKENNY
- Glebe Gallery
- Glenveagh National Park

LIMERICK
- Hunt Collection
- Lough Gur Stone Age Centre

★
- Landschaftsbild
- Ross Abbey

LOUGH ERNE
- Landschaftsbild
- Ulster-American Folk Park

LOUGHREA
- Turoe Stone

LOUISEBURGH
- Croagh Patrick

MONASTERBOICE
- Tall Cross

NAAS
- Castletown House

NEW ROSS
- Kennedy Memorial Forest Park
- Dunbrody Abbey

RING OF KERRY
- Staigue Fort
- Derrynane National Historic Park
- Skellig Experience

ROSCREA
- St. Cronan's Church

SHANNON
- Schiffsfahrt

SLIGO
- Sligo Abbey
- Parke's Castle
- Dromahair

TARA
- Hill of Tara

THURLES
- Holy Cross Abbey

TIPPERARY
- Athassel Priory

TRALEE
- Crag Cave

TRIM
- Trim Castle

TUAM
- St. Mary's Cathedral

WATERFORD
- Reginald's Tower

WESTPORT
- Ortsbild
- Westport House

WEXFORD
- Johnstown Castle

WICKLOW
- Mount Usher Gardens
- Devil's Glen

WICKLOW MOUNTAINS
- Landschaftsbild
- Russborough House

Notes